Filomina C. Steady, D.Phil. (Oxon.)

WOMAN IN ACTION

❖

Autobiography of a Global African Feminist

MEREO

Mereo Books

2nd Floor, 6-8 Dyer Street, Cirencester, Gloucestershire, GL7 2PF
An imprint of Memoirs Books. www.mereobooks.com
and www.memoirsbooks.co.uk

Woman in Action: Autobiography of a Global African Feminist
ISBN: 978-1-86151-652-7

First published in Great Britain in 2023
by Mereo Books, an imprint of Memoirs Books.

The address for Memoirs Books can be
found at www.mereobooks.com

Mereo Books Ltd. Reg. No. 12157152

Typeset in 11/16pt Times
by Wiltshire Associates.
Printed and bound in Great Britain

In memory of my parents, Filomeno Whitfield Forster-Jones and Kezia Letitia Lolloh Forster-Jones.

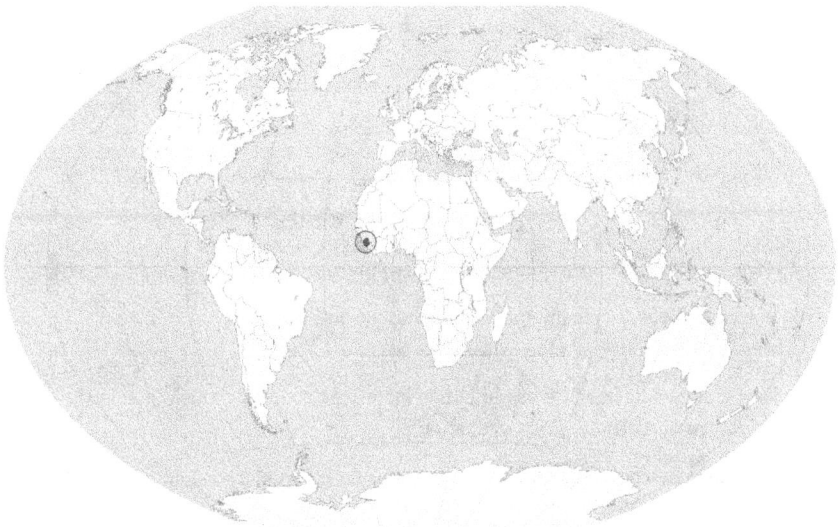

Map showing Sierra Leone's location

Contents

❖

Introduction

This memoir is a result of numerous requests to write my autobiography from my family, faculty colleagues, alumnae, students and friends from around the world. The request was strongly reiterated during the Filomina Steady Symposium, held in honor of my retirement as professor and Chair of Africana Studies at Wellesley College in April, 2019.

The symposium was spearheaded by Professor Layli Maparyan, the foremost authority on 'Womanism' and other members of Africana Studies and the Administration of Wellesley College and co-sponsored by numerous departments, centers and programs of the College. This memorable symposium was titled: 'African(a) Feminism and Women's Leadership in a Global Context: Honoring the Work of Professor Filomina Steady.' President Paula Johnson of Wellesley College paid a special tribute to me as a trailblazer and commended my contributions to Wellesley College as a professor and researcher. I am grateful for this commendation from a distinguished Harvard-trained cardiologist and head of an esteemed institution like Wellesley College. The program and a summary of the highlights of the Filomina Steady Symposium are included in this book under chapter 28, titled 'Retirement and Beyond.'

The book is intended to be accessible to a general and diverse audience. It is reflective and subjective in part and portrays the depth and breadth of my upbringing, educational and professional experiences on three continents – Africa, Europe and North America. It portrays me as a composite of various histories, cultures, traditions and experiences with a solid cosmopolitan outlook reinforced by my ethnic identity as a Krio woman. The Krios of Sierra Leone are descendants of Africans formerly enslaved or en route to enslavement in England, the Caribbean and the United States and later freed and settled in Freetown, Sierra Leone in the eighteenth and nineteenth centuries. The book also discusses my professional life as a university professor and as an international civil servant serving as deputy director of the United Nation's Division for the Advancement of Women and as Special Advisor to several international agencies. Above all, my role and experience as a daughter, woman, wife, mother, sister and family member shine throughout the book.

My journey with feminism has been an exhilarating and challenging one as I have grown to appreciate its many dimensions and permutations, and its uniqueness and complexity.

I realized very early in my career that the prevailing Western feminist paradigms did not seem complete and left out many women whose definitions would be more inclusive and have a more profound and complex perspective grounded in history and lived experiences. African feminism to me was closer to a feminism that was humanistic with a mission to free all of humanity from hegemonic global oppression, regardless of gender. For the African woman in Africa and the Diaspora, the history of transatlantic slavery, colonialism, Jim Crowism and structural racism affected both Black women and men and presented oppression and discrimination in compounded, multiple, intersected and nuanced forms. These needed to be deconstructed, revised and reconstructed, a task that became part of my mission and that of many other scholars and researchers from Africa and the African Diaspora.

My study of women in leadership, especially in West Africa, helped me to unearth models of leadership that are unique to Africa's history and tradition. These include a legacy of female-sanctioned executive authority in some indigenous political systems. Also revealed were models of leadership that can be described as parallel or complementary, such as the Queen Mother's paradigm in Ghana and Swaziland which presented power bases for women that were parallel to that of men. Another finding was about the role of armed conflict and the quest for peace as catalysts in the emergence of women's leadership in Africa. Finally, the centrality of motherhood and its 'matriarchal' association with leadership resonates within Africa and has provided inspiration for female leadership in ways that linked motherhood with statecraft in Africa. It was also clear from my interviews of women leaders of West Africa that moral leadership, defined as giving priority to what is right and just for everyone, was central to their definition of authority, statecraft and enlightened decision-making.

My work at the United Nations provided me with opportunities to lead research and policy analysis teams preparing documents for evaluating progress made and obstacles remaining in promoting gender equality and women's advancement by governments. Some of this work also involved supporting the monitoring of the Convention on the Elimination of All Forms of Discrimination Against Women and collaborating with other UN agencies on mainstreaming women in the work of the United Nations. I also worked as Special Advisor on Women, Environment and Development to the Earth Summit held in Rio in 1992. I am grateful to have been part of the teams that helped to develop three plans of action emanating from United Nations' World Conferences on Women, including The Copenhagen Programme of Action of 1980; The Nairobi Forward Looking Strategies for the Advancement of Women of 1985 and Agenda 21: The Program of Action from Rio in 1992.

This involved working directly with three Secretary Generals of United Nations World Conferences, namely Dr. Lucille Methurin Mair from Jamaica for the Copenhagen World Conference for Women in 1980; Mrs. Letitia Shahani from the Philippines, Secretary General of the Nairobi World Conference, for Women in Nairobi in 1985; and Mr. Maurice Strong, Secretary General of The Earth Summit in Rio in 1992. I owe a deep gratitude to all of them and to my other United Nations colleagues for their work on gender equality and the advancement of women. They include Dorota Gierycz, Sjamsiah Ahmed and Philomena Kintu of the Division for the Advancement of Women; Angela King of UN Women; Sharon Caperling Alakija, Thelma Awori and Beti Astolfi of United Nations Development Fund for Women (UNIFEM); Olubanke King Akerle, Atchouk

Tcheknavorian Asenbauer, Remi Toure and Marian Martin of the United Nations Industrial Development Organization (UNIDO); and Viola Morgan of the United Nations Development Programme (UNDP).

I want to acknowledge other people and institutions that have supported me and provided me with opportunities to learn, grow and serve. Foremost are my African women research colleagues, especially Dr. Achola Pala Okeyo, Professor Ndri Assie Lumumba, Attorney Gladys Mutukwa, Sarah Longwe, Marie-Angelique Savanne, Betty Melinygi, Professor Omolara Ogundipe-Leslie, Dr. Hussainatu Abdullah, Josephine Beoku-Betts and Dr. Staneala Beckley. Many of them are members of the Association of African Women for Research and Development (AAWORD) of which I am a founding member. The United Nations Economic Commission for Africa, especially its women's programs, provided consultancy and other advisory opportunities for me to be in close contact with the research and policy analysis work on the African continent and to participate in several expert group meetings, workshops and conferences.

Special thanks to my faculty colleagues at various universities in Africa, the United States and Europe that are too numerous to mention, some of whom participated in my retirement symposium presented later in this book. I also want to thank my Alma Maters, especially Annie Walsh Memorial School in Sierra Leone, Smith College and Boston University in the USA and Oxford University in England. Special appreciation is given to The Wenner Gren Foundation for Anthropological Research; The Ford Foundation; St. Anne's College, Oxford University, Wellesley College and The Kezfil Foundation for funding my various research projects over the years.

I also want to thank Elly Pradervand, the founder, and members of the board of Women's World Summit Foundation, (WWSF) an international NGO based in Geneva, Switzerland whose main objective is empowering rural women's creativity all over the world. I was president of this organization for a few years and worked with vice presidents Gulzar Samji from Canada, Bunny McBride from the

US, Wu Quin from China and a representative from SEWA, an NGO in India. As founder and current president, Elly Pradervand, a Swiss national with exceptional leadership and organizational abilities, continues to lead this important global work of empowering rural women.

I am blessed to have been born and raised in Sierra Leone and I am spending a large part of my retirement in my homeland and enjoy working with the Krio Descendants Yunion (KDY) as a member. I am particularly grateful to my parents, Filomeno and Kezia Forster-Jones, my siblings, Wordsworth, Frankwin, Glenna and Wilfred, for being sources of support and encouragement throughout my life. My thanks also go to my life-long school friends, who include Juliet Davies, nee Jonah; Imodale Burnett, nee Caulker; Theodora Songo-Williams, nee Davies; and Tita Morgan, nee Dougan. Finally, my deep gratitude and enduring love and appreciation go to my wonderful and talented family, especially my husband, Dr. Henry Maduka Steady, a physician and a thoroughly good, generous, suave and classy guy; my loving and devoted sons, Chinaka and Duka and my warm and charming daughter, Azania for their love and devotion over the years.

CHAPTER 1

Birth and Upbringing: A Cosmopolitan Orientation from the start

"God schedules a birthday, not man." — *Robert A. Bradley*

❖

I was born into a global family. My father was a reserve in the Sierra Leone Regiment for the British campaigns against the Japanese in former Burma, now Myanmar, during the Second World War. My mother, a teacher and businesswoman, was a descendant of female merchants who successfully participated in the famous Kola nut trade throughout the West African region in the 19th and 20th centuries. My citizenship is both Sierra Leonean and American and I belong to the Krio ethnic group, a quintessential entity of the African Diaspora.

Krios are descendants of various groups that were repatriated to Freetown, Sierra Leone from Europe, the Caribbean and North America. Others were rescued in West Africa from slave ships headed for Europe, North America and the Caribbean. Like most Freetown residents of Krio heritage, both of my parents had ancestral connections with West Africa and beyond. My mother, Kezia Lolloh Letitia Forster-Jones with groups of Nigeria and my father, Filomeno Whitfield Abiose Forster-Jones, with the Akus of the Gambia and the Yoruba of Nigeria. The kinship group extended beyond the shores

1

of Sierra Leone and included living relatives as well as departed ancestors. The fact that we could not see our ancestors did not seem to matter, because they were always present in conversations and lived through the memories and names of their descendants. As Africans, we operated in both a physical and metaphysical world embedded in African cosmological notions of being that connected the living, the dead and those yet to be born. From an early age, I had a global, cosmic and spiritual world view that came naturally to me.

Also endemic in the family was a consciousness of the agency and independence of women. I am descended from strong women who gave priority to economic, artistic and personal independence and believed in what today we would call 'gender equality and the advancement of women.' My maternal grandmother, Clarice Fynch, and likely great-grandmother, Kezia Williams, successfully traded in the well-known kola nut trading Diaspora of West Africa as well as with the hinterland of Sierra Leone. My paternal grandmother, Fanny Ann Forster-Jones from the Gambia, was a musical icon and pioneer and a prominent violinist who gave concerts in Freetown, a rare occurrence for women at the time. My mother was a tennis champion.

Women occupying and performing in the public sphere for professional, economic and artistic reasons are part of my DNA. Inherent in this legacy are a curiosity, restlessness, drive and activism that permeates a female cultural and social space in which a young baby girl was born, nurtured and destined to emulate all her life. It is no surprise then that my future would include working at the international, regional and national levels to promote gender equality and the advancement of women in Sierra Leone as a lecturer, in the United States as a Professor and at the United Nations as a director and special adviser.

Another consciousness which was not apparent in my growing up in Freetown was about racism. Since the majority of people were Black, race was not really an issue among Sierra Leoneans, but it was apparent in the colonial structure of political and economic domination by Britain. It established both a visible and an invisible color bar that resulted in a social pyramid with Whites at the top a few Africans in the middle and the majority of Africans at the bottom of the political and economic ladder. Racism was also apparent in the devaluation of African culture and the validation of everything British, White and European. The British colonialists tried to separate themselves from Africans geographically by living mainly on hilltops, such as hill stations with housing designed to enhance British gracious living, complete with a ample supply of servants and gardeners. Socially, their separation was manifested in their attitudes of White superiority and in their degrading treatment of Africans.

Christian missionary activity was extensive and dominated by the Anglican Church Missionary Society (CMS) of Britain and the Methodist missions. Part of their mission was to evangelize Africans, reinforce Christianity among the converted and devalue African religions as superstitious and satanic with a heavy dose of racist disdain. As Africans began to take over the ministries and Africanize some of the ritual and forms of worship, the racist overtones diminished somewhat. In fact, over the years, Christianity has survived remarkably well in Sierra Leone and in Africa in general and the Africanized 'born again' evangelical variety is now arguably, a major *tour de force* all over Africa. Some have objectives that are clearly more than spiritual and exploit the misery of poor Africans who would give their meagre earnings to the church in the hope of divine intervention for a job, a scholarship, a life of affluence or an escape from hardship.

Colonial racism was also embedded in the curriculum which prioritized the history and languages of Britain, Europe and America rather than those of Africa. A major part of the educational system was designed to assimilate Africans into the British way of life and brainwash them about White superiority. At school we were even taught to identify with the British and to sing colonial songs of British conquests and pay tribute to the White Man's Burden of civilizing Africa and other parts of the underdeveloped world. I remember singing 'Rule Britannia, Britannia Rules the World' gleefully with the other pupils at the Annie Walsh Memorial School, not realizing that we were indirectly endorsing colonial domination over us.

I came to realize the depth of racism and appreciate our colonially-imposed institutions only after I left Freetown for Britain and the United States, as will be discussed later. I did not associate the injustices in the colonial legal systems pertaining to land ownership and so forth or to the patriarchal ideologies embedded in racist institutions until later. Going overseas awoke my consciousness about racism and helped shape my life and my devotion to joining the struggle against ending racism in the Academy, the United States and at the United Nations.

From all accounts I could not wait to make my entry into the world. The plan was for my mother to give birth at the hospital where my older brother was born. However, labor pains came unexpectedly and swiftly and my birth had to take place at home. Home births were quite common and constituted important cultural spaces for women under the guidance of midwives. My mother had as birthing assistants and supporters her mother, Clarice; a grand aunt, Gramma Ida; and an inexperienced nanny, known locally as 'Mammy nurse.' There was no time to get a midwife, so the 'Mammy Nurse' nervously attended my mother and apparently almost dropped me right after I was born in 1941. 'Yu wan kil di pikin?' (You want to kill the child?') shouted Gramma Ida. 'No ma. Na fred a fred Ma' (No ma. I was just afraid) replied the Mammy nurse. So right from the start, it was clear that I was going to lead a challenging and risk-taking life.

My birth was greeted with joy for a baby girl and a sense of relief, since my parents already had a boy, my brother Wordsworth, as the first child and culturally-expected 'son and heir. 'This however, is to a large extent a myth, since inheritance is based on imported British statutory law, prevalent in most former British colonies. In this legal system, wills are usually made which may not show gender preferences. In the event of death without a will, the interstate laws prescribe that the surviving spouse receives one third of the estate and the children the remaining two thirds, regardless of gender.

Being born a girl was not a disadvantage, according to the system of descent practiced by the Krios. In the bilateral system, descent is traced through both the father and the mother, thereby giving girls a status as important as that of boys in terms of *de jure* inheritance and other rights. This is not the case with many other ethnic groups in Sierra Leone which are mainly patrilineal, with society organized around the father's descent group. Nonetheless, many of the sixteen or so ethnic groups in Sierra Leone exhibit a certain degree of 'matrilineal' proclivities and permutations through the kinship system, which allows descendants from the mothers' line, especially women, to have influence and some advantages over other blood relatives.

It is also not unusual for patrilineal groups to have women in high political and public positions. For example, the Mende and Sherbro are famous for having women chiefs and paramount chiefs in high political positions with executive power. The picture of a strictly patrilineal or strictly matrilineal society portrayed in most anthropological studies is not a clear-cut binary designation as one has been led to believe. There are many cross-cutting permutations that dilute a strictly patrilineal form of social organization. Human societies are invariably complex, nuanced and malleable and Krio society is a good example of this flexibility and unpredictability.

There were seven members of what sociologists would refer to as my 'family of orientation,' with three boys and two girls and my parents. I was the second child and first girl. With the exception of girls receiving extra protection and subject to more restricted outings in the evenings and at nighttime, there were no real gender differences in our upbringing in terms of equality of opportunity to education, artistic development and participation in associations. Ours is what can be regarded as a middle-class family in Freetown.

My father, Filomeno Forster-Jones, a Methodist Boys High School graduate, was a telegraph inspector and is credited with supervising the establishment of the first trunk lines for long-distance telephone calls from Freetown to the Provinces. He made the first-ever long-distance call in Sierra Leone from the Provinces to the Governor in

Freetown. He later established himself as a successful architect, builder and businessman and managed a number of petrol stations in the city, two of which he owned. His mother was from the accomplished Forster family of the Gambia and his father, Emmanuel Jones, was an administrator who worked with the British Government in Sierra Leone and in other parts of Africa, reinforcing the pan-African roots and consciousness of the family, which no doubt influenced my life.

My mother, Kezia Letitia Lolloh Forster-Jones, was a trained teacher, having attended the Teacher Training College after the Annie Walsh Memorial School. Her mother, Clarice Fynch, née Williams, for whom I was named, was very successful as a long-distance and wholesale trader in foodstuffs, especially cola nuts, from which the drink Coca Cola is derived. My maternal grandfather, who died very early, worked in administration. All of my grandparents died in my infancy and I did not know any of them. All of them appeared to have excelled in life and served as pioneers in various fields, including administration, education, commerce, music and engineering.

I know more about my mother's ancestry than my father's because of the efforts of my cousin, Harold Faulkner, to trace the family tree of the Benjamin family, the great branch from which my mother is descended. On my father's side, there is no such attempt to work on a family tree and in fact there is little or no information beyond the level of my grandparents. My father's mother, Fanny Ann, the violinist, died at a relatively young age and the children had to be 'farmed out' to be raised by various relatives, as was the practice among some families. I was told that the early death of their mother and the separation of the children led to less unity among the brothers, Eben, George, Filo and Chuchu. They also had an older half- brother, Wilson. After their mother's death, I was told that their father Emmanuel had two more children, Congo and Modu.

My parents' romance had a rocky start. They met when they collided with a bang in a bicycle accident in Freetown. As the story goes, after the accident, my father searched high and low for one of the few girls riding bicycles at the time until he found my mother again and they started dating. They eventually married and had five children in all, three boys and two girls. My oldest brother Wordsworth and my youngest brother Wilfred are both lawyers. Frankwin, whose name is a combination of Franklin Roosevelt and Winston Churchill, was born eighteen months after me and later studied hospitality sciences and became a businessman. Unfortunately, he passed away in 2017 after a brief illness. My sister Glenna, the fourth child, is an accomplished actress and businesswoman and lives in England.

Music is an essential part of my family history through my father's line. My father's mother Fanny Ann passed on her violin-playing talent to my father, and all of his brothers played at least one musical instrument. The next generation also displayed this talent in two of my brothers, Wordsworth, an accomplished jazz pianist and Frankwin, a talented guitarist, as well as my first cousin, Ade Forster-Jones, a gifted musician and songwriter. The successive generation carried the tradition through my niece Yasmin, an acclaimed saxophonist, and my daughter Azania, an award-winning international singer and songwriter. Alas, I did not inherit any of this rich musical talent whatsoever and cannot even carry a note. However, I remain an ardent fan and cheerleader of all my musically-talented family members and relatives.

Birth Rites of Passage, Childhood and Upbringing

Like all babies, I had to go through all the rituals associated with welcoming a new life into the family. The management of pregnancy and birth belong primarily to the woman's sphere, although most women are increasingly relying on pediatricians, midwives and nurses for advice and delivery. A number of female relatives are usually around to help take care of a new baby and fathers have specific ritual functions to support the development of the child. One such ritual is symbolically called 'cutting of the baby's tongue'. This is intended to transfer the 'father's wisdom' and linguistic prowess to the child to aid in its acquisition of language. There is clearly a subtle but significant gendered implication here, suggesting that men have priority in terms of linguistic responsibility and transmission of language to a child.[1] But women are also revered and celebrated for their wisdom and some notable icons are discussed later.

Kɔmɔja or 'pul na do' (outdooring)

Kɔmɔja is a ritual for formally celebrating a new life and introducing an infant to its kindred and society at large. Although it may vary, the timing of the ceremony is usually gendered – seven days for girls and nine days for boys, which could be interpreted in many ways. It could signify that girls are stronger and can be introduced to the world earlier than boys. It can also mean that boys are more precious and need more time for their public presentation. This underscores the fact that gender is socially constructed and therefore can be flexible and subject to interpretation.

For the outdooring ceremony, the baby would usually be dressed in white and wrapped in a shawl. An elderly woman would say prayers and give a short speech of welcome to the baby, calling her by her house (African) name. Among the Krios, children are usually given at least two forenames. The school name is likely to be Western and used at school, where the English language is usually enforced. The house name is usually African and generally of Yoruba or Igbo origin. Naming is important, since each African name has a specific meaning. In my case, I was not given an African house name but instead the name of my grandmother Clarice. In fact, none of my siblings were given African names for reasons unknown to me. I was named Filomina Clarice Fanny Ann Jones. Filomina after my father Filomeno, Clarice and Fanny Ann after my maternal and paternal grandmothers, and Jones as the family surname.

The important part of the ceremony is when the baby, accompanied by the people present, is taken outside and shown the natural and

---

1. Steady, F. 2001, **Women and the Amistad Connection: Sierra Leone Krio Society,** Rochester, Schenkam Books and Steady, F. 2018, **Krio Women of Sierra Leone: Embracing a Culture of Many Parts,** Linus Learning, Ronkonkoma, New Jersey, for further elaboration on Krio culture

built 'world' by pointing in the direction of the different landscapes, buildings and their importance. In the case of my Kɔmɔja, the location of my home was significant since we lived at Cline Town, which is very close to the Queen Elizabeth Quay, known locally as the Deep Water Quay. Our family had a clear view of the Atlantic Ocean from our veranda, with its constant parade of international ships circling the horizon. It pointed the way to other worlds and helped cement a cosmopolitan attitude that was part and parcel of the environment in which I grew up.

According to my mother, the elder in charge of showing me my environment at the

Kɔmɔja spoke of the importance of Sierra Leone having one of the few natural harbors of the world as he pointed to the Quay. He expressed the hope that when I was grown, I would be able to travel by boat to England for my advanced education. This was not a far-fetched reality since the Elder Dempster Lines started operating large passenger ships like the *Accra, Appapa* and *Aureol* from West Africa to Liverpool from the late 1940s. It was also the dream of most parents, especially in middle-class families, to have their children educated in England or to visit the colonial land themselves. He then pointed to the east where my first church, the Bishop Crowther Memorial Church, and my first school, Cline Town Elementary School were located.

Further east was the heart of Cline Town, known locally as Kanike, with a fishing community benefiting from the marine resources of the Atlantic Ocean. To the south was the Fourah Bay College, nestled on top of Mount Aureol's lush and green hills. The elder hoped that one day I would attain much knowledge from this institution. In the west lay the Central Government and Business District, where many people were employed in government and commercial jobs. All of these wonderful places were introduced to all babies, regardless of gender, with the hope that they would benefit from what the natural environment and the man-made institutions of learning, commerce and government had to offer. To balance the presentation, other institutions like prisons and dangerous areas of the city, like slums, were also pointed out to babies as places of danger to be avoided.

After the introduction to my environment, I was brought back inside. Refreshments were served and included traditional food for ritual occasions, such as beans, after which some of the guests addressed me in the following manner:

'Little Clarice, we have eaten your beans. Stay with us, O little one, so that one day you will eat with us.'

After refreshments the guests begin to depart. Close relatives stay longer and chat, or take turns in carrying the baby. It is considered a sign of goodwill and affection to offer to carry the baby, who is the guest of honor. In some families, a small basin or receptacle would be put in a prominent position in the living room for the receipt of gifts, mostly money, accompanied by short remarks like: 'This is for your comb to comb your hair', 'this is a small shawl to keep you warm' and so forth. Gifts would also likely be presented to the mother for her own use. From this day onwards the baby may be taken outside. Today these rules are not strictly followed, but many elements of this ritual are still performed by many families to ensure that the proper introductions to the landscape and people are performed.

Childhood rites of passage: christening for Christians

Since Krio culture is made up of many parts, for Christians, the way of celebrating a new life is very much in keeping with the Western aspects of Christianity through the christening ceremony. These may vary according to degree of elaboration based on the social status of the family. Two men and two women are chosen as godparents in advance from the circle of relatives and friends of the parents. One of my aunts informed me that in the case of my christening, I was dressed in a white gown and cape like all babies, and being a girl I also wore a tiny gold ring on the right little finger as well as a necklace, bracelet and tiny gold earrings. The christening ceremony was held at the Bishop Crowther Memorial Church at Cline Town, where we lived and where my mother grew up. During the service all the given names of the baby, at least one of them English and one African, are announced by one of the godparents. Mothers, including mine, usually undergo 'the churching of women' as part of the service intended as thanksgiving to God for a safe childbirth. The christening party, consisting of the parents, the godparents, relatives and friends would then return home for refreshments, speeches and dancing.

Childhood illnesses: a way of life

One of the reasons that children are so precious in most African societies is because of the high value placed on human life and the continuity of the group. The birth of a child is greeted with jubilation and the customary greetings to the parents is 'A gi yu jɔy!' (I give you joy!) Unfortunately, the high value placed on children is often threatened by the prevalence of childhood diseases and high mortality rates. Infectious diseases like malaria, measles and diarrheal diseases are common and can be fatal in children. I was fortunate to survive several bouts of childhood illnesses that daily threatened the lives of children at that time and even now. Infant mortality rates in Sierra Leone have always been high and now stand at 78 per 1000 live births.

The lives of mothers giving birth are also perilous. In 2020, maternal mortality stood at 1165, one of the highest in the world. In fact the disease burden is so high in Sierra Leone and many countries of Africa that children who die young are considered 'quick markets,' meaning that they came to this world for a certain purpose and are in a hurry and must return quickly. There is a certain fatalism that goes with death in general and people tend to attribute death to 'God's will' declaring that 'It is their time.' This is reinforced by the belief in the afterlife.

My cousin Remileku's death

Death was a mystery to me as a child and I heard so many ghost stories from an elderly neighbor that I was afraid of it. My first experience of death was at the age of ten, that of my first cousin, Remileku Thomas, who died of appendicitis. He got ill suddenly and complained of stomach ache. Three days later, we learnt that he had died. He was my playmate and I could not get over his illness and death. I did not understand what this meant, since I had never seen a dead person. The day of his funeral was a sad one but strangely, I felt some relief when I saw his corpse on the bed in his pajamas. He appeared to be sleeping. There was nothing to be scared about, until I saw his mother crying and his father's red eyes. For a number of days afterwards, I kept imagining that I had pains in my stomach and kept asking my mother if I also had appendicitis that would cause me to die. She assured me that I was all right and that I should not worry or cry for Remileku, because he had gone to heaven and was playing with the angels.

Surviving many childhood diseases must have had an influence in developing a resilience that was to prepare me well for the challenging life ahead in Africa, Europe and North America, where I would spend most of my educational and professional life as well as my life as a wife and mother.

CHAPTER 2

Krios: A Quintessential People of the African Diaspora

"Wi de fɔdɔm, grap" – (We may fall but we get up again)
A typical Krio saying.

—✵—

Krios are a product of the transatlantic slave trade and in that regard are the quintessential people of the African Diaspora and natural champions of freedom. They are the resilient descendants of Africans who were formerly enslaved in England, Canada, Jamaica and the United States, as well as those liberated in Africa on the way to becoming enslaved overseas. In Sierra Leone, they collectively became known as Krios. As a result, they have a culture of many moving parts and have developed what I have elsewhere defined as a 'pluri-cultural consciousness.'[2] This is reflected in their blend of African, Western and Caribbean cultural frameworks that are expressed in their life cycle events, belief systems, social structure, cosmology and way of life. This identity is unique and manufactured in Freetown and the peninsular villages. It is what sociologists would

---

2. Steady, F. 2001, **Women and the Amistad Connection: Sierra Leone Krio Society,** Rochester, Schenkam Books and Steady, F. 2018, **Krio Women of Sierra Leone: Embracing a Culture of Many Parts,** Linus Learning, Ronkonkoma, New Jersey

call 'sui generis' (of its own kind or of its own making.) Although other factors were important, it was the *African* cultural elements and identity that provided them with the enduring social architecture and cosmological reference point for their lives.

Unfortunately, Krios are not recognized as full citizens of Sierra Leone. They may carry the Sierra Leone passport and vote, but they are referred to in some legal documents as 'non-native' and barred from owning land in the Provinces of Sierra Leone.[3] They are also sometimes scorned as not being indigenous to Sierra Leone. This is ridiculous because, according to historical records, the majority of Sierra Leoneans are not indigenous to the country. It is well documented that most tribes or ethnic groups in Sierra Leone are immigrants and settlers, probably from the former empires of West Africa like Mali, Songhai and Ghana that flourished around the 11th to 15th centuries. By the 15th century the interior was inhabited by the Limbas. The Mende and Temne, the largest groups, were apparently living in the coastal area now known as Sierra Leone around the late 15th and early 16th centuries. In 1787 the first group that later became known as the Krios, the 'Black Poor' from Britain, were settled in Freetown.[4] Only the Bullom, who were later absorbed into the Sherbro group, can arguably make some claim to being indigenous on the basis of having been in the coastal area the longest.

The Krios may be a minority group in Sierra Leone but they are the most documented, especially by historians, and have attracted the attention of scholars from all over the world. Even non-Krio scholars from Sierra Leone seem more interested in researching and writing

---

3. Sections 3 and 4 of the Provinces Land Act, 1960 of Sierra Leone. This is a violation of **The African (Banjul) Charter on People and Human Rights**, October 21, 1986.

4   Fyfe, 1962, **A History of Sierra Leone,** New York, Oxford University Press; Wyse, A., 1991, **The Krios of Sierra Leone: An Interpretive History,** Washington, D.C. Howard University Press.) Campbell, 1993, M. **Back to Africa: George Ross and the Maroons: From Nova Scotia to Sierra Leone,** Trenton, N.J. Africa World Press. ; See also Foray, 1977, C. Historical Dictionary of Sierra Leone, London. (Cited in Wyse, A, 1991, **The Krios of Sierra Leone: An Interpretive History,** Washington, D.C. Howard University Press.)

about the Krios than about their own ethnic groups. The fascination with Krios is mind blowing. Even visitors on the shortest stay in the country seem eager to find out about this storied group. This is due primarily to their historic and significant contributions to the country. For an example, Mr. I.T.A. Wallace Johnson and Mrs. Constance Cummings-John were pioneers of the nationalist movements towards independence for African countries through their founding and leadership of the West African Youth League. Dr. Africanus Horton became the first African surgeon trained at the University of Edinburgh and is known as a political philosopher and a pan-Africanist. He provided some of the earliest blueprints for an agenda for African liberation.

In addition, there were many Krio women pioneers in commerce, education and politics, such as Mrs. Hannah Benka Coker, a beacon of inspiration in girls' education; Mrs. Abigail Jones, Mrs. Ethel Ashwood, Mrs. Lettie Forster-Jones and Mrs Princess James in commerce and Mrs. Nancy Steele in politics. Several Krio women have served as Mayors of Freetown and they include Mrs. Constance Cummings-John; Dr. June Holst Roness; Miss Florence Dillsworth; and Mrs. Yvonne Aki Sawyer. Several members of this group are making outstanding contributions to the country despite challenges of being a minority group subject to discrimination and marginalization from the political process and denial of some economic and educational opportunities. Krio women were accustomed to owning houses, some of which were inherited and some of which they built themselves. This made them the first women to exercise suffrage in the world in 1792.[5]

The story of the Krios of Sierra Leone being linked to the Abolitionists and Back to Africa movements in the United States in the 19th and 20th centuries is only partially true. It was also sparked by racism and the objection in both the United States and Britain to having Blacks living as free citizens in these countries after slavery was abolished. This later version was not taught at my school, which gave credit only to

---

5   Schama, S., 2006, **Rough Crossings: The Slaves, the British and the American Revolution**, New York, Harper Collins Publishers.

the abolitionists and philanthropists like Granville Sharpe and William Wilberforce for the repatriation of freed slaves to Africa.

I later learned while studying in the United States that racism was an important factor in the repatriation of the slaves to Africa and that slavery really ended because it was no longer profitable and because of violent insurrections for freedom primarily by enslaved Blacks. In addition, these relocated Africans were meant to serve as agents in the political and economic agenda of colonization, disguised as a mission to spread Christianity and 'Western Civilization' to Africa.

Under the leadership of the Sierra Leone Company, in which a number of the so-called abolitionists were financially involved, and the Church Missionary Society, the idea of establishing a Province of Freedom materialized at Granville Town, later Freetown in Sierra Leone. The early settlers were of three main groups. The first were the Black Poor and socially undesirable from England who came in 1787. The next group were the Nova Scotians, who included African-American loyalists and runaway enslaved Africans from the United States, as well as some Jamaican Maroons who arrived in 1800. Jamaican Maroons and Barbadian rebels were also deported to Sierra Leone in 1819.[6] During the early years the settlers faced adverse conditions and severe hardship from an inhospitable climate, hostile attacks by King Tom, the Temne chief, and a siege by a French frigate. In addition, there was general administrative disarray.

Over the years a number of settlers died, but enough of them survived until 'Liberated Africans' or 'Recaptives' (freed by the Admiralty Courts) from the slave ships from other parts of West Africa en route to Europe and America were brought in to join them. Most of the Liberated Africans were settled in the peninsular villages around Freetown, where Christian missionary activities were vigorous and widespread. These Krio villages became the incubators of Krio culture and heritage and produced many Krio families and individuals of distinction, such as

---

6   Blyden, 2000, **West Indians in West Africa, 1808-1880: The African Diaspora in Reverse**, New York, University of Rochester Press.

Africanus Horton of Gloucester. The Liberated Africans were mostly from West Africa, especially Nigeria and particularly from the Yoruba ethnic group. They contributed many of the African elements of Krio culture, including life cycle events and naming traditions.

The communities in the villages and in Freetown were unique in terms of the architecture of the wooden houses, known locally as 'bodos', and the quaint churches around which the society was organized.[7] Families were primarily composed of a core nuclear unit and some extended relatives sharing the same household. The division of labor was by gender, with men doing much of the work related to construction, land clearing, fishing and so forth and women planting, weeding, harvesting, doing domestic work and caring for children for the most part. The cuisine was largely influenced by Yoruba and Igbo dishes as well as popular Mende and Temne dishes. Palm wine was harvested and sold, as well as some minor food processing of local crops like palm kernel, raffia, coconut, gourds, leaves and so forth.

By 1808 Freetown, as the settlement became known, was made a crown colony with the governor appointed by the British monarch. The Krios then became the *first* Sierra Leoneans, as pointed out by Nigel Browne Davis in his keynote speech at the Krio Descendants Yunion Family Reunion in Boston in 2019.[8] Some Krios worked in the hinterland of the country as civil servants, traders and missionaries and built alliances with the people in the interior of the country. They fought on the side of chief Bai Bureh in the Hot Tax War of 1898, and many of them lost their lives. They went on to make history by becoming the first doctors, lawyers, educators and administrators, not only in Sierra Leone but also in West Africa and in Africa as a whole. My paternal grandfather, Immanuel Forster-Jones, was one of these early civil servants. The Krio group, fashioned in Freetown and the peninsular villages was unique and became the reference group.

7   James, E. et. als., 2006, **Den Ol Bod Os: Creole Architecture in Sierra Leone,** Freetown, The British Council.

8   Brown - Davies, N, 2019 'The Emergence of Creoledom and the Future: 1792 to the Present,' Keynote Speaker, Boston, Krio Descendants Union Global, Family Reunion.

The pioneering contribution of the Krios towards ending colonialism, not only in Sierra Leone but also in West Africa, especially Ghana, Nigeria and the Gambia, was noteworthy, and is amply documented as noted earlier.[9] Armed with Western education and knowledge of Western societies and habits, the Krios were motivated to challenge the indignities of colonialism and its racism and to push for self-governance. The National Congress of British West Africa (NCBWA), founded in the former Gold Coast, now Ghana, in 1917, was the first Pan-African political association of its kind. It grew out of a political consciousness about racism and had an anti-colonial ideology that promoted nationalism and political awareness and set the stage for decolonization. Although the membership of the Sierra Leone branch was largely Krio, the Congress sought members from the Protectorate and represented the interests of the Protectorate in the Legislature and elsewhere'[10]

The Krio Descendants Yunion (KDY)

The Settlers Union which was active in the period prior to independence in 1961 is the antecedent of the Krio Descendant Yunion (Union) which was registered as a charity in 1992. It was founded to promote Krio culture and heritage and provide mutual support and encouragement to its members, and has an extensive constitution. Its motto is 'Le wi ep wisef' (Let's help each other and share each other's burdens.) One of its most established leaders is Canon Cassandra Garber, JP, who served as its president for many years. Krio Descendants Yunion Global was founded to be the Diaspora extension of the association and has almost twenty branches in North America, Europe and other parts of Africa. The association holds family reunions every year, including a Homecoming held in Freetown in 2017.

---

9   Spitzer, 1974, The Creoles of Sierra Leone: Responses to Colonialism, 1870-1945, Madison, University of Wisconsin Press; Wyse, A., 1991,

10 Wyse, A. 1991, The Krios of Sierra Leone: An Interpretive History, Washington, D.C. Howard University Press.

There are several standard annual activities which include a thanksgiving service, a fundraising dinner and dance, and health outreach, picnic and awujo feasts to honor the ancestors. The association is currently engaged in the construction of a museum and headquarters building in Freetown. The following are five pillars around which the business of the association is organized: 1) Preservation of Krio culture and Historical Background; Fundraising and Financial Accountability; Programme Management; Institutional Governance and Human Resources Management and Dissemination of the Narrative. I would have liked to see a pillar on Youth Development since the association is made up of predominantly middle-aged and senior citizens which does not guarantee continuity, expansion, renewal and strengthening of a group for the future.

Another group, known as 'Krio Community' and based in Freetown, broke away from the Krio Descendants Yunion in 2017 in order to become more politically active in the country and to demand rights of Krio participation in the decision-making and political governance of the country.

A Very Brief Political History of Sierra Leone

Briefly, the political history of Sierra Leone from the third decade of the twentieth century until independence in 1961 went as follows: In 1923 the Legislative Council, which for the most part administered the colony by the British with a few Krio representatives, was reconstituted and enlarged to accommodate representatives from the Colony and the Protectorate. In 1950 the Sierra Leone People's Party (SLPP) was formed with Dr. Milton Margai, a Mende, as its leader. This party, which received much of its support from the Protectorate chiefs, had a majority of members in the new Legislative Council. Already in the minority, the Krios organized around three main parties -- the National Council, the United People's Party and the Sierra Leone Independence Movement. In the 1957 general elections, the SLPP won 26 of the 39 seats in the House of Representatives, and Dr. Milton Margai was appointed the first

Prime Minister. The national political scene has been dominated by non-Krios ever since and the Krios have been largely marginalized in terms of political positions at the national level. The governance of the city of Freetown has tended to be headed by Krio mayors, four of whom have been women. The current mayor is Mrs. Yvonne Aki-Sawyer, an outstanding and visionary leader of our city.

Krio Kinship 'Fambul'

Krio social structure can be defined as gender neutral to some extent, with important roles for both men and women. I grew up realizing that both my mother's and father's relatives of both genders had equal status and importance in my life. This is because kinship is bilateral, with descent traced through both maternal and paternal lines. Unlike many African ethnic groups, which are patrilineal with descent traced through the father's line only, inheritance and succession, as well as one's jural status, did not depend on gender. As a result, kinship is flexible and highlights the maternal line, despite having a few patrilineal proclivities indicated in the surnames of the father. However, the practice of using double-barrelled surnames whereby the mother's surname is combined with the father's has always been fashionable and popular.

Most Krios have British family names on account of early missionary influence and the early repatriated groups from the Americas, Europe and the Caribbean. Among the most popular are Coker, Cole, Davies, Johnson, Jones, Macauley, Smith, Taylor, Thomas and Williams. The predominant African forenames are from Nigeria, of Yoruba origin, followed by Igbo, and from Ghana, of Ashanti origin.

Kinship is important for classifying relationships and for identification, security and cooperation. Very strong social pressures ensure conformity to kindred obligations. Even though the society does not conform to a cohesive corporate group, kinship plays an important part in social relationships. When I was growing up, all relatives, regardless of gender, were important, even departed ones. Gender differences were apparent in some social events when men and women tended to segregate themselves and socialize separately. This, however, was not true of dinner and dancing parties that were oriented towards couples or mixed groups. Some gender differences were apparent in the socialization of girls, who were subject to more 'curfews' than boys, who could go out at night more often and stay out until later. For adolescent girls the fear of premature sexual activity that could result in pregnancy was the main driving force behind these restrictions.

A high value was placed on good relations with relatives and a certain amount of reciprocity was expected in terms of exchange of goods and services. In the absence of adequate welfare institutions and social services, the more well-to-do relatives were encouraged to help the poor relations in exchange for services and moral support. A type of informal adoption of children of poorer relatives was quite common as well as wards from other ethnic groups that sometimes become incorporated into the Krio family, including changing their names to Krio names.

Legally, if a man dies without leaving a will, the property is divided two thirds to the children and one third to the spouse. The situation in rural villages of the peninsula could be different, since inheritance of family farmland is usually passed on to the youngest son, instead of the oldest son. This extends the tenure of the land and serves to protect the younger members of the family. Other flexible elements are evident in the inflationary and eclectic nature of kinship, which tends to regard anyone distantly related or even non-kin as kin.

This presents an extensively overlapping network, known anthropologically as 'the kindred' and locally as 'fambul'. It consists of persons related to one another through blood lines from both the father and mother. In most bilateral societies the range of kindred or 'fambul' is reckoned in degrees of cousinship. It is well known that if a kindred is bounded by third cousins it will include an individual's eight sets of great-grandparents and their descendants. The kindred grouping tends to be unbounded and can include as many categories of cousins as an individual wishes to trace.

Other instances may be cited when one set of kindred can dominate an individual's relationships in spite of formalized kindred organization. For instance, where there has been no legal marriage, the maternal kindred of a child born out of wedlock may assume importance for the child. Singular stress on one gender of a kindred is also noticeable when the marriage tie is weak, or in villages where there is a shortage of males. In short, wherever women are bringing up children single-handedly or with limited paternal help, the maternal kindred tends to assume greater significance in their children's lives.

Another example pertains to the birth of the first child, where it is customary for a woman to go and live with her mother at this time and for a period afterwards. In my case, my parents lived in my grandmother's house already and my mother did not have to move away upon the birth of her first child or subsequent children. Much of the help she received would likely come from her mother and her mother's kindred. Despite those instances when one set of kin features more prominently than others, the general rule is one of a bilateral system in which both sets of maternal and paternal kindred are important in kinship organization.

Family and household types

Various types of families function as household units. These include the nuclear family with the male as the assumed breadwinner, common law marriage, single-parent households and faithful concubinage households. The first type is the nuclear/extended family which is considered the norm. It is based on Christian marriage, is monogamous and is backed by statutory law. This is the family to which I was born and raised. Common Law marriage is recognized by statutory law after proof of a couple having lived together for five years. Another type, the single-parent family is often headed by a woman and rarely by a man.

Single-parent households may result from divorce, loss of a spouse, or origination without marriage. Single women bearing children with married men are usually identified as 'The bearer of Mr. so and so's children.' Faithful concubinage is the fourth type of household and has a *de facto* status of living together as man and wife for less than five years. It bears a lower status than Christian monogamous marriage or common law marriage, which presupposes a breadwinner role for men and greater stability. Both the single-parent household and the faithful concubinage household have certain economic and social disadvantages but have demonstrated a fairly high degree of stability in some families.

Flexibility, individualism and charisma

The bilateral kinship structure and the tendency for kinship to be inflationary results in other factors such as individualism, personality, charisma and choice to be influential in kindred relationships. There is also a tendency to incorporate as fictive kin godparents, wards, friends and even neighbors in kinship occasions. This flexibility allows for an expression of choice in terms of how committed one wants to be in relationships with kindred. It also provides much scope for personality, sentiment and charisma to influence and act upon the pattern of kindred behavior. This allows for a wide range of kindred expressions and facilitates the impact of strong personalities on the relations among kin, regardless of their position and gender in the kindred system. For example, although my mother was more invested in maintaining 'fambul' relations, my father saw some of them as conflict prone and hypocritical and advised me to prioritize good friendship over troublesome blood relatives.

Of special significance to women is the tendency for this flexibility to provide opportunities for women who possess and express charisma and qualities of leadership to assume high positions of authority and respect in kindred groups and during kinship occasions. As I grew up, I noticed that a woman with a strong personality and charisma may acquire status and authority even among her husband's kindred. She can orchestrate most kindred activities and dominate most decisions of importance and play a prominent role in kindred consultations. She may also hold several 'functions' at her home at which both her kin and those of her husband are present. This provides her with a platform and an opportunity to demonstrate her charisma, leadership qualities and high status among the kindred and also in the community. Post-menopausal women and old women are ascribed a high status and can assume leadership roles often based on seniority. Women over sixty, in particular, are frequently sought after for advice on family and kindred matters and play important roles in life cycle events. In addition, I grew up seeing many women role models holding high positions in the professions, especially as teachers, nurses, midwives community leaders, business women and leaders of voluntary associations.

Social class and changes in kinship

Krio society is class conscious and internally differentiated. The groups range from the very poor 'Poporiopo' to the middle class 'good krio' and to the very rich 'aristo', and the degree of kinship affiliation and adherence to some extent reflects class. I grew up in a middle-class family. My father worked in the Civil Service as a telegraph inspector and my mother was a teacher and businesswoman. Significantly, Krio class structure is not rigid and many in the rich or middle-class categories have poor relatives. As a result the class structure can change over time by both upward and downward mobility. There is no guarantee that class can be reliably reproduced from one generation to another.

Class is not the only indicator of status, however. Behavior is a better indicator. The ideal behavior of the 'Good Krio' is someone in the middle of the extremes and is defined by adherence to religious beliefs, good upbringing and manners and respect for the elders, rather than economic status alone. Seldom do people admit to being poor and even the obviously poor tend to adopt an air of pride by saying: 'Po, I am, bɔt bita blod in mi.' (Poor I am but bitter blood in me.)

Kinship has undergone some changes but continues to have significance in social relationships and in gender dynamics. In a community like Freetown where most people are not affluent, kindred relationships are valued for their potential resources in human and social terms and particularly for mutual aid and moral support. However, this is changing due to the challenging economic situations that affect all strata of society. This makes it difficult for the poor to have their children fostered in the homes of better-off relatives in exchange for school fees and other opportunities. The usual 'asylum' offered to poor relations and financial help is also not as forthcoming or obligatory because of the erosion of many of the assets of the better-off families.

In my generation, as opposed to my parents', it appears that the development of other relationships based on friendship has become more important than relationships based strictly on kindred ties and obligations. New economic values which stress a higher standard of living for the nuclear family are tending to curtail extending financial expenditure to Fambul. The trend for young people to spend several years overseas receiving higher education can also negatively affect the importance of the kindred. In time, they may lose touch with the relevance of these institutions. Those who have enjoyed the isolation of the nuclear family life overseas may even dread the re-integration into a pattern which prescribes the involvement of fambul in their family life. Some tend to see this involvement as a move that would eventually interfere with their harmonious marriage and family relationships.

Development of an Ethnic Identity

Life cycle events are important in the development of an ethnic identity because of their strong social and cultural significance and what can be referred to as 'a highly degree of 'fambul' involvement.' 'Fambul' are people who can be demonstrably proven to be related by blood or marriage, or even in fictive terms to the person being honored in these life cycle events. Usually, they will wear the same ashɔbi (uniform dress) at these events so that they can be easily recognized and are the most active in terms of moving around, serving guests, making arrangements and discussing plans and arrangements. It is a display of the density and extent of the cohesiveness and pride of the fambul network.

Fambul networks are expected to be maintained carefully as a norm but in reality, many fambul networks are weak and full of tension and conflicts. This is mediated by a common saying in Krio: 'fambul tik kin bɛn bɔt i nɔ ba brok.' (A family tree can bend but it must never break.) Fambul also serve in multiple parenting, especially the mothering and upbringing of children, and tend to have a specialist within the group to handle issues of extreme disciplinary problems, preparing girls for the 'talk' about the menarche and often serving as sponsors in the form of godparents during the life cycle events of christening and marriage.

The elements of a multidimensional heritage from African, Caribbean, Western and North American cultures are expressed in the way of life and behavior of the people. Listening to Western classical music by Beethoven, Mozart and Bach on Sunday at church services and in some homes is commonplace, as is dressing up in Western attire and hats for women and suits and formal tailcoats for men as the need arises. It is also customary in a few families to speak English at home. During most formal ceremonies of the Western tradition, such as christenings, weddings, funerals, dinner parties and so forth, the English language is used. In typically African ceremonies like kɔmɔja, mared, awujɔ and so forth, Krio will be spoken.

Nowhere is the juxtaposition of African, Caribbean and Western and African culture more poignantly expressed than in the culinary traditions of Saturday and Sunday. Saturdays and Sundays are especially important days that express a multidimensional heritage and diversity of Krio culture. Important cultural symbols, values, norms and beliefs are accentuated during these two days as salient attributes and distinctive features of the society. These features pertain to the organization of family life on Saturdays when a special African meal is cooked and eaten, known as 'Satide fufu ɛn plasas' (Saturday foofoo and plasas) and other foods such as fried fish and cassava bread, reflecting Caribbean influences. In addition, it is the day on which major housework and cleaning activities take place and the evenings are devoted to cementing social bonds and entertainment. Events relating to the Christian religion and Western culinary traditions are observed on Sundays by attending church, cooking and eating of the 'Sunday Stew' and Krio salad in some homes and visiting relatives. Sundays also cement social bonds and provide opportunities for relaxation and entertainment.

The distinction between the outside and inside is marked, as many anthropologists have observed for other cultures. For the Krios, the home represents the inside and is seen as safe and secure, an oasis of nurturing, good upbringing and instilling moral values as well as a place of religious observance, ancestor reverence, informal education and spiritual growth. The outside is more complicated. It can be seen as a place for public participation, education and professional achievement and at the same time as unsafe, wild and prone to immoral and other undesirable temptations. As a result, children are warned against the evils of the outside, especially in an urban environment prone towards immoral and felonious acts and the likelihood of coming into contact with unsavory characters. Children are carefully supervised to make sure that they do not fall into the wrong company.

In addition, it is not unusual for children to be secretly observed by members of the 'fambul' and others when they are outside to ensure that they are behaving in accordance with the approved norms of behavior. The outside is particularly dangerous at night, where thieves and pickpockets may lurk and where, according to ancient popular myths, evil agents, especially the Ronsho devil, roam around in chains doing harm to people. The myth of the Ronsho devil is believed in some circles to be a throwback to the days of slavery when Africans were caught and put in chains for shipment overseas as enslaved people. Women are believed to be particularly at risk at night since they are considered more vulnerable to violence. Incidents of young girls from poor families being raped while fetching water at night, when the public taps are usually open, are not uncommon, even today.

Churches as the center of the community

The church was the center of life for Christian Krios. Voluntary associations, known as 'kɔmpins', provided mutual aid and support in times of life cycle events like births, marriages and funerals, as well as financial aid for legal disputes, illness and general economic hardship. Law, order, the fear of God and family unity were the central organizing principles of these communities and to some extent, they represent the real essence of Krio culture and heritage. Agricultural production was one of the economic activities of these villages, as well as blue-collar occupations like plumbing and carpentry and white-collar occupations like teaching, health care and the ministry. Rural villages were linked to Freetown through a marketing network that supplied fresh fruits, vegetables, household goods and so forth to the markets in Freetown on market days. Some of the inhabitants were also linked to people in Freetown through kinship ties and many so called 'villagers' gradually migrated to Freetown over the years. So, despite their rural connections, Krios developed an urban orientation in general and a cosmopolitan outlook derived from a history of a transatlantic experience; rural to urban trading and internal migration.

Churches were organized in parishes and became the center of Christian life from birth to death. Church attendance on Sundays and other holy days was mandatory, as was Sunday school for children. Adults and children were divided into classes where religious instruction would take place, including Bible study sessions. The church was also a place for entertainment during the holidays, when plays and pageants would be performed. My mother was a regular member of the theatre group at Bishop Crowther Memorial Church. Candlelight vigils on Christmas and New Year's Eve, as well as fireworks on New Year's Eve, were popular events. On Christmas day, church services would be well attended and churches elaborately decorated with Christmas ornaments. Most people would put on African attire for the service as part of the celebration. The service would consist mostly of the singing of Christmas hymns and carols. A special birthday competition for every month of the year has become popular in most churches, including a special birthday contribution for 'Baby Jesus', who is often the winner.

Children are usually presented with toys by the minister or his wife and the choir sings special Christmas songs for the occasion. After church service, the rest of the day is spent in celebration by families at home. At home, children are usually presented with toys, in addition to those given by 'Father Christmas' (Santa Claus) the night before. Since many Sierra Leoneans live in the Diaspora, Christmas is a time when a number of them return home to spend the holidays with family and friends. Most families have a Christmas meal of jollof rice, Krio salad and other delicacies. Others serve the traditional Krio Christmas meal consisting of boiled soup, yam and other root crops, served separately.

The next day, Boxing Day, is usually but not necessarily devoted to parades of schools and masquerades of masked 'devils.' Parties and picnics at the many peninsular beaches around Freetown are also popular. Easter is extensively and jubilantly celebrated with elaborate church services. Easter Monday is a holiday known for its picnics along the beaches and for the flying of colorful kites. The festivities of other religions, especially Islam, are also celebrated by Christians and vice versa.

I grew up with a vibrant and extensive church family from the Cline Town Community at Bishop Crowther Memorial Church. The church has always been a special community of family members, relatives and neighbors and served an important socializing function for children and youngsters. The relationships formed lasted into adulthood and continued even after people moved away from Cline Town to college, overseas or to other parts of the city. Although some churches, like St. Georges Cathedral in Central Freetown are supposed to reflect economic class affiliation, most churches do not. There are certain financial requirements, like regular class dues, which may vary from church to church, but no one is turned away from membership in a church. The only rule that has financial obligations is to be up-to-date with one's class dues to ensure that a church service will be conducted as part of one's funeral. Otherwise, the corpse will be shamefully taken to the cemetery by what is known locally as 'direct boat.'

Okus: Muslim Krios

Although the majority of Krios are Christian, there is a Muslim minority, known as Oku, with strong Yoruba connections, like some of their Christian counterparts. Historically, they constituted part of the 'Liberated Africans' or 'Recaptives' that were freed from slave ships en route to Europe, the Caribbean and the Americas in the nineteenth century. According to the official policy, Freetown, and its surrounding villages, was to become a Christian city with intense and extensive missionary activities, involving conversion to Christianity. It is generally believed that those who were already practicing the Muslim faith either resisted conversion to Christianity or felt it was redundant. Adherence of the Okus to Islam and resistance to conversion to Christianity led to their marginalization by the European Christian missionaries and administrators.

The Okus were generally denied equal educational opportunities by Christian missionaries who controlled many of the educational programs in the city. Those desiring an education either had to become Christians or to adopt a Christian name as a cover. The majority of the Muslims among the Liberated Africans were known as Okus and because of their Yoruba ancestry and Muslim affiliation were sometimes referred to as 'Oku Marabou', evoking their Muslim affiliation. They adhere to some cultural traditions that are different from the Krios who are Christians and monogamous. Islam allows polygamy and female secret society initiation is an important part of the rites of passage for women.

The majority of Okus settled in Fourah Bay around Savage Square and 'Krojimmy' in the east end of Freetown, near Cline Town, where I was born and raised. The remainder later settled in Foulah Town (south east) and Aberdeen Village (far west). In general, their conversion to Islam occurred before settlement in Freetown and a few became Muslims later through the influence of the Foulah and Mandingo ethnic groups in Freetown. By the beginning of the 19th century the Oku community maintained its distinctiveness primarily through its adherence to the Muslim religion. As members of the larger Krio group, Okus have maintained close ties with Krios who are Christians and with whom some share kinship ties. It is well recognized and acknowledged that the Oku contributed significantly to the development of Krio society, as Cole's book rightly points out.[11] Many returned to Nigeria and were known as 'Egba Saros.' Some were part of an influential middle class in Lagos and elsewhere and consisted of both Muslims and Christians.[12] In Freetown also, a number of Oku men and women achieved success through the professions as well as in political and economic leadership positions and constituted an influential middle class among the larger Krio society. Abdul Fatah Rahman was the first Oku Mayor of Freetown.

There is a high degree of religious tolerance in Sierra Leone among Muslims, Christians and people that practice African traditional religions exclusively. Intermarriage among Christians and Muslims is common and both participate in each other's religious festivals, especially Christmas and Ramadan. In the past, Ramadan prayers and the eve of the Ramadan were celebrated by all, regardless of religious affiliation. One particularly popular event was the parade of lanterns by the Muslims on the eve of Ramadan with different communities competing for the best lantern. Unfortunately, this event is no longer celebrated. The Ramadan day of prayer was also a spectacular event with Muslims dressed in their colorful gowns and marching to the open fields in different parts of the city for prayers. Today, most of these prayerful events are held in mosques or at the Stadium attended by heavy traffic jams of cars loaded with people, rather than by marching parades.

11. Cole, G., 2013, **The Krio of West Africa: Islam, Culture, Creolization and Colonialism in the 19**[th] **Century**, Athens, Ohio University Press.

12 Dixon-Fyle, M., 1999, **A Saro Community in the Niger Delta, 1912-1984: The Potts- Johnson of Port Harcourt and Their Heirs**, Rochester, University of Rochester Press.

CHAPTER 3

Home Life, Discipline and Childhood Experiences

"Fambul tik kin bɛn bɔt I nɔ ba brok" – (The family tree may bend but it never breaks) – Krio Proverb

❖

Growing up in Freetown was a beautiful experience for me. The feeling of being loved came naturally and was taken for granted. Many children, like myself, had a good sense of belonging to a caring community, despite the emphasis on discipline. A 'social comfort blanket' was evident in the care, compassion and order of life and children could sense the sacrifices being made every day for them by their parents and relatives. Older siblings and relatives served as role models and often helped in the raising of younger children. Although education was stressed, there was room for play time and storytelling. These events helped to promote the good values of our society, such as respect for elders, good manners and knowing the difference between home training and growing up 'wild' in the streets. These disciplinary rules came with accountability, since children had to prove themselves through their behavior and also their performance at school. Not all children obeyed these strict rules, and some families had challenges in raising their children and faced the consequences of a child going bad or becoming 'spoilt.'

Playing games was a favorite pastime, although many of the games I played are not so popular today and have been replaced by electronic games. Our traditional games include the typical hide and seek and catch games such as 'A kɔmin O, yes O;' (I am coming O, yes O) the 'Akra' game, played mostly by girls, which is a clapping and jumping game in which teams are identified as 'English' and 'German' in imitation of the Second World War. Football was always popular with boys from a very young age. Listening to the radio in the evening was also a favorite pastime and visiting relatives and friends, especially on Sundays, was routine. During the 'cricket season' children would go out hunting for crickets, roasting them and joyfully eating them. We also sang many children's songs, the most popular being 'The tren fɔ Bo i nɔ wan gri fɔ go' (The train for Bo refuses to move) and 'A kuk fufu, i tɔn to stach. A kuk agidi I tɔn to wax' (I cooked fufu but it turned into starch. I cooked Agidi but it turned into wax.) The lesson here is that one has to be careful to do things properly. Most songs carried hidden values and moral lessons.

As children grow up, their progress is watched very closely by parents and close relatives. As a rule, a mother does not bring up her children alone. Multiple mothering by kindred, friends and neighbors is the norm. In addition, older daughters are expected to help with the raising of younger siblings. A child is a playmate for the kindred and children are usually allowed a great deal of freedom and indulgence until they are about three years old. From then on they may receive small doses of discipline and an occasional spanking. Discipline increases in severity according to age and the need to instill it. Caning is the preferred form of discipline, but the size of the cane has to fit the age of the child. Twigs are used for small children and as they grow up, the size of the cane gets bigger. Canes do not always have to be used directly but are usually put in a prominent position in the home so that just a glance at the cane can serve as a deterrent. Discipline can also be subtle and effective with the use of the eyes to signal a command to the child. An undisciplined child would sometime be scolded as follows: 'Yu kɔ no yay' (You can't even read the eye signals of behavior). At the same time, being expressive and emotional is not discouraged as it is in some Western cultures. It is viewed as essential in the development of compassionate and socially-conscious human beings.

My elder brother, Wordsworth, and I started piano lessons when we were in elementary school and he excelled and completed the Smallwoods tutorial book in one month, while I was still on page two. He became an accomplished jazz pianist and played all over Europe while studying law in Dublin, Ireland. He has continued his love for music to this day and has his own jazz band in Freetown. He is one of the most senior and successful lawyers in the country and once served as a judge for a special tribunal.

Frankwin, the brother after me, was regarded as the nicest and most helpful child. He studied hotel management and business in England and Holland and took over my mother's business as distributor for the Sierra Leone Brewery, which earned her the award of best distributor one year. She and my father also ran Kezfil Enterprises, named for both of my parents. Frankwin was also an accomplished musician and played the guitar as well as composed original songs. Unfortunately, he died in 2017 after a brief illness.

I got along well with all of my siblings but my younger sister, Glenna, was closest to me and we played together a lot. My mother dressed us in similar clothes, which Glenna appreciated, but it left me rather lukewarm to the idea since I wanted to be recognized for my seniority. Glenna was the social butterfly of the family and very gregarious. She made friends easily and was always smiling and had a positive outlook from a young age. I adored my little sister and tried to be the protective older sister. I sometimes wished I could be as sociable as her since I was more reserved and tended to have my face hidden in books. Glenna and I were different when it came to cooking, which she loved and I hated. As soon as it was cooking time, I would disappear and Glenna would stay close to our mother in the kitchen.

My youngest brother, Wilfred, was born at home and I was called into the room soon after to see him. We were all filled with joy, especially my mother, and I remember wondering how his face could be so small. I watched them give him the usual African bath every day and felt sorry for him as he was tugged and massaged and rubbed down in what seemed to me at the time a very rough way. I was told that this would make him strong and healthy. What did I know? I loved carrying him, taking care of him and playing with him. He was so adorable!

The five of us lived in a three story concrete house with our parents and were considered well-to-do by local standards. Our parents used to call us by ringing a bell by the number associated with our birth order. Since I was the second child, my number was two, but we used to play tricks on our parents and not answer right away, so that they would ring another number for the next child. Naturally, there was sibling rivalry, which was reinforced by being in a large family. Scarce resources had to be distributed and followed the line of seniority, rather than gender. However, there was no curtailment when it came to expenses for schools and school fees for every child. We grew up in a family of love, but I never heard my parents say 'I love you' to any of us. They did not have to. We just knew it. I remember being surprised at hearing a mother say those words to her daughter when I went to the United States later. I thought, "How unnecessary. Of course you love her. She is your daughter!"

In the typical home, the parlour is the center of the home, with a family bible prominently displayed on a table in the center of the room. It usually has the name of the ancestors and the current parent or parents to whom it has been passed down. On the walls would be photos of the extended family, representing various life cycle stages, especially weddings and graduation portraits of the children. In addition, it is not unusual to have photos of the British monarch also on display. The furnishings would consist mostly of a sofa, armchairs and decorative items. A dining table would be in another room or part of the parlour. Most families are devout and parlours can serve as spaces for religious gatherings and public events, as well as for recreation. Children are usually not allowed in the parlour, except on special occasions and for family gatherings. They are expected to be out of sight when their parents are entertaining visitors and echo the saying that 'children are seen and not heard.'

Krios pride themselves at being good at imposing strict discipline on children and giving them 'good training.' A child carries the badge of 'good training', which is a reflection of the family. I remember my siblings and I being told not to do anything to disgrace the family and to be on my best behavior at all times. Much of this training is inspired by their religious faith and reinforced by the Ten Commandments but also by African-centered values of respect for the elderly, support of the weak and less fortunate, and building family solidarity. Children are taught to behave properly at all times, both at home and outside it. It is important that older people are respected and given the correct salutations and responses during conversations.[13]

Older male relatives of the father's age group are called 'uncle,' whether they are related or not, and women of the same status as the mother are called 'auntie.' Almost always the terms 'ma' and 'sir' are used for older people or 'sista' and 'brother' to designate respect for a slightly older relative or friend. Words have to be used carefully with the correct pronunciation and no foul language or curse words are allowed. Talking back to your parents is strictly forbidden and quarreling is to be avoided at all times. Some families have been known to move from neighborhoods where the language used is replete with curse words or where there is constant fighting for fear of influencing their children.

Education has top priority, even for parents of low means, and exhibiting the right behavior is believed to a prerequisite for good and proper learning. Parents tend to monitor the company their children keep and the friends that they spend time with to make sure that they have the same priorities in terms of good behavior, faith and education.

---

13 Steady, F. 2001, **Women and the Amistad Connection: Sierra Leone Krio Society,** Rochester, Schenkam Books and Steady, F. 2018, **Krio Women of Sierra Leone: Embracing a Culture of Many Parts,** Linus Learning, Ronkonkoma, New Jersey

The fireworks story: A call for disciplinary action

My mother attended the Teacher Training College and worked for a while as a qualified teacher. She gave up teaching after she got married and started having children. She went into business on her own, using as capital the financial help from my father and bank loans backed by collateral on the house inherited from her mother, Mrs. Clarice Fynch, also a businesswoman. She ran a shop on the first floor of the house and sold a variety of goods, including beverages, textiles, groceries and seasonal goods, such as toys and fireworks. In addition, she later operated a restaurant and became a top wholesale distributor for the Sierra Leone Brewery and a soft drinks company. As children, we would help in the shop and in the house and enjoyed selling toys to our customers. The unsold toys would be taken upstairs to my parents' bedroom and put under the crib in which my youngest brother, Wilfred, who was still a baby, slept.

One morning, my brother Frankwin and I went upstairs to do our Saturday chores, which involved cleaning our bedrooms. The rest of the family had gone downstairs for breakfast, taking our baby brother Wilfred with them. Frankwin and I decided to have some fun with the fireworks and light one of the harmless sparklers. Unfortunately, one of the sparks fell into the basket that contained the rest of the fireworks and ignited the other more explosive and harmful ones. The whole room became a display of all types of fireworks, igniting in all directions and making all kinds of noises. Soon, smoke filled the room and was escaping through the open window. People outside ran to my parents downstairs and alerted them about the smoke. As children, we were petrified and decided to move the flaming basket from under the crib and take it downstairs. At the same time, my father was coming up the stairs with some of the neighbors and helped us to take the basket outside until the flames subsided.

Needless to say, my brother and I were punished and had some of our privileges revoked, such as visiting our relatives on Sundays and going to birthday parties. My father also threatened to send us to boarding schools up country in the rural areas so that we would have to work on farms and perform other difficult tasks. He thought children were spoiled in the urban environment of Freetown, which could contribute to this type of outrageous behavior. The family was grateful that our baby brother was not in his cot when this happened and that no one was harmed. We learnt a lesson of the dangers of disobedience and how easy it was to risk our lives and the lives of others.

Discipline can sometimes be excessive or outdated

Values like respect and strict discipline for children, including corporal punishment, are the norm, although there is variation from family to family in terms of degree of severity of the punishment. Behavior in the ideal home has to be well ordered and follow prescribed rules. These rules often include exercising restraint at all times and are observed automatically from a very early age. Children are loved, but discipline is seen as a way to avoid spoiling them. A spoilt child or 'brat' is an abomination and can bring shame to the family. The extended family, the kindred and even neighbors play an important role in the discipline of children. Within the fambul circle there are usually adults with known expertise in discipline whose skills would be used in cases of very stubborn or difficult children, or whenever there is a crisis of discipline.

The rule has been to impose strict discipline whenever it is needed, although this is rapidly changing. Children that are too bold are likely to be reprimanded, and rudeness is never tolerated. It must be noted, however, that serious challenge to discipline is resulting from rapid social change; the impact of the rebel war and so forth. When a household is very large the mother assumes a dominant role in supervising its organization. As a result, women with many children and wards are constantly issuing orders and recriminations, and tend to be dictatorial.

Using a critical lens, it can be said that extremely strict methods of socialization of children can undermine their creativity and depress their ability to take initiatives. This can lead to a certain degree of conservatism that defines many Krios and is carried from generation to generation. It can derail their ability to negotiate changing social situations that require more assertiveness and innovation, and too much 'training' can be viewed as a weakness by other groups that are less constrained by convention and convictions. This is particularly true of children being raised in the Diaspora, especially in the United States, where good behavior can be misconstrued as weakness and respect for authority as disloyal to the peer group.

In addition, some of the discipline was extreme and differentially imposed on the biological children and children who were wards in their care, many of whom were from poor relations or from outside the Krio group. It was believed that wards, as 'adopted' children, required a stricter discipline as a form of protection, since they were likely to be more prone to outside influences and less equipped to cope with difficult situations and challenges. The idea behind strict discipline was that it provided children with ammunition to ward off aggressive and uncouth behavior without losing their dignity. Good decorum ranked high in the system of merit and reflected on the family and not just the individual child.

My family did not raise many wards and those that came to stay with us did not last for long. One of them fought with the pet dog over a bone and one day poured hot water on it, which caused a lot of pain and anguish to both the dog and my family. My parents asked the ward's parents to take him back. The other was a girl in her teens who was a relative. She was beginning to show too much interest in boys and was difficult to discipline. My parents feared that she would get pregnant, so they sent her back home. One year later, she became pregnant while living with her own parents. The third case was of a relative 'adopted' by my mother after her parents died. Unfortunately, my mother died when she was about six years old and all of her children were overseas, which would have made it difficult for them to get visas for the child. The informally 'adopted' child had to go back to her closer blood relatives.

England: the Promised Land

England was seen as the promised land in many of the English colonies and Sierra Leone was no exception, despite its colonial and authoritarian relationship with its colonies. Everyone aspired to go to England and if possible to send their children there for an education. The connection with England was strong among the Krios, who were among the first in much of Africa to become acquainted with English culture, education and the Christian religion as well as Western values. They were Africans first and foremost with a culture and identity that was cosmopolitan and multi-dimensional, and England was a central part of it. This gave them a unique identity as a group which came into being in Freetown and the peninsular villages.

Most people in the Civil Service aspired to the rank of 'Senior Service', which would elevate their status and earn them a vacation in England. I remember my family giving a big party to celebrate my father's promotion in the telecommunications industry. They decided to take my youngest sister, Glenna, who was ten, and youngest brother, Wilfred, who was five, with them to continue their education in England. It was considered fashionable at the time and my father explained to me the importance of having Africans growing up and going to school with English children so that they would be able to deal with them as equals, especially after independence from colonial rule. My parents decided to leave my siblings with an English family and a Sierra Leonean family, combined with boarding school to continue their education while they returned to Sierra Leone. This was all seen as normal and aspirational for the elite families and anyone who could afford it.

Since my parents did not have a lot of money at the time the older children were born, my two brothers and I did not have the same English experience as our two younger siblings. I remember having mixed feelings on the day of their departure. On one hand, I felt sad as my youngest brother and sister boarded the ship with my parents, but on the other hand I was happy for the opportunities that lay ahead for them. After they left I missed them very much, until I was able to see them when I myself went to England as one of the representatives of Sierra Leone at the Windsor World Camp of 1957.

CHAPTER 4

The Gendering Framework

"Men may be the heads of the household but women are the necks that turn the heads." – Yoruba Proverb

Socially-constructed distinctions between boys and girls start at birth with the gendered forenames given to babies. Other gendered attributes include a baby boy being circumcised within the first two weeks of birth, while a girl is distinguished by the piercing of her ears and the wearing of small earrings within the same period. Generally, the wearing of pink for girls and blue for boys is not a typical tradition, except for those that have lived overseas and adopted this Western style of distinguishing the gender of babies. Traditionally boys are taken out formally on the ninth day and girls on the seventh day. The types of toys given to babies also show gender distinctions, with girls being given dolls and boys balls and so forth. Other ways of becoming gendered pertain to child care responsibilities, which for the most part are assigned to women during childbirth and infancy. It is not unusual to have relatives help with child care or have a paid 'mammy nurse' to help look after children. Wards and older children, especially girls, also assist with child care.

Gender is also constructed along the lines of who is to be protected and who can take risks. Girls are to be protected at all cost, often against being sexually aware too early and avoiding sexual exploitation by boys and men. This involves stricter controls over girls from an early age, ranging from not dressing too provocatively or being too familiar with boys and men who are not relatives, to adhering to a curfew. Boys, on the other hand, can be out late at night and are free to go to late movies, parties and so forth. These distinctions were also marked in the organization of the church. At the time I was growing up in Freetown, girls did not serve in the choir, which meant that boys could go out to choir practice in the evening and attend other late activities in the church. This has now changed and many churches have girls and women in their choir.

Girls were clearly more restricted in their personal and physical mobility and freedom than boys. Although I appreciated the reason behind these restrictions, I never saw them as fair and felt that women's biology should not be an excuse for these restrictions. My consciousness of gendered biases may have started at this early stage of my life, but it was measured. I realized that despite these restrictions girls received the same amount and level of education and had access to equal opportunities, especially in my social circle.

The division of labor

Division of labor in terms of household work in the private domain is by and large by gender, in that women are generally responsible for the household and the raising of children. During their adolescent years and above, fathers and other male relatives are likely to be more actively involved in the socialization of boys. As a rule, men do not help with housework for a simple reason: many households have paid domestic help. In this sense household tasks are not strictly gendered, especially in the urban areas. Although women supervise the work involved in the domestic sphere, hired men are the predominant domestic workers known locally as 'month boys.' In families with small children there is likely to be hired help of women known locally as 'mammy nurses.'

Consequently, the gendering of the domestic or private sphere as essentially female in the West and the non-domestic and public sphere as essentially male does not strictly obtain in the African sense, especially in the urban areas. Children do not grow up seeing domestic work as exclusively the domain of women. Working outside the home is also not usually associated with men being more active in the public sphere than women. Women have been working outside the home in commerce, professional jobs, especially teaching and nursing and in the informal sector for many years. Several women own small and medium enterprises employing numbers of men and women, and several own houses and other real estate in their own right. Women in rural areas in the Western Area provide most of the agricultural labor on family farms and play a major role in taking the goods to the markets for sale.

Menarche – the mark of womanhood

An important aspect of gendering is the menarche for girls, which is not part of the biological process of maturation for boys. Menarche marks the beginning of adolescence, a period of transition for girls and can lead to pregnancy. It is therefore approached with caution, requiring further attention and protection of girls from sexual activity and ultimate premature pregnancy. Some mothers prepare their daughters for this event, but most do not. In some extended families, there would be a designated female adult 'fambul' with special nurturing attributes and communication skills that would be assigned this task by the larger extended family as each girl reaches maturity. In other instances, girls learn from each other and manage the best way they can to take care of their monthly periods.

I had my period at the age of twelve when my parents were in England and received help from our 'Mammy Nurse' who was taking care of us. I had tried to hide it from her, but I was very careless and she found out. My mother had told me about it but did not give many details. She only said that I should avoid sitting on concrete steps so as not to catch cold. I asked her if my brothers had it too and she said no. I then thought, how unfair! Boys seemed to have all the fun and did not have to bleed like girls.

My nanny showed me how to use the napkin safely and securely and how to keep it clean. She also warned me that now that I was a *woman*, I should refuse any boy who asked me to lie on the bed with him. I remember thinking, why should a boy want to lie with me because I was bleeding? This made me very frightened of men without really knowing why. Sex education was not taught to me in the way it should have been, and when I learnt about reproduction in my biology class later in secondary school, it made no connection to real-life situations.

Today, little has changed with regard to the poor level of sex education in the country, as reflected in the epidemic of teenage pregnancies and sexual violence. I was once involved in a research project on teenage pregnancy and maternal mortality at a health center that had a program for poor pregnant teenage girls and mothers. One thing was certain. These girls, who were from all ethnic groups, had no fear of men or getting pregnant as my generation did. For them the greater fear was poverty and destitution and sex was one way of getting out of it, at least temporarily. Most of them were stuck with their babies afterwards and had little or no support from the babies' fathers. Ironically, this reinforced the poverty from which they hoped to escape in the first place through engaging in sexual activities.

Women's associations

Women's formal associations are expressive of the gendering framework and are widespread in Freetown. For the most part, they support the traditional roles of women or serve as social welfare agencies, augmenting the work of the government. They often focus on educational and philanthropic goals and provide an avenue for the development and expression of female leadership. A number of them are linked to churches, such as the Mother's Union, the Dorcas Association and so forth, and render important services to the churches, including fundraising and the maintenance of the church. In some cases, they also provide opportunities for the development of female religious leadership, which tends to be dominated by the male clergy in some of the churches. Over the years, several women have become religious leaders in their own right and been ordained as ministers.

A number of women's associations support political organizations and are styled as 'women's wings' of political parties. Others are stand-alone lobbying groups for gender equality and the advancement of women, such as the Women's Forum and the 50/50 group, which campaigns for equal representation of women in government. Commercial associations catering for the needs of women in business and women traders are popular among market women and provide supportive services and resources, such as access to credit and technology for women-owned businesses. Educational organizations of women tend to be of the Old Girls Association type supporting the Alma Mater and raising funds for the school.

A number of associations aim at representing the whole country and started with the Sierra Leone Women's Movement in the 1950s, led by Mrs. Constance Cummings John. The aim was to empower women economically by creating a network of women farmers and traders throughout the country in an attempt to bring down the high cost of food and of living in general. Due to the initiative of the Sierra Leone Women's Movement, a number of Women's Associations, such as The Sierra Leone Federation of Women, the Muslim Women's Federation and so forth, have operated at the national level. Some of these are branches of international organizations, such as Zonta International and the Women's International League for Peace and Freedom.

For men, the most popular all-male associations are the Freemasons, which are popular among Krio men but are multi-ethnic in their membership. They promote a strong fraternity with guaranteed loyalty throughout life and are especially important during funeral and burial services for their members. They also function as social clubs with a focus on entertainment and feasting and have 'ladies' nights' events to which women are invited. Other male-only associations are known locally as 'dinner clubs' and were started primarily by the British during the colonial era. The English ones operated a color bar which prompted the formation of dinner clubs for Africans. Their focus is on speech making, political debates and feasting and there are special events to which women are invited that are usually recreational and entertaining in nature.

Double standard of morality

Gender differences are most clearly felt in the double standard of morality, whereby men are given the freedom to openly date more than one woman and have affairs outside of marriage with impunity, while women are not. This constraint is played out in ways that can be humiliating to a woman, regardless of her social position in society. She may even be taunted by remarks like 'you hold the ring, we hold the man' from the mistress or her friends. Fathering children out of wedlock when married is not rare and some of these children are accepted eventually by the wife, especially if she cannot have children of her own. Ironically, the standard of morality is not only one-sided. For example, a married woman having a child outside of wedlock also receives some immunity as expressed in the saying 'Mared uman nɔ de bɔn basta pikin' (A married woman does not give birth to a bastard). This is because anthropologically speaking, her legal status recognizes the child as the child of her husband, 'the pater', even if he is not the biological father, 'the genitor.'

Some women pursue married men for financial and other reasons and because of the general feeling that there is a surplus of women in society and not enough good men to go around. This is a result of the monogamous system of marriage practiced by Christians. In polygamous societies there are hardly any 'single women' per se, since they can become second wives. Some of these 'outside women' and 'outside children' in monogamous systems can undermine the stability of the marital home and are often considered a threat. Despite the occurrence of these out-of-wedlock liaisons, there is a high degree of marital stability among the older generation. Younger couples are more likely to break up and get a divorce, especially if the woman has a career of her own and the marriage has irreparably broken down.

Women's achievements in the professions and the economy

One area in which women have tended to achieve a measure of gender equality is in the professions. Although men may have an edge in terms of promotions and benefit from the 'old boys' network', there has never been a serious issue of gender gap in terms of pay equity in the professions or a woman being held back for promotion because of her gender. Women have risen to the highest levels of leadership in medicine, education, law, government, commerce and in many professions. At least four women have served as mayors of Freetown and four as chief medical officers. There is a woman brigadier in the army and several women hold positions of seniority in the police force. In the rural villages of the Western Area to which Freetown belongs, women are the backbone of the agricultural economy and some serve as 'Head Women' and 'Mama Queens' who are specialized in settling disputes in the community.

Regardless of gender, those who possess qualities of leadership have been able to achieve high status and authority. Many of them became important role models for me as I was growing up. As society changes and becomes influenced by modern norms, moral obligations towards kin are becoming diluted and tend to be interpreted in individual terms. They are gradually being modified by the experiences and attitudes of the younger members of society, who increasingly emphasize the element of choice rather than prescription in kinship relationships. All of these changes have an impact on eroding gender roles and expectations, loosening the 'breadwinner' responsibilities for men and opening up opportunities for women.

CHAPTER 5

Formal Schooling, Education and Civil Unrest

Bishop Crowther Memorial School and Tabernacle School

"Learning is better than silver and gold"
Inspired by Proverbs,16:16 - Bob Marley

❖

My first day at school was significant because I was not yet eligible for entering class one, the first grade. At the age of four, my mother and I were walking by our church, the Bishop Crowther Memorial Church and Elementary School at Cline Town which my older brother Wordsworth attended. I insisted that I also wanted to go to school. My mother gave in and took me to the school and asked the teacher if I could join the class. I was put at a table with other first grade pupils and could not contain my excitement on being accepted in school. Right from the start, I took to it like a fish to water. I adored my teachers, most of whom were female and provided good role models for both girls and boys. I knew that this environment was where I belonged, a fact that would be borne out for the rest of my academic life.

I enjoyed every aspect of school life, including following an inflexible academic curriculum as well as an agenda in which play held a special position. Sporting events were important and were featured in celebration of special occasions like graduation and prize giving ceremonies. I participated in many sporting events and even played football, which was usually a game for boys. Interestingly, I was assigned the role of goalkeeper, which was seen as non-essential and therefore could be held by a girl. The main focus of the boys was to make sure that the ball never got to their goal in the first place. As I grew up and understood soccer better, I realized that the role of the goalkeeper was a critical one.

After Bishop Crowther Memorial School, I went to the Tabernacle School on Circular Road, which was about three miles from my home. My brother and I were driven to school by my father on his way to work and we walked home after school, since he was still at work. Tabernacle School provided a good learning environment and I also got to meet children from other neighborhoods and ethnic groups. The main subjects studied were English, Arithmetic, Reading, Writing, Civics, Hygiene, Biology, and Arts and Crafts in forms I and II. I did fairly well in all these subjects and maintained my active interest in the dual curriculum of learning through academic work and the lessons of the playground. My favorite playground games were 'Accra', a competitive clapping game in teams, 'skipping rope' (jump rope), clapping games 'aday' and so forth. At home, we also played these games as well as table-top games like Ludo, Snakes and Ladders and card games. In addition, we played many home-made games like slings; buttons dancing on a string; recycled toy cars from cans and so forth.

One memorable event was when my brother Frankwin and I were bitten by a dog that had rabies while playing with our home-made hoop which accidentally hit our neighbor's fence and aroused the dogs, who chased us and bit us. My family was alarmed and took us immediately to the neighborhood clinic, where we were tested for rabies and given the first anti-rabies shot. After that, we had to have daily injections, which made us celebrities in the neighborhood since this was seen as a cool thing by the other children. Our father Filo drove us to the hospital every day before school for our daily rabies shots. I gave him high marks for being a 'Kombra Dadi', which is a man with nurturing qualities like a mother (Kombra.) On the one hand I praised his parenting skills and on the other hand I was recognizing the priority given to women in the gendered roles of child rearing.

Government Model School

I then moved on to the Government Model School, where I continued my elementary school education in forms III and IV. It was a different environment with a more rigorous academic curriculum and a rigid and sometimes cruel form of discipline. Caning and other forms of punishment were part of school life and tended to get more severe as one advanced through the various grades. Most of the caning was on the hands, while students were also made to stand in the corner on one leg for periods of time or carry a chair over their head for five minutes. Most of the punishment was for disobedience, talking in class, failure to turn in important homework and quarreling or fighting in school. Some discipline required the dreaded visit to the Headmaster's office for some serious scolding. Extremely bad behavior made a pupil subject to being suspended or expelled from the school.

Expulsions were extremely rare and tended to happen only in the event of a girl getting pregnant. Boys who impregnated girls, if known, were never punished by the school and allowed to continue their education – another blatant and unjust form of gender discrimination. The double standard of morality regarding sexual behavior was learnt early as girls came to realize their biological vulnerabilities and to view their bodies as potential barriers to their education. Sex education was superficially taught in secondary school through biology classes and lacked depth and pragmatism.

Standard IV was an important stage in the school system of Sierra Leone, as it prepared students for entry into secondary school, which required a general examination. I did not enjoy Model School very much because I found arithmetic to be challenging and had problems concentrating in school. The student population was diverse, with some students placing a higher value on education than others. I also had problems with the discipline, which tended to destroy initiatives of pupils that wanted something more than the rote learning approach. The teachers did not seem as motivated to try new approaches and school for the most part became boring, leading to a loss of interest. The examination to secondary school was seen as an escape from the last stages of elementary school.

Private lessons were not uncommon at that time and are still popular today. I had them at the homes of my teachers in both elementary and secondary schools; they were given to enhance learning and to prepare pupils for their external exams. They were expensive and could only be afforded by well-to-do parents. Less well-to-do families would pull their resources together to pay for private tutoring wherever possible. A high premium was placed on education as the sure and only means of social mobility in Sierra Leone and the whole educational system was built on integrity and accountability.

The same is not true of the educational system and attitude of parents and pupils today. Cheating is rampant in public exams and students are not motivated to learn. There is too much emphasis placed on social media, on which students spend too much of their time. Discipline is lacking and disrespect for teachers from some students poses major problems of classroom management and control. Lack of discipline at home also undermines the school system as teachers are forced to become both disciplinarians and educationist, an almost impossible task in present-day Sierra Leone.

The 1951 Sierra Leone Women's Movement uprising – an awakening!

My feminist consciousness was probably first stirred at a massive demonstration by women against the high cost of living in central Freetown. This was my first exposure to the public power of women and to the realization of the potential of women to bring about change through direct action. One day after school, some of my friends and I were fortunate to witness a historic event of female activism on a major scale in Freetown. In 1951, as a result of the alarming rise in the cost of food caused by the involvement of Lebanese traders in wholesale food distribution, a group of 10,000 women staged a massive protest demonstration in Freetown. Dressed in colorful African clothes, they marched in procession, singing songs and hymns and carrying banners protesting the high cost of living to the secretariat building, the country's administrative headquarters at that time. They were led by Mrs. Mabel Dove Danquah, who had worked with women's movements in Ghana, and Mrs. Hannah Benka Coker, who founded the first Federation of Women's Associations in Sierra Leone. The protesting women handed over a petition requesting that they be given the monopoly to trade in rice, the staple food. Since the end of World War II this trade had been taken over by Lebanese merchants who were demanding exorbitant prices. Some of the women who were directly involved in food production and distribution as traders in the city markets and farmers in the rural areas were flouting their economic clout and demanding more control over the cost of food.

As a sequel to this demonstration of solidarity, the women not only secured the monopoly of buying directly form the government agricultural station at Newton but also formed one of the largest and most legendary women's associations in Sierra Leone, known as the Sierra Leone Women's Movement and led by Mrs. Constance Cummings-John. It developed an extensive network of rural women farmers and urban women traders to cut out the Lebanese middleman and trade directly with each other. Not only did this movement mobilize women against economic exploitation and the high cost of living on a large scale, it also galvanized women; it built many bridges across ethnic and class lines and united women farmers and traders all over the country.

Another development of the movement was political. It became the first economic association of women to become linked to a political party. Under the influence of Mrs. Constance Cummings-John, the Movement aligned itself with the Sierra Leone's People's Party and she became a candidate in the 1957 elections for the House of Representatives. She won, but later had to give up her seat following a challenge to her victory. Many members of the association were not pleased with this political alignment and preferred to be an apolitical movement. in 1966 she became the first female Mayor of Freetown. The Women's Movement continues to function to this day, but with a much lower profile. The building at Charlotte Street still serves as its headquarters. Members receive advice on business and professional matters. The association also runs a nursery school and a cafeteria which provides some funding for economic projects involving women.[14]

Annie Walsh Memorial School

Having acquired a new consciousness about the power of the so-called 'weaker sex' I moved on to an all-girls secondary school, the Annie Walsh Memorial School, in a grade that was called 'prep,' short for preparatory at the time. After 'prep' I was promoted to form 1 and on to the upper grades until Form 5, where I took and passed the School Certificate exam, earning a grade 11, although I felt I had done well enough to earn a grade 1, the highest grade. I do not recall anyone in my class earning grade 1. Pupils who earned grade 1 were regarded as stars. The certificate covered all the important subjects like English, Math, History, Geography, Biology and French. It was administered in Cambridge, England until 1952, when it was administered by the West African Examination Council (WAEC) based in Accra, Ghana.

I went through several transformations at the Annie Walsh School. In the beginning I had difficulty keeping up with the academic work and concentration was a problem. I also had disciplinary problems

14 Steady, F. 2006, **Women and Collective Action: Development, Democratization and Empowerment,** New York, Palgrave/Macmillan

Cummings-John, C., 1995, **Constance Agatha Cummings-John: Memoirs of a Krio Leader,** Ibadan, Sam Bookman

Denzer, L., 1981, 'Constance Cummings-John: Her Early Political Career in Sierra Leone,' **Tarikh,** vol.7, no. 1

when I was in form 2, which were resolved by my going to boarding school. I started off in prep and not form 1 like the majority of students from secondary school. Prep was designed to give students who did not perform very well in the School Entrance Exam a chance to prepare for a better performance in Form 1. The principal, Miss Pole, took a special interest in me because she felt that I had the potential to do well, and encouraged me to try harder. I was appreciative of the special interest she took in girls that were struggling, and I tried hard to keep up with my classmates. I had my biggest challenge in Math and believe that if I had a better teacher I would have done better. I worked hard in prep and after a while started making progress and my performance improved in all my courses.

My time at the Annie Walsh was one of the most memorable of my educational experiences and I enjoyed it immensely, despite some academic and other challenges. The school was very formal, starting with daily gatherings and prayers in keeping with its Christian missionary orientation. These would be led by the Principal and assisted by the other teachers and the senior prefect, all of whom would assemble on the stage after a procession down the aisle of the main hall. When I first went to the Annie Walsh, I regarded the people on stage with awe as they held the highest authority and served as excellent leaders of the institution. Little did I imagine that one day I would become the senior prefect of the school. I made lasting life-long friendships with students like Juliet Davies, nee Jonah; Imodale Burnett, nee Caulker; Tita Morgan, nee Dougan; Theodora Songo-Williams, nee Davies, and many others.

The Annie Walsh Memorial School is reputed to be the oldest secondary school for girls in Africa. It was named in memory of a real Annie Walsh, who dreamt of becoming a missionary in Africa but died at the age of twenty. In 1849 her parents contributed funds to the Church Missionary Society (CMS) to establish a private school for girls in Sierra Leone. The goal was to educate them with an emphasis on academic excellence, performance and discipline. Its male counterpart, Sierra Leone Grammar School, was founded by the Church Missionary Society four years earlier in 1845. Annie Walsh Memorial school produced many eminent alumnae with high achievements in all spheres of life at the national and international levels. Pupils are divided into houses named after previous principals, such as Sass, Dunkley, Bissett, Caspari, Hamlette and Pole. These houses engaged in debating contests, sporting events and other cultural activities and are distinguished by their colors of red, blue, mauve, yellow and green.

The pupils in the various houses were encouraged to maintain their relationship throughout their stay at the Annie Walsh and afterwards. Sporting activities were very popular and I was fortunate to be on the sports team both for my house, Dunkley, and for the school as well as the gymnastic team. I ran in the 100 yards relay with Frederica John at the start, Rosalind Nicol at the second spot and myself in the third position. I handed the baton to Juliet Jonah, the anchor, who was one of the fastest students on the track field. We always won in competitions with other secondary girls schools at the time. I was also very competitive in high jump for my house.

I pushed myself hard in all my sporting activities but overdid it in gymnastics. At one 'closing function' event to mark the end of the school year, I tried to jump higher on the horse than all the other students and sprained my ankle. I did not notice it at the time but later that evening I was in excruciating pain and could not sleep at night. The next day, my father had to carry me to the car for the trip to the hospital where an X-ray was taken. Fortunately, there was no fracture and I was treated for a severe sprain and sent home. Once again, I was fortunate to benefit from the nurturing qualities of my father. That evening my gymnastics teacher, Miss Eudora John, visited me at home and I was impressed by her care and concern for one of her students.

Going to an all-girls school was important in developing outstanding academic as well as leadership qualities. The environment also promoted confidence and encouraged girls to become more articulate and less shy. The system of prefects was an institutionalized way of developing leadership skills, because it put the responsibility on student leaders for others and charged them with the task of ensuring proper decorum, collective discipline, moral integrity and accountability. No student was considered too young to take on the responsibility of policing herself and developing good manners and effective study habits. Problems of discipline were recorded on students' report cards. 'Order marks' were for bad behavior and 'language marks' for speaking languages other than English while on the school premises. Speaking the Krio language at school was outlawed because of its proximity to the English language with the potential of preventing students from speaking 'proper English.'

Annie Walsh was the most prestigious school during my time there. The academic curriculum was rigorous and we had excellent teachers both from Sierra Leone and abroad. The most widely taught subjects were English, Math, History, Religion, Geography, Science, French, and English Literature. Home Economics was taught both as a core subject and as a particular stream, which was meant to prepare girls for vocational education. Social Science was not taught and the curriculum on the whole tended to focus on England, Europe and America, with little attention to African or Sierra Leonean history. I remember challenging my history teacher, who was English, for constantly praising the military victories of Britain over other European nations. She would say 'we defeated the French, etc.' One day I asked her what she meant by 'we' and she said 'all of us as members of the British Empire.' I said 'but we are not the rulers, we are the colonized.' She replied that we were still united under the British flag. At that point, I thought it best not to continue the argument.

We were taught English history, including the history of the English Royal Family, read English authors, playwrights and poets and learnt about American history, European history and the geographical features of many countries. By the end of the Annie Walsh education, students were more knowledgeable about the world outside Africa than the one within it. The process of Western acculturation through learning was seductive yet uncritical and to some extent not centrally relevant. In fact, Africa was so marginalized in the curriculum that we unconsciously internalized a sense of invisibility of our history and culture and confusion about our identity.

The only language courses taught at that time were English and French, not African languages. Fortunately, since independence in 1961, African languages, especially Sierra Leonean languages have been taught in the schools. Despite this gap in our education, our French classes were enjoyable, especially since we all had French names that closely matched our first names and we learnt a lot of French idioms that we used regularly to impress and tease each other. We enjoyed acting skits in French and singing French songs, and read about France and French society as well as its culture, cuisine and fashion. Ironically, none of the French lessons included countries in French West Africa, like Guinea and Senegal, our neighbors.

Exams were held at the end of each term and also at the end of the school year. The exam culture introduced by the British was dominated by cramming close to the time of the exam and staying up all night the day before it. It took a toll on our nerves and turned us into jittery, zombie-like creatures. The final public school-leaving exams such as the School Certificate for fifth formers and the Higher School Certificate for sixth formers, were major life-changing events that could make or break a student's future potential. The whole city was tense as students try to prepare for the impending exams. Those who had already taken the exam the year before sometimes served as mentors, and many parents tried to encourage their children to study hard and prepare well for the exams.

We did not read books by African authors and instead read many of the popular English classics by authors like Charles Dickens, William Shakespeare, John Keats, Charlotte Brontë and Jane Austen. We also studied critical analysis of these books and learned about the societies that had formed the social and cultural contexts of the stories. I remember wondering how people could spend all their time doing nothing because they were rich and why women were so obsessed about getting married to rich men like the proud and obnoxious Mr. Darcy in *Pride and Prejudice*. Although I liked English literature and did very well in the regular exams I was very critical of the lives of the women and felt sorry for their limited ambitions at that time.

I remember experiencing an exam 'freeze' at the start of the School Certificate Exam in English Literature, which was one of my favorite subjects. As the exam approached, I studied hard and was ready. Yet, for some reason, on the day of the exam, I blanked out and froze as soon as the command was given to start the exam. I read the questions and had to answer two out of four essays, but just could not start. I panicked, froze and stared into space. The invigilator recognized that I was sitting still at the desk while all the other students had started writing. She walked towards me and gave me a tug on my shoulder, which seemed to jolt me to attention and I was able to start. I ended up doing very well in the exam, which was on English Literature, for which I had studied hard.

Most of the students at the Annie Walsh were from Freetown, but there were a few students from primary schools in the Protectorate who attended the school for their secondary education. Most of them lived in the boarding home and were very bright, which earned them a lot of friends. There was only one exception that I can remember, a student from the Provinces who was extremely shy and felt out of place. She was not accustomed to modern facilities and had difficulty expressing herself. Looking back, I think the teachers, the house mother of the boarding home and the other students should have worked harder to make the student feel welcome and provide a supportive environment for her to succeed. She eventually left the school. No one knew what happened to her, but I hoped she was able to continue her education.

We also had students from England, and there was some excitement and curiosity about them joining our class. It was strange to me how concerned the teachers were to make them feel welcome and comfortable. We had several discussions with the teachers to prepare us in advance of their joining the class and a few students were selected to sit with them in the dining hall in the boarding home during lunch. Upon reflection, I believe they were being careful to be hospitable because the students were coming from overseas as opposed to students from other areas of Sierra Leone. I was surprised to see our teachers displaying such toadying behavior to the English students by flattering them and treating them differently. I wish they had offered the same consideration to the student from the Provinces who was having a hard time fitting in.

Today, Annie Walsh does not have the same sterling academic reputation that it once did, nor is it credited with character building and leadership development of its students as it once was. It was the premier girls' secondary school in the sub-region, attracting students from elite families in West Africa, especially Nigeria, and was the beacon of educational excellence for girls. Today, its standards have dropped dismally, as well as its discipline, with complaints of low performance in academic exams and unruly behavior by students showing disrespect for their teachers. This has been made worse by the deterioration of the neighborhood in which the school is located. The center of the East End of Freetown that once displayed a flourishing area of schools, churches, and orderly traffic flow is now an overcrowded junction where there is extensive petty trading on four streets adjacent to the school. The school itself has become a car park, with encroaching peddlers and vehicles littering the once elegant driveway and playground. Most of the foundational buildings of the school are dilapidated and lack regular maintenance and upkeep.

Another problem for the Annie Walsh that was not present during my time there is the relatively sizeable number of male teachers currently teaching at the school and at other all-female secondary schools in Freetown. Although many of them perform a valuable service, most institutions of learning, especially those with female students, are rife with rumors and incidents of sexual harassment by male teachers and pressures of 'sex for grades.' Having male teachers at the Annie Walsh is a major change since my days at the school, when we only had one male teacher in science with impeccable manners, who later became a highly accomplished physician in Sierra Leone. There was no incident of sexual harassment of students by teachers in any of the schools at that time and any behavior of this type was strictly prohibited and would have been subject to dismissal.

Boarding school

Most of my years at the Annie Walsh were spent in the boarding school. Since it was fee paying, it tended to have pupils from the more well-to-do families in Freetown, including a few from the Provinces. This created a class of privileged girls who were conscious of their status in society but also felt an obligation to study hard and get an education that would benefit others. Many internalized the motto of the school, which is *'non sibi sed omnibus'* (not for self but for others.) Many students had a sense of mission and worked hard, nurtured in part by the culture of academic due diligence promoted by parents, teachers, role models and peers.

Academic performance was given a high priority, with a lot of pressure from the school itself. We had an extended study period after the regular school hours that was monitored by one of the teachers who lived in the boarding house or one of the prefects. The study period took place in one of the classrooms in the school which was not far from the boarding house and would start after dinner and end at 9 pm. Most of the students welcomed these study hours, but one incident caused a lot of consternation. As it got darker outside, we heard some strange moaning sounds and some students claimed that a strange non-human looking man was staring at us through the window. Immediately, the terrified students started screaming and running back to the boarding home. Some were sweating profusely and truly believed that they had seen a ghost that night. Fortunately I did not see the ghost, but I thought I heard the moaning sound and I also ran as fast as I could. Some students were so shaken that they talked about it for days and the study classroom was switched to one closer to the dormitory.

Another memorable and frightening incident was the initiation ceremony for new boarding school students. The new boarders were told of a special party that would take place outside one night at bedtime. We were told to wear our nightdresses and no footwear and come downstairs to the common room around midnight. One of the senior girls made a speech about this special party and we were all told to line up and led outside towards the school building. As we approached a wooded area, one of the older girls cut a branch from a tree and I thought I had to do the same. Suddenly, she started whipping me, followed by others, and I was unable to fight back.

I noticed that the other new students were also being whipped and wondered what we had done to deserve this. After about fifteen minutes, the beating stopped and we were asked to go back inside to the common room, by which time some of us were crying. We were then told that this was an initiation to welcome us to the boarding house. In what seemed a bizarre incident to me at the time, we were praised for our courage and made to feel that doing this to the next year's new boarders was something we could look forward to with glee. I did not think so. This was followed by laughter by the older girls and hugs and kisses from them for the new initiates. I thought this was bizarre and unnecessary; I had never been through any form of initiation before. Refreshments were then served, followed by music and dancing and we finally went to bed, with most of the new initiates rubbing their sore bottoms.

During my time at the Annie Walsh, we lost two students, Grace Williams and Josephine Gilpin. My only experience of death before that was the death of my first cousin, Remileku Thomas, from appendicitis at the age of ten. The deaths of my classmates at the Annie Walsh was different. I was older and more sensitive, so I was badly shaken. I felt a deep sense of loss and had no family members around to console me as in the case of my cousin. The loss of Grace Williams hit me hard, because she was a dear friend and one of the most popular students from the Provinces who had made a very strong impact on the school in terms of her brilliance, charisma and popularity. She fell ill and died during one of the long holidays. We were all devastated.

I did not attend her funeral, but I did attend that of Josephine, who died after a short illness that was widely believed to be appendicitis. The funeral was at Kissy, a town outside Freetown where she lived with her family. We were dressed in our school uniforms and warned not to go into the house, as this would upset her mother. Some of us did anyway and were reprimanded afterwards at school, but we did not mind. We wanted to offer our condolences to the mother. As soon as she saw us, she hugged us and started crying. At the funeral, we marched behind the hearse during the procession to the cemetery, but we had to rush because according to local tradition 'the corpse is in a hurry to be buried.' I really believed then that Josephine was causing the hearse to speed up. In reality, we were going down a steep hill which affected the speed of the hearse, but the story fed into a popular local legend that the dead are rushing to be in a better place, which serves to comfort the bereaved.

In boarding school, privacy was a luxury, since we lived and slept in large dorms of about twelve beds and shared common facilities like bathrooms, dining rooms, living rooms and recreational areas. Showers were in stalls that accommodated two or three girls at the same time and although the water was cold, we got used to it and even preferred cold showers because it tended to make us more alert for class.

We knew when someone was having her period since sanitary napkins were more commonly used and made of cloth and washable, with each girl's initials sewn into them for identification. In this regard, we shared a rare kind of intimacy as we managed our monthly periods in common and groups of girls tended to have their periods about the same time. In a strange way, this reinforced our identities as females and resulted in a kind of bonding and consciousness that marked our difference from boys and served as a sign of impending 'womanhood.'

We were divided into families in the boarding school, led by a senior pupil. Families took turns in running the boarding school during the weekends to allow the House Mother, 'Mama Williams', to have the weekend off. Families had to cook the traditional fufu and plasas meals on Saturdays and the stew on Sunday. In addition, they had responsibilities for cleaning the dorms and for disposing of sanitary pads through incineration in a special metal drum. Fortunately, not many girls used sanitary pads at that time, reducing the workload and discomfort involved in their disposal. Ironically, it seemed much more unpleasant incinerating other people's sanitary pads than having to wash one's own sanitary napkins by hand.

Boarding school culture was fascinating because it led to an appreciation and consciousness of one's gender and at the same time led to an awareness of some of the disadvantages faced by girls. It was fraught with the biological and psychological challenges of adolescence and teenage life. Many girls were developing breasts, wider bottoms, menstrual cramps and pimples while in boarding school and dealing with strange hormonal changes. Some developed crushes on each other in the absence of boys and it was not uncommon to have girl-to-girl romances, which were for the most part platonic and at best involved some light kissing only. The idea of being sexually active was rare and in some ways discouraged. All touching and petting was limited to areas above the waist. Realizing that girls going through puberty are likely to have some romantic and sexual urges that may need to be safely channeled and expressed, it was not a surprise that girls would have crushes on each other. In some ways, this kind of adolescent crush was seen as safer than being sexually involved with boys, which could lead to pregnancy.

I remember my aunt telling me that when she was a girl, it was nicer to have a girl kiss her and play with her breasts than a boy. At the time I did not quite understand where she was coming from and why it was necessary to say that. I was too determined to study hard and as we say in Freetown, 'learn book.' Getting romantically involved with boys at an early age was seen as a path to pregnancy and an end to one's education and dreams of a professional career. These girl-to-girl relationships sometimes got complicated if triangles were involved and some girls were very popular and received a lot of letters from other girls who wanted to be their 'friend.' Adults were usually not involved except in the rare case of a house mother and a student whose relationship was regarded as too intense and questioned by most of the residents in the boarding school, but they were not reprimanded.

Visits from family members and friends were allowed on Saturday and Sunday afternoons, during which time 'lunch', which was snacks, would be brought for the week. They consisted of fruits, locally made sweets and delicacies, such as coconut cake, groundnut cake and gari, a local cereal, eaten with milk and sugar. The lunches often reflected the socio-economic background of the pupil, with the more affluent ones having biscuits and other imported snacks as opposed to the local foods. It was not unusual for students to share their snacks or exchange them with others.

We looked forward to visiting time with excitement, especially since some boys our age would likely bring snacks for their sisters or cousins. We used to discuss them and how handsome they were and make believe that we were already dating them or dreamt that those we admired would one day be our 'boyfriends.' We were also allowed to go away on a few weekends, especially for special family occasions. Since the school had a strong Christian orientation we had special services on Sundays, and attended a nearby church on significant Christian holidays.

There were also daily prayers and singing in the school chapel, often led by the teachers and assisted by prefects. At any given time, there would be one or two teachers living in the boarding house with students, including the missionary teachers from the United Kingdom and Canada. Boarding school life was highly structured with strict periods for homework, prayers, meals, recreation and visitors. Taking long walks in pairs through the streets of Freetown for three or more miles was a regular activity. These walks would involve stopping for a rest at some recreational sites, such as King Tom, Tower Hill, Brookfields and Congo Cross. These excursions were taken during weekends when there was little traffic. It was one of the highlights of the week and boarders looked forward to them.

The 1955 Labor Riots outside the school

During my time in boarding school, one of the most significant labor strikes took place in Freetown just outside the school. The main gate to the school was locked and we were told to remain inside the compound. Nonetheless, we were able to see a large agitated crowd, mostly of men, faced by a bank of police officers with truncheons, determined to restrain them from any acts of violence. That terrified us! For the first time in our young lives, we were witnessing what industrial action for fair wages with a potential for violence looked like. This was an educational moment and helped shape my views about the supreme role of labor in the economy; the evils of colonialism; the tensions inherent in class relations and the role of violence in seeking to advance freedom and justice.

The following account of the strike is titled: "Reflections on Sierra Leone by a Former Senior Police Officer: The History of the Waning of a Once Progressive West African Country", given by Exekiel Alfred Coker, a former senior police officer, helps to expand on these thoughts about industrial action.

"In February 1955, very serious riots and looting occurred in Freetown – the worst in Freetown in living memory up till then. Sierra Leone was in transition to independence. The top minister at that time was Chief Minister Dr. Milton A.S. Margai, who was leader of the Sierra Leone People's Party (SLPP). The minister of mines and labor was Siaka Stevens. But the country was still effectively under British colonial rule. The police force and the army were still under the control of British colonial officers.

"The riots and looting occurred between Friday, 11 February and Saturday, 12 February 1955. They started following a pay increase request by Marcus Grant, the secretary general of the Sierra Leone Labor Congress a coalition of several trade unions. Member unions included United Mine Workers Union, Railway Workers Union, and Mercantile and General Workers Union. Grant was asking for an increase of six pence in the daily wages of workers in the various trade unions. But the government's minister of labor seemed to be stalling, insisting that negotiations with the Sierra Leone Labor Congress, should continue.

"In exasperation the secretary general of the Labor Congress called for a general strike, apparently in the hope of exerting pressure on the government so that it might relent and grant the wage increase. Unemployed youth and hooligans, who then spread mayhem throughout Freetown, quickly hijacked the strike. Substantial parts of the city were seriously vandalized. Telephone and radio rediffusion wires were cut.

"Widespread looting of Lebanese as well as Foullah shops followed. But by late Saturday, 12 February 1955, the police and the military had the situation under control. Several people, all of whom were suspected looters and other hooligans, were killed and several were wounded.

"During the riots, assistant superintendent of police, Everett, a young British colonial police officer, was in charge of a riot unit in the eastern part of Freetown. The mob overwhelmed the forty-man unit in Everett's charge. He himself was captured and then lynched. Several police personnel were seriously wounded. Ironically, Everett had just been transferred from Malaya (now Malaysia) during the violent and bloody insurgency in that former British colony. Sierra Leone, which had hitherto been considered peaceful, was the place where this young British colonial officer was to meet untimely and gruesome death at the hands of the violent mob. The riot was finally brought under control by late Saturday with the intervention of the army.

"During the peak of the riot and looting on Friday Deputy Commissioner of Police Anthony S. Keeling, a British police officer together with a handful of policemen fought their way along Kissy Street, where many Lebanese were being looted. After considerable difficulties battling their way through violent mobs along Kissy Street, they finally arrived at Eastern Police Station, where a few policemen were based. By then the mob had almost surrounded Eastern Police Station and had set part of the building on fire. Keeling and the handful of policemen inside the station had no way to escape.

"Just then, a contingent of soldiers under a British officer arrived and dispersed the mob. Keeling and other policemen who were inside the station were rescued from what may well have turned into lynching. The deputy commissioner was therefore saved from meeting the same fate as the young British officer Everett who had earlier in the afternoon been captured and lynched not too far away at Upper Kissy Road.

"I did not personally witness these incidents. But the details were in the report of the commission of inquiry, which was set up by the government after these disturbances in Freetown. Particulars about the incident involving Keeling were also in one of the files at Special Branch headquarters.

"However, a customs officer at the time, I did not personally witness some of the rioting and looting that spread through Freetown on those two fateful days.

"The Freetown riots were followed a few months later by very serious revolts in the protectorate. From 1955 to 1956, people, mainly in the northern province, were rising up against the chiefs. The revolts were centered mainly on Lokomasama Chiefdom."

Boarding school protests

In many ways, this event and the protests by the Women's Movement against the high cost of living in 1951 influenced the boarding school protests that took place two years later over complaints about food and other issues. I was one of the ringleaders. We had been complaining about conditions in the boarding school for years, especially the food, which was too heavy in starches like rice and less on proteins and concentrated unsaturated oils found in the old-fashioned margarine used for breakfast at that time. The students wanted a variety of starches that would include sweet potatoes, cassava and yams in addition to rice and wanted the margarine mixed with butter to make it more palatable. We also requested more free time and more weekends off. We staged a food strike and protest march and presented our list of demands. Much to our surprise, the administrators agreed to meet our demands and students felt a sense of relief and empowerment as well as a level of comfort in living in the boarding house. It was a victory that we, the senior ring leaders and those after us, treasured for years to come.

Teachers

Our teachers were a combination of Sierra Leoneans and British or Canadian White Christian missionaries, all of whom were women. During my time, Miss Pole and Miss Colbeck were principals from England and Miss Maitland, also from England, taught history and lived in the dorms with the students. Miss Strudwick was an English missionary who taught Math and Miss Holland from Canada taught the sciences. Both of them lived in the faculty house with the other international teachers. These women were dedicated and highly educated teachers.

We also had Sierra Leonean teachers who excelled in their fields and were essential role models. These included Miss Lulu Coker, later Mrs. Lulu Wright, who received her university education in England and spoke with an English accent. She was very popular and taught the students not only how to be proficient in French, which was her field, but also how to develop a good character and be of value as a citizen. Other Sierra Leonean teachers included Mrs. Eudora Garber, Miss Jan John, Miss Enid Smart, Miss Lois Thompson, Dr. Enid Forde, Mrs. Muriel Davies, Mrs. Christiana Nicol, Mr. Ishmael Peters and Miss Sarah Johns.

Transformations at the Annie Walsh

While at the Annie Walsh, I went through several stages of transformation. At the beginning I did poorly in my classes and had to be mentored by the teachers and the principal to really overcome the challenge of school work. I also went through a personal crisis when I was in form two, about the age of thirteen which resulted in rebellious and bad behavior for no obvious reason. I would be talkative in class, disobey teachers' orders and fail to turn in my homework on time. I was also the ringleader in a number of disruptive behaviors in and out of the classroom. My parents received several complaints about my behavior, which they and the teachers thought were not in keeping with my family or religious upbringing.

Being a religious school of the Church Missionary Society, discipline was strict and conformity to the required behavior and standards taught at home were paramount at the school. This was the reason my parents decided to send me to boarding school, which I resented at first but grew to appreciate over the years. During my time as a boarder, I experienced a complete personal and spiritual transformation and improved significantly in my academic work. I also developed important leadership qualities that led to my becoming senior prefect and a winning member of the school's athletic team. I also earned the high title of 'First Class Girl Guide' and was selected as one of the two Girl Guides to represent Sierra Leone at the Windsor World Camp in England in 1957.

CHAPTER 6

Windsor World Camp in England, Graduation and Falling in Love

"Love conquers all" – Virgil

❖

I was an active Girl Guide at the Annie Walsh Memorial School and had earned first-class status, which was the highest honor given to a Girl Guide in Sierra Leone at that time. We met regularly and learned leadership skills and acquired practical tools for survival in difficult environments. We went camping frequently and enjoyed challenging hiking expeditions. For all of these activities, we earned badges of honor that were sewn on the sleeves of our uniforms. Girl Guides were an elite group of young girls who had visions of becoming good leaders in the future. Character development was an essential part of being a Girl Guide and qualities like integrity, discipline, a sense of duty and preparedness were instilled in us. The motto was 'Be prepared,' and Girl Guides were distinguished by greeting each other with a handshake of the left hand. We felt very special.

In 1957, Sierra Leone was going to participate in one of the largest international camps of Girl Guides – The Windsor World Camp in England. Two representatives were to be selected, one from Freetown and one from the Provinces. We had a weekend camping event at the boarding house of the Annie Walsh school and were divided into competing teams. As head of one of the teams, I worked very hard to ensure that we won, but I was aware that this meant some excellent Girl Guides would be left out and this made me uncomfortable. At the same time, I was delighted to be selected and was joined by Isatu Kamara from another Girl Guide troop to represent the Provinces. I was overjoyed and looked forward to traveling from the shores of Sierra Leone and going to England for the first time as a teenager.

I could not contain my excitement after boarding the *Apapa*, the ship that was to take Isatu Kamara and myself to England. At that time, there were no passenger planes and everyone went to England by one of the large ships of the Elder Dempster Lines. The major ships were named after several landmarks and cities of West Africa such as Accra, Apapa and Aureol.

Our excitement was doubled when we realized that the Ghanaian contingent of Girl Guides and Boy Scouts were also going to be travelling with us. Ghana had just gained its independence from Britain and so their Scouts and Guides were the center of attention right from the start. I remember thinking how smart, mature and dynamic all four girls and four boys looked. Like us, they had their adult scout or guide leaders with them as supervisors.

We soon became well acquainted and spent a lot of time together playing games and exploring the decks and various public rooms of the ship. We even managed to get the cooks to prepare special African foods for us, including fish, which they caught right from the deck of the ship. Naturally, we were curious about the every aspect of the ship and asked to go to the captain's deck where we were allowed to take turns in steering the big ship. A bunch of teenagers having a lot of fun on a ship and playing captain is not something that happens every day. This was paradise!!

As we approached Liverpool, England, the port of our disembarkation, we could feel the change from the warm, bright and sunny tropical weather of West Africa to the cold and foggy dampness of England. We were met by representatives of the Girl Guides

Association of England. They greeted us warmly and enthusiastically, but it was clear that the Ghanaian delegation was the one they were eager to meet, Ghana being the first country in Africa to gain its independence from England. As the reception party climbed onboard, they eagerly asked 'Where are the Ghanaians?' and rushed over to greet and interview them. It was a special moment as both Ghana and Africa were being recognized and celebrated and the delegation from Sierra Leone was proud to celebrate with them.

After the immigration and customs formalities, we were warmly met by our escorts outside the harbor as we tried to ignore the fog and mist that made it difficult to see. We were taken by train station to the first host family stay at Northampton in the East Midlands region of England. The train ride was exciting and we could not get over the large size of the train, compared to our much smaller trains in Sierra Leone. We enjoyed looking at the trees, shrubs and houses, all of which looked so different from what we were used to in Freetown. The English countryside was particularly lovely with the farms and animals grazing and stopping to look at the train as it went by. Even the cows were much bigger and fatter than our cows and the sheep with their long and thick hair was nothing we had ever seen before. I wondered how much grass they would have to eat to be that size. No wonder they seemed to be eating all the time! We also saw barns loaded with hay as well as tractors for the first time. Our farmers in Sierra Leone had very few farm tools and most of them were simple tools like hoe, cutlass and knives. We also saw milk trucks and other farm vehicles loading and unloading agricultural produce. Unlike in Sierra Leone where a lot of women worked on the farm, I did not see many women and later learnt that rural women tended to work indoors doing housework or milking of the cows and looking after small animals like chickens.

Northampton – host family stay

Upon arrival in Northampton, we were met by our host family, a husband and wife with three teenage children, one boy and two girls. They greeted us warmly and drove us to their home on a large estate with a large house in an area that was between the suburbs and the rural area. It had a tennis court and a vegetable garden as well as a small area where a few rabbits and chickens were being reared. Although this was summer time, the weather was cold to us and we had a special heater brought to our room as well as hot water bottles for our beds. After a good night's sleep we woke up to some singing birds and the smell of bacon. We had the famous English breakfast for the first time, comprising bacon, eggs, kippers, fried tomatoes, toasted bread, jam and butter and two hot cups of English tea. As this was a weekend, the family drove us to the town and the market for shopping and we got our first glimpse of what it was like to live in a small and quaint English town. We were stared at a lot since everyone was White and we were the only Black people around. Some smiled at us, but most of them simply stared and then looked away when we caught them staring.

One thing that was strange to us was the fascination with our hair by people we met as well as those within our host family. Some would remark afterwards that it felt curly or like wool. One day, Isatu and I decided to have our hair straightened for a special social occasion to which we were invited. We had brought our hot irons with us so we asked our host mother to use the stove in the kitchen to heat it up. She was fascinated by the whole idea and decided to watch. As we started straightening our hair, she looked alarmed and shouted 'No no, you are taking out your beautiful curls. Please don't do that. Your curls are beautiful and you may not be able to get them back.' We assured her that after a few days our hair would go back to its beautiful curly state.

Our stay with this hospitable family was a good introduction to British culture and society and some of it seemed familiar to us, especially the way the home was decorated and the warm interactions among the family members. The food was different in that it hardly had any spices and we had hoped to eat more rice than potatoes. We also could not get used to the idea of the food being regimentally separated on the plate so that the meat stood on one side, the potatoes on another and the vegetables on a third side. They got mixed in your mouth and not in the cooking like we were used to in Sierra Leone. We got used to it and once we added some black pepper that we bought in town, we generally enjoyed our English meals.

One of our highlights was going to school with one of the children of the family who was closer to our age of sixteen. It was quite an eye opener in terms of the social aspects but the academic program and curriculum were fairly similar to what we had in Sierra Leone. The girls were very curious, but nice and felt honored to have us in the school.

We discovered a type of behavior that was very strange to us, that is the public kissing and making out on the grass of the school yard by girls and their girl friends. It was open and indiscreet and seemed to be accepted by everyone, including the teachers. It seemed to me like a strange ritual and occurred without fail during recess everyday among a large number of coupled girls.

I became aware of the fact that some private acts are public among the English, unlike in Sierra Leone, and that did not seem civilized to me. I have seen romantic expressions by girls with each other during my days as a boarding school student but kissing among girls was private, even in dormitory settings. My consciousness about being female was enhanced only to the extent that I appreciated the fact that girls in England went through adolescence in the same way we did but had no problem expressing it publicly. Maybe it was their way of warding off the boys with whom such a relationship could end in pregnancy. I never felt these expressions of love were permanent but transitory and related to adolescent development to some extent but never understood it fully. It never occurred to me to ask whether boys had similar crushes on boys. In the culture in which I grew up, that behavior would have been taboo. I later found out that intimate boy-to-boy relationships were not uncommon in British public schools which are in effect fee-paying and elite private schools.

Windsor World Camp

After two weeks with this family we left for the big event by train – the Windsor World Camp at Windsor. The camp was attended by 4000 Girl Guides from almost eighty countries. The guides were divided into ten sections which were further divided into eight groups. It was officially opened on July 30th by Lady Baden-Powell, wife of the founder of the Boy Scouts and Girl Guides, and visited by Queen Elizabeth and her sister, Princess Margaret. It was a thrill to see them both and the head of each country delegation had the opportunity to meet the Queen. In the case of Sierra Leone, our leader, Mrs. Remie Terry, was delighted at the opportunity to meet with the Queen and to have her photo taken with her.

The experience of sleeping in tents was strange because of the problem of scarcity of water. Coming from Sierra Leone, we were used to bathing every day and had to make do with a small amount of water at the camp. It did not seem to bother the English girls, who were minimalists in terms of daily bathing and felt fine with it.

There were many nationalities and at first I was overwhelmed by the differences, but later I realized that we had a lot more in common as teenage girls than differences. The girl guides from the Nordic countries struck me as being extremely tall, while the girls from Asian countries were smaller in stature. Girls from the Caribbean were mostly mulattos, which I thought was strange since these were countries inhabited by formerly enslaved people from Africa who were black. They were not very well behaved and gave me a very bad impression of people from the Caribbean. Fortunately, this impression changed in my later years when I had the opportunity of going to the Caribbean and enjoying their kindness, warmth and hospitality.

The Americans were also rather boisterous and thought they should be the center of attention. The Scottish girls were the most popular because of their friendliness and beautiful Scottish line dances. Once again, I found myself in a community of people of my gender and received a lot of support and appreciation from many of the guides.

We held camp fire gatherings, accompanied by the singing of Girl Guide songs every night, and went hiking regularly as well as on bus tours to areas around Windsor. There were several major events, including the donation of contributions from each country towards a fundraising efforts for the international Girl Guide Association. I was selected to make the presentation of fifty pound sterling from Sierra Leone to Lady Baden Powell on a stage in front of all four thousand participants. Photos were taken of each presentation and at that moment I felt the weight of my country on my shoulders and was proud of representing Sierra Leone.

On one occasion, we went sightseeing in London, and as we drove around London on double-decker buses, we saw many young male and female couples kissing and fondling each other on buses, in the parks and just about everywhere and were shocked at their lack of modesty and propriety. We wondered why they were not embarrassed and were reminded of similar but less intense behavior by some of the girls in the all-girls school that we visited earlier. Isatu and I discussed this behavior and agreed that if Africans behaved like that, they would probably be seen as uncivilized and arrested. Despite these unwelcome sights, we did have enjoyable sight-seeing visits which included Buckingham Palace, Trafalgar Square, Madame Tussauds and The Tower of London, where I was told that some of the diamonds on the Crown Jewels came from Sierra Leone. It was one of the times during the trip when I was reminded that my country was a colony of Britain, exploited for its mineral and natural resources. We were therefore subjects of the Queen and the British Empire in ways that were not unique to us.

A woman heading the throne of England was something of importance in the evolution of my understanding of gender and gender relations. At the same time, she was head of an imperial system that dominated my country and people, with hierarchical formations that constructed unequal and hierarchical power relationships. So in my mind, I was conflicted between being proud of a woman in power and realizing that this woman was at the head of a system of domination of my country and people through the colonial process. To me, it was a contradiction between the idea of patriarchy and male dominance and their representation by a woman heading an imperial patriarchal system. I came to view these contradictions as an uncomfortable reality as a young girl entering womanhood.

Visiting Glenna and Wilfred

I had the opportunity of visiting Glenna and Wilfred, my younger sister and brother, at the Collins' family home in Grayshott, Surrey, England. We were excited to see each other again and I remember wanting to keep hugging them for as long as I could. They looked different, taller but also thinner in keeping with their growth spurt and the fact that I had not seen them for a few years. I spent a weekend with them and their host family and they seemed happy enough, but tended to go to bed very early. They did not seem to eat much which may have accounted for their slim look, but I also wondered if they were having enough to eat as growing children. They were the only Black children in the town, so they were easily recognized and people were intrigued by their presence.

It was very difficult to say goodbye to them when I had to leave for Sussex. They both did very well at school, which earned them a lot of respect. Soon after my visit they finished their schooling and moved to London to stay with a Sierra Leonean family, the Aubees. Glenna went on to Upton Hall, a boarding school in Duston, Northampton, where she did well academically and athletically and helped supervise a number of young students in her leadership role as a prefect. Later she went on to the Central School of Speech and Drama in London and became an actress, while Wilfred studied and practiced law in England.

Sussex host family stay

After the Windsor World Camp, we went to our second home stay with a family in Sussex in the south-east of England, with two parents of advanced years and three adult children, one son and two daughters. Being a blue-collar family, they were not as affluent as the first family with whom we stayed, but were equally hospitable. It was a much smaller house and our tiny bedroom had bunk beds, but they felt comfortable. Once again, we experienced the lack of regular bathing and felt conscious of imposing our Sierra Leonean habit of daily bathing. We realized that it cost money for heating the water, which is not the case in Sierra Leone, where baths are usually with cold water and relatively free but in England the water is much colder.

We also had moments of acute gender awareness when we had our periods. The practice at the time was to burn used sanitary pads in the fireplace. The problem was that the fireplace was only lit when the father was home and reading his newspaper or watching television in front of it. For us it was a challenge trying to put our used and carefully -wrapped sanitary pads in the fireplace when the father was in the room. It was most embarrassing and we often wished he would leave the room for a moment so that we could get the job done. Unfortunately, he just sat in his armchair and let us get about our business of burning our sanitary pads without flinching for one second. As an insight into gender consciousness development, Isatu and I would discuss these incidents with embarrassment and wonder why our host father was not embarrassed as a man. We decided that it was because he had two daughters and a wife and was used to them burning their soiled sanitary pads in the fireplace in his presence. He probably saw us as his adopted daughters doing the same 'monthly woman thing' and thought nothing of it.

During our stay in Sussex we went out several times to the town sightseeing and shopping but hardly saw Black people, as they were rare in that part of England at that time. I remember our excitement when we saw the first Black woman in a store. We ran towards her and greeted her grinning with enthusiasm. She gently smiled and greeted us in return but showed no excitement. We wondered why she was not excited to see us. We figured that she must be used to being a rare presence in that area and either did not appreciate having other Blacks around as competition or our presence was of little significance to her. We also considered the possibility that she might have been in England for a long time and developed the English 'stiff upper lip' attitude. Whatever it was, it still made our day to see another Black person in that part of Sussex.

As our stay drew to a close, we realized that we were going to miss our host family and their warmth and kindness and we all cried a lot in saying goodbye. They saw us off at the train station to Liverpool to board our ship, the *Apapa,* back to Sierra Leone. We were fortunate and excited to travel once again with the Ghanaian contingent of boy scouts and girl guides, whom we saw only once at the Windsor World Camp. We had all changed a little, noticeably in the way we spoke. We tended to be more formal and to adopt a more English-sounding accent. It was as if we were preparing to make an impression about being a 'been to' (someone who has been to England) when we got back home. We had also adopted some English mannerisms and demeanor that looked affected but were accepted. Anything to make us look different when we got back home was fine – after all, how many teenagers from West Africa had the chance to travel to England and participate in the Windsor World Camp?

We had a great time on board the ship and had fun listening to music, dancing, fishing from the ship with the cooks and playing deck games. After a week on board, we started approaching Sierra Leone and saw the mountains from afar. I was reminded of the story of Pedro De Cintra, the Portuguese explorer who was supposed to have 'discovered' Sierra Leone. The mountains, so close to the shore, reminded him of lions on a misty morning. He then heard the sound of thunderstorms, which are evident during the rainy season and thought they were the roaring sounds of the lions. As a result, he named the country 'Serra Lyoa' meaning 'Lion Mountains.' I always wondered about that story since Ironically, there are no lions in Sierra Leone.

When the ship landed in Freetown, a large number of people came onboard to meet their relatives and friends. I was delighted to see my parents and the Girl Guides representatives and media that came to welcome us home. The media had a lot of questions for us and wanted to know about our experiences. It felt good to be the center of attention and I could sense my parents' pride in my accomplishment of successfully representing Sierra Leone, with Isatu and Mrs. Terry, our leader, at the Windsor World Camp of 1957. It was a wonderful experience for two young teenage girls from Sierra Leone. What an opportunity! What an adventure, and what an honor!

Sixth Form at the Annie Walsh

Returning to school was quite a challenge as I was now moving up to the sixth form, which prepares students for college. While in England, I had been impressed by the academic dedication of the sixth formers of the school we visited. I also noticed that they had a different uniform from the rest of the students. I felt that this would be a good idea for the Annie Walsh School and suggested it to the principal and senior teachers. They liked the idea and involved me in selecting the material and designing the uniform. It was quite an honor and everyone was pleased with the final result, which kept the general green color of the uniform but divided the sixth form uniform into a skirt of the same shade and a blouse of a lighter green color. I felt very proud to have been an innovator of sorts and to have taken the initiative to suggest this change and distinction for sixth formers that is still used to this day.

Sixth formers are in the most senior rank of the school and serve as role models for other students. They are generally respected and admired by students and teachers alike. Much is expected of them and many of them play important leadership roles as prefects, who help in the management, guidance and running of the school. I was fortunate to become one of these prefects and in my senior year became the senior prefect, the highest honor bestowed on a student. Sixth form was as special an experience as it was academically challenging. It was an important milestone since students had to take and pass the Higher School Certificate exam in preparation for college. I worked hard but always felt that I could do better and was happy to pass my Higher School Certificate exam, which qualified me for entry into college.

Infanticide at FBC by Alumna

One of the most disturbing events during my sixth form years was a scandal that involved an Annie Walsh alumna who was a student at Fourah Bay College. It brought into sharp focus the differential role that gender played in the educational prospect of young men and women. Women's biological vulnerabilities put them at risk of ending their educational goals and careers whereas men can continue their education and even deny paternity for an unwanted child. The sixth form students gathered at the back of the room to read about this tragic event in the newspaper. It reported an incident whereby an Annie Walsh Alumna at Fourah Bay College delivered a baby on her own in one of the bathrooms of the college. Apparently, no one knew that she was pregnant since she had concealed it well by wearing loose fitting clothes.

As the story goes, she gave birth to the baby and then killed it by tying a scarf around its neck and strangling it. She eventually got very weak from the delivery and fainted on the floor of the bathroom, to be discovered later by another student who reported the matter to the college authorities. This tragic event got us talking about the vulnerabilities of being a woman, as this would never happen to a man, and we wondered where the father of the child was and why he was not also in trouble. We then started blaming the mother.

Around that time one of our missionary teachers walked into the room and asked what all the excitement was about. We informed her of the tragic case of infanticide at the college and showed her the newspaper. Her immediate comment was, 'Poor child. How badly she must feel at this time. They should not have put it in the newspaper.'

We all looked at each other with astonishment at the realization that this English missionary woman felt more sympathy for the student than we did. We were ready to join in scandalizing the 'murder' of an innocent child by its own mother. We all felt ashamed! From that day on, I saw this missionary woman as a compassionate human being who displayed good moral character and sympathy and admired her.

The student was arrested and tried for murder, but was acquitted. Apparently, her lawyer argued that the child was stillborn and the tying of a scarf around the infant's neck was a customary act performed by members of the defendant's ethnic group upon the delivery of a 'still born' infant for the protection of the mother and baby.

I also learnt other lessons from our missionary teachers that are valuable to me to this day. At that time, I was not critical of missionary activity in Africa because we were not taught about their role in the colonization process. In fact, we did not have a critical insight into colonization at all and did very little or no analysis of colonialism both inside and outside of our classes. It was seen as a given. After I leant more about colonialism, mostly through my studies in the United States, I wondered if those nice missionary ladies knew how much they were complicit in the colonization process. Somehow I believe that they were as naïve about it as we were and felt driven by their desire to contribute to the education of African girls.

I do remember two things that were said by one of these missionary teachers that have stood with me till this day and that I practice in my life. One is that negative gossip was bad and that if we were to be part of a conversation that was deriding someone, we should come up with one good thing to say about the person to break the cycle of negativity. Another lesson was not to be disappointed if the things we wished for in life did not happen right away because if we work hard, our dreams are likely to come true.

All of the missionary teachers were unmarried and we assumed that this was a criterion for missionary work, but we knew that one of them was dating a Sierra Leonean academic and we used to spy on them kissing in the car when he visited the campus to see her at the faculty residence.

Being in sixth form was prestigious, because it was the preparatory stage for college and was very competitive. I succeeded in gaining high marks in the final public exam and received a Higher School Certificate after a rigorous exam. The prospect of attending university filled me with excitement and made my parents very proud. The plan was to study overseas since sociology, the field in which I was interested, was not offered at Fourah Bay College. There was also pressure from other students to study overseas and the prevailing view was that being educated overseas, especially in England, was more prestigious than being educated at the local college. In addition, a university degree from England was preferred to one from the United States since it was more competitive.

Falling in love

Sixth form was an important milestone because I fell in love for the first time with someone who later became my husband. We met when he was in upper sixth form at the Prince of Wales School for boys studying science in preparation for a career in medicine. I was in lower sixth at the Annie Walsh, studying History, English and Literature and planning to concentrate on the social sciences, especially sociology, in college. We met at the famous Prince of Wales (POW) School Dance held at Gooding Hall every year by senior students of the POW. I had seen him before at a fair at Victoria Park many years ago when I was about thirteen years old. I had just won a teddy bear and this young man walked up to me and asked me whether it was for him. I said no and asked my friend who he was. She said 'His name is Maduka Steady.'

At the dance years later, he came up to me and asked me to dance and introduced himself as 'Henry Maduka Steady.' He said I reminded him of the actress Eartha Kitt and asked for my name. He then wanted to know if I had come alone and I said, 'no, my father dropped me off'. He looked at me strangely and said, 'no, I meant did you come with a boyfriend?' I said 'no, I don't have a boyfriend.'

He then asked for my address and permission to come and visit me at my house, because he did not think I should be alone anymore. I felt very special and was struck by his voice, which was low but clear with a tinge of a British accent. I was right about his voice, because he would recite poems at school functions and later worked at the Sierra Leone Broadcasting Service after sixth form before going to university abroad. We dated for about a year before he had to leave for Monrovia to join the rest of his family. His father, The Reverend Dr. Isaac C. Steady, a Sierra Leonean, was the chaplain in the Liberian Army and bore the rank of major.

Henry had a reputation for academic brilliance and skipped one class through a system of double promotion for gifted students. He graduated with a School Certificate and a Higher School Certificate as one of the top students in his class and planned to study medicine. He came from a family of religious ministers and academics whose ancestry can be traced to Waterloo Village in the Western Area. His grandfather, the Reverend Dr. Henry Metcalfe Steady, was one of the founders of the African Methodist Church (AME) in Sierra Leone and his father, Rev. Dr. Isaac C. Steady, was a minister at the church for several years. Henry himself was ordained a Deacon of the church and lived in the family house in the back of the church from childhood on, with responsibilities that included opening the doors for service and ringing the bell. His mother was Agnes Steady, nee Noah, a teacher at the Annie Walsh Memorial School who unfortunately died when he was only three years old. His father remarried Edna Johnson and had three children, Thelma, Elizabeth and Onikeh, and an adopted son, Joseph. He had moved to Liberia, where he was appointed as chaplain of the Liberian Army.

Henry was someone who stood out not only academically but also as a broadcaster for the Sierra Leone Broadcasting Service. He was an anchor for the news and also a continuity announcer and won the Leslie Peronne Cup for excellence in Broadcasting. He also taught briefly at the Prince of Wales School, but did not like teaching because of the challenge posed by disruptive students. He lived in Freetown with his paternal grandmother, Hannah Steady, who was in her late eighties while he attended the Prince of Wales School. She lived until her early nineties and he told me how proud he was to be seen going out with his grandmother and running errands for her. Henry stood out because of his sterling character, integrity and decorum, credited to being raised by his grandmother in Freetown. He is a classy guy who is also an innately good, nice and a suave gentleman in every sense of the word. After his grandmother died, he moved briefly to Liberia to join the rest of the family until he won a scholarship to study at Yale University in the United States.

Graduation from High School after Sixth Form

After the final exams, students got ready for the long holidays during the months of June, July, August and September, most of which is the rainy season. This was usually marked by a 'Closing Function', which was the culmination of a student's secondary school career for graduating students of the fifth and sixth forms. In my case I graduated from the fifth form with a School Certificate and two years later from the sixth form with a Higher School Certificate. It was an honor for me and my family as the first girl and second child destined to go to college, which was a rare opportunity at that time. However, the school calendar of Sierra Leone ended in December and universities in England started in the autumn months of the following year, which gave me ten months of waiting time in Sierra Leone.

I decided to get a job as an assistant teacher at the government Municipal School, an elementary school on the street where I lived, and to learn typing in the evenings. I had my first taste of teaching and knew that this was my calling, even though my goal was to teach at university level. I discovered that teaching five and six-year-old children required more than just the basic knowledge of reading, writing and arithmetic. One had to have other skills and attributes, such as patience, a keen sense of observation and the ability to talk a lot and give orders constantly. Teachers also had to keep the children safe, especially during recess when they are likely to get involved in playing wild games and getting into accidents. This happened to one of my pupils, who ran through a glass door and suffered serious wounds on his legs and arms. I had to take him to the emergency department at the Connaught Hospital, the main hospital in Freetown, for treatment. His mother came later and cried a lot when she saw his wounds. She thanked me profusely and said that being a mother brought a lot of pain beyond the pain of childbirth. I felt a close bond with her as a woman. Little did I know that several years later I would experience a pain of motherhood that would almost tear my heart from my body.

I also learnt the skills of shorthand and touch-typing at this time at the Technical Institute of Sierra Leone. Most of the students at the typing school were planning to have secretarial careers. It was a skill that I am grateful to have acquired as most of my work now requires typing on my computer. All in all, I am grateful for the education I received in Sierra Leone and for the teaching experience and the opportunity to learn typing and shorthand skills before embarking on my university education overseas.

CHAPTER 7

Going to England for the Second Time
for a University Education

"The only way to resist colonialism is through education"
Tariq Ramadan

—◆—

My second trip to England was on one of the cargo ships on the West African route that took few passengers. There were three other Sierra Leoneans, a dozen Nigerians and about two dozen Europeans. The fact that recreational activities were limited made it somewhat interesting, since our activities were not highly structured and we had time to roam around on deck and watch the waves go by.

With one notable exception, relations among the passengers were cordial. The exception was provoked by friction between the Nigerians, most of whom were Yoruba, and someone from another African country who felt they were too loud and confrontational. As a result, the Nigerians sent a delegation to apologize to the offended passenger. I learnt then that in this kind of exchange the person wronged can only say 'thanks for your apology' and not try to start a new argument or the delegation will leave abruptly. That was an interesting take on the African diplomacy for which the Yoruba of Nigeria are famous. It taught me a valuable lesson in social relationships that was to prove useful to someone intending to study sociology.

After about ten days, the ship docked at Liverpool harbor on a cold and foggy morning.

My mother met me at the harbor as well as Laureen, an English friend that I had made during my first visit to England and her fiancé. Although we were the same age, I remember thinking how grown up she looked with heels and stockings compared to my shoes and socks. After a nice warm breakfast my mother and I took the train to South Norwood, London. We lived in a big apartment building which had several families as tenants from England and all over the world, such as Burma, Jamaica, India, Ireland, Nigeria and Sierra Leone. In addition there were two Englishmen who shared an apartment and kept very much to themselves. There were very few pay phones shared by all the occupants. One of them was located just outside our apartment, which meant that one of us had to answer it most of the time, and this became annoying.

Each of the families had their own characteristics, which made them unique in many ways. The Burmese family was the quietest and most rarely seen, with the husband and wife appearing to be amicable and the two children well behaved. The Jamaican family was more lively and played Jamaican music from time to time with the sound at a fairly low volume. It was a female-headed household with a strong mother well in charge of the home and family of three children, two girls and a boy. The teenage son tried to get my attention on several occasions and suggested taking me out but I declined. At the time I already had a boyfriend back home and I was too focused on getting ready for my university education in any case.

The Irish family was the only one without a working wife and mother. The wife stayed home, cooked and cleaned and kept having babies, but we never saw her pregnant. She always wore housecoats and aprons when at home and a big winter coat when she went out. We only heard the cry of a newborn baby after she had given birth. She would often put the newest babies in one of the drawers, since the only cot was already occupied by the toddler. One distinguishing feature of this family was that the four children were very pale, as was the mother, which indicated to me that most of the nutritious food was probably eaten by the father, who did not have a pale complexion.

The Nigerian family had a bright but overactive three-year-old son and a mother who was very good at her job at a Phillips electronic factory. It was never clear to me where the father worked, but he left for work every morning in a car bought on higher purchase which was later repossessed. He always seemed to have financial problems. We called him Mr. G. He found out that the British did not eat many parts of the cows, such as the feet and intestines, which were delicacies in Africa, especially West Africa. Mr. G realized that he could make a lot of money by selling these parts to other West Africans and even some people from the Caribbean, rather than having them thrown away by the slaughterhouses. He would collect large amounts of these parts of the cows and bring them to the house for preliminary cleaning. This entailed burning the hairs off the legs of the cows in the backyard, which left a strong smell that soon found its way through the house. The other tenants hated it but did not complain very much because Mr. G. had a nasty temper and was sometimes heard quarreling with his neighbors and rent and other collectors. His clients would then come to the house to collect their food, from which he made a lot of money. I learnt later that over the years as the immigrant population grew in England, the meat industry realized the profits to be made from these parts and started processing and cleaning them and selling them at some butchers' shops and grocery stores in England.

Most of the families lived amicable and wholesome lives. However, one family that will remain unidentified had a serious problem with domestic violence that shocked me and the rest of the tenants in the building. I had noticed that the father was always scolding his wife and raising his voice, appearing to be in a bad mood most of the time. The wife endured much of his aggressive behavior but would occasionally answer back and argue with him. One day, things escalated to the point where he was battering and wounding her in the face and shouting at her. Surprisingly, no one came to her rescue or called the police, and I was afraid to do anything in case I also became a victim of his one day. I had heard that domestic violence was a problem in Sierra Leone but I had never witnessed it first hand while I was there. I was in shock and later tried to console the wife, who decided to do nothing about it. This was my first real encounter with violence against women, something that was to become an important part of my work at the United Nations many years later.

Race relations in England

There was clearly racial discrimination in England and it was not unusual for Black people to be called names like 'Darkie' or 'Blackie.' England was a colonizing country and many of the people of color in Britain were from British colonies. Racial prejudice was structural and sustained by a biased curriculum in the schools about Empire and notions of White supremacy as well as ignorance and stereotypes about Black people in general. Curiosity about Black people was another motivating factor fueling racism. This was manifested by fear of the unknown and negative projections about Black people being somewhat different and living strange lives.

In one instance, our family encountered a peeping Tom who had climbed up the window of our living room from outside and was looking in, curious to see how Black people lived. I locked eyes with him and frightened him away. We later informed the police, but he was never found. From that day, we made sure that we pulled our curtains shut once it became dark outside.

West Indians from various Caribbean Islands, especially Jamaica and Trinidad, were the majority of Black people in England at that time, followed by Africans. People from the Caribbean who first came to the UK between 1948 and 1971 on the MV *Empire Windrush* from Caribbean countries are regarded as the 'Windrush generation.' The ship carried 492 passengers to England to make up for the shortage of labor after the Second World War. Several groups followed and worked mainly in factories and other low paying jobs, although a few came as students and higher-skilled professionals. In April 2018 a major scandal broke which deprived the Windrush immigrants of British citizenship and some of them were deported back to the West Indies. Under tremendous pressure, Prime Minister Teresa May was forced to reverse this policy and offered an apology in August 2018. Some form of compensation was agreed on, but to this day a number of the 'Windrush Generation' have apparently not received any compensation. The struggle for equal citizenship and racial justice still continues for Blacks in the United Kingdom to the present day and has been reinforced by the 'Black Lives Matter' movement.

The most popular profession for African women at the time was nursing, which offered training combined with accommodation and a stipend. This helped to fill the void in the shortage of nurses in England and was an inexpensive way for many women from Africa to go to England and train for a reputable and economically rewarding career. At the time I was in England, Africans in general went as students and returned home after receiving their degrees and professional qualifications. Although it was customary for West Indians to immigrate permanently to England at that time, it was rare for Africans to immigrate permanently to England as there were better opportunities at home. Succeeding generations of blacks, especially from the Caribbean, had greater expectations of living in England and in time started to demand better educational and professional opportunities and representation in local and national government. For Africans in general, permanent migration came later and has been increasing over the years as opportunities have begun to decline in their own countries.

Like most countries in Europe, North America and elsewhere in the Global North, racism is endemic and is a constraining factor in the ability of Black immigrants to fine jobs and get decent accommodation and services. Many Blacks in England continue to experience racism in housing, social relations, employment, social services and opportunities to this day. The color bar exists in the spatial segregation of some public facilities and the British tend to hold separate social gatherings and live in segregated communities. Brixton and Notting Hill in London are known as the most segregated areas of London and racial tensions in these areas have always been present; they led to the Notting Hill race riots in 1958 and Brixton race riots in1982. Blacks in England have increasingly faced harassment by the police over the years.

During the period that I was in England, South Africa brought the problem of racism to the fore. The apartheid system in South Africa, which meant strict legally sanctioned racial segregation from birth to death, had been formally established in 1948 by Afrikaaner regimes. Prior to that a series of oppressive racial laws against the African majority had been put in place, after years of murderous genocidal acts and land seizures propelled by imperialistic policies led by Cecil Rhodes, a brutal English imperialist, and others. The Sharpeville Massacre on March 21 1960, when 69 Africans were shot dead during a peaceful demonstration, brought global attention to the Black Holocaust being perpetrated in South Africa by the White minority. Blacks in England at the time also felt the impact of such racial terror and England became an uncomfortable place for many because of the historical, economic and ethnic links between England and South Africa and the large settlement of many people from Britain in South Africa.

The class system in England

The English class system is an entrenched institution and defines English society in many ways. It continues to be maintained by the economic system in which the labor of the working class remains a fundamental requirement for the generation of wealth for the higher social classes. All of the institutions, especially the educational system, were designed to maintain the class structure and cultural boundaries were instilled in the areas of residence, marriage patterns, speech, decorum, fashion and culinary traditions. Interestingly, most of the well-known English dishes, such as fish and chips, steak and kidney pie and the famous English breakfast, are believed to have been derived from the peasant and working class segments of society rather than the upper class.

The geographical landscape is designed to reflect the class structure in terms of housing, land ownership and the size of one's property and land holdings. Rich neighborhoods are marked by large houses and estates with huge spaces between the houses and tend to be on the outskirts of London. The working class neighborhoods are often close to the city and in industrial urban areas in the form of terraced houses or flats close to public transportation or discount shops. In industrial cities the skyline is often obscured by billowing smoke from nearby factories, and when combined with foggy weather, visibility could be very low. The popular British sitcom 'Coronation Street' was an apt description of life in industrial England, complete with the terraced houses, blue-collar lifestyles, cultural expressions and a working class community set in a fictional North West town in Manchester, England. Neighborhoods reflected class divisions as well as educational institutions and employment. Council housing for low-income families tended to be in high density inner city areas. The English countryside is also structured residentially according to social class and distinctions can be also glaring when comparisons are made between the landed gentry and the peasantry.

Britain's class society structure contributed to reinforcing racism, since it served as a model of differential value of human beings based on one's economic standing or lack thereof. It stratified English society in a way that was similar to racism in terms of notion of 'superiority' and 'inferiority' with negative projections about people of the lower class or a darker complexion. One's educational level, especially one's language and pronunciation, were markers of social class and can serve as symbols of exclusion and inclusion. The story of 'My Fair Lady' and its forerunner 'Pygmalion' by George Bernard Shaw best typify the subtle and overt nature of the cultures of British class society. The school system was divided by class, with public schools being designated as fee-paying schools for the rich and regular grammar schools and secondary modern schools for everyone else. Within these public schools was the system of prefects, which was designed to develop leadership that would feed into the prestigious universities of Oxford and Cambridge and later into public service in the government and the colonial service overseas. Class was determined primarily by birth and economic status as well as education, linguistic dexterity and ability to speak the 'the Queen's English' properly with the right accent. This was accompanied by an expected level of decorum that reflected good upbringing, restraint, manners and a touch of snobbery.

Gender in the UK and factory work

Gender relations in England at that time were very much along the lines expected of the nuclear family formation. Men dominated the public sphere and women ran the domestic sphere. The gender division of labor was also expressed in the home with women responsible for most of the domestic work and for staying home and raising the children. The picture of the typical English housewife at the time was someone who constantly had on an apron. Mothers with young children would be seen in town pushing their infants in prams and strollers and hopping on and off buses, which were the main mode of transportation for the majority of the English at the time.

Men did little domestic work besides helping with washing the dishes and taking out the garbage. Women were dominant in professions like teaching, nursing and secretarial work. Some worked in factories in the tasks requiring assembling and food processing. The patriarchal model operated on the premise that men should be the breadwinners and women the homemakers. At the same time, Britain was able to produce two female Prime Ministers in my lifetime, Margaret Thatcher (1979 to 1990) and Teresa May (2016 to 2019). It is widely believed in some circles that Margaret Thatcher acted more like a man than a woman. 'Thatcher, Thatcher, Thatcher, Thatcher, no other man can match her' was a song heard by children jokingly endorsing this reputation. During my pre-university time in England, my ambition to go to university was not uncommon for women, especially women of the middle and upper classes. Not only did a number of women attend university, many held leadership positions in several professions. In the aristocratic and upper classes, women were often preoccupied with making good marriage alliances that often linked wealthy families, increased their assets and consolidated their class positions.

I had an opportunity to observe the gender division of labor in a factory where I worked on the recommendation of one of the universities to which I was applying to study sociology. This was intended to gain some experience of the working world and the social relations that helped to define the working class in England before studying sociology. I got a job at a factory making stoppers for bottles that contained soft cordial drinks. Our job was to put the pink rubber band on the black stoppers by using a simple machine operated by one foot and both hands. It did not require too much skill, but one had to be fast and accurate to produce enough trays of stoppers to quality for a bonus. The pay was good for an eighteen-year old, but I wondered how the others with families managed to live on a factory wage.

The division of labor was by gender, as all the labor-intensive machines were operated by women and all the work of lifting the heavy trays of rubber stoppers to the work benches was done by men. Some women were very good and produced large numbers of completed trays of stoppers and became the envy of other women, like myself, who were much slower. It was a dirty job, so we were given aprons and had to wash our hands with a special soap at the end of the day to remove the black tar contained in the stoppers. There was little socializing at work and the lunch break of half an hour gave us just enough time to eat our sandwiches at our work stations. After work, everyone was so tired that the only concern was how quickly they could get out of the door and on to the bus that was going to take them home.

Sierra Leonean Community and Independence celebrations

There was a vibrant Sierra Leone community in London at the time, which was mobilized by the Chargé d'Affaires, Dr. William H. Fitzjohn, and his wife, Mrs. Alice Fitzjohn, in preparation for the independence celebrations of Sierra Leone. My mother and I attended all the preparatory meetings organized by the ambassador's wife, known affectionately as Aunty Alice. The women would meet regularly at the home of the Fitzjohns to plan the social events, including a church thanksgiving service and a grand ball on the day of the independence celebrations. We also learnt and rehearsed the new national anthem 'High We Exalt Thee, Land of the Free' written and composed by Clifford N. Fyle and John J. Akar. This would be followed by history lessons about the country, its new constitution and its preparation for independence. My mother was appointed as a member of the committee to plan the Thanksgiving Service and I was assigned the responsibility of helping to look after the children at the Sunday School that was held in an adjacent room at the same time.

On the day itself, we all dressed up in various forms of African attire, reflecting at least one color of the national flag of green, white and blue. The service at Saint Martins in the Fields and other churches were packed with Sierra Leonean, British dignitaries and well-wishers. It was a glorious day and everyone sang heartily, especially when it came to singing the new national anthem.

After the service, there was much jubilation outside the church that spilled into the streets with many British onlookers cheering us on and offering congratulations for our independence. The new flag was flying outside the church, next to the British Union Jack. That evening we had a grand ball and celebration at one of the halls of London with two live bands, lots of food, especially Jollof rice, the national dish of Sierra Leone and lots of drinks. There was a lot of merry making and that day went down as one of the most memorable days of my life. After independence, Dr. William H. Fitzjohn became the first High Commissioner of Sierra Leone to the Court of St. James in England.

Since the main purpose of my coming to England was to prepare to go to a university there, I filled out application forms to two universities, Durham University, which was affiliated to Fourah Bay College in Sierra Leone, and the University of Leeds to study sociology. I was interviewed by the faculty of sociology and Deans of both universities and told to be prepared to work very hard, as the first year could be challenging for many international students. The curriculum showed a progression from introductory courses to more difficult seminars and research projects. I was admitted to both universities and decided to go to the University of Durham.

Meanwhile an opportunity to study in the United States came from out of the blue. One day my father called from Sierra Leone and informed me about a special American scholarship to study in America and asked if I would like to apply for it. At the time I was not very keen on the United States because I had heard so many negative things about it. The most scary was the high crime rate, and another was racism. I had read a lot about the terrible ways in which Blacks were treated and had learnt about the transatlantic slave trade. One of my friends at the Annie Walsh had studied in North Caroline and hated the racism so much that she had left after one year. In addition, the academic degrees from American universities did not have the same high value in Sierra Leone as those from Britain and Europe, which were considered to have more rigorous academic standards and tougher admissions requirements.

Durham and Leeds did not include scholarships that paid for everything like the American program. I realized that it would probably be a bit of a burden for my father to pay my university fees in England and decided to apply for the American scholarship called 'African Scholarship Program of American Universities (ASPAU.)' The Committee in Freetown considered my application in my absence and recommended me for one of the scholarships, but required me to take the test and be interviewed like the other candidates. The American envoy from the African- American Institute in New York,

Dr. Wyatt, agreed to stop over in London on his way back to the States and administer the test as well as give me an interview.

He sent a limousine to pick me up at my home in South Norwood and take me to his hotel office in the center of London. Some of the neighbors came out to look at the limousine and realized that our family must be important or have a lot of money to be picked up by one. I waved and smiled at them like the aristocrat that they thought I was.

I had the interview with Dr. Wyatt, who also gave me the test followed by a business lunch. He told me that he would have to present my credentials to the African- American Institute (AAI) which administered the program. He assured me that everything would be all right and that they would get in touch with me.

A few days later, I received news of my acceptance for the African Scholarship Program of American Universities (ASPAU) scholarship and information about travel to the United States to attend Bennett College in Greensboro, North Carolina. The program was fully funded through a tri-partite agreement. The African governments paid for travel to the States; the universities paid the tuition and the American government paid for room and board, plus an allowance. The program was administered by the African-American Institute, based in New York City.

I was conflicted about going to a country that I knew so little about and whose university degrees did not have the same reputation in Sierra Leone as those of the English universities. I was also concerned about facing American-style racism, which from my history classes and friends who studied there seemed more blatant, potent and destructive than the more low-key, hypocritical but ever-present British racism to which I was accustomed. I also saw it as different from the colonial racism which operated in Sierra Leone as part of an imposed superstructure of political and economic domination. Colonial racism maintained an informal color bar and practiced discrimination at a structural level. This was cushioned to some extent for many Africans by the strong family and kinship networks and bonds that deeply influenced one's daily life. Such protection was not readily available in England and even less so in America. I was conflicted about leaving my family in England but was looking forward to joining my boyfriend, Henry, who had also won the same ASPAU scholarship and was heading to the United States to attend Yale University. He was going to fly to the States from West Africa instead of going by sea like most of the other students.

CHAPTER 8

Going to America by Sea, Homestays and Orientation

Irpinia: A ship of students

I boarded the ship M/v *Irpinia* at Southampton, England to the United States in the summer of 1961, along with other ASPAU students from West Africa and American and British students returning from Study Abroad programs in Europe. In addition, there were passengers going to the US on business, vacation and for other reasons. The African-American Institute that was in charge of the African Scholarship Program of American Universities (ASPAU) program sent a team, including an ASPAU student of the previous year to provide orientation sessions on the ship for the new students.

I walked into my cabin to find two bunk beds for four people, three of whom were already in the room. I heard a sigh as I entered the room and saw three Irish women who were going to the States to work as nurses staring at me in shock. They were obviously not pleased at the prospect of sharing a room with a Black woman. Neither was I pleased at having to share with them, but I did not make any sounds of consternation because I obviously had a better upbringing. I greeted them politely and asked which was my bed and proceeded to unpack.

The next day, I met other ASPAU students, two of whom were female students from Africa sharing a similar room with two bunk beds for four. I was invited to join them and happily accepted their invitation.

All the African students shared rooms with other students from Africa for the most part, until some romantic encounters started between African men and White women on the ship, leading to some changes in bunk bedding arrangements. All kinds of relationships were taking place on board the ship and it was not unusual to see couples making out on the deck at night. It became rather embarrassing at times, and those like myself who were not interested in these fleeting relationships tended to stay in the common areas and listen to music, read or play card games at night, rather than encounter one of the orgies taking place around the desks.

One of the female students was reputed to be carrying on relationships with two guys on the ship, which created a lot of tension. Later, it was rumored that she allegedly seduced the husband of a nice couple who were returning home from vacation in Europe with a small child. This reputation went with her to her university in the United States, where apparently her report card noted that she was extremely 'promiscuous.' I wondered why a young woman would be so willing to give away her body to any useless man that showed an interest in her. I was not raised that way and I had a sense of disdain for women who did not value themselves and their bodies.

I was to learn later in my psychology classes in America that these types of behavior were not so much a sign of promiscuity or excessive eroticism but of a deep sense of insecurity, some of which may come from sexual abuse as a child. This strengthened my commitment to working for gender equality, and I began to understand the sexual undertones of such inequality.

Orientation sessions had been organized by the African American Institute team for the ASPAU students and consisted of lectures, exercises, working lunches and social events. The lectures were designed to acquaint African students with life in America and university life in particular. Some of it seemed normal to me, such as the advice to attend classes regularly, studying hard and participating in out-of-school and recreational activities. Other experiences in America were new to me, such as facing the stereotypes about Africa and Africans and facing American-type racism and racial discrimination that seemed more pernicious.

We were presented with a less frightening history of slavery and Jim Crow laws as well as segregation, but told that most White Americans were generally nice people and that we should make the most of the opportunity to study in the United States. I remember being advised not to accept any general invitation from an American to lunch or dinner unless a specific date and time were provided. This apparently was a way of Americans being hospitable but the African students saw it as insincere. Some of the lectures discussed budgeting and how to make the most of our scholarship allowance. The lecture on budgeting was quite an eye-opener; we watched a highly paid female lawyer demonstrate how little she had left for recreation and savings after paying her bills for housing, utilities, car loan, gasoline, professional dues and contribution to health insurance and social security. It was quite a shock to most of us from Africa, where salaries dd not have to cover such a wide range of expenses.

I found most of the lectures interesting and useful, but some were offensive and racist, such as the repeated drum beat message of the importance of using deodorants. We were warned that Americans were very sensitive to body odor and that personal hygiene could make or break our success in the United States because we would be ostracized and further discriminated against if we smelt badly. I felt uncomfortable with these particular lectures and pointed out that in most African cultures daily bathing and washing is the norm and will prevent perspiration smells. The response was that perspiration and body odor can persist even with daily bathing. Americans, I was told, were great bathers but still feel the need to use deodorants as this was a sure way to eliminate perspiration odor than just using soap and water.

After a while, we got used to the repeated talks about deodorants and decided to just listen and make funny faces.

Since there were so many international students on board, discussion sessions were organized around various topics, some of which centered around colonization, decolonization, racism and the American political scene at that time. John F. Kennedy was the president and inspired a lot of youthful exuberance, which was felt by the young students on the ship. There was a sense of optimism and hope for better democratic changes and opportunities for marginalized groups. The Civil Rights Movement was at an active stage in the United States and the debate about equality and White superiority were beginning to take center stage. The discussions on colonialism put the English passengers on the spot and some of them eagerly defended the British Empire and its contributions to the world, while others sided with the anti-colonialists. The reaction from the Irish passengers was more measured as they had had their own history of domination by the English.

Lunchtime was another opportunity for lively discussions. We ate as a large group and this provided an opportunity to socialize across nations. I was thrilled to meet students from all over the world, but particularly from America. I met Jewish students for the first time and would not have been able to distinguish them from the other passengers if they had not identified themselves as such. I had no idea what a modern Jewish person looked like since my only image of Jews were those from biblical photos. I told one of the Jewish students that it was the first time I had met Jews in person and did not know what to expect. She told me that although there is a so-called typical Jewish look, Jews come in all physical types and that she had a sister who had blond hair and blue eyes.

American students on the whole were very approachable and eager to tell us about their country. They exhibited a kind of uncritical patriotism that I felt was not typical of young and educated people and more characteristic of older and less educated folks. They seemed knowledgeable about America, but I thought that their knowledge of the world, given their recent travels to Europe, was rather superficial. They had a lot of stereotypes about Africa and relied too much on Hollywood's depiction of Africa, with pictures of animals, natives, Tarzan and jungles.

Cultural shows were organized by the ship's crew and members of the orientation team that gave an opportunity to students and other passengers for cultural expression through music, dance, food and fashion. We took turns teaching other dances from our respective countries and performing sketches in different languages, with translations into English. We also had several parties and dances that gave opportunities to form relationships and make friends. For some students this was seen as a grand experiment of cross-cultural communication. For others, it was a time to explore Black/White dating for the first time and many of them approached it with a kind of clumsiness and apprehension, but a few seemed to adopt a cool 'so what?' attitude about it all. Needless to say, some of these interracial romantic encounters soon came to an end as we approached New York City.

Landing in New York City

On the day we landed in New York, there was a lot of excitement about seeing the United States for the first time. However, not everyone was happy about reaching their destination and giving up their orgies and newly-found romantic encounters on board the ship. There were stories about some of the interracial romances being brought to an abrupt end by the White women who felt that their White parents who had arrived to meet them would not approve of their daughters dating Black men. In a number of cases the men were told to make themselves scarce and not to be seen by the parents upon arrival. Many Africans were outraged at these developments, especially those that had carried on hot and steamy romances onboard the *Irpinia*. It was quite a slap in the face and a rude awakening to racism in this land of opportunity. Welcome to America!!

The American press greeted us on our arrival and interviewed a number of the African students with a great deal of enthusiasm and interest. The next day, the newspapers had headlines like 'Blacks that Walk like Kings,' when describing the sense of pride and the dignity displayed by the newly-arrived African students. I wondered how this would make Blacks in America feel and got my first taste of the disdain with which many Blacks in America were viewed. That made me very angry and uncomfortable and evoked many of the reservations that I had had about coming to America. That was my first taste of the American media. I thought the press were trying to throw a wedge between the Black Americans and the Africans who had barely set foot on American soil.

We were met by a team from the African-American Institute after going through immigration and customs. We spent two nights in New York city, hosted by the African-American Institute and the National Association for the Advancement of Colored People (NAACP). They 'wined and dined' us in the most hospitable and friendly way and I was impressed to meet so many accomplished and successful African-American professionals. They seemed happy to be hosting us and to be connected to Africa through us and showed a lot of pride in their African heritage. I was to discover later, when I attended a college in the South, that not all African-Americans thought so highly of Africa.

We were taken on tours of the city and many of us acted like country bumpkins, staring with wonder at the skyscrapers in New York city until our necks hurt. We had never seen anything like this in our life! The buildings were so tall and we wondered how people could live so high up in the sky and never fall off. We wondered what kind of foundation the buildings were standing on to keep them standing upright for so many years. Our tour of the Empire State Building was mind blowing. What a beautiful sight it presented of New York City! We were filled with awe.

We ended our day with a visit to Radio City Hall for a concert that thrilled us, especially the dancing by the Rockettes. These tours of the city left us tired enough to have a long, restful and beautiful night's sleep every night and to catch up with 'jet lag', which was a new experience for most of us.

Home stays with American host families

We then boarded buses and trains for trips to our American host families, where we spent about two weeks before our orientation programs. The host family part of the program was to acquaint African students with life in America, through living with an American family. It was organized by an organization called 'Experiment in International Living' which had carried out the task of securing suitable host families and placing the students with them to ensure a certain degree of compatibility. It was hoped that there would be a good fit, but there were some tricky and uncomfortable situations which involved cultural clashes and uneasy living experiences, although these were surmounted for the most part. Many of the African students, with very few exceptions, lived with White families, some of whom were recruited from their churches.

My host family in Rensselaer, New York, was a widowed woman in her sixties and her daughter, a nurse in her forties. They met me at the train station and took me to a house on a large piece of land with an extensive garden of vegetables, fruit trees and flowers. They had a part-time gardener and a handyman helped with repairs on the house from time to time. There were no houseboys as is the case in Freetown, and most of the housework was done by my hostess and her daughter. Although they were very nice and hospitable and made me very comfortable, I felt homesick for the first time in my life as so much around me felt strange. I had grown up in a city and this was a farm-like area, which was not quite rural. There was a shopping center and offices and hospitals in the center of the town. I went to church with the family and met people in the community, some of whom were curious about Africa and wanted to know how come I spoke such good English and had such straight white teeth.

The meals were interesting to me as most of them came from the home garden of my host family. We had salad twice a day, but their salads were made of lettuce and tomatoes only and a salad dressing of oil and vinegar. Salads in Sierra Leone were more elaborate, usually served on Sundays and festive occasions and were very rich in protein, such as canned salmon and eggs with dressings of mayonnaise diluted with olive oil. Dinners were quite spectacular, because the meat portion was very large and took up almost half of the plate. The potatoes and vegetables, also in large portions, made up the other half and gravy was often served with the meal. Looking at the food on my plate for the first dinner at the house made me realize that Americans ate a lot. The amount of food on my plate could probably feed a family of three back home if instead of potatoes, a larger helping of rice was added. No wonder there were so many fat people in town, I thought!

I was introduced for the first time to hamburgers and hot dogs, which soon became my favorite American meals. We occasionally had sausages and eggs for breakfast in my family back home, but this was a different type of sausage from the one that is used for hotdogs. The idea of adding relish, mustard and ketchup made it more exciting. The huge hamburgers for lunch blew my mind. I would watch as the family made a sandwich of hamburgers, tomatoes, onions, pickles that grew so large that you had to turn your head sideways to make sure that your open mouth would be large enough to accommodate the sandwich. The family took delight in eating and this was reflected in their generously-proportioned bodies.

On the whole, I did not notice any racial attitudes in my host family and when they spoke of Black people, it was always positive. They often even remarked about having good and bad people in every racial group and disapproved of stereotyping. My hostess was a widow and had a very close relationship with her daughter, who was equally kind and hospitable. It all seemed very normal to me, except that the daughter, who was in her forties at the time, had never married and had no children. It is not unusual for women of that age in Sierra Leone to have children with or without marriage for fear of their biological clock ticking away. Africans place a high value on motherhood in general but women who cannot have children biologically may opt for social motherhood and raise other people's children. The idea of motherhood as a woman's destiny is, however, changing and some women have more options and choices nowadays. Besides, overpopulation is a concern, as so many unwanted children are being born all over the world.

The daughter informed me later that she had been unfortunate in love and had been engaged once, but it had not worked out. At the time, she was secretly in love with a married doctor with whom she worked, but there was no future in it for her. Besides going to work at the local hospital and going to church and shopping and the occasional visits to friends, the family stayed home for the most part. Visitors to the house were not a regular occurrence as in Sierra Leone, where people are usually in and out of each other's houses, often uninvited. Houses in the area of my home stay were far apart and required an invitation and a car for visits. One day, we had a visitor who seemed surprised that I was an integral part of the family, because she had assumed that I was the live-in maid and even asked me how I like taking care of the house and my host family. I told her that I was an international student and that they were my host family as part of my education. The idea of a Black person staying with a White family, other than as a maid, was not very common at that time.

Orientation

Students going to universities in the North had their orientation at the University of Pennsylvania in Philadelphia, and those going to the South at the University of Atlanta, in Georgia. Since I was going to attend Bennett College, an all-women's Historically Black College in Greensboro, North Carolina, I joined the group of ASPAU students going to Atlanta, Georgia. It was a thrilling experience as this was the first time I had ever flown in a plane. I could not get over how small all the houses and streets looked as we got higher in the sky and liked the feeling of flying through the clouds. It was a delightful flight and most of us were equally thrilled to see the city of Atlanta rise up to meet the plane as we landed at Hatsfield Atlanta International Airport.

We were taken to Atlanta University for the orientation and lived in one of the dorms while the students were still on vacation. We had daily sessions, outings and social gatherings. The purpose of the orientation was to prepare us for living and studying in the States as African students. All of our mentors were African-Americans, some of whom came with us on the plane from the African-American Institute in New York City. The lectures centered around American history and culture and what can be called 'The American Personality.' We were informed about the specific history of slavery in the South and the impact of Jim Crow laws and segregation from the perspective of the African-American victims, and they did not try to whitewash slavery as had been done on the *Irpinia*.

As we drove around town on our many trips, it was clear to see the legacy of slavery and segregation in some of the poorest houses and neighborhoods inhabited by Blacks. The poverty in some areas was striking. Some of the houses were dilapidated and some children ran around with no shoes on and wore clothes that were torn and shabby. I could not believe that this was America, the land of opportunity!

Our orientation continued the drum beat of the importance of using deodorants that had been a theme on the *Irpinia*. We were advised to buy them the next time we went shopping, if we did not already have them. Most of the African students were offended by this repetition of the need for deodorant use and outraged when they learnt that some members of the orientation team had conducted clandestine inspections of our rooms and bathrooms to make sure that we were using deodorants. One student spoke out at one of the orientation sessions in protest at the violation of their privacy. In response, the leader of the team quietly and in a soft voice informed us that America was a racist society and that we would experience discrimination because we were Black. They were only trying to protect us from further discrimination on the basis of body odor, since we would already stand out as Black and foreign. We appreciated her candor and decided to ask those not using deodorants regularly to do so. She made me realize their commitment to supporting us and shielding us from additional racism. It made me realize the extent of American racism and how much Blacks in America had suffered under Jim Crow laws, segregation and the cruelty of lynching in the South and how they continued to experience discrimination, racial terror and police brutality everywhere in the United States.

Atlanta University is a historically Black university and from what I was told, had a handful of white students and a few White faculty members. With regard to dating at that time, inter-racial dating was strongly discouraged and many Black parents looked on the idea with trepidation. It was rather disconcerting then when a female student from East Africa at the university started dating a white male student from a White university nearby. It caused a lot of consternation every time they showed up on campus, especially if they were holding hands. No one wanted to see that, and I remember one of the African-American students telling them to be more discreet with their public display of affection. They protested and she reminded them that if they dared to do that on the campus of his White university, there was no telling what would happen to them. She added, 'If you can't hold hands at his White university, you should not do it here either.'

A number of things were new to me and sparked my curiosity. I had never seen American football played before and used to watch the players rehearse outside my window. I noticed that they had huge shoulders and thought they must be built that way; I did not realize that their shoulders were padded. Another discovery was attending a football game where I saw cheerleaders for the first time. I thought they were a distraction and looked out of place, until I realized that their purpose of cheering their favorite team was a cultural tradition and a vital part of the game. The people in the crowd, who were almost all Black, were enjoying themselves, which made me feel comfortable and happy. I realized that Blacks could be discriminated against, but they knew how to put it aside and have a good time.

I made friends with one of the women serving in the dining room and she invited me home with her after work one day. It so happened that she also sewed, and I needed a dress altered, which she agreed to do. She was a single mother, living in one of the low-income areas of Atlanta with her two pre-teen children. Their father had left the family some time before and did not offer much financial or other support. She served us hamburgers for dinner, which I thought was strange, since I associated hamburgers with lunch, but I realized that the children liked them and would eat them every day if they could.

When I got back to the group, I was praised for my initiative in making friends with the locals but advised to be cautious about going to the inner city on my own. On Sunday, we went to a Black church, which reminded me very much of home in terms of the people, their dresses, the fancy hats worn by the women, music and chanting and the warm fellowship that was apparent during and after the service.

CHAPTER 9

Bennett College, Greensboro, North Carolina and Beyond

"The ultimate measure of a person is not where one stands in moments of comfort and convenience, but where one stands in times of challenge and controversy." – Martin Luther King, Jr.

✦

Greensboro and Bennett College in the history of the
Civil Rights Movement

After the orientation sessions, we left for our respective colleges and universities by train and bus. I was going to attend Bennet College, a historically Black private women's college, founded in 1873, in Greensboro, North Carolina. Although the college was located in a city, it had a clearly defined campus of sixty acres with beautiful landscapes. It was adjacent to North Carolina Agricultural and Technical University (A&T) with a predominantly male student population. This facilitated a social life and male- female interactions that are not usually characteristic of female-only colleges at that time.

The town of Greensboro holds a special place in the Civil Rights Movement of the 1960s and is regarded as the city where mass protests against racism by students started. It involved four students from A&T University in Greensboro refusing to leave the 'Whites Only' lunch counter at Woolworth's store, even after the police were called, on February 1st, 1960. The owner eventually closed the store early rather than serve the Black students. They were known as 'the Greensboro Four.' Later, similar protests were held in Greensboro, including students from Bennett College, known as 'the Bennett Belles.' The efforts of these students inspired other sit-ins in fifty five cities in thirteen states and galvanized a nationwide student movement. According to some scholars, the Greensboro sit-ins were a calculated act of rebellion that involved planning between students at A&T University and Bennett College. They were inspired by the legacy of slavery, Jim Crow laws, segregation and civil rights activism, sparked by the lynching of Emmett Till in 1955 and the Montgomery bus boycott of the same year.

Bennett College had a striking building that served as an assembly hall for meetings of the entire college population of faculty, staff and students. The president at the time was an unmarried, distinguished woman who pulled her hair back in a bun and looked serious most of the time. The American students were all Black, mostly from the South, and many came from families where their mothers provided domestic and child care services to White families. All had a rural background with historical ancestry of enslavement that made some form of farming or sharecropping a significant aspect of their background. A number of them displayed what I came to know as 'the southern charm', through which they displayed a politeness that was mixed with a subtle shyness. I was thrilled to see so many young Black women like myself in America who could be my cousins. In fact some of them reminded me of people I knew back home and I often reflected on how much history and geography had separated us.

Although a few of them had parents in professional jobs like teaching and nursing, most had blue collar jobs or jobs related to farming and food processing, or jobs that were mostly in the service sector. Many of them were the first generation of college students in their families. It appeared that a number of them had grants and scholarships and some worked on campus to supplement their tuition and other fees. A few had benevolent individual donors, including one student who informed me of that her parents could not afford to send her to college so her fees were being paid for by a friend of the family. This was not strange to me, since many children have their school fees paid in Sierra Leone through a system of wardship and informal philanthropy.

Skin color, identity and racial complexities

Despite the role of Bennett College in the Greensboro sit-ins of the early 1960s, African-American students were not able to overcome the impact of the ideology of White supremacy on their self-esteem. The obsession with skin color, colorism and hair texture permeated their lives. The history of slavery and its association with colorism in the United States, the Caribbean and South America, where slavery was established between the fifteen and nineteenth centuries, was very much evident at Bennett College. The students were obsessed about being light-skinned and would ask me to compare their complexion with another student and determine who was lighter. Those who were of a darker complexion would go to great lengths to convince everyone that they had White ancestors somewhere. Those who were too dark would settle for Native American ancestry as well, rather than admit to being descended from Africans alone. It was pathetic. The African students felt sorry for them and among themselves, they often referred to the African-American students who wanted to be White as 'lost souls.'

Many of them knew very little about Africa and with very few exceptions they had no desire to be identified as having an African heritage. I would often ask them where they thought their dark skin came from and would get all kinds of answers, like the Caribbean, Native American bloodlines and so forth. As Africans, we were looked down on as coming from a primitive and backward place. The majority of African students were of a darker complexion and wore their hair naturally. This was before the 'Black is Beautiful' movement of the late 1960s in the United States that celebrated Black beauty and aesthetics and instilled pride in being Black.

At the time I was at Bennett College, there was also a high value placed on fashion and looking glamorous. African-American students seemed obsessed with dressing up and having their hair straightened and permed, even when going to class. Skirts would be worn instead of pants and jeans, and shoes and sandals were preferred to sneakers. To some students, looking pretty and fashionable was more important than being academically accomplished.

Academics

All the African students excelled academically, as that was their top priority. Some of the American students could not understand why. Most of the classes seemed easy to us, having gone through sixth form in Africa, based on the British system of a rigorous academic curriculum. There was a huge deficit in the learning process for some of the American students, which reflected the inefficiencies of their high schools. Some of the required courses for all students included courses in language, arts and science and an introductory course on 'How to study.' All the African students felt the course was a waste of time since they already had very good study habits and considered it a 'gut' course that was too easy and guaranteed to earn a student an A grade.

I enjoyed my biology classes, which made us explore the world of nature and our part in it. I remember the mixed feeling of trepidation and excitement when we dissected a frog for the first time and saw the poor animal's tiny organs and guts. Biology also included trips to forested areas where we learned about American trees that I had not seen before. My favorite courses were in the social sciences and history. English literature was enjoyable, since I was exposed to American authors like William Faulkner and Margaret Mitchell for the first time. It gave me a good insight into American society, the American South,

American history, and American values. Unfortunately, we did not read many novels by Black authors.

Most of the professors were true to the texts in their teachings, but a few had a critical approach and challenged the substance, context and background of the authors. I liked that and the way some of the social science professors taught us how to analyze what we were reading and how to read critically and to evaluate books on many levels of merit. My favorite professor taught history, but did not restrict it to American or Black history. His courses expanded to include world history and how American history and Black history were derived from, and closely linked to, world history.

He showed how the fact that most of the books on Blacks were written by Whites also explained the history of racism in education and that many of these books were biased and motivated by racism. He would analyze the race theories of the nineteenth century and was the first professor who taught us the concept of the 'social construction of racism.' One of his most convincing ways of putting it was to point out that there was only one human species – *Homo sapiens* – based on the indisputable fact that we can breed together and produce human offspring together. He would then underscore this by pointing to the failed experiments of the Nazis, who tried unsuccessfully to breed humans and animals, using Jews as guinea pigs. He spoke about the evils of Nazism that took place in Germany but regretted the fact that not enough attention was given to the Black Holocaust of American slavery that happened on American shores and soil.

Another professor who taught social science subjects was very critical of Blacks and the South and felt that they were too conservative and passive. He thought that some of the institutions, like the Black Church, promoted a brand of conservatism that placated Blacks, although the role of the Black Church in the struggles against racism was also emphasized and appreciated. He attributed Black conservatism to the legacy of slavery and segregation the Jim Crow laws that followed and that were deeply entrenched in the South. In his view, the college was not progressive enough and was indoctrinating the students to accept their second-class citizenship position in society.

I remember challenging him on that and pointing out the historic role that Bennett College and A&T played in the early days of the Civil Rights Movement through sit-ins and other forms of protest. He acknowledged the importance of the sit-ins but felt that they were cosmetic and did not alter the structures that upheld racism. Later, as I grew to understand the enduring features of systemic racism, I came to realize that he was right. I thought it was ironic that the city of Greensboro, which became famous for its resistance through the sit-ins, was in fact a very conservative city. The students, from various parts of the South and North, gave it the activism for which it became known, but some did not challenge the root of the problem, which was systemic racism. This professor was to play an important role in a change that I made after one year at Bennett College when I decided to transfer to a college in the North.

Dorm life

Dorm life was interesting, but I often felt homesick. I wondered what my family was doing and if they were missing me as much as I was missing them. I missed both London and Freetown, since Greensboro seemed very remote and strange to me. I realized that this was the price I had to pay for an advanced education. I shared a room with Leila Gonzales, a student from Panama who spoke Spanish as well as English and felt a strong affinity with African students. We got along very well and exchanged stories about our families back home and helped each other overcome our homesickness. Both of us had good study habits and like me, she also found the curriculum less challenging than she had expected.

Most students lived on campus in dorms that had two or three students sharing one room and bathrooms. Each dorm had a small lounge and kitchenette which was used to make snacks and some modified African dishes to help us cope with our homesickness. There was no television in the recreation room in the dorms to prevent binge

TV watching by some students and distract others from studying. Once a year the dorms had 'Open House', to which family and friends were invited. Rooms that were usually untidy became beautifully decorated.

During a tour of one of the dorms it became clear that two students who were suspected of being lesbians and shared a room were no longer going to hide in the closet. Their beds were put close together with two heart-shaped pillows displaying the words, 'I love you.' No one spoke about lesbianism or appeared to be concerned about it. In fact there may have been more lesbian couples on campus than was evident, but there was no outward display of it. This was a time when homosexuality and lesbianism were frowned upon and carried on secretly and discreetly, with people living 'in the closet' because there was no strong social movement backing it. Looking back, I believe these two students were among the first LGBTQ activists, even though they did not make such a claim and may not have even realized the impact of their symbolic pillow statement on others at the time.

African students and other foreign students would go to the city center for shopping and to check out the locals. Three events stand out in my encounter with downtown Greensboro, North Carolina. The first is a shopping spree that the college arranged for the ASPAU students to get us some winter clothes. We were told that some of the stores did not allow Blacks to try on their clothes, so a college administrator who accompanied us selected the 'safe' stores for us to visit. It was quite an adventure going through a large department store in America which was even bigger than some of the well-known stores like Marks and Spencer that I was familiar with in England. We made sure we got enough warm clothes for the winter, which though milder in the South, was still very cold for most of the students coming directly from Africa.

The other event was getting my photo taken at a studio for my twenty-first birthday. The photographer was White and had his studio in the center of town. At that time, portraits were taken in black and white and then painted in color afterwards to match the dress and image of the subject. The photographer was very patient and arranged the studio lighting and his camera in a careful manner. I did not see the finished product right away and had to come back for the proofs, after which the selected photos were finalized. The finished product was beautifully done and I was impressed by the professional service I received. My family was delighted to receive the photo, painted in color, and thought I had grown up to be quite a lady.

My next memorable visit downtown was not so pleasant because it was to have my impacted wisdom tooth extracted. I had been suffering from toothache for a long time, especially at night, and it was interfering with my studies. The ASPAU program provided us with very good health and dental insurance. The college medical clinic referred me to a dentist who had a good reputation in town and who was Black. I was pleased with this recommendation and was not disappointed. The dentist was very nice and had a photo of his lovely family on his desk. He looked prosperous and successful and I was pleased to see that there were Black families in Greensboro doing so well and belonging to a small but elite and affluent group in the city.

Extracting my wisdom tooth was a challenge because of its strength. After a long struggle to finally get it out, the dentist remarked that if many of his patients had teeth as strong as mine, he would have to enroll in fitness classes. What a cute sense of humor, I thought!

Gender consciousness at Bennett College

The Civil Rights Movement had started but was not in full bloom at the time I was at Bennett, although the College and A&T played an important role in its initial stages with the sit-in. Despite this pioneering role, Black students for the most part were totally committed to emulating Whites and White values and did not see the contradiction between wanting to be like Whites and trying to gain freedom from the White supremacy that had oppressed American Blacks through slavery and racism. Since sexism is embedded in White cultural frames where gender-based hierarchies and gendered discrimination prevail, it was difficult to develop a feminist consciousness among students who were trying to be White. I believe that some of the reasons for their failure to embrace their own culture and beauty were because at that time, very few Blacks had travelled outside the United States and they were mired in institutions and ideologies that elevated Whites while devaluing Blacks.

Women being automatically resigned to 'playing second fiddle' to men was also evident in male/female relationships, as I observed in the dating patterns, which clearly showed the men in control of their girlfriends. The female students seemed to be trying very hard to project a feminine image in terms of their dress and decorum. A woman appearing aggressive, ambitious or pushy was considered unattractive by men at that time. In many of the households at that time and in the domestic sphere in general, the division of labor was clearly along the lines of gender. Even though a lot of Black women in the South went out to work, many were employed as domestic workers in White homes or in low-paying factory jobs or in the service sector. Those who worked in the professions were few and mainly concentrated in female-type jobs, such as teaching, nursing and secretarial work. Adherence to Christianity also helped to reinforce gender roles and expectations that prioritized male dominance. Ministers and leaders of the churches were all men at that time and the scriptures were interpreted in a manner that prioritized men and made them heads of Christian households where wives and children should be obedient to men.

So although Bennett College was a women's college, there was no sense of the development of a feminist consciousness or outrage about the secondary position of women in society. Most of the students were studying for professions that were characteristically seen as female professions, like teaching, nursing and social work. A few aspired to be doctors and lawyers and followed their dreams, but it was difficult at that time for either Blacks or women to achieve full equality in the more challenging professions. There were Black sororities that offered support to their members and promoted achievement and success, but they were not oriented towards dealing with sexism or racism as a priority.

In spite of the lack of an environment that promoted values of gender equality, feminist theory and praxis, I was still interested in studying these aspects of society and trying to understand why there were gender gaps and why all the top leadership positions in the country were held by men. I had developed some gender consciousness in Sierra Leone from the interactions within my family and social group and from attending the Annie Walsh Memorial School, an all-girls boarding school. In addition, the demonstrations in 1951 of the Sierra Leone Women's Movement against the high cost of living had awakened a consciousness about the power of female consciousness and solidarity. Further development of a gender perspective on life would have to wait for the Second and Third Wave of the Women's Movement that started in the early 1970s and that was to have a major impact in the development of my future academic and international careers.

Tension between African-Americans and Africans

The very few African students tended to hang out together often. Most of them shared rooms with other African students or foreign students. The Liberian students were the most adjusted, since Liberia was a 'pseudo colony' of the United States. It was founded in 1822 by the American Colonization Society in response to the 'Back to Africa' movements for enslaved people that had been freed. Over a period of forty years, 12,000 Blacks, later known as Americo-Liberians, settled there and promoted an American and Christian way of life. They faced many challenges initially, but for the most part they grew and prospered. The capital city became known as Monrovia, after President Monroe of the United States, and the country became the Republic of Liberia in 1847. It was modelled after the United States and many of the social and cultural traditions and institutions of America were reinforced in the new country. For the students from Liberia at

Bennett College life was similar to what they were accustomed to in Liberia and the adjustment was easier for them, compared to the students from other African countries.

Many of the African students from countries other than Liberia had very little prior knowledge of America and knew more about England and Europe. Most of the African students were going through culture shocks about some of the differences between their countries and the United States. They also had a strong sense of identity that reflected their cultural and national identities but were at the same time developing new identities as Africans in the United States. This was what set them apart from the African-Americans and created many challenges for them. African-Americans at Bennett at that time did not really identify with Africa, as this was before the Civil Rights Movement. As a result, many African students felt unwelcome, and this led to discontent and disappointment at the manner in which they were perceived and treated by some African-American students.

African-American and African students got along for the most part and were generally gracious and polite towards each other. Some became friends in due course but initially there was tension and the occasional verbal clashes and complaints between the two groups based on differences. For an example, a few African-American students tried to get African students to straighten their hair or wear more 'American-type' clothes, which the African students sometimes resisted. This was strange to me since the Whites that I had encountered during my homestay appeared to admire our African clothes and hair as well as our accents. Despite these challenges, we were admired by some of the African-American students and many of our professors were impressed by our strong academic performance and knowledge about the world.

The tension between the two sets of students came to a head after complaints to the administration by the African students went unheeded. A large meeting was planned by the students and one of the more pro-Africa professors to allow students to air their grievances to the campus community. African students complained of being treated badly and ridiculed as being backward and refusing to straighten their hair. The African-American students complained of Africans looking down of them and using negative stereotypes used by Whites about their being inferior, lazy and wanting to be White. Both groups blamed the other for the negative projections on each other and for the hostile climate that this produced on the campus. Both groups demanded mutual respect and an attempt to get along.

The criticisms of the Africans were challenged, not only by some students but also by a German professor. Her family had fled from Nazi Germany and she had found a position at Bennett College and had a successful career there. She took exception to the African students criticizing the college that had done so much for her. The response from the African students was that she had received those special privileges and respect because she was White and from Europe, whereas the African students had been treated badly because they were Black and from Africa.

The president was not pleased with the meeting and was particularly angry with me, since I had played a major role in planning it. To show her displeasure with me, she stopped calling me 'Filomina' and referred to me as 'Miss Jones.' I felt hurt by that and could not gracefully accept her anger. I told her to please call me 'Filomina'' and she replied that I was acting like a stranger and so she was going to be formal with me. She treated the other African students with the same reservation and cold shouldering and felt that we were ungrateful for the opportunity Bennett College was giving us. Three of the seven African students were on scholarship, including two ASPAU students whose scholarship was paid for by the college.

Things became very difficult for the African students and many of us started talking about transferring to other schools. We also had problems with living in the South and could not deal with the segregation and racism that still existed in blatant forms in most cases. Shopping was difficult, since we had to find stores that allowed Blacks to try on clothes and despite the sit-ins, there were restaurants that still maintained segregation. Some cinemas and theatres were segregated and a Black person felt like a stranger walking down some of the main streets and some neighborhoods in Greensboro. The most obvious form of segregation was in housing with Blacks living on the less desirable, more crowded and less affluent areas of the city and Whites in the more spacious and more affluent suburbs with large houses and lawns. Schools were for the most part segregated, as were universities.

Woodstock, Connecticut

During my first winter and semester break, I went to Woodstock, Connecticut on the invitation of my boyfriend Henry's host family to spend Christmas with them. They had heard a lot about me from Henry and wanted to meet me. Henry was part of the ASPAU program and was attending Yale University in Connecticut. We had a great time with the Holts, a White family with a son and an adopted daughter. Woodstock is a small semi-rural town with large houses and yard space where most families grew vegetables and flowers and some tended small animals like rabbits and chicken. Almost all the houses had dogs and cats as pets which, unlike in Sierra Leone, spent a lot of time in the house, rather than outside. It was a tightly knit community with the typical division of labor by gender whereby most of the men worked in mostly white-collar jobs outside the home and often at some distance from Woodstock and most of the women stayed home as housewives. Very few of them worked, as there were not many jobs available for women in Woodstock.

Mrs. Holt was from England and had met Mr. Holt when he was stationed there during the Second World War. They fell in love but did not marry before he left, and then they went their separate ways and married other people. Mr. Holt had had two sons by his first wife but later divorced, and Mrs. Holt's husband had died before they had any children. Fate brought them together again and they got married and had a son and adopted a daughter.

Henry and I were treated like children of the family and admired the love that they shared with each other. Mrs. Holt was not the greatest cook, but she did her best and we all adjusted to and enjoyed her cooking. Her children did not help much with the housework, so I did my best to make things easier for her. Whenever we went shopping and attended a number of events in the town we were always objects of curiosity, since very few Black people lived in Woodstock, Connecticut at that time.

Christmas in Connecticut

Christmas was a special time of year and included a custom of elaborate gift giving which went beyond the family circle and included friends and neighbors. This made buying and wrapping Christmas gifts an enormous task that could take weeks. The Holts made it fun by including refreshments and music every time we wrapped presents. Unlike in Sierra Leone, where Christmas Eve was seen as party time and usually outside the home, Christmas Eve in the US was a festive time, especially reserved for family with a main purpose of opening Christmas presents that had been stacked beneath the huge Christmas tree in the living room, next to the glowing fireplace.

Henry and I were excited to receive so many presents and did what we could to give as many as we could ourselves to our host family. We also sang Christmas carols and I drank eggnog, a Christmas drink, for the first time. One of our neighbors was a physician and he and his wife had a lot of children, three of whom were of college age and spent some time with us during the holidays, including joining the Holts in their holiday home in Martha's Vineyard for a weekend. On Christmas Eve they dropped by to share some Christmas cheer and exchange gifts with the Holts.

Christmas Day was very special and quite elaborate. The Holts usually spent the day with Mr. Holt's sister and her husband, who were very rich and lived in a big house and extensive garden and pool about three miles away, complete with a live-in maid from Sweden. The house and garden were beautifully decorated with numerous Christmas lights and garlands, the likes of which I had never seen before. A sister of Mr. Holt who lived in a pink house nearby and was active in politics was also present, along with other relatives and friends, making a total of about twenty people. There was a lot of curiosity about Henry and me and about Africa and whether or not we celebrated Christmas in Africa and how come we spoke such good English and so forth.

After cocktails and lively conversation, we sat down to a sumptuous traditional Christmas meal, served on two large tables and attended by a catering company hired for the event. We had soup, salad, turkey and all its trimmings topped off with all kinds of desserts, including pecan pies, a special Christmas treat and after-dinner mints to help with digestion. Unlike English Christmas dinners where turkey is also served, the traditional English Christmas pudding and butter sauce were not served, nor did we open Christmas crackers with Christmas hats and presents in them. After dinner, there was drinking of liquor and smoking accompanied by music, to which some people danced and sang Christmas songs. We all left at night, having had a wonderful American Christmas Celebration.

Boxing Day is not celebrated in the States as is the case in Sierra Leone and England, so life continued as usual after the huge Christmas party until New Year's Eve. We spent New Year's Eve also with Mr. Holt's sibling and his family in their huge and beautiful house. This time the party was larger and held later to be closer to twelve midnight when the old year would roll over to the new. There was a lot of dancing and drinking on a very cold night. As the New Year arrived, people started kissing each other and I thought it was strange, especially as Henry and I were also included in the kissing celebration of the New Year. We took it all in our stride.

Life went back to normal after New Year's Day. Henry would accompany the physician neighbor to the hospital since he was planning to be a doctor to gain some experience and observe what goes on in an American hospital. With the exception of one daughter, all of his remaining five children were boys. They lived in a house big enough for all of them and kept a vegetable garden surrounded by fruit trees. It was always a pleasure to visit the family because although it was a large family and the mother was very much a housewife, she exhibited a lot of control and was the main disciplinarian and practical head of the family. Her husband seemed to enjoy this arrangement and supported her in every way. In fact, most of the men did not exhibit macho complexes and created a home environment that supported and complimented the women of the house.

Mr. Holt had a long commute to work and when he came home in the evening he would sit next to the small pool in the backyard with a drink to unwind before dinner. During these moments, he and Henry would have quiet conversations and would be joined later by Mrs. Holt and myself.

One day, I told them about the tense situation concerning racism in the South and about the dissatisfaction of many African students at Bennett College, many of whom wish to transfer to colleges in the North. Interestingly enough, although the Holts were not pleased with the fact that I had to study in the South as an African student and deal with the racial situation there, they were equally concerned that it kept Henry and me too far apart and that it would be good for us to be closer together. They encouraged me to transfer to a college in the North and promised to help in any way they could. I was grateful for their concern and willingness to help and was appreciative of the fact that the two White families with whom I had stayed in the United States so far did not exhibit the racism which I had feared before coming to America.

Going back to Bennett College for the second semester was not something I looked forward to, but I was energized by my determination to transfer to a college in the North. I sent out a few applications, assisted by one of my professors, and other African students did the same. I was accepted at Smith College in Northampton, Massachusetts as a transfer student with a tuition scholarship paid for by the college, according to the conditions stipulated by ASPAU. Unfortunately the other African students who wanted to transfer did not succeed and I felt guilty about leaving them behind. The second semester at Bennett

College was a little better and my homesickness was not as acute. The tense relationship between the African-American students and the African students improved slightly, and although I was getting used to life on the campus I was determined to leave.

Sexual harassment – first summer working in New York

I spent the summer in New York with a White family. The husband was a American-born White professor at an Ivy League university and the wife a nurse of European descent from a foreign country who worked in a local hospital and whose mother lived with them. They had no children and their marriage was obviously sour and the relationship strained. I did my best not to make things worse and spent most of my time with the wife's mother, who was a good cook and taught me how to make international dishes. The ASPAU program had arranged some summer internships for us in the New York area and I needed to get to the city every day. My host family arranged to have one of the neighbors give me a ride to the city and back. This worked for a few days, but then I realized that the wife was not happy about her husband giving a ride to a young Black woman and she would call every morning to check if I was still waiting for the ride.

One day, she brought all four small children in the car with us for the ride to the city and looked uneasy and angry. I then realized that she was not happy with the arrangement but could do nothing about it. I was happy when the program ended and I no longer needed the ride, but was very grateful for it.

I noticed that some of the White neighbors that came to visit were surprised that I had been accepted at Smith College, especially one family whose daughter had not gained admission there. They tried to scare me by asking a lot of questions about how someone like myself managed to get into Smith College and saying I was going to find it very difficult and so on and so forth. I calmly replied that I liked challenges and studying and planned to enjoy every minute of my time at Smith College. That quickly put an end to the constant questioning.

Something happened one day that shocked and angered me and made my stay with this family extremely uncomfortable. I had grown to like television in the United States because it had more programs than in England, and I liked to watch TV in the evenings. Since the relationship between the wife and husband was strained, she was hardly ever in the living room watching TV and would retire to another room in the big house. One day, my host father, who was sitting in his favorite armchair came and sat next to me on the sofa which surprised me, and suddenly put his arm around my shoulders, pulled me close to him and asked me to kiss him. I was shocked, said 'no' emphatically and ran out of the living room and into my bedroom. Panicking, I pushed the dresser against the door and locked the room from the inside for fear that he might follow me to my bedroom.

I was shaking all night and could hardly sleep. The next day, I told his mother-in-law what had happened and she was shocked and angry and told me to continue to lock my door at night. Needless to say, it was very uncomfortable staying with the family after that, but I was too ashamed and scared to tell the organizers of the program. I was also worried that they might not believe me.

Realizing that nothing was going to happen between us, the horrible professor started acting in a rude manner towards me and one day suggested that I switch places with the other female student from Africa in the ASPAU group who was staying with another family. I thought to myself "What a horrible man! He has no respect for women!" I refused and vouched that I would never allow this harassment to happen to another female student, nor encourage his sick plan to upset and outrage someone else. Unfortunately there was no Women's Movement or 'Me Too' movement at that time to take on issues like this and I wondered how many young women, especially his students, had had to go through similar sexual harassment from him. I protected myself as best as I could by refusing to be in the same room with him except for the communal meals with the family. Watching TV was no longer an option but more like a horror show. It never happened again until I left for Smith College. I lost all respect for him and pitied the wife, who must have endured a lot of betrayal and bad behavior from him. What I could not get over was why she was still with him!

CHAPTER 10

Smith College, Northampton, Massachusetts and Boston University, Boston, Massachusetts

'In this country, American means white. Everyone else has to
hyphenate" - Toni Morrison, Nobel Laureate.

❖

An African student at Smith College: A White, elite female college

Smith College is the largest of the elite Seven Sister Colleges which are seen as the female equivalent of the Ivy League male colleges and universities in the United States. It is a private college located on 147 acres in a semi-urban area of Northampton in west-central Massachusetts. It was founded in 1871 and usually has an undergraduate student enrollment of around 2,500 students. Among its most famous alumnae are Betty Friedan, Gloria Steinem, Barbara Bush, Otelia Cromwell, Margaret Mitchell and Julia Child. The campus was in an area sometimes known as 'The Valley' comprising four other colleges and universities including Amherst College, Mt. Holyoke College, the University of Massachusetts and Hampshire College. Over the years, these institutions developed close collaborative relationships that include class enrollments for credit.

I arrived at Smith College for my first semester in the fall of 1962 by train to Springfield, Massachusetts and then by Greyhound bus to Northampton, Massachusetts. I was met by the Foreign Student Advisor, who turned out to be like a second mother to all the foreign students. I was then taken to my dorm, in a large building called Martha Wilson House on the Quad which was the center of important campus-wide events and graduation ceremonies. This was the original part of the campus that later spread out and included a gym, a pond, a chapel, a theatre, a science building and a huge library next to the administrative buildings.

Living in the Quad was desirable because of its history and beautiful landscape, and it was the ceremonial heart of the college. The buildings were large and majestic looking in their brownstone architectural style and surrounded by large trees. With few exceptions, most of the students had single rooms that were spacious and comfortable. We took pride in decorating our rooms in an aesthetically-pleasing way because we spent a lot of time in them studying. There was also a large dining room and a spacious living room with a grand piano on the first floor. On the third floor of the building was a large apartment which housed the cooks and maids who were responsible for meal preparation and cleaning.

Dorm life

Martha Wilson House was on the far side of the campus from the classrooms and administrative buildings, and most of the students had to have bicycles. At the beginning of the fall semester the students would organize a sale of old bicycles as well as new ones that were brought in from the bicycle store in town. The bicycle sale started very early in the morning and you had to be among the earliest risers to get the best bargains. I remember waking up at 5am to be one of the first people in line and ended up with a good bike for a good price. I rode it everywhere on campus and even to town. In many ways, you can describe the campus and town as a biking town. There were coffee shops and a small grocery store and restaurants close to campus on

Green Street which provided convenience shopping and recreation for the college community.

Like all the houses on campus, Martha Wilson House had a housemother, Mrs. Chandler, who was very kind to all the students, and a junior professor in residence from Italy, who taught Italian. Our housemother was in charge of running the house and taking care of the students and liaising with their parents as necessary. She also supervised the domestic staff and was responsible for planning the meals. After dinner, she would serve us regular coffee in demitasse cups in the large lounge. This was aimed at promoting a style of 'gracious living' to which Smith students were supposed to aspire as ladies in the making and as future society women. A number of students had been introduced to society through debutante balls whose agenda included facilitating matchmaking between the eligible single people in elite society. Part of the art of gracious living included piano playing by a student after dinner, to the delight of the other students assembled around the piano.

On the whole, we hardly spent time in the lounge since there was always a lot of homework to be done and students preferred to stay in their rooms to study or go to the library, especially during exam time. Making popcorn in the evening to facilitate studying was a favorite pastime. Smoking was a habit that some students indulged in, especially after dinner in their rooms. It was considered chic, cool and sophisticated and there was little or no publicity about the health risks of smoking, especially for young women at that time. On the persuasion of one of my friends, I tried smoking a cigarette for the first time and hated it. This deterred me from doing it again and being stuck with a bad and unhealthy habit.

Drinking was a pastime for a few students, but it was not really an obvious problem. The drinking age at that time was twenty-one and younger students would borrow the IDs of older students so that they can go out to bars and drink. I was one of the few students of that age but no one asked me for my ID because the photo was of a Black student and the vast majority of students at Smith College at the time were White. Drinking alcohol on campus was banned, but some of the dorms were on the edge of the town of Northampton, which made it easy for students to take a few steps outside the campus to be technically 'off campus.' They would then be in a public place where they could drink their hearts out, and some of them did just that!

We would all congregate in the lounge on special occasions, such as during open campus, when prospective students and their families would visit. One of these times was memorable because the Beatles were on the Ed Sullivan show during their first visit to the United States. It was the first night the TV had been turned on since I took up residence in the dorm. What a night of loud jubilation!

The students at Martha Wilson House, like other houses, were divided into groups which took turns in setting the dining table for dinners and waiting on their fellow students some evenings. Other student tasks included manning the desk that monitored the movements of students in and out of the dorm at night. The rules about having male guests in dorm rooms were very strict and in fact men were not allowed to be in the bedrooms except on two occasions during the year, when the door has to be opened half way and all four feet were supposed to be on the floor. We used to laugh about this and thought it was silly, but no one dared to break the rule, at least not when it was in effect.

Academics

I was excited to go to my first class, which was an introductory course in sociology, which I had decided would be my major. I took other courses in the social sciences, such as Government, and in history and the humanities, such as Philosophy, English Literature and French. The intention of taking French was to fulfill my language requirement, but I later regretted not continuing my French courses, especially French literature, so that I could become proficient in the language. Many years later I worked for the United Nations as a Deputy Director for the Earth Summit and was stationed in Geneva, Switzerland, where

French is the spoken language. I would have also benefited from being able to communicate with Africans from Francophone countries. I had fulfilled my science and math requirements at Bennett College and was exempted from them.

There were other courses that were rumored to be easy courses or 'gut courses' that some students took to increase their grade point average. A number of these courses were in the humanities and included speech and music. Not all students, however, found these to be easy courses, especially those in music, which required long hours of studying and listening to music or learning to play a musical instrument. I do regret not taking any course in music to better understand music theory and the development and history of different musical traditions, since I come from a musical family. I also regret not taking a course in Art History, which would have expanded my appreciation of the aesthetic aspects of human expression in the visual arts. Philosophy was my worst course and even though I had a passing grade I felt that I could have done better if I had had a different professor.

Grading at that time was very strict and grade inflation was unheard of. A grade of B average was considered good enough to be on the Dean's list. With the prevalence of grade inflation as the norm in later years at many institutions, a B average at Smith would be considered an A minus average from the 1990s on. Some schools are now trying to impose policies to bring down grade inflation or do without grades altogether. Very few students made it onto the Dean's list when I was at Smith and I was delighted when I made it. The African students did well on the whole and made the Dean's list at least once, and a few more than once.

The volume of reading in the social sciences was mind blowing, something I had never experienced before. At a minimum, we were reading at least 25 pages a day per course in full concentration, because there were usually assignments attached to the readings. The practice of writing long research term papers was also something new, since we had only thirteen weeks to develop the concept and plan the research.

Unlike the British system where most courses covered the whole year, one semester seemed too short a period for a good research paper but the American students seemed used to it. I remember taking a course on world history in thirteen weeks and finding it difficult to keep up with all the reading that was required.

One of my favorite courses was Comparative Religion, in which we studied the three main universal religions of Judaism, Christianity and Islam that were rooted in the Abrahamic monotheistic tradition. These religions also shared the belief in the soul and the promise of the rewards of having lived a good life in the afterlife. The concept and actions of the Devil or Satan are also elements of these religions which were discussed and debated. Within Christianity we examined Catholicism, Protestantism and Evangelism and the role of Martin Luther in the 16th Century Protestant Reformation. We also touched on other religions like Buddhism, Hinduism and Zoroastrianism, but did not dwell on them. I remember asking the Professor why Catholicism needed so many intermediaries like Saints and the Virgin Mary in-order to reach God and if this meant that God was too far away and unreachable directly. He thought that was a good question and agreed that the intermediaries made the difficult and complicated path to God more accessible.

We also studied the main differences between Judaism and Christianity being the belief in the oneness of God in a non-human form by Jews and the Holy Trinity which divides God into the Father, the Son and the Holy Spirit in Christianity. Islam also discounts the division of God into a Trinity and does not accept Jesus as the son of God but rather as an important prophet. We had long discussions about the nature of the deity in the three religions, since in Judaism the deity seemed stern, authoritarian and punitive and in the other religions, the deity seemed more forgiving and less authoritarian. Christianity seemed the most flexible, but we recognized the different sects and divisions within each of these universal religions, which made it difficult to generalize.

There was clearly something soothing about being a believer

compared to a non-believer, and one felt a sense of security and courage in facing the challenges and vicissitudes of life, especially illness and death. All religions had compassion at their core and emphasized the golden rule to 'Do unto others as you would have them do unto you.' This made me wonder why so many religious wars were fought and why there was so much discord in some of the religions, such as between the Shiites and the Sunnis of Islam and so forth. I came to understand that religion is about power and the continuing link between religion and politics, despite attempts to separate religion from the state in many countries. Most liberation struggles such as the Civil Rights Movement and the Anti-Apartheid Movement are rooted in religion, as were the political/religious wars of history like the Crusades of Christianity and the wars or 'Jihad' of Islam. I came to the conclusion that all religions have a veiled political stance that could divide rather than unite humanity.

Student diversity and race relations

The majority of the students that attended Smith College at that time were very wealthy and of White, Protestant and Anglo-Saxon heritage, referred to in the US as 'WASPS.' Most of them were nice, accessible and smiled a lot but some of them were snobs and hardly smiled. A number of them were ostentatious about their wealth, some even bringing their horses to school and keeping them in a nearby stable so they could ride them on the weekends. Several took expensive holidays with their parents to Europe every summer and many attended expensive private high schools and lived in exclusive and affluent suburban communities. Although there were some Jewish students, I was told that there was an attempt to limit their numbers through a clandestine quota system but I had no proof of that. There was little economic diversity because very few scholarships were available for students of low income at that time. Ethnic minorities holding American citizenship were few, many being of Asian descent and not necessarily on financial aid. Italian American students came in sizeable numbers during my junior year and did not seem to have the same reserve as the other White students. Those in my dorm would play their music loudly and contrary to the practice of refraining from watching TV in the lounge after dinner, would turn the TV on regularly during study hours. They also exhibited blatant racist attitudes towards me that were not typical of the other White students. I felt that the other White students who had racist feelings would act in the following ways: either ignore Black students altogether, stare at them from a distance, or display their ignorance by asking them stupid questions about living in trees and being surrounded by animals. I put an end to it once and for all by a simple sarcastic response indicating that living in trees was fun, especially if you had some animals as neighbors because they made better neighbors than some human beings.

The total number of Black students was six and four were from Africa. There were two African-American but one was of a 'high yellow color' and I am not sure whether or not she considered herself Black . She avoided hanging around with Black students and always seemed lonely and miserable because she was not part of the White group either. The rest of the students that provided some diversity at that time were the international students, many of whom came from Europe. The international students participated in a number of social and educational activities, including the popular 'International Students Day' celebrations. All international students wore their national dresses and were presented to the whole college assembly on stage once a year. During lunch, they organized an international buffet and sold foods from their various countries to raise funds for charity.

One way in which African students stood out was in their inability to swim, even though some of us took part in the athletic programs offered by the college. One requirement for graduation was to pass a swimming test which included jumping in the Olympic-size pool, swimming four lengths using any stroke and floating on your back for five minutes. With very few exceptions, all American students could swim by the time they got to college and passed the test during the first week. African students and a few other foreign students made up the majority of those needing swimming lessons. Some of us made progress but one African student could never float, even though she took swimming lessons for three years. In recognition of her efforts, she was given an honorary pass so that she could graduate in her fourth year. Usually most students required only one year of classes to pass the test. In retrospect, I wish I had continued taking swimming lessons so that I would become better at it and gain more from it in later life.

Ethnic diversity among Faculty and South Africa

There was hardly any ethnic diversity among the faculty. The history department had one Mexican professor who taught Latin American History. One professor from Iran taught in the sociology department and the government department had one professor from Egypt. They were all extremely popular and their courses added much-needed diversity to the curriculum. Students were excited to learn about other parts of the world and there were very few study-abroad programs at that time to countries outside Europe and North America.

African students were excited when a Black professor from South Africa was hired as an exchange faculty member for a couple of years. He came with his wife and four children and opened his house to us for meals, relaxation and discussions. As he and his family spoke of the evils of apartheid and about the unjust pass system as well as state-sponsored crimes and regimes of racial terror, we latched on to their every word. They also spoke of the resistance and the struggle against apartheid by the Liberation Movements like African National Congress (ANC) founded in 1912, the Pan African Congress (PAC) founded in 1959, and about Nelson and Winnie Mandela and other icons of the anti-apartheid struggle.

Apartheid was at its height at the time and his courses covered the history and political ideology of apartheid and its impact, not only in South Africa, but also on Africa as a whole. The students decided to have a conference on South Africa and I was very active as a member of the organizing committee. I learnt a lot researching who the speakers should be as well as the readings that we should suggest to students in advance. We also raised funds and were able to bring Miriam Makeba to campus to give a concert at the end of the conference. On another occasion, we invited a touring group of dancers from South Africa to perform on campus. The tragedy of apartheid in South Africa was actively debated on many campuses at the time and students held a number of protests against apartheid on many campuses.

At Smith College, African Studies was introduced by Professor Dr. Gwendolyn Carter, whose area of specialization was the emerging field of 'Non-Western Studies' which focused on what later became known as the 'Third World.' She taught a popular introductory course on Africa which almost all the African students took. Her courses were very popular and Africa in the early sixties was very much in the news as several countries gained their independence during that period. African students felt very proud that their countries were being studied and showcased at Smith College and provided opportunities for us to contribute our own personal experiences to the discussions on Africa. Programs in African Studies were established in many institutions in the United States, and the African Studies Association, which was founded in 1957, expanded in membership and organized annual conferences at the national level. Similar developments in promoting and strengthening African Studies were also taking place on the African continent.

Homesickness

Air travel to Africa was not as frequent as it later became and was very expensive. As a result, African students did not go back home for Christmas or other religious and summer holidays and would spend four or more years in America or England without seeing their families back home. Homesickness was consequently a problem. To make up for it, the few African students on campus tended to spend a lot of time together and reminisce about home and family. On a few occasions, we would cook African food in the small kitchenettes in our dorms which would offend some students because of the strong smell of onions, pepper and other spices. A few of them complained of the smell getting on their clothes, but we ignored them for the most part. We also coped with homesickness through the special events for foreign students organized by our foreign students' advisor, including outings and dinners at her home. Some of us went to churches in Northampton and developed friendships through fellowship with young members of the church. African students also took trips to Boston and Cambridge to attend conferences and events celebrating African independence days.

In addition, we were assigned to host families in Northampton by the Foreign Students' Office that we visited from time to time, including spending some weekends and short holidays with them. Mine was a very nice and hospitable White family of a physician, his wife and three small children that lived in a large house, not far from the campus. I always looked forward to spending time with them, especially the short holidays, and playing with the children who, with the exception of the toddler, were all in grade school and curious about Africa. I was probably the first Black person they had ever met, so they wanted to touch my hair, and one of them was apprehensive every time I took my bath, fearing that I would lose my chocolate color if I stayed too long in the bathtub! He was so relieved when I emerged from the bathroom with my color intact. It was all so innocent and charming, and I loved spending time with this very special family. They would host my boyfriend, Henry, whenever he came to visit and I invited them to many of the social events on campus. To some extent, their kind hospitality helped me deal with whatever homesickness I had left after two years at Smith.

Yale and Henry

I also visited my boyfriend Henry in New Haven, Connecticut, where he was studying for a degree in the biological sciences at Jonathan Edwards College at Yale University. The mode of transportation at the time for students was the Greyhound bus with a stopover at Springfield, Massachusetts. Henry had a host family, Ned and Gus Thomas in New Haven, with whom I stayed whenever I visited him. They were Jewish and had no children but were extremely kind and hospitable and treated Henry like the child they never had. The husband worked as a newspaper reporter and the wife as a school teacher. They belonged to a closely-knit Jewish community in New Haven and later moved to the suburb of Hamden. They told us a lot of stories about the Jews and their suffering and how they had migrated to many parts of the world because of that.

Ned and Gus were both very religious and observed all the Jewish holy days, to the point where both Henry and I became quite familiar with them. They liked traveling to other parts of the world during their vacations and their house was decorated with many of the souvenirs from their numerous trips abroad. They had many friends and entertained a lot, so we got to meet many people, including their African-American friends. Henry invited them to many of the social events and public lectures at Yale and they were honored to be among his 'American family' at his graduation at Yale University.

Yale was an all-male university at the time but there were several social events which included female guests. Students had to wear a tie to dinner since being a gentleman was stressed and required a dress code. Most of the students simply left a tie in the cloakroom just outside the dining hall so that they would not forget to wear it at dinner time. I attended a number of social functions and balls as well as outings and mixers which were organized by students and the administration alike.

Interracial dating was not the norm, so the administration would make sure that Black students who did not have a date for a special dance were provided with Black females for a date. Most male students simple brought their own Black date rather than have one selected for them. This was all very strange to me at the time and made me realize how deep-seated racism was in all aspects of American society and the hypocrisy and contradictions that fueled it. Notions of equality, freedom and democracy were always touted but were more symbolic than real.

Henry visited me at Smith on several occasions and stayed with my host family some of the time. He would usually take the bus from New Haven or share a ride with other students heading to Smith or other colleges in the area. On one such occasion, he missed his ride and did something that was unbelievable. My boyfriend decided to make the eighty-three-mile trip from New Haven, Connecticut to Northampton, Massachusetts on his scooter in the middle of winter! When he arrived, his hands were cold and almost frozen and he had to sit in front of the fireplace in Martha Wilson House drinking soup and coffee for several hours to recover. He became 'the hero of love' in my dorm and won the admiration of the students. I decided then that there was no one else I would like to marry and spend the rest of my life with than Henry.

The gender factor: dating and emphasis on marriage

Like Bennett College, Smith College was a women's college but not a feminist institution and did not have the same concern or understanding of gender issues as we do today. For a start, the principal was a White male, referred to as 'Uncle Tom', and most of the professors were White men. Since this was before the second and third wave of feminism, there was little consciousness about gender asymmetry or gender hierarchies. Although many women had career plans, a number were seeking education with the purpose of marrying men of high standing and becoming highly educated housewives. Ideally, these would be men enrolled in Ivy League institutions and heading for careers in the most lucrative professions and in politics. A female culture at the time was one that prepared women for roles in the domestic sphere, designed to support husbands and children.

Betty Friedan, founder of the National Organization of Women (NOW) and author of *The Feminine Mystique*, was a Smith College alumna and one of the leaders of the second wave of feminism in the United States from the 1960s to the 1980s. She captured this dilemma in her book, which explores 'the problem without a name.' This defines women with high levels of education stuck in boring and unfulfilling lives as well-to-do suburban housewives and marinating in their fancy college degrees. The quest for the 'Second Wave of Feminism' was primarily for greater equality in the laws, norms and professions of society and greater public awareness about gender-based discrimination. It would take the third wave of feminism from the mid 1990s to delve deeper into the systemic divisions among women along the lines of economic inequality, racism and the negative legacy of colonialism for Black women and women of the Global South to expand the scope of the bourgeois and liberal feminism of the second wave. Third Wave Feminism took a historical perspective and examined how feminism intersected with race, class and other differences to produce compounded forms of institutionalized discrimination against women.

Social life

Being a women's college put a strain on social life in a small and conservative town like Northampton, which lacked the bright lights of cities like Boston or New York. In order to have interactions with male students, Smith students ('Smithies') would either go away on weekends to the Boston and Cambridge area or attend mixers in which male and female students would take turns organizing social dances at their respective colleges. Usually, the event would start with students milling around or one male student asking a female student for a dance. It would continue like this until most of the students were paired and stayed together for the rest of the night. This might or might not be followed by another date.

As at Yale University, attempts would be made to link Black female students with Black male students from other campuses. I found the mixers to be bizarre and did not participate in them, mainly because I was not accustomed to the excessive coupling culture of the United

States. Although we had boyfriends in Sierra Leone, we would tend to socialize in groups and interact with more people, rather than be confined to one person on social occasions.

I remember being visited by a male student at the University of Vermont. He was a friend from Norway who I had met at an international conference at Michigan State University, East Lansing. The other students assumed that his purpose for visiting me was to help him find a White date and were flocking around him. They were surprised when in response to their question about why he was visiting Smith, he replied 'I came to see Filomina.' That evening, the Italian-American students started teasing me by singing 'stick to your own kind' from West Side Story. This was the first time I had experienced such crude racism from other students so directly. They could not get over the fact that we were just friends and not romantically involved, even though they knew that I already had a boyfriend. In their eyes, this was a date in the American sense and they disapproved of such 'interracial dating,' a notion I found to be racist and told them so.

Having a boyfriend was a sort of status symbol at the time since many students did not have any steady relationships. Crushes on male professors made up for the drought in the scarcity of eligible and age-appropriate men. A few senior Smith College students were engaged at that time and were viewed with admiration and some envy, since marriage was a goal for some students. Graduating with an engagement ring on one's finger was a sign of achievement and these students were held in high esteem. The graduation celebrations even included competitions in which the prizes were geared towards a life of marriage and raising a family, such as baby strollers, cribs or household-related items. An enviable achievement would be to land a man from one of the Ivy League schools before graduation. I remember one of my friends telling me that her father was angry with her for wasting his investment by failing to have a boyfriend and fiancé with the potential of having a successful career and leading an affluent life. Although I had a steady boyfriend, marriage was the farthest thing from my mind, since I was determined to go to graduate school and my professional goal was to become a college professor.

Rape of a student in the library and reactions to it

The library was a popular place for students to study, especially in preparation for an exam. Students would sometimes organize special study sessions in groups for class projects or to prepare for final exams. The college library was one of the largest libraries I had ever seen and had an impressive collection, including publications on Africa. Students were assigned study carrells according to seniority and some spent hours after dinner and during the day doing assignments in the library, although some preferred studying in their rooms.

Since the college bordered the town and there were many entrances, it was easy for anyone to enter the campus from the street. One day, a student was attacked and raped in the library stacks as she studied late at night, when very few other students were still around and most of the library staff had gone home. The library desks were usually manned by students at night and campus police provided security by walking around the campus and buildings but were not permanently stationed in any one place. I remember students being terrified when the news broke and almost everyone was shocked that something like that could happen at the college. The name of the victim was never disclosed for her protection and privacy, and as far as I know the rapist was never caught.

Students were traumatized by the rape and had several discussions about it and how to avoid such assaults. We felt that the violation of one student was the violation of all students. After that incident, students hesitated to go to the library for a while and a new rule was established to ensure that no fewer than three students should be in one study area of the library at any given time after dinner. Campus security also examined the stacks of the library more often than usual during their patrol of the campus.

The incident led to several discussions about the vulnerability of women because of their sexuality at a time when there was not as much consciousness of gender-based violence as we have today. Rape was also not as common, or not as widely reported, so it was not something we thought much about. As I reflected on the incident, I became more determined that the area of women's rights and equality was one that I would like to pursue as a career.

During my second year, a student from West Africa was admitted to Smith and became one of my best friends. My friend B was not on scholarship and all of her expenses were being privately financed by her father, which was unusual for African students. She hoped that she would obtain some financial aid during her second year. We spent a lot of time together talking about home and consoling each other on our homesickness. She had the most winning smile and bubbling personality and made friends easily. Her first year was difficult academically and socially but she did very well during her second year, by which time she had received full financial aid from the college.

She had a host family in Cambridge, Massachusetts and used to visit them on long weekends and holidays. While there, she met and fell madly in love with another African student who was studying at Harvard at the time. Just before the end of the second semester of her sophomore year, we spent time together talking about how far we had gone and how well we had done at Smith. She was a rising junior and I was a rising senior. We had a habit of walking and talking from one end of the campus to the other several times, since our dorms were so far apart. As we said goodbye around Paradise Pond on the campus, I remember turning to look at her and experiencing a strange feeling as she walked away. I had no idea that I would never see her again.

Summer as a Social Worker in Westchester County –
another host family

I spent my first summer from Smith College working in Westchester

County as a paid intern in a social work agency dealing with aid to welfare mothers and dependent children. ASPAU had arranged summer jobs for African students with various agencies and educational institutions in line with their courses of study and future career plans. We lived with host families who arranged transportation for us to and from work. I stayed with a White family with two working parents. The father worked in insurance and the mother was a nurse, who worked part time. They had three grade-school children and a live-in Black maid who really raised and disciplined the children.

Unlike children in Sierra Leone, they had a lot of freedom and were empowered in many ways, often giving orders and getting their own way, even with their parents. In my view they were spoiled brats who were given a lot of material things and toys and refused to eat anything they did not like. This bothered me a lot and I found myself trying unsuccessfully to correct the children's behavior. I attributed it to the fact that the mother would often say 'I love you' to her children, which I felt was unnecessary and contributed to their lack of discipline, since there was no accountability for their actions. They needed 'tough love.'

I did not sense any racial prejudice with this family and certainly not with the children. However, after a party hosted on my behalf for all the ASPAU students that lived and worked in Westchester county that summer, I saw a difference. One of the male African students came with a White girlfriend to the party and this seemed to shock my host parents, especially the mother. She later asked me where the interracial couple had met and I told her that I did not know. My host mother bluntly told me that she did not approve of interracial dating, although she had nothing against Black people. She then added that if her daughter were to ever date a Black man, it was the Black maid that would put a stop to it. I told her that if she felt that way then it would be her daughter visiting the Black man at his home and not the other way around. She had never thought of that possibility and was astounded. It was as if I was talking to a complete stranger and I saw her in a different light from that day on. Our relationship, which had once been warm, friendly and easy going, was no longer the same, but at least I got to see the real person behind the facade.

CHAPTER 11

The Dangers of Social Work in Urban New York; Social Activism on Campus, and Graduation

"How wonderful it is that nobody needs to wait a single moment before starting to improve the world." – Anne Frank

❧

Summer Job at a Delinquent Children's Home

That summer, I got a job working at a home for delinquent young girls and boys in The Bronx, New York. I worked with the girls, who were in a separate section, but had no idea what I was in for. I convinced my ASPAU sponsors that it would be a good experience for my interest in sociology. I lived at International House in New York City and commuted to work every day. Although these were teenagers, they had been forced to grow up too quickly and had gone through a lot of difficult situations in their tough neighborhoods. Many of them had serious behavioral problems and had had encounters with the law. Almost all of them were sexually active and some of them were pregnant. Others had serious psychological problems, involving eating disorders, self-mutilation by cutting themselves and acts of violence. I was told that there was a riot in the home several years ago during which the girls had beaten up their counsellor, broken her arm and cracked her skull.

There were about twenty girls in the dorm, for which I was the assistant counsellor working with a specialist in the area of juvenile delinquency among girls. The doors to their dorm unit were always locked and the counsellor closely guarded the bunch of keys as a means of controlling their movement. Another important task was checking the cutlery in the dining room to ensure that they did not take any items up to their dorm and use them as a weapon to harm themselves or others. One of the biggest fears was that the girls would escape and get into more trouble on the outside. The typical routine was to wake up, shower, have breakfast in the main dining hall, have reading sessions, home economics courses, lunch, recreation, dinner, TV viewing and bedtime. Occasionally they would watch a movie in a large hall, and I noticed that they were more interested in the women in the movies than the men and would blow them kisses and remark on their beauty. I was puzzled that so many of the sexually active ones had obviously been with men and wondered whether the confinement with other women was producing lesbian feelings, although I never noticed any obvious lesbian activities among the girls.

I was always scared of going to work, especially when we had to be locked inside the dorm with the girls. They received psychological counselling and medical attention, but some of them had serious mental problems and needed more specialized attention. Since their home environment was not conducive to leading a normal and safe life, some of them were repeat offenders and saw no way out.

One day, I went to work not knowing that I would face one of the most terrifying experiences in my life. I worked the afternoon shift from three to eleven in the evening, so I was responsible for supervising dinner and bedtime. Unfortunately the counsellor was ill and I was the only one on duty that day. To make matter worse, one of the male counsellors who I would consult when I had problems was not at work that day.

After dinner, I noticed an eerie silence among the girls as they washed up and got ready for bed. All of a sudden they put out all the lights and attacked me, wrenching the keys from my hands and opening the door. Strangely, they did not walk out of the room but instead went back to their dorm and sat on their beds. I was wounded and bleeding on my face and arm because they had thrown me on the floor. I got up and composed myself, then went to them and asked the reason for the violent attack. They told me that it was not against me personally but an expression of their anger and outrage at being locked up all the time. They just wanted to show that they could snatch the keys and open the door whenever they wanted to demonstrate their need for freedom.

When I went to work the next day, I resigned. I pleaded with the administration to provide better protection for the staff, especially those in direct contact with the young women and men at the center. I probably could have taken legal action for the violent attack and harm done to me by the girls but I never really thought about that and felt that it was in my best interest to move on.

Summer School at Columbia University

I decided to go to summer school instead, since ASPAU was sponsoring summer courses. I enrolled at Columbia University's summer school to study intensive French, while living at International House nearby. The course was fast-paced, focused on intermediate French and lasted eight hours a day. I remember dreaming in French towards the end of course. Most of the students were American students working on their language requirements and were attending Columbia University. We had an opportunity to also learn a lot about France and to visit the French Embassy. Two students from France attending Columbia University served as teaching assistants and helped us with the conversational aspect of the course. At International House, I met a lot of foreign students as this was a popular hostel and often organized tours, speakers and social events. It was a good time to be a foreign student in the United States.

The death of a dear friend

One day, I received a phone call from Boston informing me that my dear friend from West Africa at Smith College had died. I was in shock and wondered how this could have happened, since she had looked healthy and happily in love with her boyfriend and was doing very well in her courses. I was told that she had had appendicitis, which brought back memories of the death of my cousin Remileku from the same disease as a child in Freetown. Once again, I started feeling stomach pains on the right side of my abdomen as a sympathetic reaction to the death of my friend. I was told that mine was phantom pain and represented my close relationship with her and my deep mourning for her. I decided to go to Boston for the funeral and had a difficult time throughout all the events that were organized for her. This was the second corpse that I had seen and again she looked so natural in her African dress and head tie, but she was silent and gone forever.

Her boyfriend was distraught and I found out that he was being prevented from leaving his apartment for fear of him committing suicide. I wondered why he would want to do that. Much later I learnt to my dismay that my friend had died from an illegal abortion and that the profound guilt being felt by her boyfriend might lead him to take his own life. I was in utter shock as I went through the motions of attending the funeral, which was not a burial. The family in West Africa had decided to have her buried in the States to avoid the commotion of having her body flown home for burial. Two months later, her father visited Smith College and her grave and was very angry with the college for failing to teach its students about contraception and reproductive health, especially being a women's college. I was also disappointed in the college, especially in their attempt to hide the real cause of her death and pretending that it was appendicitis to save the reputation of the college.

The loss of my friend from West Africa was a blow to me, since I did not know that she had been pregnant or ill. She had confided in me her concern that her boyfriend belonged to another ethnic group and that their families would not approve of the match. I wondered if that was the reason she decided to abort the pregnancy or because it would interfere with her studies and disappoint her parents. In my grieving for her I imagined many scenarios in which she would have still been alive, including marriage against her parents' will; taking a year off to have the child and returning to school; having the baby and taking it home to her mother to raise so that she can continue her education at Smith, and so forth.

My consciousness of gender asymmetry was heightened in realizing that my friend had had to sacrifice her life because she was a woman, while her boyfriend continued his life and pursuit of a career, even though he was equally responsible for the pregnancy. I thought it was unfair. Like her father, I also felt that the college had let her down and by extension, all the students, and that she did not have to die. Abortion was illegal in the United States and at that time was also legally restricted in her country. Abortion has been a central focus of the Women's Movement since the 1970s, which has resulted in court battles leading to the landmark victory of Roe versus Wade in1973. It is one of the main contentions in the culture war between the Republicans and the Democrats and is strongly opposed by the religious right. Given the majority of conservatives in the Supreme Court, Roe versus Wade could be overturned one day, thereby undermining the reproductive rights of women.

When I was growing up in Sierra Leone, teenage pregnancy was rare, unlike the epidemic that it is in the country today. I heard of a few girls having abortions then and in fact there was a rumor of one girl at the Annie Walsh dying of a botched abortion when I was a student there. As a rule, unmarried women tended to take their pregnancy to full term rather than have an abortion as children were viewed as gifts of God, not to be thrown away through abortion. Abortion is still illegal in Sierra Leone, despite pressure from various women's and human rights groups.

Although a bill supporting abortion was unanimously passed in Parliament in March 2016, the then president, Earnest Bai Koroma, refused to sign the bill legalizing it. One of the arguments made by politicians, women and human rights groups was that legalized abortion would reduce the perennially high maternal mortality rate in Sierra Leone, which has been over 1000 deaths per 100,000 live births for many years. It has always been my view that although women have access to abortion in many countries now, and I am pro- choice, the best and safest approach is prevention of pregnancy through contraception. The need to emphasize and make widely available the many natural and technological approaches to contraception cannot be emphasized enough.

Assassination of President John F. Kennedy

The assassination of President John F. Kennedy was an incident that I will always remember. African Students from Smith College and Trinity College were invited to participate in a seminar on Africa that included a radio interview. I enjoyed the bus ride to Trinity, which was an all-male college at the time and was located in Hartford, Connecticut, a more urban setting than Smith College. During the radio interview on November 22, 1963, we were interrupted and informed that President Kennedy had just been assassinated in Dallas, Texas. We were all in shock and the African students let out the loud screams that were characteristic of the reaction to announcements of deaths in Africa. The interview was abruptly ended and we went upstairs crying and terribly upset.

Much to our surprise, although there was a gathering of students who had also just heard the news in the hall of the building, not a single sound was heard. In fact, there was complete silence. This was a culture shock to me and I interpreted it to mean that they did not care that their president had just been shot dead. I later learned that they were probably as upset as we were but that crying and wailing were not a typical American cultural response to death and grieving. Later, we joined the students in watching the events as they unfolded on television and I did see a few of them with tears silently streaming down their cheeks. In some ways it made me feel better, and I could empathize with them for revealing their grief this way.

The legacy of John F. Kennedy was significant in the United States as well as in Africa and the African Diaspora because of his role in helping to advance Civil Rights and his progressive policies on the African world. He also appealed to youth all over the world through his optimistic views about the future. He embodied the myth of Camelot, which provided a romantic feeling of hope and a vision of world unity. Camelot made it possible to fantasize and look back to a previous era for inspiration, but also to look forward to the promise of a utopian world that would be fair, inspiring and benefit mankind.

The events of Kennedy's death gripped the nation for several days and weeks to come and most people were glued to their television sets for the duration of the saga, including the arrest of Lee Harvey Oswald and his murder a few days later by Jack Ruby in an unbelievable live television drama witnessed by millions. The swearing in of President L.B. Johnson as his successor, the blood-stained dress of Jacqueline Kennedy, the state funeral and the memorable salute of John Kennedy Jr. to his father at the age of three, together seemed like a sad fairy tale. It took me and many other students and most of America a long time to get over this unbelievable and profound tragedy.

Campus activism – civil rights and the Vietnam war

The decade of the sixties was the decade of the Civil Rights Movement, of which student movements were an integral part. I remember going to a Student for Non-Violent Coordinating Committee (SNCC) conference in New York city with some students from Smith College and seeing up close what student activism looked like in the United States. The leaders were mostly men, but a few women also spoke and contributed to the development of a plan of action and an agenda for activism on their various campuses and beyond. I also joined students who would charter special buses to join large demonstrations against racism in big cities like New York and Washington. On the Smith campus there were many organizations working on advancing civil rights that organized discussions on the injustices posed by racial discrimination and racial ideologies and the legacy of slavery and Jim Crow laws. Some of the discussions also took place in some social science classes, but it was always difficult to be the only Black student in the class in these situations, especially if the professor was not well equipped to create a safe space in the classroom for these discussions.

One of the most memorable political events was the visit to the campus of Democratic candidate Hubert Humphrey in 1964 when he was on the ticket as Vice President to Lyndon Johnson and campaigning on some college campuses for votes. Known for his oratorical skills, his presence electrified the campus even though there was a sizeable number of students who were Republicans. To me, both the students of the Republican and Democratic persuasion appeared to be conservative, even though Smith was viewed as a liberal college. They were resigned to the fact that politics at the highest national level was reserved for men only. There was no discussion about the absence of female candidates or candidates of color to achieve full democratic representation in the United States. Politics was not part of the aspirations of many students, who generally viewed it as aggressive and unsuitable for Smithies, who wanted to be gentle ladies; good and academically accomplished wives, but also skilled in the art of gracious living.

The Vietnam War was another issue that received much student activism in the form of demonstrations and protests. Smith College students, including myself, participated in several of these protests both on and off campus. The Vietnam war lasted for twenty years from 1955 to 1975 and the involvement of the United States started in 1961 and continued to the end. During this period, there were numerous anti-war protests in the United States that were energized by the youth, especially students, who felt that Americans were dying needlessly and they could not justify the war. The gendered dimensions of the war were significant, since most of the military personnel were men as were the casualties of war, although women also participated in the war as soldiers, administrators, health workers, journalists and general service workers. According to The Vietnam Women's Memorial Foundation, about eleven thousand military women served in the Vietnam war.

To many students at Smith, the fact that many more men were dying in the war made it even more unjust, since it was having a negative demographic impact. They argued that the war was destroying the lives and potential of young men whose future they felt was intertwined with theirs as members of the next generation that would be productive citizens of their country. Although some gender issues were raised, they were not considered as central to the questions about the uselessness of the war and the waste of human lives. Americans started seeing the folly of the war while I was at Smith, and a lot of young people lobbied for its end.

It was not until ten years after I graduated from Smith that the war finally ended. The final toll was 882,000, of which 655,000 were adult males, 143,000 adult females and 84,000 children. Americans and their allies lost about 64,000 military personnel. For young women attending college and looking forward to a career and motherhood, the Vietnam War left a general feeling of skepticism and trepidation about the future.

Senior year and graduation from Smith College

The senior year was a very busy year. I had declared my major in government in my second year and abandoned sociology, because most of the courses were about American society and were depressing. The behavioral approach appeared to be the favorite; it resulted in blaming the victim, instead of society. Poverty was presented as a failure of individuals to pull themselves up by their bootstraps. I also learnt that poverty and crime were intertwined, a concept which bothered me a lot because in Sierra Leone at that time, the two were not necessarily connected. In general, the poor children with whom I went to school in Freetown were among the best behaved and most dedicated to learning and succeeding.

I remember challenging my professor in a class titled 'Social Disorganization', which focused on African-Americans and their propensity towards poverty and crime. I argued that criminal behavior did not automatically result from poverty and gave the example of Sierra Leone. He was not convinced and tried to explain to me that in the United States the two were intrinsically linked. Worse still, the condition of poverty resulted from some behavioral deficiencies of people who lived in poverty. He ideas were very much in keeping with what became known as the 'culture of poverty' approach of anthropologist Oscar Lewis, who pointed to enduring negative patterns of behavior and conditions associated with people living in poverty. This view has since been challenged by the sociological approach, which placed most of the blame for poverty and societal ills on society rather than the individual.

In one of my political science courses, I was exposed to critical analysis of the most extreme kind that led me to doubt every conviction I had. One political science professor insisted that there was nothing moral about the political process and that it operated on the principle of 'might makes right.' He felt that democracy was not possible because the strong and those with wealth will always have power over the weak and poor. He presented it almost like a law of nature, and I and other students had many arguments with him. In another class in Government, we studied political theory, starting with the Greek philosophers. I had a strong objection to the notion of Philosopher Kings as the best rulers, as advanced by Aristotle and Plato. It seemed to endorse a class system based on knowledge and aristocracy. Women were not included in the discussion of philosopher kings, as the assumption was that they were ill equipped to rule as they were devoid of these qualities.

Then we studied the social contract theorists, mostly Hobbes, Rouseau and Locke; once again they were all men and I wondered why women were not among the many political theorists that we studied. I was sure that there were women with political ideas at the time and some professors informed us of the social restrictions that kept talented women from expressing their ideas in writing.

I learnt later in graduate school that both Harriet Taylor Mill and her husband John Stuart Mill were philosophers and prolific writers who contributed to the early development of nineteenth century feminism through her publication of *The Establishment of Women* and his on *The Subjection of Women.* These publications challenged the inferior status to which women in Victorian England were delegated and pointed the way for feminism in the twentieth century. The Second and Third Waves of feminism would push these ideas even further and objected to the andro-centric biases in the Academy, projects in which I became intensely involved in graduate school and beyond.

I had more than enough credits to graduate in the summer of 1965. My record was good enough to earn me a place in graduate school with a scholarship at Boston University. Two of us from Africa at Smith were going to be graduating that year, and we received a lot of support from Smith College and families. I had to negotiate with my sponsors, the African Scholarship Program of American Universities (ASPAU), in order to be able to stay and go on to graduate school. According to the agreement, ASPAU students were supposed to go back home after their bachelor degrees. The problem was that many of the students did very well academically and received full scholarships and fellowships to postgraduate and professional schools (term used in the US).

The African students in the ASPAU program also felt that a bachelor degree, especially from the United States, with which many African countries were unfamiliar, would not be given the same weight as a comparable degree from Britain. Many were apprehensive that they would not have a satisfying position back home, and the lure of a good scholarship and opportunity to earn some money as a research assistant or similar position was very attractive. In the end, the African-American Institute that managed the ASPAU program realized that they could not stop the students from continuing their education in graduate school and relented. A few years later, the program was changed so that it only gave scholarships to African students for graduate study in the hope that they had already established themselves in their countries and would be motivated to return home. The new program was called the African Graduate Fellowship Program (AFGRAD.)

Graduation rituals from Smith College were a huge celebration lasting a few days, including college receptions for the graduates and their families, dorm parties, competitive games for those engaged and religious services of thanksgiving. At the special college assembly, the candidates were presented and celebrated and given instructions by the college marshal about the procession and other requirements for the ceremony. A special Smith tradition is the procession of graduates and alumnae in white dresses on the eve of graduation, carrying red roses and lined up in the order of their year of graduation with the oldest in front. It was difficult to see the students with their families and mine not being there, but my host family attended the ceremonies and the graduation. It was a wonderful feeling to hear 'Filomina Clarice Jones' called before I marched up the stage to receive my degree of Bachelor of Arts from the president. All my hard work had paid off. I was a college graduate. What a wonderful day that was!

CHAPTER 12

Graduate Study at Boston University and First Encounter with United Nations

"One book, one pen, one child and one teacher can change the world." Malala Yousafzai

⬦

The summer before Graduate School

After graduation, I left for New York City. I worked for the summer as an assistant teacher at a day camp and attended some of the summer events sometimes hosted for Sierra Leonean students by the Sierra Leone Embassy in Washington, DC. In the fall of 1965, I started graduate studies at Boston University in Anthropology and African Studies on a fellowship. I chose not to continue in government or political science because they did not offer a lot of opportunity to learn about Africa, which was my goal. Sociology also had limitations, since the emphasis was on the United States and other industrialized societies and not on Africa. I felt that Anthropology would be an advantage for several reasons. First, I would learn more about Africa in a holistic way; second, anthropology emphasizes the comparative method; and third, it studies human social and cultural system through a cross-cultural approach.

I enjoyed the summer in New York and spent a lot of time with the Sierra Leone community there. I wish I could have gone home that summer, but there were very few flights going to Sierra Leone at that time and they were very expensive. Once again, I stayed at International House and got to know the upper west side of New York City very well. At that time, Harlem was considered an area in which one had to exercise caution because of its high crime rate. At the same time, it had an admirable reputation for being the center of the arts and a cultural icon for Black America. It had benefited from the Harlem Renaissance, known as the golden age in African-American culture, that lasted throughout the first three decades of the twentieth century. It left a rich legacy in literature, theatre, the arts, music and dance and was associated with famous artists and writers like Langston Hughes, Zora Neale Hurston, Louis Armstrong, Paul Robeson and Josephine Baker, among others. I also enjoyed taking tours of New York City, visiting the Empire State Building, the Rockefeller Plaza, Radio City Hall, Greenwich Village, Spanish Harlem and the United Nations.

My first encounter with the United Nations

The visits to the United Nations were special as I held the institution in high esteem because of its promise for world peace and its social and humanitarian efforts. I felt that although the UN was not a truly democratic institution because of the veto power of the five permanent members of the Security Council, the General Assembly gave every nation of the world, regardless of their relative size and wealth, visibility, relevance and importance. I went to several sessions of the General Assembly and the Committees of ECOSOC (The Economic and Social Council) as well as meetings of non-governmental organizations (NGOs). Little did I know then that one day I would be working for the United Nations myself.

The Sierra Leone mission to the United Nations was active in a number of the negotiations that took place in the mid to late 60s when many African countries gained their independence.

Some countries were governed by the Trusteeship Council, which provided international supervision for eleven Trust territories in their preparation for self- government and independence. The Cold War from 1947 to 1991 between the Soviet Union nations and the Western Nations divided the United Nations in a way that forced the other countries to strike out for a non-aligned position. In 1961 the Non-Aligned Movement was formed, followed by the G77, which was also a neutral bloc from the Cold War countries.

Political decolonization was very much on the agenda of the United Nations in the 1960s and some progress was made in facilitating political independence by African countries from their former colonial rulers. Economic independence was not given the same priority, despite the central role of economic domination in the colonization process. The Economic and Social Council was not willing to dismantle the structures of economic exploitation which remain till the present. This resulted in African countries in a state of economic colonization by their former colonial rulers despite their political independence. In many cases the economies of African countries became even weaker, especially in the subsequent development of economic globalization propelled by industrialized countries, multinational corporations and International Financial Institutions like the World Bank and the International Monetary Fund.

During the 1960s issues of economic development assumed a position of importance on the United Nations agenda, due primarily to lobbying from non -aligned countries, sometimes referred to as developing countries or Third World Countries, or the Global South. Many of these countries had been previously colonized and their economies continued to be dependent on the Global North, especially European countries.

The UN's General Assembly established the First Development Decade from 1960 to 1970 to accelerate progress towards self-sustaining economic growth and social advancement in developing countries. To this end, all member states were asked to intensify their efforts and mobilize support to achieve this goal. The problem was that global economic imbalance put the developing countries in a weak position, as their economies were forced to liberalize and compete in an unequal and unjust single global market engineered by the powerful and rich countries of the Global North. These rich countries and multinational corporations controlled and ensured the unfettered flow of international capital throughout the world. This weakened the sovereignty of the developing countries of the Global South and the ability to protect their economies, their currencies and the labor of their citizens.

The UN was also championing the campaign against apartheid in South Africa. In 1962 the General Assembly established the United Nations Special Committee Against Apartheid to keep the oppressive racial policies of South Africa under review by the organization. The Sharpeville Massacre, which took place in 1960, brought global attention to the evil system of apartheid, based on a brutal racial ideology of separation of the 'races' into four main groups: Africans, Whites, Coloreds and Asian. At Smith College I had helped to organize an international conference on South Africa and was very much involved in the activism against apartheid. I was able to participate in many of the meetings on it held at the United Nations during the summer of 1965 and as an activist with student organizations fighting against apartheid.

Graduate study at Boston University's African Studies Center

By the time I started preparing for graduate work in Anthropology and African Studies at Boston University, I was quite knowledgeable about African political systems and their status and performance on the world stage. The goal of multinationalism was very popular and the increasing numbers of African countries that gained independence and joined the United Nations gave them visibility and some clout in terms of their numbers and novelty. However, the United Nations is not a democratic institution, as mentioned earlier, due to the domination of the permanent members of the Security Council. In addition, the advantage that many countries of the Global South had in the General Assembly by virtue of their greater numbers was gradually undermined by the insistence on reaching consensus on decisions rather than voting. This not only diluted the positions of the countries of the majority but also gave advantage to the countries of the Global North that are in the minority.

Boston University was a bustling and noisy urban campus with trams and buses running through it and shops, restaurants, office buildings and hotels lining the streets. It was quite spread out and had dorms, administrative buildings and departments scattered all over the city, primarily around Commonwealth Ave and Beacon Street. Since I was in the African Studies Program, which was set off from the main campus at that time, I found myself crossing Commonwealth Avenue, a very busy street with a tram running along it, to and from my classes several times a day. This was quite a contrast to Smith College with its lush green lawns, trees, clean air, paradise pond, flower gardens, walking paths and hardly any vehicles on campus. I felt a special connection to Boston because it was the area of America to which I was first introduced at the Annie Walsh School in Freetown, Sierra Leone. I remember learning about the Boston Massacre of 1770 and the Boston Tea Party in 1773 and its role in the American Revolutionary War against the British.

My major for my Master's Degree was anthropology, which included cultural anthropology, archeology and physical anthropology. I also took courses in Political Science and Sociology and attended seminars on African Studies, which hosted a number of speakers from American and African Universities, as well as African dignitaries and politicians. One of the most popular majors in graduate school was economics, which was seen as important for understanding Africa's problems of development and would provide some of the answers to underdevelopment. I was disappointed with my first class in Economics because it emphasized some of the ugly aspects of capitalism and presented it as the only path to development. It followed the Adam Smith philosophy of laissez-fair free market capitalism and was critical of the Maynard Keynes proposal for a role of the state in the economy under certain circumstances. It attributed American success to greed and competitiveness and a desire for accumulation of capital. It blamed Developing Countries for lacking the motivation for greed and aggressiveness. According to the professor, this was the reason for their economic backwardness of the Developing Countries. I dropped the course after four weeks.

My other courses were mostly in anthropology (cultural, social, physical and archeology) and sociology, but I also took courses in political science and African Studies, including history. In cultural anthropology I studied the foundational aspects and the discipline of anthropology, especially the American school of anthropology, which emphasized cultural anthropology. The norms, values, belief systems and symbolic aspects of societies received significant attention and notions of 'cultural relativity' whereby each culture is considered important in its own right, was emphasized. We also studied physical anthropology and the evolution of *Homo sapiens* from its origins in Africa and Africa's contributions to tool making, agriculture and so forth.

Sociology courses focused on the United States for the most part but some sociology courses covered Africa, especially those taught in conjunction with the African Studies Center. The focus was on the rapid social change taking place in Africa, especially through urbanization. Political science courses explored the independence movements of Africa and nation building efforts of the new nations. Very little coverage was given to indigenous Africa pollical systems or social systems as the emphasis was not on pre-colonial but on post-colonial Africa. There was a strong emphasis on modernization and modernity and African societies were presented as being on the path towards becoming Westernized and adopting and domesticating Western institutions, systems and values. There was little or no criticism of the deleterious effects of colonialism on the economies of Africa or attempts made to rescue some of the valuable African institutions that had been destroyed by colonialism or to examine the erosion of the role of women who had held important positions in the pre-colonial political, economic and social systems of Africa.

The majority of the graduate students working on a Masters' degree or a doctorate degree were White, as were most of the professors teaching in the African Studies Program at the time. There was only one Black female professor, an African-American who taught sociology and had been to Africa more often than her White male colleagues who were boasting of being experts on Africa. I always wondered how they could be so sure when they spent so little time in Africa; only a few had lived continuously on the continent for more than one year. I started questioning a lot of the material that they were teaching and was surprised how stereotypical the views of the students and some professors were, even after 'studying' Africa.' They assumed that all Africans lived in rural areas and that all the women had gone through female circumcision. One White male student had the nerve to ask me if I was circumcised. I told him that if he had been so smart about Africa, he would have known that many ethnic groups, mine included, did not engage in this practice and that it was rude of him to ask me that question.

I had a lot of work re-educating some of them and made some headway, but I did not feel that they were taking African Studies to be enlightened about Africa. Their main objective was to land a job with the government in foreign affairs, African development or with the CIA. Others were pursuing their doctorate degrees in the hope of teaching at a university. There was a lot of media attention on Africa in the mid 1960s as many countries were gaining their independence and embarking on nation building. This coincided with the Civil Rights Movement in the United States and the anti-apartheid movement in South Africa and beyond. This spurred an evolving academic interest in Africa leading to an expansion of research activities and publications and a mushrooming of African studies programs in America, Africa and the world at large.

Boston – an academic mecca

The academic environment in the Boston area was rich, as it was saturated with many well-known institutions, which included Harvard University, Massachusetts Institute of Technology (MIT), Northeastern University and Boston College. In addition, Boston is the mecca for medicine and surrounded by several medical teaching hospitals and scientific research centers. Its teaching hospitals and research output are considered to be among the best in the world. With regard to higher education and the professions as a whole, the Boston/Cambridge area is reputed to have a surfeit of highly educated professionals. In addition, there are many institutions of higher learning in the state of Massachusetts as a whole. At the same time, Massachusetts has a serious problem of social inequality that is not addressed by its abundance of knowledge. Boston has a reputation of being one of the most racist cities of the world, and It made national headlines in its violent opposition to racial integration of the schools through busing in the 1970s.

Despite its lack-luster image on racial justice, Massachusetts represents important aspects of New England history and culture and is home to sports teams like the New England Patriots and the Red Socks. It also has some of the most famous families in the United States, like the Kennedys, as its inhabitants. It attracts tourists every year visiting historical landmarks like the Freedom Trail, Faneuil Hall Market, the Old North Church, founded in 1722, Boston Tea Party shops and museum, Fenway Park, USS Constitution Museum, the Bunker Hill Memorial and the African Meeting House.

Boston is also known for its ethnic neighborhoods, comprising descendants of immigrants from Italy, Ireland, China and neighborhoods of African-American descendants of enslaved

Africans in both the South and the North. Unlike other groups, they are not part of the population that migrated from other countries to the United States. Theirs was not a story of migration of any kind since they were involuntarily brought to the United States as a result of the transatlantic slave trade. Blacks have a long history in Boston and are among one of the earliest inhabitants of the area. The African Meeting House in Boston is one of the oldest Black Church Buildings in America. The story of Black migration to Boston was an internal one, related to the Great Migration from 1916 to 1970 of Blacks from the South to the North.

My scholarship at Boston University included full tuition and a small stipend. It was supplemented by a position as resident counsellor in one of the dorms, which was not salaried but covered the cost of my room and board. It was a job which carried a lot of responsibility, because most of the students did not abide by the rules and much time was spent keeping them in line. Those who broke the rules, such as returning to the dorm after hours, had to spend the next weekend confined to the dorm. This meant signing with the resident counsellor every hour to ensure that they stay in. Many of them resented this and when they came to my room to sign they would write 'Mickey Mouse' or 'Donald Duck' or something outrageous in protest. Instead of getting into an argument with them, I decided to accept whatever signature they wrote down as long as they were confined to the dorm for the weekend. Knowing how they loved their freedom, I thought that confinement to the dorm for the weekend was punishment enough.

Unlike Smith College, which was an all-female college and located in a small town in Massachusetts, Boston University was a co-educational, urban campus surrounded by other educational institutions as well as museums, theatres, shopping centers, historic buildings, monuments, famous churches, the Boston Harbor cruises, cultural sites and the state government building complex. Many social functions were held at Boston University and in the community, including conventions and banquets. There were many social activities for students in the numerous colleges and universities in the area and some of them had a lively fraternity culture, known for outrageous parties. The dating scene was active but complicated for those who did not already have a steady mate. It was rumored that some students lived promiscuous lives and that incidents of sexual harassment and date rape were not uncommon.

It was not unusual for some of the students in graduate school to be married and have families. African students, of whom Nigerians were in the majority, tended to organize occasions to get together and celebrate their respective independence days. They also formed associations on the basis of their country of origin or their ethnicity, thereby increasing the number of social events held in one year. Ethnic markets selling African foodstuffs were located in the Black area of Roxbury. Black churches, such as the African Methodist Episcopal Church (AME) and several Baptist churches and other denominations which served the spiritual needs of many African students, were abundant in the Boston area. Boston has had Black politicians in the state and city government as well as in leadership positions in all areas throughout the Commonwealth of Massachusetts.

As I approached the end of my first year at Boston University, I realized that I would have earned enough credits to obtain my Master's Degree in Anthropology. I had written long term and research papers for most of my courses and decided on the option of taking a rigorous exam or spending another semester working on a thesis. I decided to take the exam along with one other student. My other reason was that Henry and I had been dating steadily and we were thinking of getting married. He was planning to continue his studies in medicine at Oxford University and it would be a good idea if I speeded up my Masters degree so we could get married that summer and move to England, where I could also continue my studies towards a doctorate degree.

The Master's exam at Boston University lasted for one week and was quite grueling, but in the end both of us passed and together with our credits for the other graduate courses, the other student and I were awarded Master's Degrees in Anthropology. I was overjoyed and happy and took a studio photo with my Masters cap and gown, but did attend the graduation ceremony because I left Boston for New Haven, Connecticut to join Henry. My parents were overjoyed about my success in obtaining a Master's Degree and our pending nuptials.

CHAPTER 13

Wedding Plans, and Getting Married

"A perfect marriage is just two imperfect people who refuse to give up on each other." – Unknown

❖

I went off to New Haven, Connecticut where Henry was working as a researcher in the Ophthalmology department at Yale University Hospital. Together, we were going to plan our wedding for August 20th, 1966. Henry had written a letter to my parents asking for my hand in marriage and I remember him writing at least three drafts before he was satisfied enough to mail it. Computers were not around then and mistakes made on typewriters were difficult to correct, so he would rewrite the whole letter until he got it right. This impressed me a lot and reflected patience and thoroughness, which are character traits he has exhibited for as long as I have known him. My parents wrote back giving their consent and expressing their extreme joy at our pending wedding. They knew Henry and his family and held them in high esteem so in their eyes, this was a good match.

We became engaged the summer before at a grand party in New York, organized by some friends and family members. We decided to have an Afro-centric ceremony for the engagement and the wedding to the extent possible. As a result, my engagement ring was made of gold, which is typical of my culture and was in the shape of the popular V-shaped rings from Liberia, the second country of Henry's family. Planning the wedding was not easy because we did everything ourselves. I do not know if there were wedding planners at that time but if they existed, we could not afford them anyway. In addition to making wedding plans, we also had to arrange the hosting of our parents from Sierra Leone and my brother and sister from England.

I had bought my wedding dress at Filene's basement in Boston, famous for its bargains that get cheaper as the days go by. It was a beautiful ivory dress in lace and silk with a train of adequate length. I got my pearl jewelry, shoes, veil, gloves and flowers elsewhere in New York. The bridesmaids were to be my sister, Glenna Forster Jones, and sister-in-law, Thelma Steady. The best man was Henry's cousin, Frederick Noah, and the groomsmen were Felix Downs-Thomas, a Yale colleague of Henry's from the Gambia; Peter Sylagi of Hungary and Henry's roommate from Yale University; and Akin Aboderin, a Nigerian scientist friend, also from Yale University.

The wedding ceremony was to take place at Riverside Church in New York and be led by the Reverend Paul Cordes, who gave us a couple of counselling sessions about the importance of God in our marriage and virtues like patience and forgiveness. Many of our friends from Sierra Leone played important roles in our wedding, including Ayo and Ivy Hamilton, Jeredine Williams, Aisie Williams and Ahovi Kpounou. Although our wedding did not follow the strict order of the traditional Krio/Christian wedding, we tried to adhere to many of its main features, which are recounted below. In the first place, marriage is a union not only between individuals but also between families, so we made sure that representatives from both sides were among the wedding party and the hosts at the wedding and celebrations.

At this stage, I would like to discuss the importance of marriage in the Krio context. Even though our wedding and marriage took place in the United States, we adhered to some of the ceremonies but skipped the traditional 'put stop' and 'gage ceremony' which established, in a ritual way, the intention or betrothal of marriage. I thought it would be important to discuss the main features, normative expectations and significance of marriage in our culture and have outlined them below.

Typical Krio Marriage

In the past, marriages were arranged by parents or members of the 'fambul' (kindred) on the basis of similarities of background and future ambitions and expectations. If not arranged, they are likely to be facilitated by introductions of the couple or through social contacts by the families and fambul. Parental influence and approval of the choice of a prospective spouse for their sons and daughters still prevails in many families and for the most part most marriages are based on romantic love.

Gej and Put Stɔp (Engagement)

Like many Krio institutions betrothal procedures display a mixture of Western and African ritual observances. Once again, Yoruba influences are particular marked in the African component of these rituals. Although a woman's consent may have been secured in private between the couple, this can only become official after the proper customary procedures have been followed. As in most African societies, marriages customarily occur in a number of stages. In the Krio context, the initial stage is the 'put stɔp' ceremony, which literally means the exclusive dating of the couple. This lasts for about a year, followed by the 'bible and ring' or 'gej' ceremony (engagement ceremony) about two months before the wedding. In our case, we blended the two ceremonies, since we were in the United States and had to modify some elements of the rituals and just had an engagement ceremony.

The engagement ceremony was held with a small group of friends who stood in for our families. Instead of the elaborate ceremonial white satin cloth, lace, ribbons and calabash containing alligator pepper, cola nuts, bitter cola, needle and thread and a pin, we only had the bible, ring, lace and a pin. Each of these items symbolize the roles both parties will play after marriage. Some of them like the cola nuts are usually used in rituals celebrating the dead and are intended to invite the ancestors to bless the impending union. The pin symbolizes the good intentions of the man to support his wife financially by ensuring that no future complaint could ever be lodged for lack of support. A bride is henceforward forbidden to say 'He never gave me even a pin.'

The gage ceremony itself is quite elaborate and involves the formal request for the bride's hand in marriage in a theatrical performance involving presenting several young women of the prospective bride's age to be refused by the groom's family before the prospective bride is finally presented. The imagery of a rose garden is used as follows:

Groom's family: 'We have spied a beautiful rose in your garden and would like to have it.'

Bride's family: presents a number of young women asking 'Is this the rose?

This goes on until the prospective bride is produced and the groom's family consents that she is the one, followed by much jubilation.

At this stage the calabash would be handed over to the prospective bride's mother. The mother's consent is crucial. If she agrees, she then consults with the father of the prospective bride and together they agree to the match on condition that a promise is made that she will be well taken care of. Good intentions are then expressed on both sides. The engagement Bible and the ring are presented to the mother on behalf of her daughter, and presents are given to the bride's mother with the intention of 'tying the calabash' (finalizing the deal). The bride's people may also present a gift to the prospective groom's family, such as a bottle of whisky and so forth. The delegation of the prospective groom is then formally received. Introductions to the other kindred are made, and refreshments are served. In the past, the prospective bridegroom would not attend the ceremony but stay at home awaiting the return of his representatives with the news of his acceptance. Afterwards there is some celebration and the following refrain is shouted repeatedly with jubilation: 'The bride's mother has given the answer 'yes'!'

Like most engagements today, ours was not as elaborate as in the past but we did our best to capture the main elements of the rituals. The Bible is given as a demonstration of faith in the Christian religion in which the union will be blessed. The ring serves as a seal to demonstrate a man's commitment. As with most institutions, the extent and elaboration of formality and ritual on ceremonial occasions differs from family to family.

A significant factor worthy of note here is the important role played by the prospective bride's mother in the 'gage' ceremony. Since my mother was not in the States at the time, an older friend represented her. Usually, It is the mother who receives the gifts on behalf of her daughter, and the ratification of the betrothal is contingent upon her approval. On the representatives return to the home of the prospective bridegroom, it is the consent of the mother of the bride-to-be that is proclaimed in the song, not that of her father. A mother's consent is essential in a betrothal ceremony because she is primarily responsible for her daughter's upbringing and preparation for womanhood and marriage. After the mothers' consent has been secured the father is free to 'give her away' at the Christian wedding ceremony.

The Eve of the Wedding - 'Kuk' and Bachelor's Eve

A 'cook' and 'Bachelor's Eve' are usually held on the eve of the wedding. In our case it was more in keeping with the bachelor's eve in the United States where the groom and his male friends celebrate his last night as a single man. A group of friends from home cooked the traditional meal to honor dead ancestors and to ask for their support, guidance and blessing for the new couple. This consisted of beans and other ceremonial foods and the pouring of a libation to the ancestors at the entrance to the house. It is a ceremony that also symbolizes the value placed on the solidarity of the kindred, which includes the ancestors.

The Wedding Ceremony (Mostly Christian and Western)

In the Krio wedding ceremony, which can vary from family to family, the events would likely proceed along the following lines: On the day of the wedding the bride is bathed very early (about five o'clock a.m.) by her mother (a nostalgic gesture symbolic of motherhood). In the absence of her mother she may be given a bath by a female relative, usually on her mother's side. She is then dressed by female relatives and friends. She is forbidden to look at her reflection in a mirror, as this is believed to bring bad luck to her marriage. The bridal dress is usually floor length, and made of white satin and lace. She wears a short white veil, white gloves and white shoes. Jewelry is simple and is usually white in color. The bride's hair, which has been pressed and curled, is then combed out and arranged under a crown or tiara.

A bouquet of flowers, usually artificial, complements her outfit. A few brides import their dresses from England as this is supposed to carry more status, but the majority have their dresses made by one of the many highly skilled dressmakers in Freetown. The bridal attendants usually dress in pink, blue or yellow, with nylons, gloves, gold jewelry, and flowers in their hair. Each carries a bouquet of flowers and the chief bridesmaids carry white fans to keep the bride and groom cool during the service. Young children act as bridesmaids and pageboys and may number as many as ten for a big wedding. They carry small baskets of confetti to be thrown at the bride and groom after the ceremony. A feature that has been added to the ceremony is a junior bride – 'lili yawo' (little bride), who is dressed like the bride and is part of the bridal party.

The Christian wedding ceremony (mostly Western) is usually held in the bride's church during the afternoon hours. Formerly weddings were on Wednesdays or Thursdays, but they now tend to take place more often on Saturdays. The groom and best man, dressed in dark lounge suits or formal wear, arrive early at the church to await the arrival of the bride. There are no formal rules about seating arrangements. Guests sit on either side regardless of their relationship to the couple. The first two or three rows are usually reserved for close family members and relatives of the bride and groom, as well as for the sponsors (Godparents). A choir is usually in attendance, with two or three clergy officiating.

Upon the bride's entrance the congregation stand and sing the hymn which begins: 'Lead us heavenly Father lead us, O'er the world's tempestuous sea...'

As a rule the bride is escorted into the church by her brother, and is followed by her chief bridesmaids, bridesmaids and pageboys, in that order. In recent times, the bride tends to enter the church after her attendants. She is usually 'given away' by her father or male relative. Subject to denominational modification, the service then follows the proscribed order of the marriage ceremony of the Christian religion in which vows are exchanged, the bride is given a wedding ring, and the union is blessed. A number of brides today also give a ring to the groom.

Almost all of these hymns stress the notion of romantic love, which continues to be a strong influence in mate selection and marriage. One of the ministers then gives the sermon, usually directed to the couple who by this time are well known to the officiating clergy. At the end of these marriage rites the bride and groom walk arm in arm to the church vestry for the signing of the church marriage register. Relatives and sponsors are then called by the groomsmen and ushers to sign the church register as witnesses to the marriage.

Sponsors and relatives are among the most distinctively attired and when called to sign the register are given an honor that is so cherished, that several people may be summoned to sign the marriage register. This tends to make weddings very long, lasting about an hour to two hours. During this time the wedding fans carried by the chief bridesmaids become fully functional. The bride and groom and their attendants then emerge from the vestry to the accompaniment of the wedding march and proceed down the aisle, the nuptial couple arm in arm. Confetti may be thrown at them by the bridesmaids and pageboys just before they enter the cars and head for the wedding reception, known locally as the 'cake and wine' ceremony.

Cake and Wine Ceremony

The 'cake and wine' ceremony is usually held in a large hall to accommodate all the guests (usually 100-200), some of whom may be uninvited, sɔniɔgi (wedding crashers.) The program consists of the cutting of the wedding cake by the bride and groom, speeches and toasts and responses to the bride and groom; their families; the wedding party and the guests. The highlight is usually the speech of the groom when he says 'My wife and I' to a loud applause. This is usually followed by the reading of telegrams and other messages, and lasts about one and a half to two hours. Gifts from the guests may also be presented to the bride and groom at this time. The Chairman then makes a closing speech, and the benediction is said by one of the ministers.

The bride and bridegroom and their attendants leave for the bride's house. The guests disperse to reappear at the home of the bride or groom, or that of one of the sponsors or relatives. Up to this stage much of the wedding ceremony reflects a marked Christian or Western influence, with some modifications. From the time the bride and groom enter their respective homes after the wedding, the African aspects of the marriage become more manifest. Today, some weddings continue the celebrations with music and dancing after the cake and wine ceremony and may forego the celebrations at the home of the bride and groom, except in a much more simplified version.

Mared (Marriage) - mostly African

Upon the arrival of the bridal party, her parents and her guests at the bride's home, groups of women who have been doing the cooking and getting the house ready greet them with dancing and singing of the congratulatory chant:

> *Yawo mami ebi so! Yawo dadi ebi so!*
> *awo ɛn ɔkɔ ebi so!*
> *(Mother of the bride how grand and honored you look!*
> *Father of the bride how grand and proud you look!*
> *Bride and bridegroom how grand you look!)*

The women each hold out their skirts to form a receptacle into which money from the bridal party and her relatives must be thrown. After this joyful welcome the party proceeds into the house.

Giving the cold water of peace

At the entrance of the house, the couple is met by an elderly woman of the bride's family who gives the couple (kol wata) 'cold water'. This is a very serious affair and is in essence a speech of advice that may also call on the ancestors to shower their blessings on the newly married couple. In general it offers them a welcome to married life and shows the desire of all for their happiness, peace and fecundity.

This was the gist of the ̲k̲o̲l̲ ̲w̲a̲t̲a̲ speech after our wedding given by my mother at the International House in New York:

> *'Henry and Filomina you are now man and wife.*
> *May God bless you both and bless your marriage*
> *with children so that I can live to see them*
> *and to carry them on my back. May you have*
> *both love and respect each other always.*
> *Do not let anyone interfere in your marriage*
> *whatever you do. No one should know of your*
> *troubles except your pillow. May the ones who*
> *have gone ahead to the 'true world' bless you and*
> *guide you always. May you always have peace and a*
> *cool mind--as cool as this water.'*

In the typical situation in Freetown, the bride and groom would then go into the parlor and later may proceed to a private room with the bridal party. After a while, the groom would leave with his groomsmen for his own family house. Meanwhile the bride and her bridesmaids change into their ashuɔbi (uniform dresses) of similar material which will also be worn by their relatives and friends. They then join the rest of the family, relatives and guests arriving intermittently throughout the day for the mared celebrations. At the home of the bridegroom a similar celebration is in progress with his relatives and friends.

The Mared Celebrations (Mostly African.)[15]

The layout of the celebrations in the homes of both the bride and the groom is usually as follows: Men tend to congregate on the veranda; adult women in the parlor; young adults downstairs and children outside. It is customary for sponsors and relatives also to have celebrations in their respective houses, with their own families and friends. The ashuɔbi (uniform) for women is used to identify groups of family members or friends of the bride and groom.

Music at the various mared celebrations is usually of three types. In the parlor there is music from all over Africa and the Caribbean, including Reggae and Zouk. Among the younger group the latest pop tunes are played. Outside in the yard the typically Krio music the gumbe, of possible Caribbean origin, or the more updated mailo version is provided live. From time to time women and sometimes men, go outside to dance to the gumbe. One of the cultural heroes of gumbe music is the late Ebenezer Calenda who had a unique style and made several recordings of his music before his death.

The basic gumbe band is made up of percussion instruments, a drum, a saw, (scraped by an iron bar), and an iron triangle and rod. There is also a vocalist. Mailo music and its variants are popular

---

15 The celebrations held at the homes of the bride and groom and their relatives or sponsors are known in Krio as mared.

among all age groups and are guaranteed to capture the mood of the celebrations. It is an innovation which started in the mid-1960s. According to several <u>mailo</u> musicians interviewed, it developed among groups of boys who belonged to a mutual-aid society. <u>Mailo</u> is very similar to the traditional <u>gumbe</u> music. It reflects the influence of the music of various ethnic groups in Freetown. A <u>mailo</u> group usually consists of eight to ten musicians who make their own instruments. These are mostly percussion instruments - a talking drum, two double drums, one beagle, a 'shine pan', one <u>kerleh</u> (a long hollow log beaten with two sticks), one <u>egugu</u> (a simple iron bar struck with another smaller bar) and a wooden box.

The preparation of food usually begins on the eve of the marriage and is completed by the time the bride returns from church. The jollof rice is the most important of the ceremonial dishes which also include a special African salad, peppered chicken, akara, meat and fish balls and cocktail onions, scotch eggs, sausage rolls, cake and rice bread. Soup may also be served in the evening. Drinks include beer, stout, spirits and soft drinks (sodas) and the traditional ginger beer. Female members of the bride's kindred help with serving as this helps to identify the members of the kindred group, who are usually dressed alike in ashuɔbi style. It is considered an honor and a sign of love to serve the guests at the wedding of a close relative or a member of the family. Guests come and go throughout the day, and may number from two hundred to four hundred total for both the bride and the groom. Towards evening - usually about 6:30 p.m., the bride gets dressed for her 'going away' ceremony. Afterwards celebrations can continue well into the night.

Going away (Mostly African.)

At about 7 o'clock in the evening the groom arrives with his groomsmen for the bride, who now wears a dress matching her husband's suit in color, usually in beige or brown. Upon the arrival of the groom's party the guests from the bride's house greet them with chants of:

ibi, ibi! answer: Hura!
(hip, hip! Hooray!)
ɔkɔ nɔ de na ya? answer: ɔkɔ de.
(Is the bridegroom here or not? He is here.)

The couple proceeds upstairs and are given some refreshment. The bride and groom then dance together, sometimes to the gumbe music and are later joined by others. Friends of the couple joke with them, and tease them about the impending consummation of the marriage as they wish them happiness. The bridal party then leaves and proceeds to visit the various sponsors in their homes. Each visit begins with the characteristic welcoming:

'ibi, ibi – ure' (Hip Hip Hurray).

Refreshments are served, and a speech of thanks by the groom follows.

Formerly the couple would drive off for their honeymoon to 'the farm', usually a country house just outside Freetown. A young girl of about four or five years would accompany them as a mascot, and for running errands. In the past, but rarely done today, other relatives would accompany them to see proof of the bride's virginity, and bring back the good news that the bride was virgo intacta (a virgin) to the chant of 'hot kɔn. Yawo du gud O' (The bride has done us proud!)

Fortunately this practice has virtually died down, but it is interesting to note the double standard of morality since the groom is not required to prove his 'virginity' on his wedding night. In the past, a bride who is not a virgin can bring shame to her family but fortunately this archaic practice is now defunct and a woman does not have to prove her sexual purity any more. In fact, it is not unusual for a some men wanting to ensure proof of the fecundity of their bride by impregnating them before the wedding.

It is customary for food to be sent daily to the honeymoon couple for a period of one or two weeks, after which they return to reside in their new home. 'Patrilocal' residence, that is, the groom's father's house used to be the general rule, although it is becoming increasingly desirable to commence married life in a new or 'neo-local' residence whenever possible. It was customary for the bride and groom to attend church in their formal wedding attire, without the veil, on the Sunday following the wedding.

There are many variations possible in a wedding and marriage ceremony but the above account represents the most ideal traditional Krio marriage rites. The degree of elaboration depends on social class as well as on the family's desire for a 'quiet' or 'grand' wedding, although having a 'quiet' wedding in Freetown is almost impossible. If a wedding takes place overseas it is customary to also have corresponding celebrations in Freetown. These vary in terms of elaboration but tend to be similar to the actual wedding celebrations which take place when the bride and groom are present in Sierra Leone. In our case, since both of my parents and my brother and sister came to the States for the wedding, only a small celebration was held in Freetown. Henry's sisters were already in the States and the oldest one was one of the bridesmaid.

CHAPTER 14

Oxford University via Honeymoon
Ship to England

"Oxford is beautiful; its beauty is its plumage, its method of procreation. The beauty of the dream of Oxford, of spires and quiet learning, of the life of the mind, of effortless superiority, all these had beguiled me." – Naomi Alderman.

❖

Studying Medicine and Social Anthropology at Oxford University

After the wedding, we spent some time with our parents in New York before their departure for Sierra Leone and the departure of my siblings for England. We had planned a honeymoon by ship to England, where both of us had been admitted to Oxford University. Henry would be studying medicine and I would enroll in a program that would lead to a doctorate in Social Anthropology.

We boarded the passenger ship at New York Harbor for Southampton, England. We had a cabin in tourist class that was nicely decorated for us as newlyweds by the ship's crew. It was a voyage of ten enjoyable days of dancing, dining, talking, participating in sports and table games on deck; having variety shows, feasting, watching the seagulls and taking long walks along the deck.

Henry and I have always enjoyed dancing and got to be very good at it. so it was a compliment when the dance teachers on the ship remarked that we must have all gone to the same dancing school. The truth is Henry and I never took dancing lessons in our lives. Like most Sierra Leoneans we learnt to dance by imitating adults from a young age and 'having rhythm' came naturally to most of us. There was a division between passengers in first class and those in the tourist section, but tourist passengers would always gatecrash the dance parties in first class, which often served champagne and abundant and delicious food. No one seemed to mind.

We landed in Southampton on a misty day and unlike many passengers, we were not met by anyone. This was fine as we viewed our seafaring honeymoon as an adventure. After clearing immigration and customs, we tried to get a train to Oxford, but this would have been difficult given the number of suitcases we had. As we waited on the platform, a taxi driver drove up to us in his classic black English taxi and offered to take us all the way to Oxford with all of our luggage at a good price. We could not resist the offer and the convenience of being driven for two hours to our first home on Divinity Road in Oxford, England. It was a beautiful ride through the big cities and countryside and a good introduction to England. As we approached Oxford, we drove through Cowley Road, on which the main Mini car factory is located. We arrived around closing time and the streets were filled with factory workers going home on bicycles, cars or on foot.

We were met by our landlord who welcomed us to our first home, a two-bedroom fully furnished apartment in a blue-collar area not far from Oxford University. After unpacking and getting over the initial stage of our jet lag, we soon figured out how to get around the town of Oxford, which was both a working class and upper class town, depending on where you lived. The center of Oxford was always lively with shoppers and much of Oxford University was in the middle of it. Both Henry and I had relatives in different parts of England, but mostly in London with whom we exchanged visits from time to time. The Sierra Leone students studying at Oxford University and other institutions in the area were welcoming and we spent a lot of time together in social events and in discussing current events in Sierra Leone.

Having this extensive network was helpful in making us feel at home and in having a successful social and academic experience at Oxford. We became members of a large Episcopalian church since our church, the African Methodist Episcopal Church (AME) did not exist at Oxford. While Henry was busy with his medical studies, I expanded my academic network to include meetings and lectures at Queen Elizabeth House, a part of the Oxford University's programs involving international study. It was popular with graduate students from Britain and other parts of the world and had facilities that included a large library, reading rooms and a beautiful garden. It also hosted public lectures, seminars and formal lunches.

Academics - graduate studies and Medical School at Oxford University

Henry was admitted to St. Peters' College to study medicine and I was admitted to Linacre College, one of the handful of graduate colleges at Oxford University, to study social anthropology. Coming back to England was a different experience for me because I was now married and had two university degrees from the United States and was planning to earn a doctorate degree or D.Phil. (Oxon.) at Oxford. I first enrolled for a diploma in Social Anthropology, which was a one-year course, followed by a Bachelor of Letters (B.Litt.) degree for two years, which, despite its title, was a graduate degree equivalent to a Master's Degree. Our graduate classes were mostly in the form of individual tutorials with a faculty member and seminars and held at the Institute of Social Anthropology on the Oxford University Campus.

Like Boston University, Oxford University was located in the city with the various colleges spread out over a wide area but unlike Boston University, the buildings provided a landscape that was historic, displaying a variety of Gothic, Saxon, Neo-classical and modern architectural styles. Also, unlike Boston University and American universities in general, most of the students wore their academic gowns when attending classes, especially undergraduate students who wore the 'commoner gowns,' a much shorter and simpler version of the full academic regalia which is conferred upon graduation.

In the English system, unlike in America, there were only a handful of 'professors,' a title earned almost towards the end of one's careers when one is distinguished and in their sixties or older. At the Institute of Social Anthropology we only had one professor, E. Evans-Pritchard, while I was there. The others were Readers, Senor Lecturers or Lecturers. They were all from England with and one from India. With the exception of Dr. Wendy Williams, an Alumna of the Institute of Social Anthropology, who had just earned her doctorate and joined the faculty soon after, they were all men. It was striking that during the inaugural lecture of the lecturer from India, only two other lecturers showed up, which was unusual and seemed discriminatory to me. He eventually left and got a position in India.

I often wondered whether the lack of attendance at his lecture by other faculty members was due to racial discrimination. The faculty would take turns at giving lectures for a week and then on Fridays, we would have a guest lecturer from another university. Some lectures were more interesting than others and since attendance at these lectures was not mandatory, you could easily tell the popular lecturers from those that drove people away. Most of the lecturers were English academics who worked in Sudan. The research area of the Middle East was covered by one lecturer, Oceania by another and South Asia by an Indian lecturer, who eventually left. The students represented many countries, including England, Germany, Japan, Sierra Leone, the United States and Ireland, and their research interests covered many areas of the world. It was quite an international atmosphere and we organized a number of social events to showcase our international backgrounds.

The theoretical orientation was centered around the British School of Social Anthropology, which was geared towards the functional/

structural approach. This approach was necessary to understand indigenous political systems that upheld law and order in order to enable the British colonial rulers to govern their colonies effectively. Anthropologists played a major role in facilitating the colonial process, which influenced the colonial policy of 'indirect rule' through the local tribal authorities, rather than the direct rule of the French and Portuguese colonial policies which ignored the local authorities for the most part and envisaged these colonies as part of France, Portugal or Belgium. The British School also emphasized customs and social systems and was closer in many ways to sociology, unlike American anthropology, which emphasized culture and symbolic systems. In fact, social anthropology was sometimes referred to in England as 'comparative sociology.'

I remember feeling conflicted, along with a few other students from former colonies, about studying anthropology, sometimes referred to as 'the handmaiden of colonialism.' We had lengthy discussions and arguments and finally agreed that we were in a unique position to both learn about these societies and chart a path that would lead them to nation-building and economic development through our understanding of their social and cultural processes. We echoed one of the basic philosophies of anthropology, which is to understand, explain and reconcile the differences among human societies, despite their similarities. We also pursued the major areas of emphasis of social anthropology, namely, a focus on customs, a holistic approach and a cross-cultural perspective. We felt we could make a contribution to understanding human societies, traditions and customs and hopefully contribute to world peace. We also sought to understand how societies were held together and how they dealt with conflict. Little did we know how difficult that task would be since anthropologists have not made an impact on promoting global understanding and world peace as I expected them to do.

We were all paired with individual faculty members for our weekly one-on-one tutorials. My tutor was the late Edwin Ardener, who had done his research in the Cameroons on marriage, divorce and kinship systems. We would be assigned some readings and a research topic for a week, and this had to be handed in two days before the tutorial. We would then spend one or two hours each week on a one-to-one tutorial session with the lecturer. I found this method of teaching to be intensive and effective and learnt a lot from these tutorials. It required a deep sense of commitment from the student and a lot of self-motivation, because the learning process was not overly-structured as most graduate programs are in the United States.

At the same time, the British system created greater opportunities for creativity and initiative and a chance to delve deeply into one's subject of research. Ironically, it also sparked interest in each other's research in a way that resulted in voluntary collaborations and discussions on research methodology, approaches, analysis and funding for field research. After the diploma at the end of the first year, successful students were allowed to register for a Bachelor of Letters Degree (B.Litt.), which was a graduate research degree equivalent to a Master's Degree from a reputable institution in the United States.

I was fortunate to be awarded a research scholarship named for Ioma Evans-Pritchard, the late wife of Professor Evans-Pritchard of Social Anthropology. Since the scholarship was at Saint Ann's College, I had to transfer from Linacre College to St. Ann's College. The research scholarship was a great honor and inspired me to produce the best work that I could. My thesis was titled 'The Social Position of Women in Selected West African Societies.' It was the beginning of my scholarly interest in the subject of women, an interest that was to continue to a doctoral program. I had spent most of my life in women-centered or women-only institutions and my consciousness about the talents and capabilities of women motivated me to study this area. I had also developed an awareness of aspects of gender-based discrimination which existed in overt and covert ways in many societies.

In many ways, I was a pioneer at Oxford University's Institute of Social Anthropology. At that time, there was little or no interest in the subject of women, although social anthropologists had written a lot about kinship and marriage systems in Africa and elsewhere. For the most part, the emphasis was on the lineage, which in the majority of cases, was the patrilineage. Matrilineal societies were seen or presented as anomalies. What was striking to me was that the reality was not as rigidly one-dimensional or dominated by one lineage as we were led to believe. In fact, maternal kin remained influential in the lives of their daughters after marriage and especially upon the birth of their first child and subsequent children. They played a major role in the rearing and upbringing of children and would mediate between their daughters and husbands in situations of marital disputes. Matrilineal connections can also lead to opportunities for inheritance of some assets from that lineage.

Matrilineal societies gave women a higher position because society was organized around the mother, but her legal authority was in the custody of her brother or male kin. This left some of the students uneasy, because it seemed to discount the 'legal' authority of women and presented them as 'minors' that needed to have custodians. On the other hand, some students saw this as greater power for women in that they were in a position to delegate authority, which is itself a hallmark of authority. The picture from the Pacific was slightly different in that there was an emphasis on wife exchange and wife circulation in addition to descent but it did not appear to make a difference to what appeared to be the dominant role of the patrilineage in patrilineal societies.

I believe I never accepted this total dominance of one lineage and kept looking for women's loci of power and authority, whether overtly or covertly expressed, and this quest remained with me for the rest of my academic career. I completed my thesis on 'The Social Position of Women in West Africa' and showed how their positions varied in three societies, based on their economic roles as well as their access to political authority and power. I was fascinated by the extent to which women and men held complementary roles among the Bemba of Zambia, held roles that were parallel to men among the Mende of

Sierra Leone and in the case of the Bakweri of Cameroon, women's roles were diametrically opposed to that of men.

I passed with flying colors and was admitted to the program for a doctoral degree. My delight knew no bounds and my husband and family were very proud of me.

Pregnancy and the birth of our first child

Soon after obtaining a Bachelor of Letters (B.Litt.) graduate degree at Oxford University, I became pregnant with our first child, Chinaka. We were overjoyed and shared the experiences of prenatal counselling for expectant parents with excitement. Henry accompanied me to many of the prenatal classes held in the Radcliffe Hospital and conducted by a midwife. In England at the time the majority of births were delivered by midwives, either in the hospital or at home, except for the first and fourth and subsequent children, in which case a hospital delivery would be likely. I read as much as I could about pregnancy and childbirth and did my best to eat well and to exercise. Since this was a first child, I would be delivering my baby at the Radcliffe Infirmary (Nuffield Maternity Home) Oxford, rather than at home, which was a comforting thought to me. We were both on the National Health Plan so all the costs were covered from prenatal care to delivery, postnatal care and early child care.

We had a very small house which we bought with the help of my father, who contributed the down payment of seven hundred pounds sterling, representing twenty percent of the total cost of three thousand, five hundred pounds sterling at that time. As graduate students, we had little money, mainly from Henry's Scholarship from the Commonwealth and from my Ioma Evans Pritchard Research Scholarship from Saint Ann's College, Oxford University. We did well with budgeting and being thrifty and had our needs met and were very happy. One of my fondest memories was Henry going out to get patterns for maternity dresses so that he could make one for me since we could not afford to buy maternity clothes. He did a good job of it on a sewing machine that I had received as a wedding present. I was appreciative and knew he would be a good father.

I made friends with some of the other expectant mothers at the prenatal counseling and exercise sessions, and we all looked forward to having healthy and happy babies, regardless of gender. My pregnancy was normal for the most part, except for the first three months when I had nausea, usually referred to as 'morning sickness', in the late afternoons. I also felt very heavy and uncomfortable towards the last two months of the pregnancy. The back pains were particularly severe at times and I tried to get rid of them by exercising and going for short walks. I could not get over how much weight I had gained, reaching one hundred and sixty five pounds and feeling sleepy and tired all the time. It was hard to get over how much my body changed and I vowed to get back to my basic weight of one hundred and twenty five pounds as soon as I could after delivery.

On March 25th 1968, I started having stomach pains, which I thought were a sign of indigestion since it was at least three weeks before my due date. The pains stopped and I went to bed and fell asleep until I was awakened by a sharp pain that was followed by another and then additional pains at regular intervals. We thought there was enough indication that I was in early labor and we should go to the hospital. I was admitted immediately, around two o'clock in the morning, and started receiving treatment for delivery, which was mostly inhaling gas from a cylinder and being given a shot or two for the pain. I was in labor for three hours and there was no progress because the position of the baby was 'face to pubis' which was abnormal and slowed up labor.

Henry had been with me in the room for some of the time but when It was decided that the baby would be delivered by forceps and I was taken to the operating room, he was not allowed to stay with me there. Suddenly, more nurses and another doctor showed up and all I could hear were knocking sounds made by the metal instruments. It went on for a while and I was wondering what on earth they were doing to the baby. Finally, he was yanked out and blood spluttered everywhere. I thought 'O my God, what's going on? Is he dead?' I then heard a voice saying 'you have a baby boy with dark curly hair.'

He was then cleaned up and put on my chest. I thought he looked traumatized and his head was elongated, probably due to the forceps, but he was the most beautiful baby I had ever seen and I was happy that both of us had made it alive. The experience was a miracle and I felt a kind of love and bond with him that I had never felt before.

We named him Chinaka, in honor of his late paternal grandfather, Chiakazia, and his Igbo ancestry which goes back to Waterloo village in the Western Rural Area of Sierra Leone. Chinaka in Igbo means 'Mankind is God's greatest gift.' Henry was over the moon with joy and also got the results of his success in his medical examination at Oxford University. He became a father and a doctor at about the same time. What joy! So much joy!!

I was then taken to the general ward at the Nuffield Maternity Hospital, where there were eight other mothers with beds facing each other in dormitory formation. It was not unusual to stay for about a week at that time. We had nurses running around all the time bringing in the babies on their cribs to be near their mothers since babies were kept in a separate nursery for some of the time. As I was the only Black mother on the ward, Chinaka and I attracted a lot of attention and curiosity, especially since he had a full head of hair and the White babies were mostly born without any hair at all.

The first day, I went to the bathroom and was so sleepy from the medication that I fell asleep on the toilet. I wondered why they allowed new mothers to go to the bathroom alone, especially since I had difficulty walking due to the drowsy feeling brought on by the drugs. I got up and went back to my bed and was glad that I did not slip and fall.

All of the mothers were breastfeeding which made things difficult for one woman, the only mother in the group who had lost her baby. I felt that it was insensitive for the hospital to keep her in the same ward with the mothers who had had successful deliveries. You could see her anguish and misery every time the babies were brought to the mothers for feeding. I really felt sorry for her and hoped that she would have a healthy baby the next time.

I had to have my son circumcised, but male circumcision was not the norm for the British. I had asked my doctor about that during my pregnancy in case I should have a boy and his reaction was 'Why would you want to do that to your baby? I told him that it was part of my culture and his response was 'What kind of culture would do that to a baby?'

Despite his disagreement, he made the arrangements for my baby to be circumcised at the hospital if it happened to be a boy. A Pakistani doctor at the hospital performed the circumcision on my son and the son of a Jewish mother on the same day. I felt a bond with her as we both prepared our babies for the minor operation. We were told not to feed them too much or put on their nappies (diapers.) I was a bit anxious waiting for the nurses to bring the babies back, since we were not allowed to accompany them for the circumcision. When the babies were returned to us, the other mothers looked at us with some disbelief and disdain, but we did not care. In our cultures, not to have a baby boy circumcised would be viewed with disbelief and disdain.

Motherhood

In most African societies, a woman graduates to the high rank of womanhood with the birth of the first child and in some African ethnic groups, she is only considered truly married at that point. Regardless of the order of birth, most families like to have at least one child of each gender. The fact that the first child is a boy is not necessarily celebrated more than a girl in my culture, for two reasons. One, Krio society is bilateral and descent, inheritance, succession, legal status and so forth are based on both the paternal and maternal lines of descent. Two, in general, both genders are valued, the boy as 'son and heir' and someone to carry the family name, and girls as first children are viewed as good role models and 'little mothers' for the younger children. They can make upbringing easier because of their propensity to adhere to rules and the general belief that they tend to behave in a less boisterous manner than boys.

Although I felt an overwhelming burst of love for my first child, feelings of motherhood came much later, when he started reacting to us and his environment. Since his birth was three weeks earlier than expected, we had to cope on our own as my mother was planning to come closer to the time of delivery to assist us. In the meantime, our prenatal classes and the books by the famous Dr. Spock, the baby doctor, helped a lot. Our son had a loud voice and so the nights were noisy, tiring and challenging. Since I was breast feeding I had to wake up every time he did and sleep when he did. I realized for the first time that babies have a certain degree of power of their own. When my mother came it was a relief and I could get more sleep since she was more experienced and good at keeping him quiet by turning on the grand-motherly charm.

Christening and nursery

The christening ceremony took place six weeks after Chinaka was born and was led by the Chaplain of St. Peter's College, Henry's College at Oxford University. It was attended by relatives and friends from other parts of England and the Oxford community. My mother, who owned a restaurant in Freetown after she gave up teaching, did all the catering and everyone had a good time. I resumed my classes the week after and my mother stayed on for three months before returning to Freetown. England had a social welfare state and democratic system of government which entitled us to free milk for the baby and a small stipend as well as home visits from the health care nurse. We were well taken care of and the baby thrived and made a lot of noise and we enjoyed being new parents. Those were among the happiest days of our lives, even though we were students and had very little money.

The child care services in England are excellent and for the most part affordable. I had to resume my studies after Chinaka was three months old and my mother had returned to Freetown. We discovered a full-time day care nursery that charged according to the means of the mother. Although we were married and technically not qualified, since this was primarily for unwed mothers, we applied and were interviewed and accepted. We were charged only one pound a week based on our meagre students' allowance. It was a relief to take Chinaka to the nursery and leave him there all day from 9 to 5pm so that we could both continue with our studies. He loved it, thrived and grew up by leaps and bounds.

A Doctorate, and an unexpected pregnancy

I had started work on my doctorate degree and it was easy for us to go to our classes knowing that Chinaka was being well taken care of at the nursery. We had decided to wait for at least four years before having another child, but two years after Chinaka was born, I discovered that I was pregnant again. We were happy and I took some time off from my studies and prepared to welcome our second child.

The pregnancy and birth were easier this time around and Duka was delivered by a midwife in the Radcliffe Infirmary (Nuffield Maternity Home) Oxford, where Chinaka was born. Henry was very happy to be having another child. He brought two of his female medical school colleagues to observe the birth, but they were turned away by the midwife, who insisted that only spouses could at present at the delivery.

I remember looking at my baby boy and counting all his fingers and toes to make sure that they were all there. I could not get over my delight at this bundle of joy! Delivery was natural compared to my previous forceps delivery for Chinaka but there was an important difference. This time, the pains did not stop after delivery. I continued to have labor pains *after* the birth for about three days, so I had to stay in the hospital for ten days, which is longer than usual. I remember my mother talking after 'after birth pains' being worse than labor pains and in a way she was right. I dreaded having them, especially at night, when they would be so intense that they would wake me up. I was relieved when they finally subsided after about three days.

I was lucky this time to have a single room as opposed to the dormitory style mass production line up when Chinaka was born. Chinaka visited us after two days of wondering where Mum and her large belly had gone. He was excited to see his Mum and baby brother and was beside himself with joy and wanted to carry the baby by himself. He was just under two years old and was not strong enough to carry the baby, but we encouraged him with some help from his dad.

We were now a family of four and it felt wonderful! Henry was a totally devoted father and family man and spent as much time as he could with his family. He gave the new baby his full name, Henry Maduka Steady, and we call him 'Duka' for short.

CHAPTER 15

Fieldwork and Lecturer at Fourah Bay College, Sierra Leone

*"Fieldwork and lecturing in Sierra Leone were among the most
instructive and exhilarating experiences of my life."*
Filomina C. Steady

⬧

Going back home, and fieldwork research

Fieldwork was an essential requirement of a doctorate in social
anthropology at Oxford University. When Duka was five months old
and Chinaka was a year and seven months, Henry and I agreed, after
much discussion, that it would be a good time to do my fieldwork in
Freetown. I would stay with my parents, who would be happy to have
us and provide a lot of support and help. I received a generous grant
from the Wenner-Gren Foundation for Anthropological Research for
my doctoral research. At that time very few planes were flying to
Freetown so I went by sea with the two children, since Henry had to
stay in Oxford for his medical studies. It was difficult to leave him,
but he would come and visit us during his holidays and we would be
returning after a year.

The sea voyage was interesting and most of the passengers on the

Aureol ship were West Africans returning home after their studies. It was most unusual at that time for Africans to stay abroad as immigrants, and many longed to return home and secure positions with the government or the private sector. There was a nursery on board where I would take Chinaka for a few hours, but Duka stayed with me for the most part. Chinaka was very rambunctious and difficult to control and did not fare very well on the ship, which was confining for an active child. There were many games and social activities on board for the adults and I spent time with some of the Sierra Leoneans returning home.

My parents and aunt met us on board the ship at the Queen Elizabeth Quay and immediately and joyfully carried the children to the arrival lounge. It felt so good to be home after ten years. Everything looked so much smaller, especially the streets and the buildings. Our house, a three-story concrete building that towered over most of the other buildings on our street at Ross Road, Cline Town, seemed to have shrunk. My mother's joy at seeing us was reflected in the beautiful way in which she had decorated the house to welcome us. She had photos of the family all over the parlour and we had a constant stream of visitors to welcome us every day for about two weeks. Some of them were former classmates, schoolmates and teachers as well as relatives and friends. Both of my parents had retired, my mother from teaching and my father as a telegraph inspector and both now owned their own businesses. They had more flexibility and could spend time with the children while I went out to work as a lecturer at Fourah Bay College and conduct my fieldwork afterwards and on weekends and when I did not have classes at the College. In addition, we hired a nanny and there were other domestic workers who helped with housework and cooking.

After about three months in Freetown, Duka, who was only five months old, got very ill with malaria and was running a very high temperature, even though we were all taking prophylaxis against malaria. I took him to the doctor at Fourah Bay College, who treated him for malaria and he seemed to improve, but later the fever returned and he was developing a cold as well. My mother consulted with one of her tenants who had raised several children, and she advised us to take him to Dr. Claudius Cole, who had a hospital on the west side of town. By the time we got there Duka was very ill and on the verge of having a convulsion. There was a large group of mothers with sick babies also in the waiting room, but none of them looked as bad as Duka. He started having strange symptoms that I did not understand and getting weaker and shaking. I was petrified and hoped the doctor would notice and attend to us right away.

The doctor called us in and told the other patients to wait because he had an emergency. He tried to bring down Duka's temperature by putting ice packs on him because a high temperature on an infant was dangerous. He also indicated that of all illnesses in children under one year, he found malaria the most difficult to treat. He admitted Duka to the inpatient section of his hospital and I stayed in the room with him while my mother joined us as often as she could. He got worse and we thought we were going to lose him, but after about a week, his condition started to improve and on the tenth day he was discharged. I believe that it was through the illness of Duka at five months and his close brush with death that I really felt and understood the true meaning of motherhood and the sacrifices that it entailed.

The title of my fieldwork for my dissertation was 'Women and Collective Action in Africa: A Study of the Associative Process among Women in an African City." I interviewed over 50 women's associations in Freetown and over 200 women from different ethnic groups. The functions of these associations included aims and objectives related to education, politics, economics, religion, culture, tradition and those that aimed to form federations uniting all women's associations. Since Freetown is the home of the Krio ethnic group, it was important to focus on this group of women, so my research included extensive interviews of Krio women, who for the most part were active members of women's associations as well as founders and leaders of a number of these associations.

Fieldwork was an awakening experience and I had students

assistants helping me with my interviews. Even though I was born and raised in Freetown, fieldwork was a discovery. I learnt a lot from the women interviewed and appreciated their worldview and their sense of theory making and theory testing that became important tools in their daily lives. For them, theory was a way to explain *how* they lived and *why* things are the way they are. The market women in the association I studied lived with daily challenges of economic hardship, especially the devaluation of the local currency, the Leone. They often made the link between the devaluation of their currencies and the increase in prices of commodities and transportation which had a negative impact on their already narrow profit margins. For them, the fault lies with the government who they felt had the responsibility of controlling currency exchanges and maintaining the value of the Leone.

My research into Freetown society as part of my doctoral degree gave me an insight into the inner workings of Krio society and culture that I had taken for granted. My training in Social Anthropology enabled me to study enduring social patterns and relationships that formed the social structure and cultural norms and values that were central to Krio life. I came to appreciate how all the various historical strands and cultural frames were woven together from 1787 when the first group, the Black Poor, came from England, until 1808, when all the other groups who were seeking freedom from the Transatlantic Slave Trade, such as the Nova Scotians, the Maroons and the 'Liberated Africans', had settled in Freetown and it became a Crown Colony of the British. I realized how special we were as a people, how resilient we were to challenges and how the focus on religion, education and African cultural norms and values played a major role in our survival and success.

I later went to Sierra Leone for several fieldwork projects and leant a lot. The women I studied over the years taught me about the link between agriculture and infrastructure and why they are sometimes reluctant to produce a lot of farm goods. Since access to affordable transportation needed for marketing their goods was not guaranteed, they did not wish to take the risk of food spoilage by producing a lot of food. The women's association in the fishing communities taught me about the need to have their fish- smoking technologies balanced with that of the men who did the fishing. They condemned a project by a European aid agency that succeeded in improving the fishing nets of the men to increase the catch without equally successful innovations in smoking technology for the women. The ovens provided for the women to smoke the fish were not efficient and caused burns to their stomach as they rotated the trays from a higher to a lower level to adjust the heat. Also, they did not have enough capacity to cope with the additional volume of fish caught by the men due to the new purse seine nets, which also caught juvenile fish and disturbed the fishing grounds for future fish harvests.

Teaching at Fourah Bay College, Freetown

I got a job teaching sociology at Fourah Bay College and felt proud and honored for my role in helping to establish the first sociology department at the college, along with Dr. Moses Dumbuya. Our chair was the head of the Economics Department, Professor William Cox George, a distinguished economist. Our offices were on the sixth floor of the Kennedy building, which had been donated to the college. Fourah Bay College is the oldest university in West Africa, offering Western-style higher education. It was founded in 1827 and was affiliated with Durham University in England. It has always attracted students from Sierra Leone as well as West Africa. It is now one of the colleges that make up the University of Sierra Leone.

At the time I was teaching at Fourah Bay College, the only other university was Njala University, specializing in agriculture and founded in 1964. It later became part of the University of Sierra Leone. Other components include the College of Allied Medicine and Allied Health, founded in 1986 and the Institute of Public Administration and Management (IPAM), founded in 1980. In addition, a plethora of universities and colleges of all stripes from all origins and of all standards have been established all over the country, but primarily in Freetown, since the 1990s. There are many discussions about the excessive proliferation of these institutions and whether their quality and standards are high enough to reach the level of accreditation.

Courses at Fourah Bay College covered a period of one year instead of a semester, in the majority of cases. Academic regalia were used during the end of year exams, special occasions and degree-granting ceremonies. I taught two classes, namely, 'Introduction to sociology' and a 'seminar on women in Africa.' I conducted my fieldwork interviews and participant observation procedures in my spare time and on weekends. I had about 100 students in the 'Introduction to sociology' class, which was nicknamed 'the United Nations Class.' There were more men than women and the classes were lively with lots of discussions and critiques of the readings, most of which were by Western authors since there was not an abundance of publications by African scholars at that time. I tried to make some of the research data that was done in the United States and England somewhat relevant to the Sierra Leonean and African situation.

On the whole, there was very little published scholarly research on Sierra Leone at the time, with the notable exception of books by Christopher Fyfe on Freetown and the Western Area, particularly the Krios; Kenneth Little on the Mende; Michael Banton on the Ethnic groups and migration to Freetown and Arthur Porter on the Creoles in his classic book *Creoledom.* As the first sociology lecturers at the college, Moses Dumbuya and I had a challenge to explain what sociology meant to the students of Sierra Leone since this was a fairly new subject at the college at that time. In general, the students felt that this was a much-needed subject that would enhance their understanding of our societies and various social processes, such as migration, rapid urbanization and ethnic group relations.

Anthropology as a subject was even more obscure and I spent a lot of time explaining the difference between anthropology and sociology. In fact, the British School of Social Anthropology, unlike the American School of Anthropology, was close to Sociology and is sometimes referred to as Comparative Sociology. One of the main focuses of the British School was on non-Western and non-Industrialized, small, tribal and rural societies. It was also linked to the colonial project as the academic arm that provided research data and analysis on how these tribal societies functioned and how they maintained law and order. This was important if the colonial powers were to rule them effectively and successfully and extract the natural resources that they needed from the colonies without resistance and revolt. Of course, this did not happen without resistance, since Africans did not passively accept colonial rule. The history of Africa's encounters with colonialism is full of resistance to European colonialism throughout the continent.

I found the students eager to learn but some complained of the inadequacy of the facilities, such as the condition of the dorms; the dining room and quality of the food; the bathroom and toilet facilities and lack of enough facilities for recreation. They also had difficulty obtaining the required books and journals from the bookstore and the library, and many of them struggled to meet their financial obligations even when scholarships and financial aid were provided. Some of them wanted to continue their studies overseas and discussed this during my office hours, when I would advise them on opportunities for graduate study abroad. This was not a subject I enjoyed discussing, since scholarships for overseas studies were difficult to obtain. They feared that job opportunities in Sierra Leone were scarce and they needed to get a graduate degree to increase their chances of employment. Social life for students seemed active to me and there were well-known couples among the student population but I believe that the majority dated people outside the college.

Among the most established departments were History, English, Biology, Chemistry, Physics, Engineering and Math. Geography and Economics were also popular fields. Although the majority of the lecturers were from Sierra Leone, expatriate lecturers from Britain, the United States and other West African countries were not uncommon. Expatriate faculty members from Europe and America tended to socialize separately, although there were general faculty meetings attended by local and expatriate faculty alike. On a few occasions seminars and lectures were held that would be open to the public, and the college was a popular venue for concerts and other social events. Students relied on public transportation to the city for most of their shopping and social events since a large number of them did not live on campus.

The dorms continued to be poorly run over the years and from time to time were closed for repairs. They also later became hotbeds for political conflicts between adherents to the various political parties, especially the two dominant parties the Sierra Leone People's Party (SLPP) and the All People's Congress (APC.)

In addition to the dormitories for students, campus housing was provided for the faculty and a guest house with a dining room for visitors to the college. The college also operated a successful private elementary school 'College School' in which many of the children of the faculty were enrolled as well as other pupils from Freetown. The campus is situated on Mount Aureol, which is hilly with winding roads and very difficult for driving. It is known for its dangerous curves and has an iron barrier along the road on the side of the mountain to prevent speeding and accidents. Vehicles breaking the barrier and tumbling down the hill would have disastrous consequences for the heavily populated valleys and mountain settlements in the areas below. The road to Fourah Bay College has had its share of accidents over the years but fortunately, not many are serious. My father made sure that he took me on several guided trips up and down Mount Aureol so that I would be safe driving to and from the College on my own.

Henry came to visit us every three months during our stay in Freetown, which was an important break from his rigorous medical studies at Oxford. We explored Freetown together again and went to all our favorite dating spots, including the Quay at Cline Town, where we had spent a lot of precious evenings together. We could not get over how much time had passed from our carefree dating days to our life together as a married couple with children. We were grateful for our many opportunities and blessings. Henry enjoyed visiting his high school, the Prince of Wales, and spending time with some of his teachers who had retired and his classmates. Freetown had changed a lot since our school days. It was more crowded with heavy traffic on the main roads. The majority of people had migrated to Freetown from the Provinces and together with the residents of Freetown and the Western Area were struggling economically and eking a living as petty traders, laborers or service workers and many were in the vulnerable informal sector of the economy.

CHAPTER 16

Return to Oxford University and Back to the US –
Teaching at Yale University

"I am an educator who thinks globally" – Paulo Freire

Doctorate Degree - A memorable and distinguished achievement –
D.Phil.(Oxon,)

❖

Back to Oxford

In 1972, after teaching and conducting fieldwork for a year in Sierra Leone, it was time to return to Oxford University, England and Henry. The children had enjoyed Freetown so much that they were not sure whether or not they wanted to return, but were delighted at the thought of seeing their Dad again. I realized that it would be difficult for me to complete the analysis, writing and completion of my doctorate degree, so Henry and I decided, with the help of my parents, to take someone with us to assist with the children. Fortunately, it was not difficult to obtain a student and helper visa at that time and Albert, a teenage son of a friend of the family, accompanied us to England. He helped with the children during the day and attended night school and became our adopted son. He later obtained a scholarship to study as a chef and ultimately became the chef for late former President Mr. Tejan Kabba of Sierra Leone.

Reviewing, analyzing and writing my dissertation was one of the most difficult assignments I had given myself. Under the Oxford University tutorial system one has to be self-motivated and disciplined. My supervisor, the late Edwin Ardener, worked with me on deadlines for submitting drafts of chapters of the dissertation for review, but it was really up to me to push myself. We were living on Henry's Commonwealth Scholarship and occasional gifts from my father, which helped us buy a small car for taking the children to day care and kindergarten and for getting me to the Institute of Social Anthropology.

The car also came in handy for visiting friends and family in Oxford and London and taking the boys for rides and family outings. Fortunately, I won another grant, the Herbert Plummer Research Award, which covered some of my expenses, and also worked part-time in the secretary's office at St. Anne's College. The job entailed helping to maintain the files of Alumnae from St. Anne's College in connection with the publication of 'The Ship', the alumnae magazine. It gave me an opportunity to learn about the various professions and graduate school programs that alumnae went into after leaving St. Anne's. Teaching, administration and healthcare were among the most popular professions at that time.

This was a busy time for all the Steadys, since the boys seemed to work as hard at playing in their nursery schools and at home as we did in our studies and raising a family. Henry was now a physician and very busy with the demands of his internship at the Radcliffe Hospital and other surrounding hospitals and had very little time to spend at home. The children got the hang of things very quickly, because he would always come home in his white coat and they waited to see if and when he would take it off. If that did not happen right away, they would ask 'Are you a doctor today or a daddy today?' He would answer by taking off his coat and they would scream with delight, knowing that daddy was going to spend a few days or hours with them at home this time.

Henry completed his internship and got an offer to continue his specialization in England, but had decided to return to the States for his residency in laboratory medicine and hematology. I also finished and publicly defended my D. Phil dissertation on "Women and Collective Action: A Study of the Associative Process Among Women in an African City." The dissertation ended up in two parts: one dealt with an ethnography of the Krios of Freetown with a focus on women, and the other analyzed the relationship between the informal associations and the more formal ones, many of which were founded or led by Krio women. Henry and I received our degrees at different times at the Sheldonian Theatre with the pomp and glory that is characteristic of Oxford University. I felt proud watching Henry march in the procession for his degree as a medical doctor and hearing the boys shouting 'There is Daddy!' We had graduation parties for both degrees at different times attended by family and friends, in addition to the celebrations hosted by Oxford University for its graduates.

Back to the States

We returned to the United States in June of 1974. Henry's residency was at the Mallory Institute of Pathology at Boston City Hospital. I had secured a visiting faculty position in Anthropology and Afro-American Studies at Yale University for one semester and another at Boston University's Anthropology Department and the African Studies Center or the second semester. Although Henry had started his residency in July, my job at Yale University did not start until September, so I had the summer to adjust to the States but this time not as a student, but as a working mom and wife. We made friends with Henry's colleagues at Boston City Hospital and their families and attended many parties that were organized by the hospital and our new friends. We also took several tours to the many historical and cultural sites that Boston had to offer. Boston had changed since the time I was a graduate student at Boston University. The number of immigrants from other parts of the Global South, especially, South America, the Caribbean and South Asia had increased and the city looked very diverse compared to Oxford.

Living in Boston

We stayed at the new housing complex provided by Boston University on Harrison Ave. in the South End, which was affiliated to the teaching hospital. The building had modern two-bedroom apartments and a large Olympic-size pool and gym. The boys and I learned to swim and spent a lot of time at the pool when Henry was at work. It was relatively safe as long as you stayed within the compound. Our boys were still only six and four years old and had lived a sheltered live in Oxford, so they had to stay within the compound for their own safety. There was heavy traffic outside the and the area was close to the inner city with a problematic safety record. We made sure that the children were driven to all their activities and avoided sending them on errands in the busy streets to which they were not accustomed.

The first summer, I enrolled them in a day camp in the Roxbury area so that I could spend some time in the library doing my research. Most of their activities were held outside Boston, to which they often went by bus. They found it difficult to adapt to the fast pace and lacked the street sense that most of the kids were used to. Their English accents attracted a lot of attention from the other children, who could not always understand them. Some thought they sounded cute and others thought they sounded funny. Chinaka and Duka were also fascinated by the American accents of the inner city kids and learnt some Ebonics and Spanish as a result.

The city of Boston was facing a serious problem of racial tension in the early 1970s. During the summer of 1974 Judge Arthur Garrity of the Federal District Court had ruled that the Boston School Committee had deliberately segregated the city's schools. This created one system for Blacks and another for Whites which was separate, unequal and unconstitutional. Busing to achieve racial equality and end discrimination was mandated the year we arrived in Boston. This created a highly tense and toxic environment for race relations, since most of the Blacks lived in segregated areas like Roxbury and Mattapan and had to be bused to areas with a predominantly White population. One of the White areas which aggressively objected to busing was South Boston, made up of predominantly Irish Americans. The leader of the opposition was Anna Louise Day Hicks, a politician and attorney from Boston who staunchly led a massive opposition to desegregate the Boston public schools by court-ordered busing. Some of these opposition tactics included large demonstrations and protest marches that bordered on sporadic outbreaks of violence.

In addition to the controversy over busing, ethnic tensions were high, as was the crime rate in Boston at that time. The murder rate for 1974 was 312,000. We lived in an apartment complex that had an extensive security system that was next to the Boston City Hospital complex but the neighborhood was not safe. I remember Henry and I taking a walk after dark in the South End and being advised by a policeman that it was not a good idea to take walks in that neighborhood at that time of night. The South End of Boston was a dangerous area requiring a shuttle service for employees at the hospital to the parking lot about a quarter of a mile away. Ironically, the South End became gentrified over the years and is now one of the most expensive and relatively safe areas in Boston.

We were assigned an elementary school for Chinaka, based on where we lived. Henry and I went to look at the school in advance. It was very close to a busy street and had so many broken windows that we felt Chinaka would not be safe in that environment. He had lived a relatively sheltered, safe and genteel life in Oxford, England and would be bullied. Even before 'the theory of broken windows' was developed, I already had an uneasy feeling about the dangers of a school with broken windows in a dilapidated environment. The broken window theory was proposed by James Wilson and George Kelling to explain how one broken window can lead to more, and indicate an unsafe environment of disorder and misbehavior, leading to serious crimes.

We decided to enroll Chinaka at Park School, a private school in Brookline, for a year. There was a day care center nearby which his brother Duka attended and which also provided after-school day care for children like Chinaka at Park School. We made lasting friendships with some of the physicians with whom Henry worked and their families, such as Dr. Ray and Lynn Clarke and the supervisor and instructor of the residents and his family, Mr. Vernon and Mrs. Iris Truell. We had many delicious dinners at the house of the Truells and attended numerous family events and parties with our friends and got to enjoy Boston and all it had to offer. We attended St. Paul's AME church in Cambridge, Massachusetts and All Saints Episcopalian Church in Brookline, Massachusetts where we lived.

Teaching at Yale University

It all worked very well as far as the children were concerned and I was able to take up my commuting job at Yale University for one semester without any difficulty. I taught 'Societies and Cultures in Africa ' for the Anthropology Department and 'Africa through African Literature' for the African-American Studies Program to well-enrolled classes. I was also a fellow of Calhoun College at Yale University. The environment at Yale was challenging because it was around that time that Blacks were being admitted in fairly sizeable numbers as students and in fewer but increased numbers as faculty. It was a period of adjustment for both Whites and Blacks and there was a sense of unease as everyone tried to figure out what to make of the new situation. But change was in the air and 'the die was cast.' Blacks would increasingly become a more visible and a vital part of Yale University. There was no going back.

I stayed with Ned and Gus Thomas, Henry's host family from his undergraduate days at Yale University, and spent three days a week in New Haven commuting by train from Boston. I made lasting friendships with some faculty members and collaborated with three of them on a book project that I had started when I was at Yale. Despite my commute to Yale I was able to spend long weekends and school holidays with my family in Boston.

It was not easy for four-year-old Duka to understand why I had to go to Yale. One day, after accompanying his Dad to pick me up from the South Station in Boston, he said: "Mum, why do you always have to go to Yale? Don't you know we miss you?" I reassured him that it was just for four months and that my next job would be in Boston and I could then be home every day. That made him very happy!

Teaching at Boston University

My next job at Boston University was a homecoming to my *Alma Mater*, the place where I had earned my Master's Degree in Anthropology. I was going to be teaching two courses as a temporary replacement for a professor on leave for one semester. I had an office at the African Studies Center and one in the Anthropology Department but spent more time at the African Studies Center because the office was a little bigger. Boston University had one of the best graduate programs in African Studies in the country at the time and probably the best collection of African books and resources, including the newspapers of some African countries in its African collection at the Muger Memorial Library. I taught 'Peoples and Cultures of Africa' and 'Third World Urbanization' and presented a paper at one of the weekly seminars in the African Studies Center Library. My courses had both graduate and undergraduate students and were conducted as interactive seminars for the most part. The Center hosted many guest lecturers and visitors from Africa and maintained close relations with universities in Africa. It received funding from Boston University as well as from the Ford Foundation and other donors, and many of its graduate students had full or partial financial aid. Occasionally, we would have visits from African dignitaries, especially Ambassadors to the United Nations and government ministers.

The Center was not academically neutral when it came to African politics and the role of Africa in the Cold War. In fact American democracy and capitalism with its free market system was seen as the solution for Africa in its nation building and development efforts, and not socialism and its centrally-planned economies or totalitarianism. It was widely believed that the CIA was actively recruiting graduate students in African Studies, especially male students, and a few actively sought employment with the CIA.

African Studies Programs in the United States were not immune to the competition inherent in the Cold War. Some of the teaching in political science and economics reflected the American preference for market-oriented democratic systems of the United States and Western democracies than the Centrally-Planned Socialist models of the Soviet countries. The African Studies Center participated in media programs that interviewed African students and subtly encouraged them to portray a glorious picture of the United States. They were encouraged to project a Western image by wearing Western instead of African attire for videos and photos. As can be expected, the African students caught on to the game and kept showing up in their African attire for photo sessions and insisting that they be accepted for who they are. It worked!

Most African countries belonged to the groups at the United Nations that were known as 'Non-Aligned', or the Group of 77 or Third World Countries, many of which were formerly colonized by European countries. One of their objectives was to gain economic as well as political freedom in the post-colonial era to maintain a neutral position between the East and West. Nonetheless, the Cold War that lasted from 1947 to 1991 was actively and clandestinely fought on the African continent for many years after most African countries gained their independence. It gradually ended when Glasnost, ushered in by Mikhail Gorbachev of the Soviet Union from 1989 on, diluted the Cold War tensions between the East and the West. The emphasis on nation building and development was front and center for many African governments and the curriculum of the African Studies

Center increasingly included research on economic development but not as much on social and human development. Those of us in the social sciences stressed the importance of having these concerns at the center of development because of the challenge of poverty faced by the majority of people of Africa. After the Boston University teaching position, which was for one year, I got a research associate position at the African Studies Center.

I tried looking for faculty positions in the Boston area that would be on a more long-term basis, but they were few and far between. I thought I would get a more secure position at Boston University's Afro-American Studies Department, but was disappointed. When I went to see Professor Adelaide Gulliver, the head of the department at the time, she told me outright that these positions were not for Africans. I was shocked, since she had been one of my professors when I was a graduate student at Boston University and used Africa for her research, which helped to advance her career. However, I was not surprised. I had come to realize that as long as Africans and African-Americans cannot unite in solidarity, they will always be fighting for crumbs from the table of the White supremacist system instead of demanding a place at the table and a large piece of the pie of opportunity. Compared to other groups and their Diasporas, such as Latinos and South Asians who generally used unity and solidarity for their advancement, Blacks have yet to capitalize on the importance and power of solidarity.

Despite this setback, I went on to secure and enjoy high-level professional jobs and illustrious careers in Academia and the United Nations.

The boys go to Sierra Leone

We decided to send Chinaka and Duka to spend some time in Sierra Leone and attend school while staying with my doting parents. We thought it would be good for them.

We were a bit apprehensive about the boys growing up in the States and thought they needed some immersion in their African culture. We were also not pleased with some of the friends that they were making in the apartment building which we moved to in Brookline, Massachusetts. The children played on Washington Street, a busy street on which we lived, and we thought this was unsafe. My mother visited us that summer and together we decided to send the boys home to Sierra Leone for two years to live with my parents and that I would accompany them for the trip home. They loved it there although they missed us but my father brought them to visit us every year. They attended the elementary school at Fourah Bay College, where I taught and received excellent care from my parents.

Although we all missed each other, we thought it would be good for them to know their culture and experience growing up in the country of their parents' birth. They made a lot of friends and felt comfortable being in the majority group for a change. They developed a sense of identity and belonging which seemed to have given them a great deal of confidence. At the College School in Freetown, Duka became a hit and the teachers were impressed by him because he loved to talk and tell jokes. They would have him spend some time with them in the Teachers Common Room during the lunch hour so that he would entertain them with his jokes and skits. It was clear from the start that he was born with a creative talent and would likely be attracted to the artistic field and decided to support him and encourage him to develop his talents. Both of the boys were academically strong. Chinaka was the one to later become the consummate scientist, interested in photosynthesis and environmental science and studied at The University of Wisconsin, Madison and Yale University. Duka studied theatre and the dramatic arts at Carnegie Mellon University and post film production, editing, digital imaging and design at New York University later.

CHAPTER 17

Women and Development Conference in 1975; Assistant Professor at Wesleyan University

"African Feminism as humanistic feminism" - Filomina Steady

⋍⋇⋍

Historic Conference at Wellesley College

Wellesley College held the first Women in Development Conference at the Wellesley Centers for Women in 1975. It was attended by women from all over the world and was in the middle of Second Wave of Feminism. Plenary sessions and several panels were held over a six days on the Wellesley College campus. Most of the presentations were delivered by scholars from the Global North, using data from their research on women of the Global South. There was an immediate tension and reaction as several scholars from the Global South felt they were being patronized and worse still, that the research was limited and lacked authenticity. They organized spontaneous meetings at Schneider Dining Hall in the evenings to discuss and express their discontent about the way in which the conference had been organized to give prominence and priority to the work of women from the Global North. The meetings were contentious because the organizers did not see anything wrong and thought they had worked very hard to plan this historic international conference.

Some of the scholars from the Global North insinuated that unlike those from the Global South, they had paid their way and had the right to present their papers without disruptions. Some of them were heard saying that the women protesting had just learnt the English language and were eager to use it in protest as a way of showing off their newly-acquired linguistic skills. Those from the Global South insisted that they were not going to listen to wrong information and inaccurate data being presented about their countries and their lives. They also resented the arrogance of the organizers in not including them in the planning process and compared the relationship to one of academic colonialism. They insisted on greater representation of women of color and The Global South in follow-up planning meetings and in the publications and editorial board that was going to publish some of the papers from the conference. All of these conditions demanded were met to some extent by the end of the conference.

In addition, groups of women researchers from various continents started having meetings at night in the dorms to discuss their own particular issues of development and the challenges facing women in their own countries. They adopted a historical perspective in which the negative impact of colonialism on The Global South and the resulting disenfranchisement and marginalization of women was central. Women became economic pawns in the colonial project as their labor was necessary to maintain the subsistence sectors of the economy which had been shared by men in the pre-colonial arrangements of the division of labor by gender. During these meetings, the African women decided to form a research group of African women that will decolonize research and present research from an African perspective with gender theories and analyses relevant to the African reality. The new association was to be called: Association of African Women for Research and Development (AAWORD.) I was one of the founding members.

During the final plenary, the regional groups that had been

meeting after dinner presented their assessment of the conference and recommendations for future conferences. I was pregnant with my daughter, Azania at that time and there appeared to have been an attempt to close the conference before all the regional groups had made their presentations. I walked down the aisle looking very pregnant and determined that all regional groups should have their say. I then announced that the Africa Group had a statement to read, which was then read by the representative of the group. The statement stressed the need to decolonize research and to end the domination of the Global North by the Global South which was a continuation of colonialization.

It added that since women were among the most affected victims of colonialism, they will continue to be exploited in the structures of the post-colonial arrangements. It asked women of the Global North to be in partnership with women of the Global South to combat Western hegemonic economic policies which continue to destroy the economies of countries of the Global South, especially Africa and to destabilize the lives of its people, especially women and children. The meeting ended with the customary statements of thanks but this time it was made clear that future conferences have to be more inclusive and diverse and organized in the spirit of partnership between women of the Global North and the Global South instead of a male-oriented hierarchical approach. It was also clear that conferences on 'Women and Development' have to have a more critical approach and condemn the injustices in the global economic system that were having deleterious effects on women of the Global South.

Birth of Azania

Two months after the Wellesley conference, I had our daughter, Azania at the former Boston Women's Lying -In Hospital in 1976. I had had premature labor pains one month before and was afraid that I would lose her. When the pain reoccurred the doctor decided to admit me which was a good idea because it was the real labor pains this time and like my other two children, It was three weeks early. The attending nurses took me to the room adjacent to the delivery room where all the mothers at advanced stages of labor were waiting. Some were groaning; some sighing and others very quiet. I had asked for an epidural so I felt little pain but the pressure got intense quickly and the nurse realized that the baby was about to be born.

She rushed with me to the delivery room, pushing the bed and grabbed a doctor on the way saying: 'Mrs. Steady is about to deliver. You have to come with us, NOW!' As soon as I got to the delivery room, Azania made her grand entrance and the nurse said: 'It's a girl.' I said 'I know, Welcome baby girl!' I recalled a woman giving me her seat on the subway some months earlier when I was pregnant and feeling bad and saying: 'Its going to be a girl. They like to make a lot of fuss and to be noticed.' I was so relieved to have my baby and a girl to add to the two boys. My family was complete. Henry was overjoyed when he came by later and saw his little girl. We named her 'Azania' after the African name for South Africa because for us, she carried the hope that South African Blacks would soon be free from apartheid.

AAWORD Founding meeting in Lusaka, Zambia

When Azania was three months old, I left her in good hands and went to the first organizing meeting of AAWORD in Lusaka, Zambia, along with some of the women who had been active at the Wellesley conference. These included eminent African women scholars and researchers like Achola Pala, (later Achola Pala Okeyo after marriage,) who was a doctoral student at Harvard University, Omolara Ogundipe-Leslie, an English professor from Nigeria; Felicia Ekejiuba, an anthropologist from Nigeria and Marie Angelique Savanne , a feminist activist and publisher from Senegal. Others who did not attend the Wellesley Conference joined us in Lusaka and represented professional African women from all fields, including law, politics, education. These included Gladys Mutuka, a lawyer and Sarah Longwe, a noted 'women and development theorist' and NGO from

Zambia Betty Milinyi, a nutritionist from Tanzania and Zen Tadesse, a researcher from Ethiopia. We had several meetings about the aims and objectives of the organization, its membership; its governance structure; its research agenda and fund-raising strategy. We received funding from The Swedish International Development Cooperation Agency (SADEC) for our founders meeting and subsequent meetings of the full membership in Dakar, Senegal, where AAWORD has its headquarters.

We were focused on approaches for decolonizing research and deconstructing the dominant discourses, while contributing knowledge that is based on African realities. We also envisaged research as a liberating process in itself and as a pathway for discovering our true selves as African women. The feminist discourses coming from The Global South are borne out of the realities of these countries and the daily experiences and economic struggles of women on the ground. They are the essence of women's movements, which are mass movements that rise up to challenge their governments and fight against oppressive political and economic forces that are undermining their livelihood and security. They are different from the kind of bureaucratic feminism that comes out of the United Nations Decade for Women and resulted in the creation of Women's Bureaus in governmental institutions. These bureaus are reformist for the most part and can only deliver limited change in the position of women due in large part to their limited resources and their marginalization within the governmental apparatus.

Book - The Black Women Cross-Culturally – Beginnings

When Azania was a baby, I had some time during 1976 and 1977 to start planning a book project I had been thinking about for some time. It was a year after the Women's World Conference in Mexico and the start of the UN Decade for Women. Research on the burgeoning field of women's studies was advancing and there was funding for women's studies. Many Black women and Black scholars did not feel very comfortable with the White and middle class aspect of the Women's Movement and some felt completely alienated from it. Clearly, the perspective of the Black woman had to be brought in. I realized that there was a serious lack of literature on Black women from Africa and the African Diaspora and that very little research was being done, despite the avalanche of writings on the women's movement featuring mostly White women's lives. The publications on Black women were few and scattered in various sources, some of which were not easily accessible so I decided to use both published and unpublished articles for the book, which was to become a prize-winning anthology.

I started working on a the research that would bring in the voices of Black Women from an international perspective. The Women's Studies theories that were evolving had to be more inclusive and take into account an essential historical perspective that would study and analyze Black women's cultural contributions to the world in terms of their talents, resilience, self-reliance and achievements. We also needed to reclaim motherhood from the radical feminists who attributed motherhood to the subordination of women, and show how the centrality of motherhood in African cultures was held in high esteem and how matriarchy was an essential aspect of statecraft in some African societies.

In order to do this, a revisionist approach would have to be adopted in which women were not only presented as victims but also as having agency and as leaders in their own right. In addition, a historical perspective would be vital to show how racial terror and oppression were administered to both African men and women through the trans-Atlantic Slave Trade that was mainly responsible for the dispersal of Africans primarily to North America, the Caribbean and Europe. Under slavery, women's oppression was compounded by their gender, which was often manipulated to produce more slave labor or as sites of sexual oppressions by the White slave master and his adult sons and White male workers. Women also had to endure the evils of slavery which did not discriminate on the basis of gender and was an equal opportunity oppressor.

Colonialism followed slavery and brought women into the process of political and economic domination in ways that exploited their labor, reducing it primarily to a position of subordination and augmentation of the work of their men. Both male and female labor were used to extract resources for export from the colonies to the European colonizing Metropoles to be appropriated in those countries. Under colonialism, some African women who had executive power, lost their status and authority as rulers and others their control over resources as a more absolute and robust form of European patriarchy which oppressed both African men and women was imposed. Regardless of whatever patriarchal norms existed before, they paled in comparison to the oppression of African women and the devaluation of their labor and worth by European colonialism. To make matters worse, they also subjugated their men and oppressed them through racial terror.

Another important perspective that was missing in much of the feminist literature at the time and had to be reflected in the book was the link and organic articulation of the world economic system that dominated the economies of African countries and countries of the Global South. The labor of African men and women was used to accumulate capital on a world scale for the Global North. This later continued and was fueled by Multinational corporations and sponsored by international financial institutions in the post-colonial era. Neoliberal policies and the debt burden were also contributing to the destruction of African economies as they were increasingly held hostage to corporate globalization, a successor to colonialism.

I started doing research for the book; soliciting articles and looking for published and unpublished authors. The book was divided into four sections: Introductory, Africa, The United States; the Caribbean and Latin America. I wrote the first article that served as a position paper on the review and analysis of the Black women in cross-cultural perspective, in which I introduced 'African Feminism as humanistic feminism' and discussed the major themes highlighted in the book and the links among them. After putting together the first draft, I started looking for a publisher and contacted Shenkman Publishers in

Cambridge, Massachusetts, which was just a few miles away from my home in Brookline, Massachusetts, at the time. The manuscript turned out to be quite lengthy, but it was accepted and I started working with an editor at Schenkman Publishers. I also looked for photos that would be illustrative of some of the themes discussed in the book. Since Azania had been a baby it had been easy to take her with me in her stroller to the publisher's office, where she was quite a hit with the staff.

Azania, Mama Marie and the boys' return to the States

When Azania was two years old, my father arranged for a friend of the family, Mama Marie, to come and stay with us and help look after Azania because he realized how difficult it was for me to balance my career and the family obligations. It was fairly easy for her to get a visa because she was in her middle years and not likely to want to stay in the United States as the younger people tended to do. We were also going to be responsible for her room and board and expenses, so she would not be depending on the welfare system of the United States. Mama Marie and Azania hit it off very well from the start and Mama Marie loved her as if she was her own child. She had never married and had no children of her own. She would make her meals, take her outside to play and for walks and sew beautiful dresses for her. Azania returned her love and the two were almost inseparable.

We felt it was important that the boys should return to the States after going to school for two years in Sierra Leone. It was very difficult for them when they realized on the last holiday trip back to the States that they were not going back to Sierra Leone. Chinaka was upset and cried, begging us to allow him to go back with his grandfather, because he did not like being in the States. Duka did not feel so strongly about staying and in the end they stayed with us and their sister Azania, whom they both loved. Mama Marie was great as an older member of the family, a friend and helper. She was an excellent second mother and took care not only of Azania but Chinaka and Duka as well, and did the housework and cooking, even without my asking her. We helped with some of the housework and the boys loved doing the laundry and were fascinated by the laundry machine and dryer, so we let them help as much as they could.

Teaching at Wesleyan University

I had been having interviews for tenure-track faculty positions in the Boston and New England areas and landed a position of Assistant Professor of Anthropology and Afro-American Studies at Wesleyan University. Although it involved commuting, I wanted to establish my career and was willing to drive to Middletown, Connecticut from Boston. I lived in an apartment in faculty housing for four days a week and would make a one and a half hour drive to Boston for the long weekend with my family. The boys were in school and after-school day care, so they had their own busy lives. Also, Mama Marie was doing a great job looking after all of the children and the housework and cooking. We decided to buy a house in Middletown, Connecticut, since the college gave low interest loans to faculty. The family would visit me on their short holidays and long weekends to give me a break from commuting.

Wesleyan was a difficult environment for me because of having to deal constantly with micro-aggressive behavior related to racism from one of my faculty colleagues. Even my hiring was contested by her for fear that I would be competing with her for the limited tenured positions available in the Anthropology Department. I even learnt of a protest organized by her at the Dean's office to block my being hired. I considered the kind of resentment I experienced a form of racism that was unsophisticated and irrational. Unsophisticated because I compared it with the more subtle and high-brow prejudices that I had experienced in England that seemed to be mediated by class and education. In other words, in England, you got some credit for being an educated Black person whereas in the States you didn't, and an uneducated White person at the lowest social strata assumed the right to discriminate against a Black person. Irrational beliefs about White supremacy gave Whites that right.

The atmosphere in the Anthropology Department was uncomfortable, but I ignored the negativity and tried to work positively with the students, with whom I always had an excellent rapport. Fortunately, I had a joint appointment with Afro-American Studies, where I also had an office at the Malcolm X house. The encouraging aspect of my work was in being one of the few faculty members that offered courses on Women at a time when Women's Studies was in its infancy. The interest of the students was overwhelming, leading to large enrollments in my class, which further annoyed my competitor, who had abysmally low enrollments and was one of the most unpopular faculty members in the college at that time.

I taught 'Sex Roles in Cross-Cultural Context', 'Medical Anthropology', 'Peoples and Cultures of Africa', a course on urbanization and another on African societies through African Literature. I was also the faculty adviser for an informal seminar on 'Critical Theory' developed by the Frankfurt School of Germany and aimed at critiquing hegemonic systems of domination, oppression and conflict, including the domination of nature. The major proponents were Max Horkheimer, Theodor Adorno and Herbert Marcuse. In the United States, this work continued at Columbia University and attracted a number of students who were also enthusiastic about understanding anti-domination theories in general and looking for critical alternatives. My other teaching assignment included supervising a Master's Thesis on the Maroons of Jamaica, focusing on the role of Obeah traditions of spiritual interactions and healing in the survival and achievements of the group and on the general ethnography of the Maroons.

The Black students were doing well generally, but they also had to deal with unsophisticated racism. It greatly affected some of them in terms of their confidence in their own abilities and consciousness about being constantly judged or evaluated. They sought refuge in Malcolm X house, a dormitory and cultural center that housed the majority of Black students by preference and provided study facilities and recreational spaces for them. The director was Mrs. Gwendolyn Lewis, who administered the house and served as a substitute parent when needed. She was a kind, friendly and compassionate woman, married to a scientist and a mother of three children. We became good friends and discussed how best to support the students and help them succeed.

On the social scene, there was not much excitement in Middletown, Connecticut for young people. It is a blue-collar town and bedroom settlement for commuting workers to Hartford, Connecticut. The University provided much of the cultural facilities, such as museums and theatre for the campus and the town. As was characteristic of many cities and towns in America, Blacks tended to live in segregated areas. The social scene on campus was difficult for Blacks, especially Black female students who had a difficult time dating. Parties were held from time to time to facilitate the meeting of students from other institutions in the area. Students would also go out of town to Hartford or New York City for social events and recreation. The Black faculty worked very hard to bring Black artists to campus as well as lecturers and organized seminars and conferences on the subject of Black history and culture and Black life.

Some Black students had a lot of interest in Africa, and many took my courses and the few courses on Africa that were offered. They also participated in study abroad programs that were offered in Africa, especially in Ghana. They were particularly interested in African forms of social organization; colonialism and its impact on indigenous African systems; economic development; and the role of women and Africa's role on the world stage. African religions fascinated students, many of whom enjoyed reading John Mbiti's book *African Religion and Philosophy*. This book explored African cosmological traditions, notions of time and concepts of collective identities, rather than the individualism of the West, among other things.

The cyclical nature of the African world view, which promoted integration rather than separation, gave them an alternative to the dualistic, oppositional and static approach characteristic of the

Eurocentric world view. The students longed for books by African authors to get a sense of authenticity, because they needed access and exposure to African voices and enjoyed the course that gave sociological insights through African literature. This was a time in the late 1970s when the Academy was being challenged for its Eurocentric imperatives and its marginalization of contributions of people of color and from the Global South. Most institutions of learning were being pressured to reevaluate their Western-oriented Canonic proclivities which were incomplete and often biased.

The interest in South Africa was particularly strong partly because of the global campaign against apartheid in South Africa and because of Wesleyan's investments in South Africa. Black students were among the many Wesleyan students who protested against apartheid and lobbied the college to divert its investments from South Africa. The university hosted some of the luminaries in the Liberation Movements in South Africa and organized lectures on apartheid and the struggle to end the most evil legal and political system ever fashioned by humankind. Apartheid, which means 'separateness' in Dutch, is the legally-mandated segregation of the four main ethnic groups of South Africa (African, White, Coloreds and Indian) from birth to death. In order to achieve this, it continuously used the state machinery of the police and the military to officially oppress, dehumanize and massacre Black Africans with brutal force and racial terror and with impunity from 1948 to 1994.

The Black Woman Cross-Culturally was published in 1981 while I was teaching at Wesleyan University and was eagerly received by Black women and men as well as some Whites in academia and elsewhere, and it became one of the few texts that were available on women who were not White at that time. It also offered a critique of White, bourgeois feminism for failing to provide a crucial analysis of how race compounds discrimination based on gender and how White women were complicit in the oppression of Blacks, especially Black women. The book sparked a lot on interest and inspired the convening of a conference by Professor Roselyn Terborg Penn on 'Women in

Africa and the African Diaspora', in which I gave the keynote address and wrote the leading article on 'African Feminism: A Worldwide Perspective' for the book that resulted from the conference, titled *Women in Africa and The African Diaspora.* The book focused more on women of African descent in the United States. Another anthology that was receiving a lot of attention and published shortly after *The Black Women Cross-Culturally* was *All the Women are White, All the Men are Black, but Some of Us are Brave,* edited by Gloria Hull, Patricia Bell-Scott and Barbara Smith.

CHAPTER 18

The Family Moves to Madison, Wisconsin, and Family Transitions

"There is nothing permanent except change." – Heraclitus

✦

After three years, I had a sabbatical of sorts and did not have to commute to Middletown for a semester. At the same time, Henry had completed his residency and was applying for jobs as a physician. He had three offers: in Boston, in Toledo, Ohio and Madison, Wisconsin. The decision was difficult and we spent many sleepless nights deciding which one to accept. We liked Boston but the position would have involved Henry in too much administrative work, which was not his main interest.

Henry and I were invited to Toledo for the interview as it was common practice to invite the spouse as well for these physician positions. We felt that it was not diverse enough and the boys were not excited about leaving their schools in Madison for the isolation of Ryan, Ohio. There were not many physician specialists at the hospital and it was not an attractive proposition.

For the Madison position, Henry had two interviews and I was invited for the second one. We liked Madison from the start, as it was a beautiful university city set between two lakes and was the capital of the state of Wisconsin. The group of physicians in private practice that he would join were enthusiastic about having Henry on board. He chose Madison, Wisconsin. It was a position in laboratory medicine at Meriter Hospital with a group of pathologists called 'Wisconsin Pathologists' in private practice.

The family decided to move to Madison, which was not easy for the two boys in their teen years but posed no problem for Azania, who was only seven years old at the time and had not begun to send down roots in Boston. Madison was a neat and orderly city compared to Boston and although it had more diversity than Toledo, Ohio, Blacks were hardly seen, except in South Madison, an area of low income public housing but far from being a slum. Instead of high-rise projects, every small house had a little garden and the apartment buildings blended in with the other private apartment complexes.

Blacks were also at the university as undergraduate students and as graduate students, some of whom had families, and many of these lived in university housing called 'Eagle Heights.' The faculty was not very diverse and had few Blacks. The university was in an urban location with University Avenue, the main street, running through it. Some of the campus centers extended to the west of Madison. Madison is on an isthmus bounded by two lakes and a few smaller lakes, ponds and parks throughout the city. The university is one of the large land grant universities and is famous for the sciences, economics, agricultural programs and veterinary medicine. We joined St. Paul's AME church in Madison and made many friends with families which included Sierra Leonean and American families and enjoyed summer outings to Wisconsin Dells and other places of interest. Our children attended West High School and Shorewood Hills Elementary School and did very well.

After my sabbatical, I was not too keen on going back to Wesleyan so I started looking for a position at the University of Wisconsin in Madison and Milwaukee. Unfortunately, there were no vacancies. I got frustrated and was beginning to get depressed. I felt useless. and the feeling was intensified when I realized that I did not belong to any institution in Madison and had no professional routine. In addition, Mama Marie came with us and did all the cooking and helped with child care, so I really did not have much to do on the home front. After two winters in Wisconsin Mama Marie was beginning to get homesick and was not as happy as she had been at the beginning when we first moved to Madison.

All the children were happy in school and adjusting well. Chinaka was fifteen and at West High School, Duka thirteen and at Van Hise Middle School, and Azania was five and was admitted to first grade after taking a qualifying exam. After a year, we moved to Shorewood Hills and Azania attended Shorewood School, where she made many friends, even though she was slightly younger than most of the students. All of our children were among the youngest in their classes and did very well academically and socially. Chinaka appeared to be the most academically-motivated at the time and as the first child and role model, this was important for the family.

My mother's last visit to us in Madison, and her passing

Soon after we arrived in Madison in June, my mother came to visit us after visiting my youngest brother Wilfred, a lawyer and his family in England and my younger sister, Glenna, an actress and businesswoman who was visiting Los Angeles from London at the time. She was her usual self for the most part and played with the children, but seemed tired. She had just turned seventy years of age, which calls for celebration, since life expectancy in Sierra Leone in 1982 was 41 years. One night, she was a bit out of breath, so we took her to the hospital where Henry worked and she was admitted for congestive heart failure. Test revealed that she had type 2 diabetes, which she did not know about. She did not like going to the doctor for check-ups in Sierra Leone but she must have had diabetes for many years, since she had always been overweight and enjoyed eating between meals, especially at night, all of which must have contributed to the diabetes, which was now undermining her heart.

She stayed in the hospital and had a series of tests which showed myocardial infarction (heart attack.) On the fifth day at the hospital, she took a turn for the worse and when I visited her, Henry was already at her side and she was breathing heavily. They rushed her to the intensive care and started working on her until her kidneys were starting to fail and it appeared that she would not make it. I whispered in her ear that we all loved her and that I had told Dad that she was in hospital. A smile lifted her tired lips and muscles and she said: 'Thank you. I love all of you." At that point, the pulmonary specialist was called in and he started giving her more and more oxygen as she gradually faded. I knew then that I did not want to be in the room at the last moment, because I was sure I could not handle it. I kissed her and left the room.

Henry stayed with her until the end and I waited in the family lounge, preparing myself for the news. The doctor came in three times to tell me that she was getting worse and each time his face looked more and more sad. The third time he came in I knew from the look on his face that my beloved mother was gone. It is hard to describe the feeling that came over me, so many emotions all at once, but I could not find my voice to cry. The tears just kept streaming down my face. "How do I tell Dad that he has just lost his beloved wife?" I thought.

Henry had called my brother to alert him of Mum's illness and made a second call to say she was critical. The last call I knew I had to make myself, because Dad and I were very close and he would want to hear the news from me directly. I could hear him scream over the phone from so many miles away in Sierra Leone and I found my voice at that moment and let out a loud scream also. We sat in the waiting room for another hour and after expressing our gratitude to the medical team, who were also very sad, we left for home to tell the children and Mama Marie.

I admired the way Henry gave the children the news. He woke each one up gently, held them tightly and whispered in their ear that grandma had gone to heaven. I could see their little bodies shaking as they sobbed uncontrollably at the news of their grandma's passing.

They loved her very much. She always encouraged them to do well at school and at home and to look after each other.

Azania was too young to understand what was going on. When she was told that grandma had gone to heaven, she said, "Can I go with her?" There was so much love that night in that house and in my beautiful family. Their grandma's death brought us even closer and made our love for each other even stronger.

We decided to dress her in an elegant outfit we gave her that was appropriate for her many functions as 'Godmother' at weddings in Freetown, and she had liked it very much when she tried it on before she got ill. When we went to see her laid out at Ryan Funeral Home in Madison, she looked so still and peaceful that Azania turned to me and said, "Grandma must have gone to heaven already because she is not talking or playing with us anymore." I said, "Yes, and she is resting now because it is such a long journey."

It was only at the memorial service held at our church, St. Paul's AME in Madison that Azania realized that her beloved grandmother had died, since she could read the memorial sheet. She then turned to me and said: " I guess you have to die to go to heaven. I am sure Grandma would like it there." I was so relieved that she could accept her grandmother's parting so gracefully.

Taking my mother home for burial

There was no question of burying my mother in the United States. Henry and I decided to take her home. We did not realize that there was so much bureaucracy in transporting someone's remains out of the country. Ryan's Funeral Home in Madison was very helpful and made all the arrangements, which included informing the Sierra Leone Embassy in Washington, DC and using a special steel casket for shipping her body overseas. On the day of the flight I felt very uncomfortable and sad. As we took off, my sadness got worse because I could not stand the thought of my mother being on the plane and not sitting next to us. We changed planes in New York for Monrovia,

Liberia and then on the Freetown, where we were met by the funeral home, some relatives and Dr. Belmont Williams, my mother's first cousin. In the typical Sierra Leone tradition, there was a crowd at the house and as soon as they saw us, they started wailing. I was so exhausted by then that I did not really notice until my father told them to stop, because it would upset us more as we had been through so much already.

The reason for taking my mother home for her funeral was that she held a special place in the hearts of her family, her fambul and so many people in Freetown. She was a popular figure, a successful businesswoman and a philanthropist. Her special roles were that of godmother for weddings and grand chief patron for Thanksgiving and other special church services. In Freetown, death has a special meaning and a cultural context that would enhance the value of my mother's life. Deaths have great social significance since they bring together a multitude of kindred, friends and neighbors and are usually mourned for one year.

Traditional burial rituals

The following gives a description of the major elements of rituals related to death, some of which were observed in my mother's case. Death rituals reflect the multi-dimensional nature of Krio society in that they contain African, Western and Caribbean elements. The African elements are most strongly expressed in the following five rituals, many of which are no longer practised: *Wek, tri de, sɛvin de, fɔti de* and *wan yia/pul munin* (the wake, three, seven and forty days after death, one year and the end of the period of mourning.) The Western elements are mostly conveyed in the Christian ceremonies, which include the funeral, burial, and post-burial communion services.

Attendance at funerals is usually large and some funeral processions are supervised by police to ensure their slow and dignified passage through busy streets. It is quite common for bands to accompany funeral processions from the church to the cemetery. In recent times it has become customary to have the communion during the funeral service for the whole congregation. Freemasonry societies, which are exclusively male, also play an important role in the death rituals of their members. The wake echoes some Caribbean elements found in 'Nine Nights', which assists the departed on their journey by singing, storytelling, eating and drinking for several days. In Freetown the wake or vigil is usually held for one day only, on the eve of the funeral. The following recounts the major features of death and funeral rituals in Freetown:

The death of a loved one is a moment of grief, but that grief is tempered by the deep belief in the continuity of life in the 'true world' or the 'next world' which is usually seen as a better world than the earthly one. In my mother's case some people saw it as predestined and her final trip to see her children in England and the United States was viewed as the first stage of her journey to the world of the ancestors. When someone dies, there is usually an announcement on the radio under 'Obituary Notices' The full names and age of the dead person are given, and a statement of where the person died. The cause of death is not usually announced on the radio. A lengthy list of names of relatives and friends is then read out. The main purpose of the plethora of kin and friends is to ensure a crowded funeral.

The high value placed on a well-attended funeral reflects the social attributes of the dead and ascribes a high status as well as a reputation of having lived a good and influential life. It also gives comfort to the relatives and reassures them that the feeling of loss is shared by many. In my mother's case, we gave the names of the members of the nuclear family and the immediate extended family and ended with 'numerous relatives and friends.' This started a trend for a while, but it did not last long. Obituaries not only recite long lists of names but also make announcements on more than one radio station and television with photos of the deceased.

As soon as a death is announced, sympathizers will call at the home of the bereaved throughout the day. It can be quite tiring for the bereaved and I remember feeling more and more depressed every time a sympathizer asked how my Mum died. I was so relieved when a group of my cousins came and started telling jokes instead. Ironically, laughing turned out to be such a relief. In some cases, visits to the bereaved could continue even after the until the fortieth day ceremony. Women play an important role in death rituals and customs as managers of the process and as ushers of the deceased to the new world. They are usually dressed in black with or without matching black head ties.

It is customary for relatives to offer their help in running the home. Some regularly bring food to the house and one or two womenfolk who are close relatives will sleep at the house of the deceased to help console the bereaved. The home will usually display the characteristic signs of mourning, such as white window curtains with the mirrors turned backwards. This is in accordance with the belief that the spirit of the dead could be reflected in the mirrors. The dead are believed to be 'roaming', and the relatives have to be protected from their power until the fortieth-day ceremony, when they are supposed to leave this earth.

Wake, or vigil

The eve of the funeral is usually set aside for the wake or vigil, attended primarily by adults. Formerly the wake was kept with the corpse in the house and lasted throughout the night. Nowadays the corpse is likely to be in the hospital morgue or a funeral home. The wake usually lasts until midnight but could go on as late as the early hours of the next day. Popular foods are served as well as coffee and alcoholic spirits. A soup or broth, known as pepper soup, is often served as nourishment to make up for lost sleep. Hymns and spirituals or 'shouts' are sung. Tributes are also offered by relatives and friends and in some cases, specialized wake attendants may provide an 'entertainment monologue' by telling light-hearted stories about the deceased.

Friends and relatives tend to congregate in small groups and the whole atmosphere reflects both a celebration of the life of the deceased and mourning for the life lost. If the deceased was a member of the Freemasonry society, a special place in the house will be reserved for their observance of the wake. The more prominent the person the grander the wake. In some cases wakes also reflect the last wishes of the deceased. If the deceased had expressed the wish for a restrained wake the vigil would be kept by singing of hymns softly until midnight. On the other hand some wakes resemble a grand soiree and may go on throughout the night. In some elaborate wakes, a trumpet player would be hired to startle people whenever they showed signs of falling asleep.

The wake recognizes that the spirit of the dead still abides in the land of the living. It is also believed to be a ceremony of uniting the living with the dead, as the dead are thought to also 'join in' during the singing and 'shouting'. Wakes for anyone over 80 are usually elaborate celebrations because of their rarity and because old people are believed to be nearer the world of the ancestors. Significantly, wakes prepare the mourners and sympathizers for the funeral which is usually held the next day.

Funeral

Most funerals take place about one or two weeks after death to allow time for relatives living overseas to attend. In addition, since these rites tend to incur great expense for many families, a long interval between death and the funeral provides the bereaved with ample time to solicit other relatives for financial help and contributions towards the funeral expenses, should this be necessary. Formerly the relatives prepared the corpse for burial at the home of the deceased but this is now rarely done, except in the rural areas. The hospital mortuary provides low cost funeral and burial services for people who died in the hospital or taken there for an autopsy. Funeral homes have been operating since the 1970s and are now widely used. In my mother's case, the Freetown Funeral Home, which no longer exists, provided burial services for the family.

In Freetown, it is important to be 'churched' after death. The privilege of being churched depends on regular payment of one's class dues. Theoretically, if there are any arrears at the time of death one is denied a funeral and gets what is known locally as a 'direct boat' burial instead. There is now considerable leniency shown to defaulters of such payments, so that 'direct boat' burial seldom takes place. If the dead person was in the service of the church as a trustee, warden, or prominent member, the corpse may be laid out in the church for viewing. This privilege is greatly courted as it adds grandeur to one's funeral. Nothing is more important than to be accorded a well-attended funeral. Since my parents were both prominent members of the Cathedral Church and my father was an usher at the church, my mother was laid out in Cathedral House which is a hall next to the church.

Funerals are important social occasions, partly because of the significance of death rituals but also because of the high value placed on a well-attended funeral. Events which involve a large number of people are attractive and provide opportunities to see and to be seen. A notable element in the society is its class-consciousness, which accounts to some extent for the spirit of competition. Occasions involving a large number of people provide opportunities for demonstrating one's success. Women in particular show this is their attire. Funerals are attended in fashionable clothes although the usual mourning colors of black, dark blue, grey or white are retained. One female bystander watching a funeral procession remarked: "bɛrin tide na fashin sho" (funerals have become fashion shows). Many funerals, including my mother's are accompanied by a marching band that leads the procession from the church to the grave. After the funeral, there is usually the repast, which is the serving of refreshments at the home of the bereaved family or at a public hall.

After-death rituals

After-death rituals express primarily African elements in rituals of death. They are called 'awujɔ' and used to include the seventh, fortieth day and one year, which usually mark the end of the mourning period. Formerly the third day was also observed but this and the seventh day are no longer observed because most funerals take place much later to allow for all significant relatives at home and abroad to be present. After-burial rituals, <u>awujɔ</u>, are associated with the distribution of protein-rich foods and therefore have some bearing on one's social status. The more affluent the deceased, the more elaborate the after-death rituals and the more food that is likely to be distributed.

Women play an important part in after-death rituals because of their central role in all matters relating to birth and death. Since they usually cook as a group, these rituals also provide them with opportunities for informal socializing. They are often seen in groups inside and around the kitchen in the backyard preparing various dishes for the <u>awujɔ</u> feast. As they cook they shuttle to and from the kitchen, gossip, complain about the high cost of living and eulogize the deceased in whose honor and memory the <u>awujɔ</u> is being held. In recent times, many awuj feasts are catered by one of the many catering services in Freetown.

The forty-day ritual used to be more frequently observed by Muslims but is now also a Christian ritual that is increasingly being regarded as the official end of mourning by some families. The ceremony is almost identical to that of the seventh day. As a rule, forty day ceremonies are far more elaborate in terms of the number of people present and the amount of food served. In some families, food is left on the dining table for the dead until the fortieth day ceremony. As this is only meant as a symbolic gesture of feeding the deceased, the food is thrown away the next morning or given to someone outside of the nuclear family of the deceased. The relatives of the dead are believed to be under the power of the spirit of the dead, and are only released from it after the performance of the ritual marking the fortieth day after death. In my mother's case we only observed a limited forty day in which the traditional foods of beans, olele, special plasas, palm oil fish stew, rice, rice pap, coconuts and so forth were served.

At the end of one year the bereaved hold a ceremony to mark the end of their mourning. This involves an 'awujɔ' feast similar to the fortieth day, but in addition the family and relatives marked the end of mourning by a special church attendance dressed in more colorful clothes on the Sunday following the end of the mourning period. The grave will also be visited on that day. For some families, African rituals would be observed at the graveside while others will simply visit the grave of and return home. For the more Afro-centric families, a divination ceremony with kola nuts would likely be performed to ascertain that all is well with the departed kin. We were not able to stay for all the after-death rituals for my mother, but the relatives and friends in Freetown celebrated the forty-day and one-year ceremonies.

Regardless of what may be the reason for the persistence of this one-way communication with dead kindred, it seems clear that it forms an essential part of a belief system that has been well integrated into the Christian religion without conflict. Dead ancestors are seen as advocates for the living in that they exist in the heavenly abode and are powerful intermediaries between the Deity and the living. The fact that they are ancestors serves to personalize the relationship and to enable the living to communicate their specific problems to them more confidently and directly. Significantly, the dead ancestors are also believed to share the burdens of the living in a way that can be therapeutically beneficial.

Both female and male ancestors are believed to be able to influence the lives of their close living relatives, and the valuable role of motherhood is elevated to a higher spiritual realm by their being closer to God in 'the true world.' In most families in Freetown there is a popular tradition of paying a visit to the grave of a loved one on Christmas Day or New Year's Day and pouring a libation on their grave, taking turns to address them and give a brief update of their lives and ask for their guidance and blessings for the future. The pouring of a libation and other forms of ancestor veneration are also observed on major events such as the opening of a new house, bidding farewell to a student going overseas, obtaining a new job and life events.

Back to Madison, Wisconsin, USA

Going back to the United States was difficult for me after my mother's funeral. The sadness was magnified at Lungi Airport in Freetown, to which her body was flown from the States. My legs felt heavy as I boarded the KLM flight back to the States alone as Henry had gone back earlier to resume his work at the hospital in Madison. After my return to Madison, I felt that I needed to get back to work as a way of helping me cope with the loss of my mother. I felt the lack of a secure academic position even more acutely, especially since I had invested so much in getting to the highest level of my university training by obtaining a doctorate from Oxford University and could not use my education in the way I wanted to.

At the same time, I knew that I had a lot to offer and wanted to make a contribution, especially to the rising interest in women's studies and to promoting gender equality and the advancement of women. I briefly became affiliated with the Women's Studies Program at the university, but felt I was only peripheral to the work going on there. The University of Wisconsin had a bad reputation for racism and there was little or no diversity in the faculty or the student body. I tried to get a position in Anthropology also, but was unable to do so. Having held teaching positions at reputable institutions, namely Yale, Boston and Wesleyan Universities in the United States and the University of Sierra Leone, I felt that I had earned the right to be considered for a teaching position at the university. The only opportunity I had was through the Women's Studies Program, but it was not yet a department and had to rely on tenure lines from mainstream departments that were reputed to be traditionally racist.

246

Otelia Cromwell Distinguished Alumna Award – Smith College

I was delighted when a letter came in the mail from Smith College to inform me that I had been selected to receive the Otelia Cromwell Distinguished Alumna Award at Smith College. The award was in recognition of my contribution to women's studies, especially the study of the Black Woman in the African Diaspora and in Africa. This line of dedicated work resulted in an anthology titled, *The Black Woman Cross Culturally*, published in 1981 and mentioned earlier. I was invited to go to Smith College for the award ceremony and looked forward excitedly to going back to my *alma mater*. Henry accompanied me and we stayed on campus for the weekend and were able to visit my favorite sites on campus and the new buildings and facilities as well as attending some events. We also went downtown to see how much it had changed. I tried to see my host family but they had moved from the area and I could only speak with them on the phone. I tried to catch up with the progress and wellbeing of all the members of the family, especially the children, who were now grown up.

The presentation ceremony was attended by the president of the college at the time, Jill Ker Conway from Australia, the Deans and other members of the administration, faculty and staff. I was being especially given this distinguished Otelia Cromwell Award, in honor of the first Black student to attend and graduate from Smith College. I accepted the award and citation and gave a speech about my experience attending Smith College as one of the few Black students at the time. I remember thinking that we were so few that we did not even constitute a minority in the true sense of the word. We were a token at best, but made an impact nonetheless and did very well academically. I noted that much had changed since then and that more Black students were now admitted, but they faced greater challenges than when we were students because they were a critical and articulate minority, born out of the Civil Rights Movement of the 1960s.

I expressed my gratitude to Smith College for providing me with the scholarship that covered my tuition as part of a special program titled

'African Scholarship Program of American Universities (ASPAU)'. The experience at Smith gave me a solid academic background on which I was able to build, obtaining a Master's Degree in Anthropology from Boston University and a doctorate from Oxford University. I had worked in academia as a faculty member and assistant professor and as a consultant for the United Nations. Smith also taught me leadership skills through its emphasis on responsible learning and sharing as well as critical thinking and problem solving. While I was a student there I took the lead in organizing a few college wide events, including conferences on South Africa and social events. I also participated in inter-collegiate conferences and students' organizations working on the Civil Rights Movement, especially the Students Non-Violent Coordinating Committee (SNCC.)

Smith also helped advance my character in terms of being more confident and self-reliant with a strong sense of accountability and integrity, all of which I had been taught growing up in Sierra Leone. I also enhanced my skills in articulation, which was made easier by being in an largely all-women environment. I therefore owe some of my success to Smith College for helping to shape my intellectual and personal life.

What Smith did not do for me was to open my eyes to the cruelty and injustice in the real world. It provided an environment that was too sheltered, in which students were more interested in being gracious ladies and potential wives for Ivy League men than dealing with the realities of hardship, suffering and challenges in life. After Smith, I encountered many challenges as a graduate student working on a master's degree, a doctoral student, a wife and student combined, a mother of three and a junior faculty member. I am glad to have risen to the challenge in all of these responsibilities and built a successful career.

CHAPTER 19

A Job Offer as Deputy Director
at the United Nations

"Mum, you have important work to do for women of the world"
Chinaka Steady

❖

Just as I was beginning to get frustrated about being unable to secure
a mundane teaching job at the University of Wisconsin in Madison, a
call came from the United Nations inviting me to an interview for a
high level position as Deputy Director of the United Nation's Branch
for the Advancement of Women in Vienna, Austria. I decided to go to
New York for the interview and was offered the position that was to
change my life and launch my career on a global scale in a manner
that I never imagined!

Now that I had an amazing dream job at the United Nations, I had
to face the difficulty of leaving my family for at least a year. One
factor influencing my decision was that the United Nations Office
in Vienna had its headquarter in New York and the job required me
to travel to New York on several occasions with long weekends in
between, allowing me to fly to Madison to see my family. In addition,
two of the great perks of working for the United Nations are family
leave and home leave. Family leave is granted once a year for your

family to visit you at your field station, and home leave allows you to visit them. This made it possible to see my family at least twice a year during the children's summer holidays and at Christmas, in addition to the long weekends when I had assignments at the UN Headquarters in New York. Still, the thought of leaving left me with many sleepless nights.

I agonized about leaving my family, but felt I needed to pursue my career and take whatever exceptional opportunities came along. In the end, what made it easier for me to leave were the loving words of our son Chinaka: "Mum, I know you are worried about leaving us and taking this United Nations job. Don't worry, you have important work to do that will benefit women all over the world. We will take care of ourselves and even take care of Daddy. We will be fine." After those words, I found the strength to make the flight to Vienna, Austria and take up the position of Deputy Director of the Branch of the Advancement of Women of the United Nations.

We hired someone to help with the cooking and housework who turned out to be White, as is to be expected in a predominantly White city like Madison. She told me after raising four children as a single mother that she was bored at home. She also wanted to help our family and said she could use the extra money. She was very good and willing to cook whatever they liked, although she tended to stick to her own favorite dishes.

However, a White maid working for a Black family did not sit well with one of our neighbors in the Shorewood Hills area of Madison. The maid told me later that the neighbor would phone the house when she was there wanting to know why she was working for us and the nature of the work. After a few annoying calls, she told the neighbor that it was none of her business, which put an end to the calls.

The whole family took me to the airport for my trip to Vienna and we decided that there would be only smiles and no tears because Mum was going to do important work for women. It was a long overnight flight from Chicago to Vienna, so I slept most of the way. I was met in Vienna by my boss, the Director of the Division for the Advancement of Women, Mrs T. from from Algeria. She told me that my office was not ready and I should not bother to go to work the next day and the day after until they had my office fixed. This sounded strange to me, especially since I was so eager to start working and to hit the ground running.

Preparing for a major world conference

The UN office in Vienna had me go through a series of procedures for new professional officers that included health screening; obtaining health insurance and signing numerous administrative forms. I was then given a tour of the Vienna International Center, an impressive building that houses a number of United Nations Offices and specialized agencies, such as the International Atomic Energy Agency (IAEA); the United Nations Industrial Development Organization. (UNIDO) and an office of the United Nations Secretariat. There was a commissary with discounted prices for UN workers and several meeting rooms for conferences, recreational lounges and a huge cafeteria and dining hall. Many of the professionals sent their children to the International School with tuition paid for by the United Nations as part of their dependency allowance.

My position was an established one but I was hired specifically to be an executive member of the conference secretariat for the third United Nations Conference on Women: Equality, Development and Peace, to be held in Nairobi, Kenya in 1985. The secretary general for the conference was Mrs. Letitia Shahani from the Philippines and Mrs. T. from Algeria was the deputy secretary general. As deputy director of the Branch for the Advancement of Women, I was the third member of the executive team of the United Nations that was to spearhead the third United National World Conference for Women to be held in Nairobi, Kenya. The branch was the secretariat for the conference, which was being organized by the Commission on the Status of Women, a committee of the Economic and Social Council (ECOSOC) that implements General Assembly resolutions. It was also responsible for monitoring the Convention on the Elimination of All Forms of Discrimination Against Women (CEDAW) organized by the Committee on the Elimination of All Forms of Discrimination Against Women.

The main responsibility of the secretariat was to prepare the documentation for the three preparatory committee meetings and the Nairobi conference and provide substantive, administrative and diplomatic support for the actual conference itself. This involved translating the resolution for the conference from the Commission on the Status of Women into workable reviews and analysis as well as research and policy analysis to form the background documentation for the conference. Preparing the documentation involved developing questionnaires to be sent out to governments to assess the progress made and obstacles left to overcome. This required changes in laws; institutional reforms; human resource development including health, education and training and promoting economic equality and opportunities for women.

Recalling a Previous Women's World Conferences experience

After the first World Conference on Women in Mexico in 1975, a United Nations Decade for Women was declared from 1976 to 1985 with a mid-decade conference in Copenhagen in 1980 and an end-of-decade conference in Nairobi in 1985. The theme of the World Conferences was Equality, Development and Peace, with the subthemes of Education, Health and Employment. I had worked as a consultant to the United Nations second Conference on Women held in Copenhagen in 1980 and prepared the document on 'women and health' based on research and policy analysis of questionnaires sent out to governments. The objective was a review and analysis of what governments are doing to improve women's health, challenges remaining in terms of health status indicators like morbidity and mortality rates; access to health care facilities and resources and the role of women as health care providers. In the preparation of the documentation for the conference, a broader definition of health was considered necessary to capture the full range of women's health needs and the social and cultural framework as well as the policy environment facilitating or impeding women's health.

At the time, I was teaching Medical Anthropology at Wesleyan University and delving into the cultural and social factors that define, diagnose and treat illness and promote health and healing. The United Nations Secretariat was looking for someone who would bring in the social and cultural dimensions to the analyses of women's health, which is exactly what I was researching and teaching. For this reason, I was selected for the job above a few physicians who had also applied for the consultancy position. After analyzing the questionnaires which were designed and sent out before I was hired, I realized that certain critical aspects were missing. One was women's excessive workload, especially in rural areas, a factor that could undermine their health especially if their nutritional intake was not commensurate with their energy output. The other one, even more significant, was violence against women as a health issue.

After preparing the first draft of the review and analysis document, I presented it to a committee of UN agency officials that included a representative from the World Health Organization. She was not happy with the strong social and cultural emphasis in the document and felt that violence against women was too much of a social issue to be included in a document on health. I argued with her, stating that violence affects women's health and could even lead to their death. In my desperation, I said: "When does violence against women become a health issue? Is it when she collapses and dies at the hospital? That would be too late." Fortunately, my colleagues at the UN secretariat for the conference supported my position and the case for violence as a health issue was included in the document on women and health. Despite the disagreement, the representative from the World Health Organization must have had a change of heart, because their document for the conference included violence against women as a health issue. The secretariat celebrated this important milestone for women.

Thirteen years later in 1993, the Declaration on the Elimination of Violence Against Women was adopted by the United Nations. Since the Copenhagen Conference, all plans of action for gender equality and the advancement of women from subsequent UN World Conferences for Women included recommendations to end violence against women as a health issue and a social issue. By the time of the Beijing Conference in 1995, the subject of violence against women had a section of its own with emphasis on its implications for women's health as one of the twelve critical areas of concern. It recommended the appointment of a Special Rapporteur of the Committee on Human Rights on violence against women at the UN's High Commission on Human Rights. It defines the term "violence against women" as ''any act of gender-based violence that results in, or is likely to result in, physical, sexual or psychological harm or suffering to women, including threats of such acts, coercion or arbitrary deprivation of liberty, whether occurring in public or private life."

Twenty years after the Beijing Conference in 2015 , two thirds of the countries of the United Nations' 193 members have passed legislation to stop violence against women, reinforced by essential services ensuring safety, health and justice. In 2018 the World Health Organization in collaboration with other United Nations agencies working on Women's Health and Domestic Violence Against Women from 2000-2018 in 161 countries found that one third of women have been subject to physical and or sexual violence. Although the problem of violence against women remains a challenge to this day, these international mandates helped to promote a climate of no tolerance of gender-based violence, especially as it pertains to women.

The Plan of Action being developed by the secretariat for negotiation at the Nairobi Conference resulted in the title: "Forward Looking-Looking Strategies For the Advancement of Women." It adopted guidelines to the conference themes of equality, development and peace. The theme of equality stressed building the legal capacity of women towards the elimination of *de jure* (by legal) and *de facto* (in practice) discrimination against women. The theme of development placed emphasis on the negative impact of unequal global economic imbalance between the rich and the poor countries and the need to eliminate these obstacles and promote equitable development. Peace, as the third theme focused on reducing increasing international tensions evident in the arms race, armed conflict, foreign domination and foreign occupation.

The Plan of Action also developed guidelines for promoting the subthemes of education, health and employment. Unlike previous declarations and Plans of Action it expanded the section on development to include new and emerging areas such as the environment and women's roles in the management of natural resources and included fourteen areas of special concern for vulnerable women, such as urban poor women; elderly women; destitute women; women victims of trafficking and involuntary prostitution; women with mental and physical disabilities; refugee and displaced women; minority and displaced women.

Tensions in the Branch for the Advancement of Women in Vienna

When I was preparing to go to Vienna, I made a visit to New York to be briefed about the position of deputy director and other personnel and administrative matters and what it meant to be an international civil servant. In effect, I was technically relinquishing my country as this would be a conflict of interest when working for the United Nations. The branch had its headquarters in New York and its main administrative office. I remember the chief of the office telling me that I was walking into a war zone because there was a major rift between the Secretary General of the Conference (ASG), who was also in charge of the Center for Social Development and Humanitarian Affairs, and the Director of the Branch for the Advancement of Women, (D2) who was also the deputy Secretary General of the conference. This was an understatement. As Deputy Director (D1) of the Branch, I was number three on the hierarchical ladder which in fact put me in a very difficult position between my two warring superiors.

I discovered that the split was not limited to the two individuals but had resulted in two major factions. In walked Filomina Steady as the third-ranked official and executive member of the conference secretariat, directly hired from New York by the Undersecretary General of the Department of Economic and Social Affairs and the Secretary General of the Conference. No matter how hard I tried to maintain a neutral position, I was swept into the conflict from the start. The first sign was the fuss made by the director about my office not being ready so I should stay home and not come to work, which was odd. I decided to go to work anyway and was told by a high level professional administrator from one of the Soviet Union countries that this was a ploy to involve me indirectly in controversy from the start and that I should take up my assignment right away. I went to my office the next day and found nothing wrong with it. This was just a taste of things to come.

I later learned that the nature of the conflict revolved around a power struggle between the two women at the top. As an African, I wanted the conference to succeed, since it would take place in Nairobi and there was much at stake for the women in Africa who were struggling for gender equality and advancement like women in other parts of the world. The Secretary General of the conference also wanted the conference to succeed and was working very hard to achieve this, so I naturally supported her. Ironically, the opposition was coming from someone who was also from Africa, from Algeria, and was serving as Deputy Secretary General for the Conference and Director of the Branch for the Advancement of Women. It was widely believed that she viewed the failure of the conference as an opportunity to replace the Secretary General of the conference and advance professionally from the level of Director (D2) to Assistant Secretary General (ASG). The tactics used were similar to guerilla tactics: underhanded sabotage and disruption to the work of the secretariat and the governments and non-governmental organizations.

In order to proceed with the work in the midst of such a contentious environment, the Secretary General of the conference would hold secret meetings with some of the professional staff at her home to plan for the conference. It was very odd and I felt that this lacked the essential team spirit that would bolster our efforts. Although we got a lot of work done, I thought that the Secretary General should have been strong enough to control the situation and assert her authority more for the good of the rest of the professional and general service staff.

Some of the junior professional staff were seriously affected by the authoritarian and warlike leadership style of the director, who boasted that she had once been a revolutionary in her country and was used to fighting. The junior professional staff were more seriously affected, because their work was demanding and the hierarchical norms of the UN left them unprotected. Unlike professionals at the higher level of P5 and the deputy director (D1), they lacked the insulation which seniority can provide. Some of them lived and worked in constant fear of the director and a few had serious emotional problems resulting from the unrelenting insults and devaluation of their work. I had to step in on several occasions to protect the professional staff and the general service staff, which infuriated the Director.

It was always a relief when the two most senior women had to travel to meetings abroad and I or the other deputy director of the former Center for Social Development and Humanitarian Affairs (CSDHA) would serve as Officers in Charge. Coming from academia, I found it difficult to understand the intrigue and conspiracy that went on at the United Nations, since none of it was based on merit but on sheer political machinations. I found out later that the most politically shrewd professionals did very well at the United Nations. It was a highly political and cut-throat environment based on the survival of the fittest. Also different from academia was the hierarchical structure and norms of the UN which gave a lot of power to those at the level of Director and above. It was similar to a military-style operation where orders and instructions have to be obeyed and attempts to 'fight back' would be seen as insubordination and could be reflected in your periodic evaluation, used for retention and promotion.

Family visit to Vienna for Christmas

It was a pleasant relief when my family came to visit for Christmas, a few months after I was stationed in Vienna. The United Nations paid the expenses for the children's fare and since I had diplomatic status and a diplomatic passport, the children were also entitled to diplomatic privileges. Henry was doing his best to look after the family in Madison, and it was such a delight to see them all again during their break from school. My colleagues at the UN were impressed by them and thought I had a beautiful and loving family. Azania, the social butterfly, was four years old at the time and made many friends of all ages, including play dates with some of the children who attended the international school. The boys also made friends with children their own ages (12 and 10) and enjoyed exploring Vienna and going on tours of the historical and cultural sites of Vienna with their Dad.

Praterstrasse was a great hit with the children, because it had a permanent fair and rides on a large scale. We spent a lot of time there as a family. The highlight of their visit came when we went to Strasbourg for the weekend and toured the city, including the 'Sound of Music Bus Tour.' The children were fascinated since they had already seen the movie and enjoyed running through the archway made of trees and jumping on the steps like in the movie. We also saw the church where the wedding was held and aspects of the Convent, graveyard and the Von Trapp mansion. In Vienna, we went on tours to several historical and cultural sites including Schönbrunn Palace, Belvedere Museum, Stephansplatz, Votivkirche and castles and the Spanish Riding School.

One day I dressed Azania and myself in identical traditional Austrian dress and went on one of the horse riding tours around the center of Vienna. It was a beautiful summer day and the streets were full of pedestrians and shoppers. The Austrians came out to look at us and word got around about our Austrian dresses. In no time at all people came out of their shops to see us and shoppers stopped to take a look at us. They were waving, taking photos and cheering us and we waved back smiling, knowing that we were all celebrating the Austrian traditional dress together. They were so happy to see an African mother and daughter dressed in their national attire. Azania really enjoyed the admiration and waved back, blowing kisses. This was a good example of inter-cultural communication and appreciation that did not require the utterance of a single word.

The city of Vienna is a joy to behold! It is the most beautiful European or North American city I had ever seen. The historic buildings are most appealing, especially when viewed from the U-Bahn trains that go all over the city. One is struck by the beautiful Gothic and Romanesque architecture; the ornate and quaint shops; the market and the busy walking streets. The culture celebrates art in many ways through its museums, theatres, concert halls and opera houses. Anyone who lives in Vienna ends up loving classical music and going to the popular operas and operettas, characteristic of the city. The tradition of yodeling is also popular, as are the many folk songs that can be heard in the local bars at night and on television. Austrians are proud of their culture and love putting on their traditional attire.

I grew to like Viennese food, especially their Wiener Schnitzel, Bratknodel mit Sauerkraut and Apfel Strudel. Some of the food with pork meat or knuckles is quite greasy, but it appears to be popular in the more folksy and local restaurants. An African-American friend of mine used to say that the Viennese like greasy foods like African-Americans but looked healthier because they had a more egalitarian health care system.

I discovered a market that sold the entrails of cows and pigs, considered delicacies in some circles in Austria and quite a favorite spot for many Africans and Asians living and working in Vienna. There was also availability of a wide variety of international foods as well as restaurants offering ethnic menus. All in all, I was very happy in Vienna, and even though I missed my family very much the heavy workload and constant controversies in the Branch kept me busy and distracted.

Mother Kezia and her children. Left to right – Frankwin, Mum, Wordsworth,
Wilfred, Ghana, Filomina (Above right)

My parents- Kezia and Filomeno Forster-Jones

Cotton Tree and buildings, Central Freetown

Women demonstrating for a political party in Freetown, 1971

Filomina at Smith College, third from left

Henry on his motor scooter while a student at Yale University

Glenna at the BBC co-hosting 'London Line'.

Henry's graduation as Bachelor of Science at Yale University, Jonathan Edwards College

Filomina in her cap and gown masters' graduation, Boston University

Henry and Filomina's wedding party outside Riverside Church, New York City

Filomina and Henry exchanging wedding rings, New York City.

Henry's graduation as Medical Doctor, Oxford University - Filomina, Henry Lande, Wilfred, Oxford

Duka and Chinaka as babies – Our Oxford Home

Oxford Park – Duka, Albert, Chinaka, Henry, Filomina

Chinaka and Duka in their College School uniforms, Freetown

Steady family, Madison, 1984

Duka and Azania with Dad, Madison, Wisconsin

Henry and siblings – Henry (top) Thelma, Joseph, Elizabeth, Nikki, Florida

Duka's Bachelor's degree graduation at Carnegie Mellon University.
Later earned a Masters' degree at New York University.

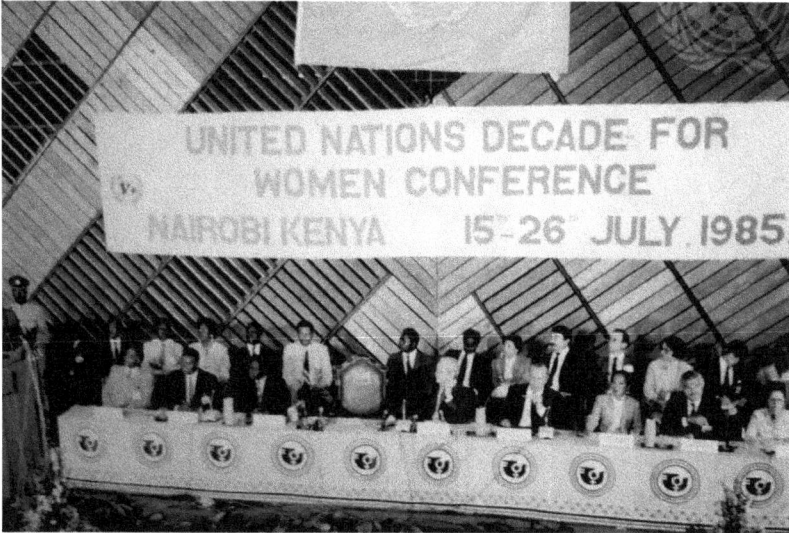

Women's World Conference, Nairobi, 1985. Filomina is on the right, back row

Earth Summit, Rio, Brazil, 1992 - opening ceremony

Azania's Masters Degree graduation, Webster University, Switzerland

Azania singing at Triad Theatre, New York City

Azania winning talent competition "Graines des Star" (M6 TV) France

Duka and Azania in Freetown

Maduka Steady and Ayo Haynes in 'A Raisin in the Sun' at Ford's Theater, Washington DC

Filomina with Julie Andrews and Sharon Capeling-Alakija of UNIFEM. UN, New York

Filomina teaching an Environmental Justice class at Wellesley College

Filomina teaching Medical Anthropology at Wellesley College

Filomina's Medical Anthropology class at Wellesley College

Filomina's Seminar on 'Africa' at Wellesley College

New Zion 'Steady' Church, Freetown

Filomina about to give a speech celebrating the 230th birthday of Freetown, 2022

CHAPTER 20

Assassination of a Turkish colleague by an Armenian at the United Nations, and Controversies

"Working at the UN is a stressful but rewarding job" – Evner Ergon, Assassinated Turkish Deputy Director at the United Nations

It was not long after I took up my appointment as Deputy Director of the Branch for the Advancement of Women in Vienna, Austria that tragedy struck. Mr. Evner Ergon, the other Deputy Director of the Division for Social Development assisted me with my transition to the new job when I first arrived. He was from Turkey and reputed to be hard working and a conscientious international civil servant. He was quiet by demeanor but had the ability to make everyone feel appreciated and comfortable. An exceptionally kind man, he approached his work with a high level of professionalism and conviviality. The tensions between the two top women bothered him and like me, he was sometimes caught in the middle of their cat fights.

One morning, we were all told to go to the conference room, as there had been an emergency. I happened to be the Officer in Charge as the two top women were travelling to meetings overseas. Someone from the Administration announced that our Mr. Ergon had been assassinated on his way to work. He had stopped by a stop sign that was at the entrance of the subway. The shooter suddenly appeared with a sign indicating he was Armenian, opened fire and disappeared down the subway steps. He was never found.

We were all in shock and some people were crying. In my statement to the group as chair of the meeting, I expressed my deep regret at the loss of such a gifted professional and mentor to many of the people in the room. I added that it was most unfair and unjust that an innocent and peace-loving man whom we all admired should become a victim of such a violent act.

The members of the Branch decided to request that his body be brought to the UN building in Vienna so that we could have a ceremony to honor him in the place he loved and to which he contributed a lot. The ceremony was attended by all the UN offices in the building with tributes from UN members, the Turkish embassy, his family and friends. The next day, there was a funeral cortege of cars driven by UN staff with their lights on escorting his body and his family to the airport for burial in Turkey, his home country. Turkey and Armenia had a long-standing feud and a few Turks had been gunned down in various parts of Europe in retaliation for what they felt were genocidal acts against Armenian Christians by the Muslim Ottoman government between 1915 and 1916, when 30,000 Armenians were killed.

The work of the Branch continues

As the UN secretariat for the Commission on the Status of women, the twelve professionals, directors and Assistant Secretary General were charged with implementing the recommendations and directives of the Commission. The professional staff were given various research assignments for review and policy analysis in preparation of the documentation for the Nairobi World Conference and the plan of action contained in 'The Nairobi Forward Looking Strategies for the Advancement of Women.' As an executive member of the conference secretariat, I was part of the team responsible for supervising this work, which in many ways was similar to academic work, without the policy aspect. Our main task was the preparation of documentation for negotiation by governments based on the themes of equality, development and peace and the subthemes of education, health and employment. In addition, there fourteen 'areas of special concern' for vulnerable groups of women and international and regional cooperation for implementation of the plan of action. This work was in cooperation with national government and coordinated with the other United Nations agencies.

The process of drafting the documents required much research primarily on UN documents, Expert Group Meetings and library research as well as analysis of questionnaires sent out to governments to assess the progress made in gender equality and the advancement of women and measures to eliminate the remaining obstacles. The three themes of equality, development and peace provided the framework as well as areas of special concern dealing with vulnerable women. Three preparatory committee meetings of the Commission on the Status of Women were held before the conference to try to reach agreement on much of the recommendations contained in the documents and the draft plan of action.

As an academic, I was influential in ensuring that research becomes an essential aspect of the measures to be adopted as there was still a need to improve the database, resources and publications on women in all countries. As a result, I was instrumental in ensuring that universities, colleges and research institutes play a major role in promoting research on women and gender issues. These findings would be important for teaching purposes as well as for providing important research findings to governments for policy development. Paragraph 168 of the draft document of 'The Nairobi Forward Looking Strategies' which was adopted by the conference states:

"The Decade has witnessed the rise of centres and programmes of women's studies in response to social forces and to the need for developing a new scholarship and a body of knowledge on women's studies from the perspective of women. Women's studies should be developed to reformulate the current models influencing the constitution of knowledge and sustaining a value system that reinforces inequality. The promotion and application of women's studies inside and outside and conventional institutions of learning will help to create a just and equitable society in which men and women enjoy equal partnership. "

The Non-Governmental Organizations (NGOs,) especially women's groups, were an important aspect of our work of coordination for the conference. An officer of the Branch was assigned to them as the focal point and for communication. They had to meet certain criteria for registration as NGOs for participation at United Nations meetings and required specific credentials to attend the meetings related to the conference and the conference itself. NGOs lobbied governments at the national level to ensure that their needs and concerns are being addressed. At the international preparatory meetings and conference, NGOs would customarily have parallel meetings to the inter-governmental negotiations. In many ways, credit is due to NGOS, especially those inspired by the Women's Movement for lobbying the United Nations and demanding that women's issues be put on the global agenda and that measures be adopted for a plan of action for gender equality and the advancement of women.

The pressure for UN conferences on women was sustained largely by Non-Governmental Organizations (NGOs) comprised mostly of the women who attended the inter-governmental meetings of the United Nations. They represent parts of the women's movement to whom some credit is due for bringing women's issues, needs and concerns from the outside to the UN's and agenda. They lobbied governments to bring some of the more controversial issues such as abortion, trafficking, inheritance, harmful cultural practices, foreign occupation and global economic imbalance and so forth to the agenda. Many of these groups represented all stripes and ideologies but came together in general to support gender equality and the advancement of women. Women NGOs organized several events, featuring lectures, panel presentations, discussions groups, informal networking sessions and participation at press conferences. Some NGOs were also active in organizing protests and demonstrations aimed at moving government delegates to action to end gender-based discrimination and gender hierarchies. A number of these demonstrations were radical and militant in nature, denouncing an end to the patriarchal architecture responsible for economic exploitation, militarization, misogynistic policies, wars and armed conflicts.

Contentious issues and controversies

Once the negotiations started between the governments, there were several contentious issues which had to be resolved at the three preparatory committee meetings before the conference. Those left unresolved are usually put in brackets and sent to the conference for final negotiation. This led to rifts between groups of nations that played out in the form of East /West tensions, inherent in the Cold War environment at the time. Many of the contentious issues were in the section dealing with peace. First, the definition of peace was highly contested as countries of the West tended to view peace as a political issue that did not belong to a women's conference but to other UN committees dealing with security issue and disarmament.

Delegates from the East and the non-aligned countries felt strongly that wars and conflict affect women 's lives even more than men in some cases and should be considered as women' s issues. They insisted that it would be unfair to ask women to leave the room when matters related to peace are being discussed, because women are often among the worst victims of wars and continue to bear the burdens of war even after it ends. They insisted that women are heavily invested in peace and should be central to the prevention of wars and the promotion of peace. The emphasis of the Western countries in relation to peace was on violence against women and unharmful cultural practices, which they argued were more appropriate women's issues than questions of wars and foreign domination.

Polarizations between the West and developing countries also centered around global economic imbalance in terms of the domination of the economies of these countries by the West, many of whom were their former colonial rulers. In the section on historical background, 'The Nairobi Forward-Looking Strategies for the Advancement of Women' called attention to this global economic imbalance resulting in a global economic crisis:

"The Nairobi World Conference is taking place at a critical moment for the developing countries. Ten years ago, when the Decade was launched, there was hope that accelerated economic growth, sustained by growing International trade, financial flows and technological developments would allow the increased participation of women in the economic and social development of those countries. These hopes have been belied owing to the persistence and, in some cases, the aggravation of an economic crisis in the developing countries, which has been an important obstacle that endangers not only the pursuance of new programs in support of women but also the maintenance of those that were already under way." (Paragraph 7)

Among the most vexing problems of the global economic crisis was the debt burden borne by many developing countries, resulting in reverse resource flows from the poor to the rich countries. Structural Adjustment Policies (SAPs) of the international financial institutions such as the International Monetary Fund (IMF) and the World Bank were also viewed as major obstacles. These policies were impoverishing many countries of the developing world and resulting in the destruction of their economies and the social fabric of their societies. The impact on women, who are often among the poorest of the poor, had been devastating.

The conference deliberated contentiously on the nature and extent of these global economic imbalances and exploitation and argued on the nature and solutions of these problems. The Eastern Bloc and China tended to side with the Developing Countries of Africa, the Middle East, Latin America and much of Asia, giving them greater clout in their negotiations. The Western European countries, the United States and Canada tended to side with each other and the international financial institutions that were responsible for generating many of the global economic problems.

Structural adjustment policies were the response to the debt crisis of developing countries aimed at promoting neoliberalism and marketization in the early 1980s by the IMF and World Bank. They were strongly condemned by Developing Countries and led to many structural adjustment riots in these countries. These policies imposed conditionalities that included liberalization of their economies through privatization; removal of tariffs; retrenchment in the public sector resulting in massive unemployment; reduction of subsidies on food and fuel; devaluation of local currencies; and an emphasis on exports. Due to the worldwide opposition to these policies, they later became disguised as Poverty-Reduction Strategy Papers in the 1990s, with equally unsuccessful and devastating results.

In addition, there were sensitive issues related to religious affiliation, such as abortion, which is not supported by Catholic and Muslim countries in general and is quite contentious within some countries. In addition, the Islamic countries were strongly opposed to the issue of single motherhood as well as inheritance of property by women as these would be in violation of Sharia law. Other contentious issues include the chronic problem of trafficking; involuntary prostitution, Lesbian rights, reproductive rights as they relate to access to birth control and manipulation of the reproductive rights of some women, especially poor women.

Two obstacles to achieving peace were among the most contested in the negotiations. These were women and children under apartheid, and Palestinian women and children. The main objection was from the United States and some European countries who were not in full support of economic sanctions against South Africa proposed by the majority of the member states of the United Nations. They were also not inclined to condemn the foreign occupation of Palestine by Israel. Liberation movements from South Africa, such as the African National Congress (ANC) and the Palestinian Liberation Organization

(PLO) lobbied vigorously at the preparatory committee meetings of the United Nations for the world conference.

The liberation movements were supported by some non-governmental organizations that participated in these preparatory meetings. In addition, the United Nations Center Against Apartheid organized a number of conferences and consultations during the run up to the conference and held several media events to raise consciousness about the evils of apartheid. Some universities and colleges all over the world were also involved in campaigns to end investments of their institutions in South Africa as an attempt to undermine the apartheid regime.

The Areas of Special Concern dealing of the Forward-Looking Strategies draft document dealt with vulnerable groups of women. It included urban poor women; elderly women; young women; abused women; destitute women; women victims of trafficking and involuntary prostitution; women deprived of their traditional means of livelihood; women who the sole supporters of families; women with physical and mental disabilities; women in detention and subject to penal law; refugee and displaced women and children; migrant women and minority and indigenous women. In some of the earlier preparatory meetings, some delegates were concerned about the prominent position given to these vulnerable groups of women in the early stages of the preparatory process but came to appreciate the importance of highlighting their position in order to lift the majority of women up.

CHAPTER 21

The Third World Conference for Women in Nairobi, Kenya, 1985

"I hope women at the Nairobi Conference do not adopt a resolution banishing all men from the face of the earth." – Comment by a Kenyan man on the opening day of the conference.

━━◈━━

Wall to Wall Women in Nairobi

The United Nations' Third World Conference on Women in Nairobi, Kenya started with a crisis. An unexpectedly large number of people, far more than anticipated, showed up for the conference, which led to a serious shortage of accommodation. Desperate attempts were made by the organizers to get people to share their hotel rooms and to look for alternative accommodation. Some people ended up sleeping in the lobbies of hotels for one or two nights before adequate accommodation was found for them, often in private homes at short notice. Almost two thousand delegates showed up from 157 countries.

The official inter-governmental conference was held at the Kenyatta Conference Center from July 15-26 under the leadership of the conference president, Margaret Kenyatta of Kenya. The Non-

Governmental (NGO) Forum was held at the University of Nairobi. The plenary sessions were devoted to the formal opening of the conference and to policy speeches as well as accounts of progress made and obstacles to be overcome in promoting gender equality from heads of delegations.

The rest of the work was done in committees and consisted of negotiations on the outcome document, "The Forward Looking Strategies for the Advancement of Women". The plan was to arrive at consensus on the guidelines for action rather than voting which was the system the UN had adopted once it became clear that the majority of the countries were from the Global South. In order to arrive at consensus, however, many of the recommendations would have to be diluted. This resulted in the West imposing its will on the other countries, but not without resistance and intense confrontations. The Cold War atmosphere reinforced the divisions between the East and the West, resulting in some high dramas between the delegations of the United States and the Soviet Union.

The Non-Governmental Organization (NGO) Forum held at the University of Nairobi attracted 12,000 participants. It facilitated network building at the national and international level and put the struggle for women's rights on a global platform as never before. Despite internal differences based on geographical divisions, historical experiences of gender-based domination and compounded discrimination for women of color, a symbolic recognition of women's needs and concerns as global problems requiring urgent global action emerged. The Forum held several discussions among women from all regions of the world relating to the themes of the conference – equality, development and peace – in a vibrant and dynamic environment that was accessible to all women. Among the most popular events were the panel discussions as well as the events held in the Peace Tent. Other popular events were the informal outdoor discussions on the lawns ranging in topics from the unjust global economic system to Lesbian rights, state-sanctioned oppression, sex trafficking and forced prostitution.

The conference had a major impact on the landscape of Nairobi. The streets were literally crowded with women from all over the world in their various national dresses. There were many stories about the reaction to Kenyan men to the invasion of their city. In one case, a woman was carrying two heavy suitcases and asked a man to help her with one. He replied: "I thought you women want equality with men. Carry your suitcase yourself!" In another case, a man was heard saying "I hope you women do not adopt a resolution to banish all men from the face of the earth." Kenyan men are no different from many other men who felt threatened by the demands of women for gender equality. It was a conference that had challenges at many levels, but it was timely and important.

The local economy benefited from the conference and business was booming, especially for shops that cater for tourists. Restaurants were full to capacity as delegates tried the local and international cuisine and the more adventurous dined to their satisfaction at the famous Carnivore Restaurant, where animal meat of all types was served. We were excited to sample meats of lions, tigers, crocodiles, giraffes and leopards, but I could not bring myself to consume zebra meat because I find zebras too beautiful to eat. Most of the meat tasted like some version of beef or pork, and the crocodile meat had more of a chicken than a fish taste.

We also enjoyed dining in the local 'meat and alcohol' bars, which were always full of men eating the typical Kenyan dish of ugali and a huge helping of meat with a bland sauce. As a rule, Kenyan food tends to be bland and not as spicy as foods in other parts of Africa and meat is usually the favorite meal. We learned that alcohol consumption was very high among Kenyan men and that the meat was necessary to absorb some of the excess alcohol and slow down the rate of intoxication. As in many countries of the world, alcoholism is a social and medical problem and has been proven to cause serious relationship problems in addition to being injurious to one's health. Women are usually affected negatively by alcohol, either as consumers or as victims of domestic violence triggered by alcoholism.

At the official inter-governmental conference, some of the controversies from the preparatory committee meetings that were put in brackets were resolved in the negotiations of the committees, but others often led to a deadlock. These had to be resolved in the final plenary of the conference where the "Nairobi Forward-Looking Strategies for the Advancement of Women" was to be adopted. These two major controversial obstacles to peace and several other sections in the whole document could not be resolved in advance of the Nairobi conference and had to be taken to the conference in brackets for further negotiation.

At the final plenary, the few remaining measures for implementing the Forward-Looking Strategies still in brackets had to be resolved for the document to be adopted. As one of the members of the executive team responsible for the substantive work of the conference, I was on the podium with the other UN officials at the levels of director and above to assist with the technical and diplomatic aspects of the negotiation. This was a critical time and the last chance of adopting the document by consensus. Time was running out and we still had some contentious issues that stood in the way of consensus. The following were among the most controversial issues that still had to be resolved. Abortion as an aspect of women's reproductive rights was opposed by countries where Catholicism was the predominant religion and by Islamic countries in general that also took a strong stand against abortion. Also contentious were the issue of single motherhood and inheritance of property by women which were against Islamic law. The conference arrived at a deadlock and there was no compromise.

An idea came to me at the time which I suggested to the Assistant Secretary General of the United Nations, who was sitting next to me. He was considered one of the most adept at negotiations and working with governments. I suggested that delegates who strongly objected to abortion, inheritance and single motherhood could state their objection and ask for a footnote to be placed on the sections of disagreement and recorded as an objection by the respective countries. He went around the room and spoke with the delegates and was able to secure their consent for this suggestion. After hours of deadlock in the middle of the night, we were able to move on and tackle the other contentious areas of the document using this method of placing footnotes on paragraphs objected to by specific countries.

Some of the other contentious and divisive issues were under the theme of Peace. One was 'Women and Children Under Apartheid' and the other 'Palestinian women and children.' These two issues dominated the negotiating process and created major schisms between the Western Countries and the Developing Countries, who often had the support of the Eastern Bloc and China. They remained in brackets throughout the preparatory process and became the major obstacle to the adoption of the Forward Looking Strategies for the Advancement of Women at the Nairobi Conference. They were deadlocked into the wee hours of the night.

The main objection was from the United States, which was under the Republican administration of President Ronald Reagan at the time. Maureen Reagan, the daughter of President Reagan, led the United States delegation. The Reagan administration had taken a rigid position in opposing sanctions against South Africa. Many of the measures proposed to ease the suffering of women and children under apartheid in South Africa were therefore rejected by the United States. Similarly, the guidelines for eliminating the negative effects of women in Palestine due to foreign occupation by Israel were not given full support by the United States and the vast majority of Western countries. Some of these countries lobbied against strong measures and sanctions on the foreign occupation of Palestine and considered many of the issues under peace to be too political for a conference on women.

In the end, the same mechanism of unblocking the deadlock by footnotes stating objections to certain paragraphs was used in the early hours of the morning of July 26th after delegates began to nod off in their seats and no end appeared to be in sight. The Secretary General of the Conference, Mrs. Letitia Shahani from the Philippines, was an astute negotiator and had worked with the delegates to find a way to agree by consensus on the document as a whole. This was intended to recognize but overcome the schisms and reservations on issues like apartheid's impact on women and children; the foreign occupation of Palestine, abortion, single motherhood, inheritance and global economic imbalance. It worked.

The delegates finally adopted the Nairobi Forward Looking Strategies for the Advancement of Women at the final plenary session of the conference. Those who were still too sleepy were awakened by the thunderous applause which signaled the success of the Third World Conference on Women in Nairobi, Kenya and the successful end of the United Nations Decade for Women from 1976 to 1985. I felt so proud and honored to have been a part of the executive in the UN Secretariat of the conference as an African woman. I was appreciative of the opportunity to have played an important role in the research and policy analysis that underpinned the preparation of the documentation for the conference and the plan of action contained in the outcome document.

Above all, I was grateful to have played a critical role during the wee hours of the morning in suggesting the idea of the footnotes on the areas that received the greatest objections by some countries. This enabled the delegates to move on to the adoption of the whole document and give the world an opportunity to advance the quest for gender equality and the advancement of women. Around 3 am on July 26th, 1985, the Nairobi Forward Looking Strategies for the Advancement of Women was adopted by consensus by the conference. A great victory for women of the world!

After the conference, there were many opportunities for the members of the conference secretariat to go on Safari tours and other sightseeing adventures. It was my first safari and I was fascinated to see animals up close in a safari van. A feeling of awe came over me at the sight of the beauty of nature and the peaceful and clean atmosphere that surrounded us. I remember wondering why people who behaved badly are described as 'animals.' I did not see any bad behavior in these aesthetically pleasing and calm lions, tigers, zebras, giraffes, lions and so on. They were surrounded by lakes and trees in savannah landscapes which they shared with various birds and aquatic mammals. They lived in peaceful coexistence in a state of balance of nature and were self-sufficient in terms of the pattern of acquiring food throughout the food chain. There was a sense of order and dignity involved, even in a process in which animals had to devour each other in order to survive. In a strange way, I remember the peacefulness of the environment and realized that even the skeptics must be aware of the presence of a greater spiritual force in nature in such a serene place.

I went back to Vienna with a sense of joy and satisfaction that the conference had been successful, despite the tensions and controversies that marked the journey from Vienna through the preparatory meetings to Nairobi. Many members of the Branch took a short leave to go to their home countries. As an executive member of the conference secretariat I had to work with the team in a number of follow-up activities that involved the implementation of The Nairobi Forward Looking Strategies for the Advancement of Women and the individual resolutions that emanated from the conference. I was concerned that the demands of the plans of action adopted would overwhelm a number of the poorer countries that lack the resources to implement many of the recommendations and guidelines for action. I hoped that The United Nations' Advisory Services and its specialized agencies would contribute resources and support to programs that assist countries in their follow-up activities.

CHAPTER 22

Back to Madison, Wisconsin, USA, Director of Women's Studies, California State University, Sacramento, and family tragedies

"The calm before the storm" – a popular saying

❈

A quiet period in Madison, and family time

Since my assignment was for the conference, I was happy to return to Madison to my family, whom I had managed to see on several occasions because of my frequent visits to the UN in New York in relation to the preparations for the conference.

This was a quiet period for me and I decided to work on some of my field research material and get some publications out. At the same time, I wanted to spend more time with my active family. I got an associate position at the University of Wisconsin, Madison and had an office in town. I also tried to get involved with the events in my daughter's school - Shorewood Elementary School, where we lived. Most of the pupils in the school were international pupils whose parents were studying in various graduate schools at the university. Many of them lived at Eagle Heights, a university housing complex for married students which was adjacent to Shorewood Village. This was good for Azania since there were many students of color at Shorewood School.

Every year, the students celebrated their international diversity by organizing a concert in which international students performed various variety shows depicting their countries and dressed in their national attire. I assisted the coordinator by providing arts and crafts for display at the Africa table and teaching the pupils a number of African dances to perform. The whole event was quite a success and Azania was proud to have her mother play an important role in this event.

Both Chinaka and Duka were in high school and Chinaka was preparing to go to university. He was admitted to several universities but chose to stay closer to home. He attended the University of Wisconsin, Madison and graduated with honors in the biological sciences. He was then admitted to Yale University's School of Forestry and Environmental Studies and was enrolled in a graduate program leading to a doctorate degree.

Losing my father

In 1986, my father's health started declining, so I was grateful to have time to visit Sierra Leone frequently to see him. He developed prostate cancer and in 1976 had surgery at a hospital in England under a special arrangement with the Freemasons in Freetown, of which he was a staunch member. After a speedy recovery from the surgery he spent some time recuperating in Boston with us. Seven years later, he started having problems with metastasized cancer that had spread to his pelvis. I made frequent trips home to spend time with him and help take care of him whenever I could. On my last visit, It was clear that he was very ill and would not make it. The doctors did what they could, but in the end he passed away, in 1989.

My older brother Wordsworth and I flew home from the States to make arrangements for the funeral according to the tradition of many cultural dimensions of Krio funeral rites consisting of African,

Caribbean and European influences. The vigil, which is held on the eve of the funeral, is a modified form of the 'nine nights' wake of the Caribbean. It was held at our house which he had built as our architect and contractor at Wilberforce, just outside Freetown. The event was a catered affair and the cuisine was predominantly African. The Freemasons played an important role in the wake and funeral, as he was one of their most senior and respected members. Freemasonry is a popular secret society among the Krios predominantly but not exclusively, with chapters that are linked to England, Scotland and Wales. I believe my father belonged to all of them. Since it is a secret society for men, it is difficult for a woman to learn anything about it. I only heard my father say once that the members that benefit most are those with a big appetite because an important part of their meetings is devoted to feasting and consuming large amounts of food. On a few occasions they would have a 'ladies' night' to which their spouses and other female guests would be invited.

It is my understanding that Freemasonry is not a religious society but a fraternity of brothers whose principles of life are divinely inspired and serve as a guide to living. They are also believed to adhere to a cult-like view of the dead, requiring special rituals to usher their deceased members to the other world through the aid of rituals performed at their funerals and at the graveside in full Masonic attire.

The Freemasons had secured a special place on the veranda of the house during the wake for their own celebration of my father's life, insisting that my Dad, Filo, had to be given a farewell fit for a king. They came in large numbers and stayed until the wee hours of the morning. They chatted, ate, drank and sang hymns and other songs and seemed to be having a great time. In the main living room upstairs there was a comedian whose purpose in attending wakes was to tell restrained jokes about the deceased and present some light-hearted biographical insights into my father's life. Chants of an African flavor were sung in the Krio language, as well as Christian hymns. A minister conducted a short service and offered prayers for the smooth passage of my father to the other world. The family took turns in reading from the bible and were joined by others in paying tributes to my father.

The next day, his body was laid out at the Masonic lodge in his full masonic attire. A year before his death, he showed me where he kept his masonic uniform and slim briefcase and asked me to give them to his doctor, a fellow Freemason, upon his death. Since my father was a 'sidesman' (usher) at the Cathedral Church, he was given a grand funeral that was well attended, and the internment was at Race Course Cemetery, next to his wife, Kezia, Lolloh, my mother. We had selected a steel casket to match that of my mother, who had died in the States and had her body flown to Freetown in 1982. After the internment, the Freemasons gathered around the grave and gave him their own exclusive farewell ritual. The repast was held at our house at Wilberforce attended by a large number of family members, friends and well-wishers.

Upon my return to the States, I received a call for an interview at California State University in Sacrament for the position of Director of Women 's Studies. The thought of another commuting job was daunting, but I knew I had to get back to academia after the United Nations job. I felt that with the weekends off and the many holidays, including the long semester breaks, Spring Break, Thanksgiving and Easter, I could handle it. So I took the position at California State University in Sacramento and taught for one year, after which I was granted tenure to strengthen my position in a department that had two combatting factions of women on the board of Women's Studies. It was a difficult environment and I tried to transfer to another institution since I felt caught in the middle.

The main rift was between women who I believe were more left leaning and women who would be considered moderate in the political feminist spectrum. There were also many who were more radical and subscribed to the lesbian philosophy of separation from men at all cost. It was a difficult position for a feminist of my persuasion who was Black, African and married with children. I taught women's studies courses, medical anthropology and courses on urbanization. As in all institutions of higher learning, racism was an issue and the power was vested in the hands of a predominantly White administration, even though there was a Black female vice-president and an Asian Dean. I built alliances with the faculty and students of the Ethnic Studies Program which had its offices next to ours. The student body was diverse and made up of a relatively high percentage of working and more mature students. California State University in Sacramento is part of the system of universities that tended to emphasize teaching as opposed to the research-oriented Universities in the State.

Chinaka was completing his senior year in biology at the University of Wisconsin, Madison and getting ready for graduate school at Yale University, his father and grandfather's alma mater. He graduated with honors in Biological Sciences from the University of Wisconsin and we were all very proud of him. That summer, he went to visit Henry's sister Elizabeth and her family in Dakar, Senegal and took part in a program involving the planting of trees in arid areas of the country. I saw him off at the bus station in Madison and remember both of us smiling and waving goodbye. Duka was in college at Carnegie Mellon University. Azania was attending Middle School in Madison. Little did we know that our happy family life would soon be torn apart by an agonizing tragedy.

A family tragedy – losing Chinaka

Chinaka started graduate school at Yale University in the School of Forestry and Environmental Studies at the age of twenty-one. He had earned a Bachelor's Degree In Biology with Honors at the University of Wisconsin, Madison in June 1989. Over Thanksgiving that November, during the first semester, he went to visit some friends of ours, Mr. and Mrs. Vernon Truell in Boston. He phoned us to say he had a wonderful time and had returned to campus.

The next Monday after the Thanksgiving weekend, the phone rang at 1.30am in Madison and woke us up. The voice on the other end identified himself as a doctor from Yale New Haven Hospital. He told us that Chinaka had been playing a game and had walked across the room for a drink of water, collapsed and fallen on the floor. When he came to, he had some problems breathing, so an ambulance was called and he was taken to their hospital. They did a CT scan which found bleeding in the brain and suspected that an aneurysm had ruptured. They had informed the surgeon, and said that Chinaka might have to have surgery.

I asked if I could speak with Chinaka and the doctor said it would not be possible but he could take a message to him. I asked if he was in pain or any discomfort and he replied that he was complaining of a slight headache. We told him to tell Chinaka that we love him and were praying for him. He then spoke with Henry and explained further about the medical plan for his treatment, since they were both doctors.

That morning around 6 am, we received another call to tell us that the surgery was over and had been successful, but that there was a lot of bleeding, due in part to the risky test to determine the exact location of the aneurysm. He said the next 48 hours would be critical.

When Chinaka woke up after the surgery, the first thing he did was to phone his professor and ask how his experiment was doing. I called the hospital and asked to speak with him but they could only take a message, so I told the nurse to tell him that he was a champion and would win this battle. The nurse told me later that he had been pleased with the message and responded with a big smile.

Henry's host family in New Haven, the Thomases, went to visit him right away while we were planning to go and see him ourselves. The surgeon called Henry often to give him an update, but they were not very encouraging. The bleeding was causing problems and there was swelling of the brain due to vasal spasms. They would have to fly him out to a specialist hospital in New York City for a more advanced procedure to deal with the complication. We decided that Henry would go first to New York and I would go later, since someone had to be with Azania and we had to make plans for her care. We had told Duka and Azania that Chinaka was very ill and had been admitted to

Yale New Haven Hospital, where he had had surgery for a ruptured brain aneurysm.

Around 10am on the 7th of December, I started feeling very anxious and decided to phone the hospital and told them that I would like to find out about my son. After stalling for a while, they told me that Henry was with the doctor and he would call me. When the phone rang, Henry did not have to say anything. I spoke and I said, "Vincs, we lost him, right?" and he said, "Yes my love. I am so sorry. When I arrived they rushed me to his bedside and I hugged him and he responded and died in my arms. He is at peace. I am coming home and we will make the arrangements together."

Henry then called Carnegie Mellon University to tell Duka and his colleagues at the hospital where he worked in Madison. One of them immediately came to the house, gave me a hug and said "Chinaka at the age of 21 had a sterling character that it takes most men as much as 80 years to develop." Later the other doctors came with heavy hearts and shared deeply in the loss of our precious child.

I was scared of having to tell Azania when she came home from school. I called her to me and hugged her and told her that Chinaka was not coming home anymore. We both cried a lot. Henry came home that night and we started planning to say goodbye to our first and beloved son Chinaka who had died at the age of twenty-one. We knew then that our family would never be the same again, but that we had to be strong for Duka and Azania and for each other.

The Sierra Leone community in Madison rallied around us, as did the members of our church, St. Paul's AME church in Madison. Sympathizers came to the house every day and we put together an album of Chinaka that showed pictures of him going backwards from being a graduate student at Yale University to the day he was born at Nuffield Maternity Home at Radcliffe Infirmary in Oxford, England on March 25th, 1968. I could not understand why, but for a long time after his death I kept thinking of him as a baby and reliving the day he was born, over and over again. The funeral was at our church, St. Paul's AME in Madison, where Chinaka attended Sunday School and was active in the choir and other activities for youth. The burial was at Forest Hills Cemetery opposite West High School, which he attended.

My grief was deep and I cried a lot until one of our church members came to the house and sat next to me on the sofa. She took my hand and said: "I lost my daughter at the same age as Chinaka and I was heartbroken like you, but I want to assure you that it does get better." Those were the best words I heard during this difficult period and I remember wanting to speak to as many mothers that had lost children as I possible could. The loss of a child leads you to experience a different kind of motherhood. Carrying a child for nine months in your womb makes them a part of you, so the love gets deeper when they leave because a part of you goes with them. There is a deep sense of loss and emptiness and you get the feeling that your heart is buried with the child. You can never be the same again.

Chinaka was a brilliant young man who at the age of twenty-one was in graduate school and on track for a Master's Degree, leading to a Ph.D program in Environmental Sciences at Yale University. As an avid environmentalist, he had spent his last summer planting trees in Senegal and enjoyed staying with Henry's sister, his aunt Elizabeth and her husband Tony Ndiaye and their children.

He was not always the brilliant student that he later became. He was 'a late bloomer' and had a difficult time in his early years of schooling. He started making tremendous progress when the family moved to Madison, Wisconsin for Henry's new position at Madison General Hospital, which later became Merriter Hospital. Chinaka was very happy at West High School and excelled in all subjects. He told me that the pupils were more serious at West High School, Madison than those at his previous school, Brookline High School in Brookline, Massachusetts.

As the capital of Wisconsin and a university town, Madison had a high percentage of parents who were university graduates. They tended to motivate their children to perform well in school and also participated actively in the academic programs of the public schools. Parents often helped to organize extra-curricular activities and provided resources and other material support for the schools. Most of the academic programs were rigorous and Madison schools always ranked high nationally in terms of their excellent academic performance.

Chinaka thrived in this kind of academic environment and received the full support of the family and his teachers. He was also highly conscious of his position as the eldest child and the role model for Duka and Azania, whom he also helped to raise.

Talk of a high energy, busy child, that was Chinaka. From infancy on, he was always on one project or another and took no breaks in between. His brother Duka used to jokingly ask him if he had considered taking a vacation. He was a 'busy bee' and always belonged to a number of extra-curricular activities in school and at the university, including sports, especially long-distance running, basketball and rowing. He was also a member of 'Forensic', a debating society, and wrote articles for the student newspaper at the University of Wisconsin. At church, he was a leader among the youth and was active in Sunday school and bible reading activities as well as helping to organize social activities for the youth.

Chinaka was a social justice activist and felt strongly about systemic racism and negative expectation of Blacks, and was a member of organizations on campus fighting for equality and justice. He graduated from the University of Wisconsin, Madison with a Bachelor of Science with honors in biology in 1989. In a predominantly white town and university that Madison was, Chinaka stood out. He told me that whenever he wore his honors ribbon with his gown during graduation time, people at the university would stare at him in surprise, as if they did not expect a Black student to be graduating with honors. He was proud and told me that he was not bothered by it but instead felt sorry for them for their ignorance and limitations.

At home, he helped take care of his younger siblings and guided them in their homework as well as in their social and spiritual development. He was very religious and would sometimes spend a long time kneeling at his bedside when he said his prayers. I remember teasing him once and saying: "Chinaka, Don't you think you have spent a long time talking to God? Other people are in line and you may be tying up the phone." He would then stand up smiling and we'd both say "Amen" together.

Chinaka was a devoted son to his parents and always made us proud. He had a strong sense of responsibility as the first child and was the glue of the family in many ways. I used to refer to him as the 'social worker' of the family who cared deeply about everyone and contributed to a loving and healthy home environment.

I went to the funeral and the memorial service that was held later at SS Morris Church, the other AME church in Madison. In keeping with the tradition of the krios of Sierra Leone, I did not go to the cemetery for the burial. Mothers are not allowed to do that for fear that the spirit of the child will not have a smooth passage to the next world and that the mother will have a hard time overcoming her grief. It took me a year before I could go to Chinaka's grave and when I did, I was shaking all over. His sister Azania, who wrote poetry and songs from an early age, had written a lovely verse on his headstone: 'The heart is never lost. The love will never die.'

To honor his love for the environment, the design on his headstone is of the earth and a bird above it symbolizing the preciousness of all living things – something that Chinaka believed in and wanted to work to preserve. Going to see Chinaka's grave was a turning point in my life because it gave me the strength to go on, for his sake and for the sake of Duka and Azania and above all, for Henry.

About a month later a memorial service was held in Madison at SS Morris Church, full of beautiful tributes from the University of Madison Community, his high school teachers, the African community in Madison and relatives and friends.

Another memorial tribute was held for Chinaka at Yale University, where he was a graduate student at The School of Forestry and Environmental Studies and was meant to celebrate his life and the impact he had on the students and faculty at Yale University. Henry, Duka and I went to the service, where a Korean dogwood tree and a plaque bearing his name and words to his memory were erected on the campus. Chinaka's professors and colleagues warmly welcomed us and paid lovely and heart-warming tributes to him. They continued to express their sympathy, which they had done before by phoning and sending numerous sympathy cards to the house. It was sad to see so many students crying. Henry gave an inspiring speech urging them to go on and finish the work that Chinaka had begun. The Dean, who was also his professor and adviser and with whom he had been working on photosynthesis, spoke of how Chinaka was exceptional. "He stood up and he stood out," he said, adding "I have taught science for twenty years and I have never worked with a student who was a more gifted and consummate scientist." I remember praying quietly and being thankful for the life that he shared with us.

For me, the only way to get over my loss was to figure a way of unburying the heart and transferring it to the head in the form of beautiful memories so that I could let the child go. Grieving is a lonely state of being. As a family, you really cannot console each other when you are all grieving with heavy hearts and feeling helpless and vulnerable. Without faith, our extended families, our church, the Sierra Leone community in Madison, our colleagues at work and our friends, it would have been difficult to overcome the loss of our beloved Chinaka. At the same time we had Duka and Azania who were equally precious to us and who would need us even more now and help lead the family to a new future. Chinaka has been resting in peace since his passing and we are grateful for having him for twenty one years. Over the passage of time, only the beautiful memories remain.

CHAPTER 23

U.N. Appointment as Special Advisor on Women to The Earth Summit – 1992

"The generation that destroys the environment is not the generation that pays the price. That is the problem." Wangari Maathai, Nobel Peace Laureate.

❖

After Chinaka's passing, I realized that only a busy schedule would help me get over my profound grief. My friends at the United Nations may have been thinking the same thing, because I got a call from Angela King, a Director at the UN secretariat, informing me about a high-level position at the United Nations for a gender expert on women and the environment with academic and research experience. She thought I would be excellent for the position, which was likely to be established for the United Nations Conference on Environment and Development (UNCED.) Apparently women NGOs had been lobbying to make sure that women's needs and concerns were included in this conference and its Plan of Action. It was to take place in 1992 in Rio de Janeiro, Brazil.

The Director of UNIFEM, Sharon Capeling Alakija from Canada, was also looking for a way to make a major impact on the work of the conference by integrating women substantively in the research and policy analysis and the plan of action for the conference. My curriculum vitae was presented for consideration during a meeting of the Director of UNIFEM with Mr. Maurice Strong, the Secretary General of the Conference, the Deputy Secretary General, Mr. Nitin Desai and his senior staff at the UN headquarters in New York. Mr. Strong apparently told them that he was interested in staffing the position of the gender expert if he could secure funding for it. In 1990, after some consultation with the Director of UNIFEM and an agreement that UNIFEM would partly fund the position, I was hired as Special Advisor on Women, Environment and Development to the UNCED Secretariat. Betty Astolfi, a senior professional official at UNIFEM and a gender expert from Wales, was to be my counterpart and major link between my work at UNCED and UNIFEM. We worked very well together to help coordinate the NGOs that formed the main outside lobbying group supporting my work at the UNCED secretariat. Professor Irene Dankelman, an ecologist and gender expert from the Netherlands sponsored by her government, completed the team.

United Conference on Environment and Development (UNCED)

UNCED was based in Geneva, Switzerland and I was hired at the Deputy Director's level (D1) as Special Advisor on Women, Gender and Environment. My assignment was to mainstream gender issues throughout all the documentation for the Earth Summit to be held in 1992 in Rio de Janeiro, Brazil. The mandate resulted from lobbying by women's NGOs at meetings of the Commission on Sustainable Development and the General Assembly at the UN headquarters in New York. My work involved one-to-one consultations with each of the professional staff at the UNCED Secretariat responsible for various aspects of the documentation, which was divided into four sections. Section one covered social and economic dimensions, and this in many ways was the easiest section for my work. It facilitated mainstreaming gender and strengthening the role of women at all levels, particularly at the level of decision making. Section one included poverty, consumption patterns, population dynamics, health, sanitation and decision-making in environment and development.

Section two was concerned with conservation and management of natural resources. These included deforestation, fragile ecosystems of drought, desertification, mountains, sustainable agriculture; biodiversity; biotechnology; oceans and high seas; freshwater resources; toxic chemicals; hazardous waste; solid waste and sewage and radioactive waste. Although gender issues ran through all of these sections, it was more difficult to convince the highly science-oriented staff of the important link between women's work, women's health and care-giving roles and ecosystem decline destruction and pollution. In the end the staff came to appreciate the important role women played in the management of natural resources and environmental catastrophes in many countries of the world.

Section three focused on the role of major groups, including women, children and youth, indigenous people, NGOs, local authorities, workers and trade unions, business and industry, the scientific and technology community and farmers. In many ways, this was the most important section for my work since it gave a clear signal of the significance of women and other major groups in issues relating to the environment. Nonetheless, these were among the most controversial negotiations throughout the preparatory process for the conference. Mainstreaming women and gender issues did not come easy or automatically.

Section four was concerned with the means of implementation in terms of financial resources, transfer of technology, science, education, public awareness, national mechanisms, international institutional arrangements, international legal instruments and mechanisms and decision making. Most of the controversial arguments in this section were related to the reluctance of some of the rich countries of the Global North to agree to transfer financial and other resources to the countries of the Global South. This was considered unfair by most of the countries of the Global South since The Global North continues to extract and benefit from many of the resources from the Global South.

Three environmental challenges were in negotiations for the development of Conventions, in addition to Agenda 21, the Program of Action to be adopted by the conference. These were the United Nations Framework Convention on Climate Change which came into force in 1994 aimed at preventing dangerous human interference with the climate system. The second was the Convention on Biodiversity in 1993, which recognized that the conservation of biodiversity is 'a common concern of humankind.' With regard to the preservation of forests a set of forest principles were generally agreed on and in 2000 became the Forum on Forests. To succeed, all of these conventions would require an integral participation of women at all levels to ensure their successful implementation.

My work also entailed securing relevant documentation on how women's participation would enhance environmental protection in the various sectors and areas. The important role that women already play in environmental conservation, though well documented, had to be communicated to the professional staff. These included managing natural resources, especially in rural areas; conserving biodiversity and deforestation; cleaning up the environment and women's pivotal role in matters relating to population and consumption patterns. The area of poverty and human settlements was clearly in the women's domain since poverty is often feminized and women are responsible for tasks relating to the immediate environment of the home. Agriculture was another area that required clear and decisive plans of action since women provide the essential labor in agriculture in Africa, Asia and parts of Latin America.

In some other areas, it was more difficult to persuade my colleagues of the importance of a gender perspective and gender mainstreaming, especially those that were trained as scientists with an orientation towards the laboratory experiments rather than social analyses. These were forestry and oceans scientists; biochemists, biologists, physicists, toxicologists and so forth. With them, the work was much more difficult as they could not see where women fit into their schemes or analysis of largely innate material. Foresters would likely see the trees only and are more concerned about the forests as carbon sinks to mitigate global warming rather than see people for whom the forest is their home and habitat providing them with their livelihood.

Ocean scientists would be more inclined to see a body of water, the marine animals and the chemicals that pollute it as well as large-scale shipping activities, rather than the women and men who depend on these resources for their livelihood through fishing, food preservation and the marketing of marine products. Scientists working on climate change and biodiversity may not always see the impact of seasonal change on the agricultural cycle that often determines the division of labor by gender in agriculture. The gender-differentiated health consequences of toxicity from chemicals and hazardous waste are also often missed. These include serious harm to women's reproductive and other organs and an increase of their workload in caregiving responsibilities for their families. These were the areas that required the most work in gender mainstreaming for policy development and coordination in preparation for the conference.

Preparatory meetings

The preparatory meetings for the conference displayed the usual polarizations between blocks of countries, but this time it was less noticeable between the East and the West due to the end of Cold War by President Mikhail Gorbachev of Russia and his policy of Glasnost from the late 1980s on. The new major rifts were between the Global North and the Global South and were reflected in almost all areas of negotiation. The Global North, consisting of the so-called developed countries, was seen by the Global South as the major destroyer of the environment and responsible for 80% of carbon emissions into the environment. Africa's emissions are among the lowest and less than 2% with most of it coming from South Africa. Other polarizing issues during the preparatory process for the conference included forest conservation and loss of biodiversity. Many countries of the Global South felt that unfair restrictions were being placed on them to conserve their forests which are needed for their own development.

They argued that the Global North benefited from its forests for its own development and could not now impose restrictions on the Global South in their development efforts. In fact, they argued that much of the heavy logging in the Global South was a result of the commercial activities of corporations from the Global North. The loss of biodiversity was also blamed on the Global North, whose development model is the exploitation and extraction of natural resources based on the ideology of the domination of nature and capital accumulation. Wherever possible a link was made between imbalances in the global economy that functions to benefit the Global North at the expense of the Global South. Some of these polarizations played out throughout the preparatory process and on to the conference on Environment and Development in Rio de Janeiro, Brazil, later known as 'the Earth Summit.'

One of the most significant developments in the preparatory process was linking the analysis of population and environmental degradation to consumption patterns. It was sparked in part by a speech by Prime Minister Indira Gandhi at the Conference on the Environment in 1972, when she stated 'the poor pollute out of need and the rich pollute out of greed.' It was important conceptually to understand how excessive consumption of the Earth's resources has to be taken into account, as much or even more than the pressures of population on the environment. Consumption patterns of the Global North were also severely criticized and examples of excessive consumption were cited. In one case, a delegate mentioned that a child in the Global North would likely consume fourteen times more of the earth's resources than a child from the Global South.

My particular challenge was working with professionals who were very good in their field but had little or no exposure to gender issues or the social construction of gender resulting in gender-based hierarchies. I had the support of the Secretary General of the conference, Mr. Maurice Strong, which helped a lot since the UN is a hierarchical organization and directives from the highest level are automatic mandates and have to be acted on without question. During our working meetings in the secretariat, Mr. Strong would make it clear that he wanted everyone to cooperate with me in my efforts to mainstream gender in all the documentation of the secretariat. This support was necessary, especially with some of the professionals who were not familiar with the women's movement or gender theory, gender analysis and gender mainstreaming. Most of them did not have the opportunity, or maybe the desire, to take courses in women and gender studies.

I did not receive the same support from Mr. Strong's deputy and experienced some resistance to a strong presence of women in Agenda 21, the outcome document of the conference. I also had challenges from some men who resented having what they regarded as 'too much focus on women.' As we prepared to start the discussions on solid waste, one of a senior male colleague said to me "Well, Filomina, are you going to mainstream women into sewage too?" He thought this was funny, but I did not. When one of the members of the press interviewed me during a preparatory meeting, I recounted this to him and it appeared in the newspaper that was covering the conference. Mr. Maurice Strong, the Secretary General of the conference was not amused and insisted at a general meeting of the UNCED secretariat that everyone must cooperate with me in mainstreaming women as an important aspect of our work.

Expert group meeting

I decided to use one of the established institutions of the United Nations which brings specialists to discuss the state of the art of research in the substantive areas dealing with the work of the organization. These are called 'expert group meetings', at which academics, researchers, policy makers and NGOs with extensive knowledge in a particular field are brought together for a week-long meeting. I organized one such meeting by bringing experts to present papers and discuss the importance of mainstreaming women in all areas under consideration for the Earth Summit. Although not all environmentalists invited, like Dr. Wangari Mathaai, were able to attend, Dr. Vandana Shiva and other well-known experts on women and gender issues and the environment were present at this important meeting.

The group explored women's roles in the management of natural resources as well as the link between environmental degradation and poverty and its gender implications. The meeting made it easier to mainstream women's environmental roles into the work of the conference dealing with forests, oceans, biodiversity, climate change, population, consumption patterns and the negative impact of hazardous waste and toxic chemicals on women and so forth. Also as a result of the expert group meeting, I edited a book titled *Women and Children First: Poverty, Environment and Development*[16], which contained the papers presented at the meeting and additional ones for areas that were not covered. The book was enthusiastically welcomed as there was very little published on the subject of women and the environment at that time.

In addition to demands for mainstreaming gender in all the work of the secretariat, especially Agenda 21, NGOs lobbied government delegates for a separate section on women to highlight their important role in sustainable development. In the end, a resolution was passed requesting a separate section on women, in addition to mainstreaming women in all aspects of the review and analysis and in the plan of action. In the end, the final version of Agenda 21 contained a section on 'Strengthening the role of major groups' led by chapter 24 on women titled 'Global Action for Women Towards Sustainable and Equitable Development.' [17]

During the preparatory meetings for the conference there were a

16 Steady, F., 1993 **Women and Children First: Poverty, Environment and Development,** Rochester, Schenkman Books

17 United Nations, 1992, **Agenda 21: The Program of Action from Rio,** New York, United Nations

few road blocks, as some governments challenged the inclusion of women in so many areas of the review documents and in the draft of Agenda 21. I was called in a few times to help defend the inclusion of women in some sections of the document. I explained the importance of women in forestry, as many rural communities depend on the forests for their livelihood and women provide the labor for food, fiber, fodder, medicinal herbs, building material and so forth. I also had to explain the importance of women for maintaining biodiversity because of their pivotal role in managing natural resources. In addition, women are usually among the first to notice the loss of valuable plant species, soil erosion due to logging of trees and the negative impact of pollution on flora, fauna and humans.

In terms of oceans and high seas, the loss of marine resources affected both men and women, but I had to explain how the division of labor by gender involved women in many artisanal fishing activities related to both fishing and the collection of shellfish on the shore. In addition, women play a vital role in post-harvest preservation and marketing of fish and other marine animals that provide a valuable source of protein for both rural and urban communities. As a result of these explanations in small working groups, all of the reservations on the inclusion of women were accepted and the negotiations proceeded smoothly after that.

Not all delegates questioned the mainstreaming of women in the work of conference. The skepticism came mainly from countries that tended to have reservations about promoting gender equality and the advancement of women. These countries are also inclined not to recognize the important role played by women in environmental preservation or the negative impact of environmental degradation on women. On the whole, many government delegates and United Nations officials welcomed gender mainstreaming and remarked that it was the first time that a major United Nations conference, not devoted to women alone or to population issues, had given women such a high profile. This was evident in the successful mainstreaming of gender throughout the preparatory meetings and in the documentation for the conference.

The United Nations Conference on Environment and Development (UNCED) was a landmark event and major breakthrough in mainstreaming women into the UN apparatus and provided a road mark for all other world conferences that followed. These included the Human Rights Conference of 1993 which declared 'women's rights as human rights.' I felt proud of being part of this ground breaking and pioneering effort to mainstream gender into the global agenda not only in all sectors of environment and development but in all other areas of policy development and coordination in the work of the United Nations. A real triumph for women!

Living in Geneva, Switzerland

Living and working in Geneva was a successful experience for a number of reasons. In the first place, there were several meetings in New York which I attended that allowed me to spend long weekends with my family, and I was entitled to family visits to Geneva that allowed me to see them for long periods every six months. In the second place, I had an opportunity to improve my French and spoke the language as much as possible, although it was difficult within the UN where everyone spoke English. Thirdly, Azania joined me in Geneva and spent two years attending Collège du Léman and later Webster University, an American/Swiss University where she earned her Bachelor's Degree and a Masters degrees.

Collège du Léman is a highly reputed international school that prepares students for an international high school diploma. Most of the students at the school were international students whose parents worked for the United Nations in Geneva or were in the diplomatic service of their countries. Others were from extremely rich families in Switzerland and other parts of the world who wanted their children to have a good international education. The curriculum was divided into a French stream and an English stream and all students had to learn both French and English to a high level. Azania earned an international baccalaureate and later a Master's Degree in International Business from Webster University.

All students had to also learn how to ski, as this is an important pastime among the Swiss and an essential recreational sport during the winter season. Azania thrived in the environment of Collège du Léman and Geneva and became fluent in French, with a working knowledge of Spanish, in addition to her fluency in English, her primary language. She also developed her love for music, took singing lessons and gave concerts as the lead singer of two bands. She achieved international acclaim when at the age of 21 she won the television singing competition called 'Graines des stars' on French television, viewed by millions. She continues to have strong ties with Geneva and is founder and CEO of Singer Elite Academy in addition to giving regular concerts, song writing and and serving as goodwill ambassador to 'All As One,' an orphanage in Freetown.

Duka, our son, also grew familiar with the Geneva scene since he and his father visited Azania and me several times when he was a student at Carnegie Mellon University in the United States. He was studying Theatre and his class presented several plays that the family made every attempt to attend. He played the lead in one of two of the plays and enjoyed the roles so much that we supported him in every way and knew that this was his calling. We met many of his friends at Carnegie Mellon University with whom he worked constantly to perfect their craft. Since childhood, Duka had a strong interest in the theatre and was a member of Children's Theatre in Madison, Wisconsin where he played leading roles in many of their productions.

He did very well in Van Hise Middle School and at West High School in Madison, Wisconsin. He attended the University of Wisconsin for two years and studied the sciences before transferring to Carnegie Mellon University to pursue a degree in theatre. He did very well at Carnegie Mellon and graduated with honors. After Carnegie Mellon he went to New York and appeared in several plays, including Amy's View on Broadway and Scapin and other plays off Broadway as well as several major roles in plays at regional theatres. He later got a Master of Science degree in Digital Imaging and Design in which he learnt skills with which he does a lot of film editing when he is not on stage. He has also acted in a number of television shows and movies, including a major role in 'Lorenzo's Oil' with Susan Sarandon and Nick Nolte. He got the part for the movie, which depicted a child with a rare neurological disease, while he was still a theatre student at Carnegie Mellon University.

As the headquarters of many United Nations Organizations, Geneva is also an international city. This is especially striking if one visits Berne, the capital of Switzerland, which is much less diverse. The kind of international landscape that Geneva presents is appealing to someone like me with an international background and a cosmopolitan outlook from an early age. It is also a city with a rich history and is itself made up of elements of three cultures, namely French, German and Italian. I learnt to appreciate Swiss culture through their cuisine and love for cheese, especially in the form of fondue.

The Swiss are also famous for their chocolates which are made in many chocolate factories, some of which I visited. The reputation of the Swiss for clock making is usually attributed to the famous Swiss cuckoo clock, but the exquisite workmanship of their watches, especially Rolex and Omega, is second to none. They are not as famous for their music as the Viennese, but they have beautiful folk songs and traditional dances, not to mention their long Alpenhorns, which are usually used for ceremonial occasions in Geneva. Their national attire is similar in some ways to that of the Viennese, especially in the German and French parts of Switzerland.

As the conference approached, it was renamed the 'Earth Summit' because heads of states would hold a summit two days earlier. There was a lot of excitement as well as anxiety at the secretariat. We knew that a number of areas of contention still in brackets in the draft document of Agenda 21 still had to be negotiated to arrive at consensus. These related to climate change, forests, oceans, toxic chemicals and hazardous wastes, biodiversity, population, consumption patterns and poverty. The controversial aspects of the negotiations were played out in polarizations between the Global North and the Global South due mainly to the global economic imbalance embodied in the debt crisis and propelled by the dominant neo-liberal development model. We wondered whether the final negotiations of the governments would be contentious and threaten the success of the Earth Summit and the adoption of Agenda 21 for which we had all worked so hard.

The Earth Summit in Rio, 1992

The conference was held in Rio de Janeiro, Brazil from June 3 to June 14 1992 and attended by 192 countries and 42,000 participants at the Non-Governmental Forum. It was presided over by the Secretary General of the Conference, Mr. Maurice Strong from Canada, and the president of the conference was Fernando Collor De Mello, President of Brazil. The UN managed to find funding for everyone in the UNCED secretariat to attend including all the administrative staff and secretaries.

There was concern about the slow pace of the work in Rio to get the premises ready for the conference. Eventually, all fears were allayed when the Brazilian government delivered a first rate venue and facilities for both the intergovernmental conference and the NGO Forum a few miles away from the official conference. There were many protests at the NGO Forum, some of them violent and targeting international financial institutions like the World Bank and the IMF and challenging the destructive impact of corporate globalization on the environment, primarily on countries of the Global South.

I was fortunate to attend the two days of the restricted Earth Summit held by 117 heads of state, thanks to the invitation of the Sierra Leone government. It was almost surreal to be in the midst of heads of states, seated in alphabetical order of their countries and listen to their five-minute policy statements. Behind me was President George H.W. Bush and his delegation and not far from him was President Museveni of Uganda, who stated that he came to make sure that no one tells him what to do with his forests. Seated in front of me was Norway, headed by Prime Minister Gro Harlem Brundtland and Prince Rainier of Monaco and his son Prince Albert. Further down towards the front was Fidel Castro, who gave a thunderous speech pointing the finger at the West for their avaricious appetite for the Earth's resources and blaming them for environmental destruction. I remember looking around and seeing all these heads of state and asking myself 'How did I get here?' It was mind blowing, and one of the memories that will stay with me forever.

The negotiations by governments at the main conference managed to arrive at general agreement by removing the remaining brackets from Agenda 21. This meant diluting the most contentious recommendations of Agenda 21 dealing with the imbalances in the global economy; the debt burden; sustainable utilization of forest resources; lowering carbon emissions to combat climate change; protecting biodiversity; promoting healthy and sustainable human settlement; combatting poverty; reducing consumption patterns and promoting sustainable population growth. In addition, The negotiations for a Convention on Climate Change and the Convention on Biodiversity were launched and advanced as were the general guidelines for discussions on Forest Principles to promote better and sustainable management of forest resources.

In the final plenary the delegates adopted 'Agenda 21: The Program of Action from Rio' and 'The Rio Declaration', which contained twenty-seven principles. These included the precautionary principle; women's vital role in environmental management, and the development and avoidance of warfare, an inherently destructive factor inhibiting sustainable development and peace. This was seen as a *sine qua non* for environmental protection and development . The Earth Summit was a success and had a record attendance of 192 nations, 2400 non-governmental organizations and 10,000 journalists. We in the UNCED secretariat celebrated loudly and felt proud of the hard work that we all did to make this historic conference a success for the United Nations; NGOs, humanity and planet Earth.

Some members of the secretariat stayed on for a few more months to work on the follow-up of the Earth Summit with other agencies within the United Nations system and NGOS. Many of us took time off to visit our families and I could not wait to get back to Madison to see Henry and the children, who had visited Geneva a few times and enjoyed my frequent home visits during my missions to New York. They were equally excited about the success of the Earth Summit and felt proud of the sacrifice we as a family made in allowing their mother and wife to take on this important assignment at the United Nations. They felt that nothing was more worthy than working on saving the planet while promoting gender equality and the advancement of women.

Returning to Madison

I looked forward to going back home to the family, who were particularly proud of my work and in some ways of continuing the work of our late son Chinaka, who was an avid environmentalist. I felt he was with me throughout my work for the Earth Summit. The family was also proud of my role in drafting chapter 24 of Agenda 21 on 'Global Action for Women Towards Sustainable and Equitable Development' with UN colleagues, government delegates and NGOs. I also published two monographs based on questionnaires sent out to governments to assess their plans and program for enhancing women's participation in environment and development projects and to evaluate the work of the United Nations in this regard. Upon my return to Madison in 1993, I took a long vacation with the family, did some short-term consultancy work with the United Nations and then started making plans to return to Academia.

Attending the UN Conference on Population and Development, 1994

In the meantime, I attended the United Nations Conference on Population and Development in Cairo, Egypt in 1994 as a Non-

Governmental Organization participant representing The Association of African Women for Research and Development (AAWORD.) I remember being driven from the airport to my hotel and given an informal tour of Cairo. When I expressed my admiration for the nice buildings, the driver informed me that those buildings did not represent the real Cairo and pointed to the areas with recently erected high walls to hide the slums from the view of the participants at the conference. So I realized the contradictions from the start and was not surprised as they were characteristic of many developing countries, especially in Africa.

As usual, the NGO parallel conference was dynamic, exciting and colorful and had a high presence of women NGOs promoting reproductive rights and the empowerment of women. Several from women's health care movements lobbied for greater control of women over their health care and their bodies and for women-centered and women-controlled health care services. There was concern about Muslim fundamentalists disrupting the conference, as they were strongly opposed to feminist aspirations and women's demands for greater autonomy and rights, especially control over their bodies.

Their presence at the conference was noticed but not obtrusive and did not really pose a threat. Some women were worried that the fundamentalists would target women for assassination, as this was not uncommon in some parts of the Muslim world of North Africa. Lesbian women from all over the world were well represented with an agenda for strongly advancing women's reproductive rights and sexual autonomy. Religious groups of all stripes were also active, particularly from Catholic and Muslim countries that are generally opposed to abortion. For Muslims, the idea of single motherhood was not accepted since according to the religion, conception should not occur outside of marriage. In addition, there was heavy lobbying against provisions for single mothers in the documents for negotiation. The Secretary General of the conference was Dr. Nafis Sadik from Pakistan.

Some of the delegates adopted the Malthusian view and were concerned about high rates of population increase leading to economic and social problems and to overcrowding, epidemics, immigration, environmental destruction, violence, wars and poverty. These tended to be from the Global North. Countries of the Global South argued that many of these problems are caused by the economic development models pursued by the Global North that destroy the economies of the Global South. They emphasized the fact that global economic policies are resulting in intractable debt burdens and underdevelopment and creating population pressures while displacing masses of people.

Others linked these policies to the vicious cycle of poverty, maternal mortality and high infant mortality resulting in high fertility rates in poor countries. Abortion was a major issue of contention as it was seen as a violation of religious beliefs and opposed by many countries where the dominant religions were Catholicism or Islam. The majority of the delegates agreed that more effective family planning methods should be developed and made widely available for both women and men so that abortion would become a last resort. Emphasis was also placed on accelerating research and development of male contraceptives and other technologies aimed at regulating male fertility.

Reproductive health and reproductive rights were center stage and received acrimonious debate. In addition, there was disagreement on family reunification as it relates to immigration. This was complicated by definitions of 'the family', which typically refers to the nuclear heterogeneous family according to Eurocentric traditions and not to the many and varied family forms found all over the world. Other objections included linking macro and micro levels of analysis that implicated The Global North for some of the unethical approaches to population control, such as sterilization without informed consent. Some delegates insisted on micro-level approaches limited to country level only and not to the international level of policy making where many of the economic imbalances and injustices that affect health, reproductive rights and so forth take place.

Negotiations around immigration in general were also contentious at times, with some delegates regarding immigration as part of the history of humanity and a basic human right, whilst others insisted on more immigration control. On the central issue of family planning most delegates were in general agreement on the importance of access to family planning aided by improving health for all and closing the gender gap in education. Despite these difficulties, the Program of Action was adopted by consensus, which was worth celebrating but agreements by consensus usually weaken the strength of some of the recommendations. The other challenge is the burden for countries of the Global South of implementation of this plan of action, in addition to numerous mandates and programs emanating from various United Nations conferences.

At the end of the conference many of us went on tours to the historical sites, visiting the Pyramids, the Sphinx, temples, palaces and so forth that are the treasures of Egypt. It was striking that many of the huge sculptures of pharaohs and other rulers had broken noses. As the story goes, Napoleon instigated some of the nose chopping campaigns during his visit to Egypt when he angrily asserted that negroes could never have ruled Egypt. One of the guides told us that this was intended to deny the racial characteristics of these rulers who had negroid features. This was an attempt to obliterate this fact of the history of ancient Egypt's Black rulers and the eminent Nubian civilization and presence in Egypt. Distinguished Senegalese archeologist Professor Cheik Anta Diop did extensive research and published volumes on African antiquity and documented the prevalence and contributions of the famous Nubians of Black African identity in Ancient Egypt.

CHAPTER 24

Fourth World Conference on Women 1995 – Beijing, China – Special Advisor to UNIDO (United Nations Industrial Development Organization)

"Women Hold Up Half the Sky"
Chinese saying credited to Mao Zedong

❖

Finalist – Secretary General, Fourth World Conference
on Women – Beijing

I was one of the short-listed candidates for the position of Secretary-General of The Fourth United Nations World Conference for Women. I felt proud of this nomination by my government of Sierra Leone and realized that it was an honor not only for me but for all women of Sierra Leone. Although I was not selected for this highly political position, I was glad that it went to an African woman, Mrs. Gertrude Mongella, a politician from Tanzania and also a strong advocate for women's rights. Tanzania has a special relationship with China as the country that led the campaign to admit China into the United Nations after twenty-one voting cycles in 1971. Her selection was therefore a politically strategic one for the two countries and gave a high profile to women of Africa, of which I was very proud.

The United Nations came calling again and this time it was the United Nations Industrial Development Organization (UNIDO) in Vienna, Austria. I was offered a position at the Director's level as Special Advisor on Women and Industrial Development for the Fourth United Nations Conference for Women to be held in Beijing in 1995. I was responsible for working with the team on gender mainstreaming in industrial development with particular attention to increasing women's educational opportunities and training in the fields of science, technology and industrial production; strengthening women entrepreneurs; expanding access to credit, technology and improving women's managerial and decision-making skills and opportunities. We were equally concerned that the integration of women in manufacturing should include provisions for their safety; good working conditions; entitlements to support their reproductive roles and child care responsibilities; career advancement opportunities and protection of their human rights, including their ability to unionize.

Work as Special Advisor to UNIDO

I was stationed in Vienna, Austria for about one year and had opportunities for missions to New York, which allowed me to see the family. It also provided attractive benefits like the other UN appointment, including university tuition for Azania.

I enjoyed being in Vienna again as it is one of my favorite European cities. This time I was a Special Advisor and worked with the team that was preparing for the Beijing conference. Our analyses were based on research done by UNIDO on women in manufacturing in global perspective; data from governments; data on industrial development; state of the art research by academics and 'grey literature' publications by NGOs. The trend showed women's participation increasing in some manufacturing industries including agro-industries; food processing; garment; leather and electronics, especially in those located in export-processing zones of countries in Latin America, Asia, Africa and the

Middle East. Despite these increases in women's participation, they were often relegated to the lower ranks of the manufacturing sector.

Studies also revealed poor and insanitary working conditions, particularly in labor-intensive industries that hire a lot of women, especially in electronics and export-processing establishments. The working hours are long with few breaks and there is a high vulnerability to industrial accidents and health hazards in cramped and poorly ventilated factories. Some agro-industries in the developing countries used pesticides that are dangerous to women and cause damage to their reproductive organs, resulting in infertility, spontaneous abortions and so forth. Many of these industries are owned by multinational corporations operated from industrialized countries in violation of the Conventions of the International Labor Organization (ILO) and the human rights of workers.

In the field of entrepreneurship, there was evidence that women were taking a more active role in this area, including ownership of their own businesses. Some of the obstacles inhibiting women entrepreneurs included their predominance in the precarious informal sector, which is often bereft of government recognition, support and protection and lacked access to resources. Women entrepreneurs in both the informal and formal sectors face constraints regarding access to credit, technology and competition from cheap manufactured goods that are being dumped in Africa, primarily from China.

I was part of the team that organized an Expert Group Meeting in preparation for the conference and invited academics, policy makers, female factory owners, managers, NGOs and women's activists. The participants presented papers on their research, case studies of women in industrial development and made first -hand presentations of their experiences in this sector. The meeting explored many of the obstacles facing women in industrial development, entrepreneurship and economic development in general. Some of the substantive discussions helped prepare the documentation and recommendations for removing obstacles and strengthening women's role and beneficial participation in industrial development and entrepreneurship.

Fourth World Conference on Women – Beijing

The Fourth World Conference on Women was held in Beijing, China from September 4-15th. It was attended by 189 countries and there were 17, 000 participants, including 6,000 governmental delegates and 4000 NGOs, at the official conference. We spent most of the time at the inter-governmental conference and with other colleagues in the United Nations System. The flight to Beijing was full of participants at the conference and government delegates and you could feel the excitement as passengers, mostly women, looked forward to a successful conference. Upon landing in Beijing, one could feel the weight of officialdom as we were processed through immigration and customs. We were met by our local counterparts from the United Nations who gave us information about China as the bus drove us to our hotel.

Beijing was an amazing experience and full of surprises. We had heard a lot of rumors about the reluctance of some Chinese people to hold the conference for fear that feminists were likely to strip suddenly as part of their campaign for equality. The police were therefore equipped with blankets to cover the naked women should this become necessary. One got the impression that there were spies everywhere, especially when going to our hotel rooms. The corridors were manned with personnel that checked every time we came in to make sure that the rooms we were entering were the correct ones. There were incidents where the press was harassed and their equipment and cameras seized. Foreigners who live in China on a regular basis were segregated and lived in separate 'walled' communities in Beijing, with their children attending international schools for the most part. The foreigners we spoke with that lived in Beijing working as diplomats and for international organizations gave the impression that the Chinese were very not very hospitable. They noted that they were very chauvinistic and suspicious of foreigners and very rarely mixed with them.

The conference started with the challenge since many of the

recommendations in the Platform for Action were still in brackets for further negotiation. During the preparatory committee meetings for the conference there were disagreements and tense negotiations on controversial issues, as is to be expected. These centered around the unequal rate of industrial development among countries; the perennial challenges in the unequal world economic system, such as the debt burden, Structural Adjustment Policies recycled as Highly Indebted Poor Countries (HIPC) initiatives and corporate globalization. Neo-liberal policies, propelled by the dominant economic model of market-driven privatization, liberalization and the establishment of a single global market have not worked. They have resulted in massive impoverishment of nations and people, especially women in The Global South.

Other contentious issues were largely cultural and appeals were made for respect and deference to cultural mores and values. Some of the points of disagreement included abortion, which was objected to by many countries where Catholicism is the dominant religion. Islamic countries also objected to abortion and single motherhood, since pregnancy outside of marriage is not accepted. Inheritance of women of property was also opposed by Islamic countries. The reason given is that women are likely to marry out and take the patrilineal property with them. The issue of quotas for women in government was not accepted by all countries as it was seen as a temporary measure that does not alter institutional norms and practices. Countries that objected to quotas for women argued that they already had laws that guaranteed women equality and that political positions should not be subject to quotas. In the final controversial plenary, the 'Beijing Declaration' and the 'Beijing Platform for Action' were adopted by consensus.

UNIDO's recommendations were considered in the negotiations and successfully integrated into some of the actions proposed for governments, the international community and NGOs in the Beijing Platform for Action (BPA.) Many of the areas of concern were of interest to the work at UNIDO and considered by the team as areas of action for UNIDO's work. These include women and poverty, education and training, women and health, women and the environment, and women and the economy. Most of the recommendations for action for UNIDO fell under 'Women and the Economy." The following are a few of the representations of UNIDO's contribution to the teamwork that I was proud to have been a part of:

- Adopt and implement laws against discrimination based on sex in the labor market, especially considering older women workers, hiring and promotion, the extension of employment benefits and social security, and working conditions; (BPA, 165, b.)

- Eliminate discriminatory practices by employers and take appropriate measures in consideration of women's reproductive role and functions, such as the denial of employment and dismissal due to pregnancy or breast-feeding, or requiring proof of contraceptive use, and take effective measures to ensure that pregnant women, women on maternity leave or women re-entering the labor market after childbearing are not discriminated against; (BPA, 165, c)

- Promote and support women's self-employment and the development of small enterprises, and strengthen women's access to credit and capital on appropriate terms equal to those of men through the scaling-up of institutions dedicated to promoting women's entrepreneurship, including, as appropriate, non-traditional and mutual credit schemes, as well as innovative linkages with financial institutions; (BPA,166, a)

- Promote gender equality through the promotion of women's studies and through the use of the results of studies and gender research in all fields, including the economic, scientific and technological fields; (BPA, 175, e)

A parallel NGO conference was held some distance away in Huairou, China and attended by 30,000 participants. Some of the conditions were strongly criticized as inadequate and poorly planned. Some women complained about the poor standard of the accommodation. Many of the rooms were ill equipped with unaccustomed furniture and arranged in dormitory-style formation with six or more women expected to share one large space. Some of the toilet facilities were also inadequate and not in keeping with those to which many women were accustomed. To make matters worse it rained heavily on some days, resulting in the collapse of some of the tents and general disarray and confusion. One positive aspect was the many regional tents representing every continent of the world which provided women with a space in which they could immediately feel welcome and participate in a number of activities that were planned to take place in these regional tents.

Shopping and sight seeing in Beijing

One of the best aspects of Beijing was shopping, a celebrated pastime for women. Women were seen everywhere, especially in the popular Silk Market and at several souvenir shops. After a few days, many women showed up at the conference wearing silk and at times it seemed like a parade of silk dresses and pant suits was the order of the day. Silk is relatively cheap and plentiful in China, so women were indulging their love for it, most of it being of very good quality. Other popular shopping items included Chinese fans, sculptures and carpets. We were surprised to visit one of the state of the art Western-style shopping malls, similar to those in the United States. We had never thought anything like that existed in China.

The ordinary people were generally polite but reserved, and the language barriers did not help. Very few Chinese speak English and many of the international women attending the conference hardly spoke even a few words of Chinese. The Chinese officials and administrative staff who worked with us for the conference were always politically correct according to Chinese perspectives and it was difficult to have any conversation that was critical of the one-child policy at that time, thanks to restrictions of the press or other limitations to people's freedoms. They often gave us the party line and denied that there was any repression in China but felt that too much freedom was also detrimental to a well-functioning society.

Whenever we took taxis, we had to have the receptionist at the hotel desk, who usually spoke a little English, write down our destination on one piece of paper and our hotel address and phone number on another in Chinese so that we would not get lost. After the conference there were many sight-seeing tours, the most popular of which were to the Walled city, Tiananmen Square, the Forbidden City, the Great Wall of China, ancient palaces, museums and the famous Panda House at Beijing Zoo.

CHAPTER 25

Wellesley College, Wellesley, Massachusetts – Professor and Chair, Africana Studies Department

"To provide an excellent liberal arts education for women who will make a difference in the world." – Mission of Wellesley College.

❖

Wellesley College

In 1996, after Beijing, I returned to Madison to the loving arms of my family, who I had seen during my visits to the United States on United Nations missions and leave. I was at the University of Wisconsin for a year as an independent researcher working on a number of research projects that I had suspended during my time at the United Nations. I wanted to get back to academia and had applied to Wellesley College in Wellesley, Massachusetts, since we had enjoyed living in New England. The following year I received a call from Wellesley College inviting me to an interview for a faculty position in Africana Studies. I felt comfortable during the interview as the campus reminded me of Smith College, my Alma Mater. The faculty, students and Deans displayed the utmost hospitality towards me and made me feel that I would be a good fit at Wellesley. I was offered the job of full professor of Africana Studies.

Wellesley College is a prestigious Liberal Arts women's college in Wellesley, Massachusetts. It was founded in 1870 by Henry and Pauline Durant, who wanted to promote higher education for women. It is one of the few colleges in the United States that was founded exclusively for women. In keeping with the evolution of thinking about gender identity, the college clarified its admission policy in 2015 and "will consider any applicant who lives as a woman and consistently identifies as a woman." Unlike my Alma Mater Smith College, which has had male presidents for years and had one while I was there, Wellesley College has always had female presidents.

As one of the oldest highly-reputed Seven Sisters Colleges, Wellesley College has an impressive roster of distinguished alumnae, including Hillary Clinton and Madeleine Albright, both of whom became Secretaries of State of the United States, and Madame Chiang Kai-shek, formerly Mayling Soong, the former First Lady of the Republic of China. The college has a magnificent campus in the town of Wellesley, with beautiful lawns and trees and a sparkling pond. The architecture represents a mixture of Gothic styles in the original Founders Building and a warehouse -style, unfinished-looking modern science building with metal spikes at the top. The majority of the students live in dormitories that also reflect various architectural styles. Junior faculty members tend to be the majority of faculty that live in college houses and apartments on the campus. The President and her family also live on campus in a large white house suitable for receptions that have become a part of the Wellesley tradition. The college has been fortunate to have three distinguished women as presidents while I was there, namely Dr. Diana Chapman Walsh, Dr. Kim Bottomley and Dr. Paula Johnson. The current one, Dr. Paula Johnson, is the fourteenth president of the college and the first Black president. Since 1916, she has been providing outstanding leadership and promoting inclusive excellence at all levels of the college. Prior to Wellesley, she was a renowned Harvard-trained cardiologist and former professor of medicine in Women's Health at Harvard Medical

School. A recipient of many awards of distinctions, Dr. Paula Johnson is one of the most popular presidents of Wellesley College.

Africana Studies and challenges

Like most of the faculty of the college, those in the Africana Studies department have distinguished academic reputations at national and international levels with strong publication and teaching records. Some are award winners for their research and publications and provide valuable service to the college and the wider Boston area community and the Academy at large. After a year of teaching, I was asked to chair the department and ended up doing it for most of my tenure at the college until my retirement in 2019.

Despite the strong academic reputation of the Africana Studies faculty, Wellesley was a challenge from the start. The atmosphere in the department was tense as I realized that rifts which at first seemed superficial ran deep. I was warned of a major controversy between one of the faculty members of the department and the Jewish community at Wellesley. Since my work has been mainly on women and to some extent on Black women and the African Diaspora, I had very little experience of the tensions between Jews and Blacks. I thought that since both had been subjected to oppression, they would be natural allies, so this controversy came as a bit of a surprise to me. I did not realize that victimization could become competitive.

Growing up in Africa, my earliest experience of the Jews was in the Old Testament, which was popular in my Anglican denomination. In fact, some Krios identified with the Jews in terms of being a minority, having a common but qualitatively different history and experience of enslavement and also being subjects of discrimination. I had stayed with Henry's wonderful Jewish host family while at Yale.

Most of the devastating events that surrounded the department occurred before I was hired. From the prevailing accounts, the problem began when Professor A, a historian and Professor of Africana Studies, used some texts in his class on slavery that were written by

Jewish authors. These books made reference to the role of the Jews in the transatlantic slave trade. When I heard of this at first, I recall my history professor confirming that almost everyone was involved in the slave trade as a major economic activity at the time.

Apparently this was seen as an act of anti-Semitism by some members of the college and a major campaign was launched which, according to those present and supporting Professor A at the time, demonized the professor. According to reports some of his opponents even lobbied unsuccessfully for his tenure to be revoked. Since Professor A was one of the most popular professors at Wellesley, many Black students, faculty and staff and even some Whites rallied in his favor and condemned the attacks, which they viewed as unjust and racist. As I understand it, the matter soon spilled outside of Wellesley and out of control and into the public arena. According to some members of the Wellesley community, the controversy was covered in the press, putting the professor, the department and the college in a somewhat embarrassing and scandalous position.

The pressure on Professor A, a leading scholar on Marcus Garvey, Race, The Caribbean and The African Diaspora was overwhelming and from all accounts would have destroyed someone less resilient. It was generally believed in the Black community at Wellesley that the whole controversy and attack left an indelible mark on the professor's health and well-being. According to Professor A, his biggest disappointment was when people in positions of power at the College automatically sided with his accusers instead of asking for his point of view and protecting his rights and academic freedom. Another blow came when, according to him, the chair of his department at the time spoke out denouncing him in Academic Council, the legislative body of the college which is made up of faculty and administrators. In his view, this was a betrayal that affected him profoundly. In his state of anguish with a sense of victimization by some members of the Jewish community at the college, he published a very angry and combative book in his defense and apparently took legal action against the college.

When I joined the department, it was deeply divided and I was immediately bombarded by negative information about Professor A by the faction that did not support him. I decided to keep an open mind because in my view, no one could be that bad and without any redeeming qualities. I noticed that he was ostracized and anxious and hesitant to come to the department. When I became chair of the department, I tried to ensure that his rights as a senior member of the department were restored as long as he was still a faculty member at the College. This was not going to be easy, but I knew that I had the strength, based on my background and experience, to do what I felt was the right thing.

I saw him suffering and compromising his strength, health and intellect to fight what I considered to be a fight that had run its course. What I saw was a quiet and brilliant man who loved his Black people and wanted their true history to be told, no matter how ugly, horrific and uncomfortable that may be for some people. As a historian, he also appreciated that human beings were not perfect and were equally capable of goodness as well as malevolence, without exception. For him, the horrific history of the transatlantic slave trade and its racial terror reveals involvement of almost everyone, especially Europeans, in a prevailing economic system, regardless of religious affiliation and denomination.

During my tenure at Wellesley College, I never came across anyone in Africana Studies who was anti-Semitic in my view. Everyone abhorred the brutal tragedy of the Holocaust. No one ever spoke negatively about Jews as a people and all valued the relationship that had been forged between the African-Americans and the Jews as allies during the Civil Rights Movement from the 1960s on. In addition, Jews were an important part of Wellesley College and were not by any stretch of the imagination seen as a group that was experiencing discrimination and marginalization. On the contrary, both Jewish students and professors seemed to be thriving at Wellesley and always had been. There was a large number of highly reputable Jewish professors, with many holding endowed chairs and wielding considerable influence in the governing process of the college. A major Jewish organization on campus called 'Hillel' provided a safe space for Jews and had considerable influence on campus.

I believe that this whole affair and accusation of a professor in Africana Studies of anti-Semitism was an unfortunate event and wish it could have been avoided. A Visiting Committee, made up of faculty from other institutions, had been invited to evaluate the department and make recommendations along several lines in 1996. This is routinely done at Wellesley every five to ten years. One of recommendations of the Visiting Committee was to restore harmony in a divided department resulting from this unfortunate event. Another recommendation was to facilitate the rehabilitation of Professor A, who had been a professor in the department since 1973 and had helped develop its curriculum and research agenda. I decided that as chair I would take on the task of restoring his constitutional rights as a senior member of the department, regardless of the opposition that I was bound to face from some members of the department. Slowly, but surely, Professor A started coming to the department more often with a pleasant smile on his face and participating in committee meetings and in the activities of the department. The students felt relieved, as he was one of the most beloved professors and they felt he had been wrongly and unjustly treated.

During the rest of his tenure at Wellesley he enjoyed relative peace and worked on a number of research projects, including finalizing book projects for publication. The controversy surfaced again after his retirement party in 2007, when a student wrote a laudable article in the students newspaper *Wellesley News* about his sterling career at Wellesley and his outstanding contribution to the education of students. This did not sit well with a handful of faculty members who denounced the article for failing to refer to the old controversy during which he was accused of anti-Semitism. The students of the department were unhappy about the attack, which was mostly in the form of acrimonious on-line postings by faculty and students on a college forum. They felt that it distracted from what was a popular and magnificent retirement celebration of his career and not related to the controversy which happened many years *before* they came to Wellesley College. Some had never even heard about the controversy.

Things eventually died down and Professor A marched in the Convocation procession with other faculty for the first time in many years, watched with pride by his wife and their young son. I had never seen him look happier and I knew he was ready to put Wellesley behind him and enjoy his retirement and his family. He wrote a long-planned book titled *Caribbean History: From Pre-Colonial Origins to the Present*, published in 2012. Unfortunately, after a short illness, he died in 2013 in his home town of Port of Spain, Trinidad. He was mourned by his many adorable fans of students, some of whom attended his funeral in Trinidad. His contributions to the history of Africana people, the study of the transatlantic slave trade, the study of race and Marcus Garvey and his love for Black people will live on and be always celebrated. May his soul continue to rest in peace!

Chairing the Department

Other aspects of chairing the department were also challenging, mainly because most of the tenured faculty at the rank of full professor had been men, a couple of whom had sexist proclivities. The department had also been chaired mainly by men since it was established in 1972. The only female chair did not complete her term because of what she described as deep-seated obstructions and confrontations from the male members of the department, motivated by what she perceived as misogynistic proclivities. I experienced some of the misogynistic culture of the department myself and had to fend off a series of attacks by one senior male faculty member in particular. Although it was tiring, I finally stopped reading insulting memos from him, copied to the Dean, and opened a special file for his emails labelled 'Professor Nuisance.' I also realized that this was a form of bullying and remembered the words of my father who often said, 'a bully is really a coward at heart' and decided to ignore him. I continued my work of chairing the department without many interruptions once I made that decision.

Chairing requires managerial and administrative work, in addition to attending meetings at all levels of the college. It is time consuming, but there was no one else who could do the job for our department at that time. One previous chair resigned before the end of her term and another was removed from the chair by the administration because of complaints of discrimination by a junior faculty member. It took a lot out of me, but I decided to do it for the sake of the department. The department had an administrative assistant, Arleen Lavene, who had been at Wellesley for several years and knew the job and coordinated well with the other units of the college. When she retired, we had problems finding a replacement for her and had to go through three others who were not efficient. We finally recruited Lizette Rodriguez Ponce, who had excellent administrative and interpersonal skills and was very popular with the faculty and students.

Founded in 1972, Africana Studies at Wellesley is described as follows:

> "...an interdisciplinary and transnational program of study of the experience and intellectual traditions of Black people the world over. Its mission is to acquaint students with a critical perspective on the Africana World that is found primarily in Africa, the United States, the Caribbean and South America and also among peoples of African descent in Asia and Europe. Grounded in the history, literature, culture, religion, and philosophy of Africana peoples, Africana Studies not only promotes knowledge of the contribution of Africana people to the world but also develops a critical perspective to examine the Africana experience, and cultivate a respect for the multiracial and multicultural character of our common world humanity."

Africana Studies has its genesis in the Civil Rights Movement the

Decolonization Movements and the Anti-Apartheid Movement. In the United States, many of these programs and departments were founded soon after the assassination of the Reverend Martin Luther King, Jr. on April 4, 1968. They were also a result of the resistance to the domination of Eurocentric systems of thought and knowledge in the canon of the Academy. This resulted in the negative representations of people of the Africana world and a devaluation and marginalization of their history, culture and contribution to knowledge production and world civilization. One of the objectives of Africana Studies is to critically appraise, deconstruct and revise systems of thought and knowledge production and to promote a more inclusive approach to learning. It is inherently multidisciplinary and operates at different levels of research and analyses, including areas that have been submerged and marginalized by the dominant paradigms. It belongs to the critical tradition and its methodology is multi-dimensional and centralizes on inter-subjectivity, authenticity, oral traditions, story-telling, testimonies, life histories and experiential approaches. Over the years, the faculty in Africana Studies has covered areas of teaching and research that have included history, literature, sociology, social anthropology, psychology, women's studies, government, economics, religion and Swahili.

Our courses attract students from a wide array of major fields as well as class levels. The enrollment in our classes is ethnically diverse and the majority of the students are White, whereas the majority of the majors are Black. Over the years the number of Asian and Latin American students taking our courses and majoring in Africana Studies has been increasing. International students are also attracted to our courses which include the fields of history, literature, religion, anthropology, sociology, philosophy, political science, psychology, women's studies, art and music. Some of these courses are cross-listed and taught by other departments which served to enrich our curriculum and build collaborative relationships with several departments. This is not unusual in institutions of higher education which show a trend towards more inter-disciplinary focus and collaboration.

Racism and sexism in academia

Academia is a microcosm of society, and is equally replete with institutional racism and sexism. I sometime marvel at the tremendous courage of African-Americans to have withstood the evils of slavery, Jim Crow laws, overt and covert segregation and institutional racism. They deserve a medal for resilience!! Not having grown up with this kind of racism, I had to find ways to deal with it. In general, interaction with White males, especially a few of those of middle or older years, tended to lead to conversations that evoked some form of subtle or overt racist remark, the longer the conversation lasted. As a result, I would end the conversation abruptly and move away. I grew tired of educating people who had biased and myopic points of view. With many White women, it was not always so predictable and conversations were a bit easier to conduct.

Direct racism is becoming rare, but it has not been eliminated and has assumed various labels such as 'micro aggression' and 'unconscious bias.' I am still skeptical about these new ways of disguising racism. Racism is racism. Another disturbing development is the possible misinterpretation of the theory of 'stereotype threat' put forward by Claude Steele. It runs the risk of Blacks, as well as marginalized groups, internalizing negative stereotypes about their group because it ignores the history of black resistance and the courageous struggle of Blacks and other marginalized groups against racism and stereotyping.

Regardless of the various indirect and subtle impacts of racism, one of the most extreme forms of overt racism took place in recent times and was witnessed by millions. The torture and murder of Mr. George Floyd on May 25th 2020 was watched on television by people all over the world. This Black man was tortured to death by Derek Chauvin, a White police officer by kneeling on his neck for more than nine minutes, despite his plea for his life. The global reaction against this evil act gave me some hope that racism could become abhorrent not only to Blacks but to the whole world. I remember thinking at the time, "maybe we shall still overcome someday after all."

Sexism is another challenge that mirrors the larger society in academia. Having spent a substantial amount of my career fighting for women' s equality and promoting feminist goals, Wellesley did not seem like a feminist institution to me for many of the years I was there, although many of our male colleagues had developed some consciousness about the odious nature of sexism and exhibited good collegial decorum. Nonetheless, some male faculty seemed to be in charge and would throw their weight around. Some tended to dominate the discussions in Academic Council. A few of them had an air of superiority and tended to trivialize women.

Although Wellesley is a women's college, it is by no means a feminist college nor did it reflect a feminist-centered environment for many of the earlier years that I taught there. I remember asking some of my colleagues the following question after a year at the college: 'Who really has power at Wellesley?' The reply was: 'A group of White men who tell the female president what to do.' It was also widely rumored in my earlier years there that some of the women in top leadership positions at the college did not believe that sexism was a problem at Wellesley, which enraged some of the female faculty devoted to teaching courses on women and gender issues. This was reinforced by a survey of 'faculty satisfaction' conducted by a Committee on Minority Recruitment, Hiring and Retention (MRHR) which found that the most satisfied faculty members at Wellesley, a women' s college, were White men. That says a lot!

When I first joined the college, there were slightly more male faculty than female faculty, but over the years, female faculty have increased significantly and now constitute the majority, although men outnumber them at the rank of tenured and tenure-track faculty. It was also discovered that male faculty on the whole earned more than female faculty. A sub-committee was appointed to look into this discrepancy, but I do not know if anything came of it. Further evidence of probable sexism is the belief that men are much more adept at negotiating for higher salaries by using the threat of leaving due to competition from other institutions that are offering them higher salaries. It is also believed that men are better at bolstering their credentials with lots of details to enhance their profile during a time of recruitment and promotion.

I served on a number of committees that are part of a governing process that has to be ratified by the voting rules of Academic Council. It is made up of the President, Provost and other administrators, the faculty and students' representatives. When I first started teaching at Wellesley, the committees appeared to be controlled by the male faculty, who seemed to have a lot of clout. Over the years, this changed as more women were hired and served on committees as members and chairs of committees.

In my personal interactions with male faculty at the institutions in which I taught, I had my share of male chauvinistic obstructions and attempted bullying in my department and on one college committee in particular that is charged with the task of faculty appointments and tenure. In some cases the sexism was mixed with racism of the subtle type, designed to keep a woman, especially a Black woman, in her place, whatever that perceived place is. I prevailed in all the bullying and used my African feminist strength to overcome these difficulties. One of the reasons for sexism stems from the culture of gentility in some academic institutions. This tends to prevent women from speaking out on controversial issues for fear of being regarded as 'difficult,' 'trouble makers' or even 'crazy.' In my experience, most liberal arts Institutions tend to be conflict averse, and Wellesley was no exception.

Being a women's college with a substantial number of male faculty, the problem of sexual harassment was bound to surface from time to time. Like other institutions, Wellesley has had its share of rumors of relations between male faculty and female students but on the whole, formal sexual harassment accusations are uncommon. As a global and African feminist, I am strongly opposed to sexual harassment and adhere to a zero tolerance policy for such odious behavior. Unfortunately, I was informed by students of differential treatment of male professors who had been formally or informally accused of sexual harassment. According to them, professors were more likely to get away with it than others, based on their ethnic or gender affiliations. The college has a title IX official dealing with matters relating to sexual harassment and discrimination and is supposed to apply the rules equally and fairly to all faculty. The Wellesley Community that I know has always prided itself in its policy of fairness and justice regardless of race, gender and other socially-constructed differences, even if the goals may be difficult to achieve and the reality may sometimes be different and elusive.

Dealing with institutional conflicts: drawing on UN experience

Having worked in a highly charged political environment like the United Nations and witnessed a lot of backstabbing behavior, I was more than ready to handle the politics of Academia which seemed like 'child's play' compared to United Nations politics. The problem of racism was always discussed throughout the time I was at Wellesley and several studies were conducted as well as special commissions and task forces set up to look at the problem. One study on 'Racism at Wellesley' examined the problem and identified the elitist White culture, which includes White women as one of the mechanisms that perpetuates racism at the college. Wellesley's culture is one of political correctness on the surface but can have a number of turbulent undercurrents since most faculty, especially female faculty, tend to avoid controversy. As a result, most problems get talked over *ad nau*seum in successive committees and this process is itself seen as a solution, regardless of whether or not the recommendations are implemented and enforced.

Being in a predominantly White community, the town of Wellesley, added other challenges to faculty and students of color at the college. There were constant reports of Blacks being followed and watched in the stores on the assumption that they would steal something. Hispanic and Black students complained of lack of hairdressers that catered to minorities and Black children in the school system faced challenges of racism. Since very few Blacks lived in the town of Wellesley there were reports of incidents of police harassment, including a case involving a sports celebrity who was arrested because of mistaken identity several years ago.

I was fortunate to co-chair the Black Task Force at Wellesley College for many years. It comprises Black faculty and staff and provides a voice and platform for activism against racism and discrimination on the campus. It was founded in 1970 to advocate for the rights and security of Black faculty and staff and to ensure Black representation on committees of the Academic Council. This was two years after the assassination of the Reverend Dr. Martin Luther King, Jr., which inspired Black activism in academia and in society at large. The nationwide protests and demonstrations by students and faculty were aimed at critiquing, deconstructing and revising the dominant Eurocentric curriculum and including critical analysis of the history, culture and experiences of Black people in the Africana World. This was bolstered by the decolonization movements, leading to the independence of many African countries. The anti-apartheid struggle waged in South Africa and all over the world added fuel to the global fight against racism, Eurocentric hegemony and White supremacy.

Despite challenges, the positive aspects of Wellesley College today far outweigh its negative features. It offers a pleasant and supportive working environment for faculty, with competitive salaries and benefits. Its academic programs strive to maintain high standards of excellence and it demands much of its faculty, many of whom are distinguished in their fields, both nationally and internationally. The students are bright and motivated and most of them welcome the challenge of a rigorous academic program, even though they may complain of the heavy workload at times. The curriculum is rich and expanding, with increasing emphasis on global education, greater achievements in STEM courses, multi-disciplinary approaches and experiential learning. There has been increasing collaboration among departments and a growing emphasis in distance learning and on-line courses, even before the advent of the COVID-19 pandemic. The education is rounded by participation in many active students organizations as well as in a variety of sporting activities, including competition with other institutions of higher education.

CHAPTER 26

Teaching and Research at Wellesley College

"I cannot teach anybody anything, I can only make them think."
Socrates

❖

Teaching philosophy and approach

Being a professor occupied much of my professional life and deserves full attention in my autobiography. Teaching was a joy at Wellesley, despite the administrative and departmental challenges. Wellesley students are special, bright and energetic with a strong commitment to social justice in general. The workload for students was heavy and demanding, but they found time to concentrate and produce work of a high quality. They also participated in students' organizations and have their own student government. Although there is a fairly recent three- college collaboration with Babson College and Olin College (BOW) which are co-educational institutions, Wellesley has historically been a predominantly women's college. Students also take courses at neighboring Brandeis University and Massachusetts Institute of Technology (MIT).

I taught a total of nine courses at Wellesley; three on Africa, two on women, two on urbanization, one on medical anthropology and one on environmental justice. My courses attracted a wide variety of students. The three most popular courses were 'Societies and Cultures of Africa;' 'Medical Anthropolgy: Comparative Healing Systems' and 'Environmental Justice.' According to my students, the courses offered something different from the mainstream academic curriculum because they reflected a wider world view, a representational presence of the knowledge and experiences of a female professor from Africa. The African Diaspora and Africa, especially African women, were pivotal subjects at the center of the discourse. Some of the courses explored why racial ideologies are usually expressed and presented in hierarchical formations, with the Black woman often at the bottom of the hierarchy. This enabled us to appreciate how one form of discrimination, such as race, not only intersects with gender, economic status, nationality, religion and so forth but also reinforces these differences.

In my course on Environmental Justice, I focus on ways that bring people, especially people of African descent, into the narrative of how the environment intersects with social inequality. By using this approach, the environment is understood as a resource that is exploited primarily by those in power for the benefit of the rich and powerful. However, the burdens of such exploitation, such as pollution and toxicity, are often borne by the poor, disenfranchised and people of color, especially women. As the commons and public lands become enclosed and privatized and are no longer open to all, some groups benefits from the beauty and bounty of the outdoors more than others, based on their socio-economic status and other socially-constructed differences, such as race, gender, class and so forth. The course also examines how the impact of climate change disproportionately impacts on people in Africa in terms of coastal erosion due to sea level rise, deforestation, desertification and dumping of hazardous waste and e-waste in Africa. Africans in the Diaspora also tend to be more affected by floods, such as the case of Katrina and other environmental disasters due to Climate Change.

My teaching philosophy has been expanding to meet the challenges of post-modern and post-colonial discourses as well as the need to appreciate the phenomenological and epistemological challenges of the social sciences in general. I am particularly interested in discourses that challenge the very process of knowledge production that has been heavily Eurocentric and prone to drown out all other discourses. Fortunately, the heroic efforts of scholars of Black studies, Africana studies and the critical theory tradition, especially critical race theory, continue to challenge dominant paradigms and their internal contradictions that overtly and covertly sanction domination and racist ideologies.

In my anthology *The Black Woman Cross-Culturally*, first published in 1981, I considered White women as conscious and unconscious partners and beneficiaries in a system of domination responsible for the transatlantic slave trade, colonialism, economic domination and institutional racism. Western feminist discourses have arisen within the context of the dominant Eurocentric discourses for the most part and therefore lack the emancipatory power for liberating women from engendered hierarchies of power. In this book, I introduced the concept of 'African feminism' for the first time and later elaborated the concept to 'African Feminism as Humanistic Feminism.' I also considered the African woman as the original feminists, those who were among the first humans destined to challenge forces of oppression and domination.

The results of research collaborations and projects with women researchers from Africa and the Global South in general provided rich and exciting teaching material for my courses. I always enjoy the stimulating atmosphere in my classrooms and value the wide range of pedagogical tools that I employ to convey and debate theoretical and empirical data. I find most of the students to be bright, motivated and hardworking. Teaching undergraduate students at Wellesley was a challenge at first because I was used to teaching both graduate and undergraduate students at my previous institutions. Although Wellesley students are very bright and some of them write theses that could pass for Masters theses, they are mostly teenagers or in their early twenties and do not have the life experiences and general knowledge that graduate students can bring to a class discussion.

I often assume that Wellesley students are conversant with the material and have the necessary skills for in-depth, complex and analytical analyses. As a result I tend to start my courses with the presumption that there is a general understanding of the fundamental issues and state of the art literature in the field. After a couple of weeks I would have to roll back my lectures to a more accessible level. Davis scholars, who are usually older students who return to complete their degrees and have benefited from some additional life experiences, usually add more depth to the discussions. Nonetheless, regardless of their age, experience and class level, Wellesley students are special in many ways and often rise to the challenge. They are curious, highly motivated, ambitious and generally have a social justice approach to their learning and plans for a future career. With very few notable exceptions, they are extremely empathetic and are a joy to teach.

Pedagogy and courses

My pedagogical style is multi-disciplinary and interactive with an emphasis on critical thinking. Most students appreciate this approach, but a few find it difficult at times, especially when they have not read the material and come to class unprepared to discuss the assignment. The critical thinking approach can present a challenge to some students and an opportunity to others. Some are uncomfortable if they are not used to critiquing dominant paradigms, especially neo-liberal or Eurocentric interpretations. For example, some are uneasy about any critique of science or about presentations of science from a multi-cultural perspective, rooted in cultural systems that also have their own scientific traditions. It is also difficult to get some students to appreciate that science is a commodity and subject to differential access based on class, race, ethnicity and so forth.

That being said, most students are open-minded and eager to learn about alternative ways of knowing, thinking and viewing the world. I try to point out the importance of appreciating the foundational texts in the field even if they are considered to be dated by the younger age group. With the internet and the immediacy of information, students tend not to appreciate texts that were written many years ago. They believe in the here and now and seek instant gratification. The world is changing so fast that social media have assumed a more exigent significance in their lives than books written many years ago. As some would often say: "I was not even born when these books were written." This reflects a cultural challenge that needs to be addressed so that students will appreciate the foundational and genealogical platforms and architecture upon which new knowledge is constantly being evaluated, critiqued, revised and built.

Our 300 level courses are among the highest level of courses offered at Wellesley. They are often taught in a seminar format with emphasis on discussion and interaction. Over the years, I have noticed a change in the expectation of students taking my 300 level courses. Some tend to have a lower expectation of a 300-level requirement now than in the past. For an example, a term paper of 25 pages or more used to be assigned in previous years. Now students expect term paper to be no more than 12 pages long and often want to know the spacing, font size and whether footnotes and references are included in the total number of pages required. I have also observed that students are not keeping up with the reading as much as they used to and sometimes complain about having too much of it. This is, however, not unique to Wellesley and is a generational change and a sign of the times.

I cannot help but think that this change in expectation of assignments has something to do with the influence of the Internet on education. As mentioned earlier, social media and Internet browsing are the norm. Students spend an inordinate amount of time on line and on social media platforms than before, leading to a deficit in the time spent on coursework and homework assignments. The faculty discuss these changes intermittently, but there is no widespread college policy to address this. It is up to each professor to set his or her own rules, since each course has different requirements and is taught independently. In my courses I have strongly discouraged the use of personal laptops during class for anything other than note taking and imposed a penalty of loss of points for internet browsing, chatting or visiting Social Media sites during class. Another fairly recent problem is the reluctance of students to purchase the required texts for the class. This is apparently not a compulsory part of the budget for college, as it was when I was a student. In addition, a number of students have figured out ways of accessing the texts on line and then informing the rest of the class. As a result, the bookstore usually has many unsold books on the shelves.

I combine lecturing, discussions, students' presentations, guest speakers, the use of audio-visual material and field trips in my courses. I emphasize the importance of contextualizing the discussion and of recognizing a variety of viewpoints and interpretations. I introduce the material gradually, using that with which they can easily identify first. My interactive approach includes students' participation in the form of teams and as well as individual presentations and discussions and videos are used for added visual impact. This is important, since most of our courses have a geographical context with which students are unfamiliar. I also encourage field research in communities around the Boston area.

At times, I use role playing and debates through which students takes sides that they would not ordinarily support. In some instances, I allow them to critique each other's presentations and viewpoints from opposite positions. I have also found it useful to have them develop questions for the class as a group. This way, students who are shy and do not like to speak in class can get support from the group. In my courses on Africa I try to enlighten students about the contributions of Black Africa to ancient and modern civilizations and the special place of the continent of Africa as the origin of humankind and human cultures. The UNESCO video series on African history by Zeinab Badawi, viewed and told by Africans past and present, is a favorite. Students appreciate critical analyses that show the political and economic factors contributing to the continuing racialization of certain groups and the denial of the contributions of some groups to human cultures and civilizations.

In my 300-level course 'Urban Development and the Underclass' it was necessary to emphasize the importance of the major texts in the field of urbanization and the foundational theories that undergird this line of enquiry. In this regard, I used the work of the Chicago School of Sociology, mostly of White scholars and the Atlanta School of Sociology, mostly of African-American scholars. The students appreciate this comparison and felt the Chicago School should not have had a preeminent position in the field of urban studies compared to the Atlanta School of Sociology and quickly realized the political imbalances endemic even in academia and in the academic publishing industry.

The seminar examines the factors that lead to urban development, primarily in the United States, and the creation of what has been termed 'the underclass.' It looks at processes and policies that contribute to an urban 'underclass' such as the history of urban migration by various ethnic groups, residential segregation, economic restructuring and suburbanization. The underclass often includes people who are chronically poor, chronically unemployed, isolated, experience extreme racial discrimination, live in Black areas of concentrated poverty and tend to experience inescapable years of inter-generational poverty. The very term 'the underclass' first used by Aluetta is interrogated in the course as well as notions of a 'culture of poverty' put forward by Oscar Lewis and 'The declining significance of race' advanced by William J Wilson.

A critical and revisionist approach is used to challenge assumptions about urban poverty by also studying the suburbanization of poverty since the beginning of the 21st century. Although suburbs have traditionally been associated with affluence, many studies are showing that suburbia now has the largest and fastest-growing population of poor people in the United States. Also studied is the rising Black middle class to restore some balance to the automatic assumption that

Black people are overwhelmingly poor. Although the Black middle class has existed in urban areas for some time, their lives are often precarious, since unlike the White middle class, their status is not likely to be upheld by inherited wealth.

In addition, we examine social conditions propelled by waves of economic recession, especially in the new millennium, that are triggering a serious housing crisis and an epidemic of foreclosures and potential homelessness. Other topics covered include the role of race and class in urban development, gendered dimensions of the underclass, family structure, social problems related to gangs, violence and homelessness, and challenges of immigration, gentrification and problems of environmental injustice. Comparative insights are drawn from Brazil and South Africa, which have similar demographic arrangements and problems of racial and economic discrimination and structural adversity.

The texts and articles used include: *American Apartheid: Segregation and the Making of the Underclass* by D. Massey and N. Denton; *There Goes the Neighborhood: Racial, Ethnic and Class Tensions in Four Chicago Neighborhoods* by W.J Wilson and R.Taub; *The Immigration Debate: Remaking America* by J. Isbister and *Confronting Suburban Poverty in America* by E. Kneebone and A. Berube; *Tell Them Who I Am: The Lives of Homeless Women* by E. Liebow and *Youth Gangs in American Society* by R. Sheldon and others.

My seminar on 'Societies and Cultures of Africa' attracts students from all disciplines and class levels and resonates well with all students, especially African students and students from the African Diaspora. It provides an opportunity to explore the richness, diversity and complexity of African societies and cultures while appreciating its unique and unifying features. The significance of pre-colonial Africa; the trans-Atlantic Slave Trade and colonial history are important in understanding the contemporary events and challenges facing the continent. Africa's problems are examined as well as the political and economic significance of Africa in the modern world.

Topics discussed include the centrality of Africa's enormous natural resources in explaining its history of extraction and exploitation primarily by European colonial rulers; the resistance of Africa to foreign domination; the resilience of Africa's forms of social organization; the relevance of kinship and marriage systems; the centrality of religion; the impact of globalization; African priorities in the 21st century; the position of women; China's role in Africa; environmental challenges; political transformation; corporate globalization; and armed conflicts. Some of the books used include Fanon's *The Wretched of the Earth*; Mbiti's *African Religions and Philosophy,* Moyo's *Dead Aid,* Rodney's *How Europe Underdeveloped Africa,* Martin and O'Meara's *Africa,* Fourth Edition and Steady's *The Black Woman Cross-Culturally,* Third Edition.

My 'Medical Anthropology: Comparative Healing Systems' course is one of the most popular courses at Wellesley. It is taken by a wide array of students but tends to attract pre-med students and those desiring a career in the healthcare field. The course examines healing systems that attempt to treat the whole person as a physical, social and spiritual being and also to promote community participation in healing and self-care. It offers new perspectives on the bio-medical model as it examines the socio-cultural context of the causation, diagnosis, prevention and cure of disease. Examples of healing systems are drawn from countries of the Global South, particularly Africa, the Caribbean, Asia and Latin America and from industrialized societies, especially African-American and indigenous communities in the United States.

Examination is made of healing systems which include Shamanistic traditions and other systems of divination, herbal medicine, folk medicine, faith healing, traditional healing and so forth. Topics studied include theories of disease causation, comparative histories of healing systems, the cultural management of pregnancy and childbirth, medical pluralism and authoritative knowledge, complementary and alternative medicine, and cultural approaches to prevention and self-care. The course also examines and analyzes the global impact of the Women's Health Care Movement, the global challenges of epidemics and pandemics, the alarming incidence of maternal mortality globally and the prospects and problems for human health posed by advances in technology.

Medical anthropology is defined in the course as a study of how people's beliefs and behavior affect their health. It emphasizes the role of culture and examines how aspects of sickness and healing differ in various types of societies. It examines how, as social constructs, sickness and healing are dynamic processes which can change in relation to the social organization, belief systems and medical practices of any given society. The course analyzes how medicine as a social institution exhibits great diversity when viewed from a cross-cultural perspective. At the same time, traditions of medicine arose from practices about health and healing which are embedded in religious and other belief systems. Although modern medicine, based on the scientific tradition, has moved away from its religious origins, there is renewed interest in faith healing, alternative medicine and other forms of healing that go beyond the biomedical model and seek to heal the whole person rather than just curing the disease. There is also a trend towards reducing excessive medical interventions in the treatment of illness.

The course starts with a definition of medical anthropology as a cross-cultural study of systems of healing that range from holistic to reductionist approaches and that centralizes culture and belief systems expressed primarily through the spirit theory of disease and the germ theory of disease. It shows how medical anthropology is becoming increasingly important for understanding immigrant communities, since people move with their health care belief systems, and also the role of medical anthropology within the academy. It explores the increasing significance of global health in multi-cultural and international settings and for holistic approaches to health. A major aspect of the course deals with cultural and biological adaptation to diverse ecological zones and diseases and explores cultural modalities for handling the challenges of life and death.

A few students, especially pre-med students, find it difficult to appreciate alternative concepts and theories about sickness and healing that deviate from the biomedical model at the beginning of the course. However, towards the end of the course, many of the skeptical ones come to appreciate the values and contributions of other healing systems. The course is taught from an interactive approach including oral presentations of case studies and team projects on various themes including medical pluralism in the modern world. It is aided by audio-visual presentations and guest speakers, including Chiropractors, Midwives and Shamans. Among the numerous texts and articles used are *Medical Anthropology and the World System:* Third Edition by Baer and others; Jordan's *Birth in Four Cultures*; Gordon's *Manifesto for a New Medicine* and Fadiman's *The Spirit Catches You and You Fall Down.*

'Environmental Justice, "Race" and Sustainable Development' is a course that often has a large enrollment. It attracts students from all disciplines, interdisciplinary programs and Environmental Studies. It adopts a critical approach that deviates from the idea of conceptualizing the environment only as the natural and physical environment and considers it as everything, according to the Environmental Justice definition. It focuses on the social aspects and the interaction of socially-differentiated people with the environment. The course examines how the impact of human activity on the planet is shaped by norms, ideologies and practices which reinforce inequality and disproportionately expose some groups of people to environmental hazards. It explores the systematic and deliberate pattern of unequal allocation of benefits and burdens emanating from economic and environmental policies and practices. In short, the course investigates the extent to which the causes and consequences of environmental degradation are influenced by normative factors and practices pertaining to social inequality and distributive injustice.

The concept of 'environmental justice' was developed in the late 20th century in the USA, primarily by African-Americans, and has focused on environment and race issues. This position argues that discrimination, exposure and lack of access to decent housing, transportation and green spaces have a significant negative impact on the quality of life on some minority and poor groups. Since race and class tend to reinforce each other in matters of environmental (in)justice, the term 'environmental racism' is often used simultaneously. Environmental justice has spawned a vibrant and growing grassroots movement made up primarily of minority groups, many of whom are women.

Their major objective is to tackle the problem of the placing of waste disposal, incinerators, depots and transportation routes in communities inhabited by people of color, indigenous people and poor people. The Environmental Justice Movement also advocates for better housing in areas dominated by slums and ghettos, in which there is high exposure and vulnerability to environmental hazards and disease, such as lead poisoning and asthma. Environmental justice concerns are global. Also of importance is the examination of the gender dimension of environmental justice as it relates to ecofeminism, the impact of environmental degradation on women and children and women's role in sustainable development.

Of particular importance is the examination of the racial and socio-economic dimensions of climate change and natural disasters and their implications for environmental justice, with particular reference to Hurricane Katrina. Overall, the course seeks to integrate knowledge and skills into practice at the college, i.e. in the dorms, in the community and at home. Whenever possible, I would take groups of students on field trips to poor inner city areas to see for ourselves the sites of dumping of hazardous wastes, toxic chemicals and diesel-using bus depots in neighborhoods inhabited by poor people and people of color. A large number of books and articles are used and include Bullard's *The Quest for Environmental Justice*; Colburn and others' *Our Stolen Future;* Maghoff and Forster's *What Every Environmentalist Needs to Know about Capitalism*; Macdonald's *Environmental Justice in South Africa;* Shiva's *Earth Democracy, Justice, Sustainability and Peace*; Steady's *Environmental Justice in the New Millennium* and Whybrow's *American Mania: When More is not Enough.*

The 'Seminar on South Africa' is at the 300 level and tends to be a smaller class in keeping with seminar formats which emphasize discussions. It attracts students from many disciplines and from Study Abroad programs that include South Africa and students with an eye towards a career in the foreign service, law or human rights. The course is designed as a study of the degree of social transofrmation and/or stagnation in the new South Africa. It is based on the assumption that South Africa is ideally moving from a racist, centralized, and oppressive apartheid system to a non-racial, democratic, and participatory system, which seeks to promote social and economic justice for all its citizens. However, there is evidence to show that the structures of apartheid which have been in place for almost three quarters of a century are still entrenched. Systemic and institutionalized racism and the economic architecture of apartheid did not disappear with the dismantling of 'de jure' (legal apartheid.)

The topics discussed include a multidisciplinary understanding of the ideological proclivities and political economy of South Africa that continue to uphold de facto apartheid which is 'aparthied in practice.' The seminar examines structural challenges to the dismantling of apartheid, such as monopoly capitalism, 'State capture' of political power and the commanding heights of the economy by foreign-controlled corporations and conglomorates and endemic corruption which has its antecedents in the institutions of the apartheid era. Other topics examined include a critical analysis of the Truth and Reconciliation Commission and the role of retributive versus restorative justice. Post-apartheid efforts at reconstruction and democratization, as well as socio-economic development and resource distribution, are also studied. In addition, an examination is made of the impact of globalization and South Africa's place in Africa and in the world at large.

The seminar also critically examines the question of whether there can be reconciliation without justice and effective punishment. Problems of environmental justice in both urban and rural areas and its impact in marginalizing the African majority population are also examined. The position of African women during the apartheid and post-apartheid periods are among other popular topics covered. Among the texts and articles used are: Kunnie's *Is Apartheid Really Dead? Pan-Africanist Working Class and Cultural Critical Perspectives;* McDonald's *Environmental Justice in South Afri*ca; Thompson's, *A History of South Africa,* Nelson Mandela's *Long Walk to Freedom,* London, Abacus Press; Winnie Mandela, W. *Part of My Soul Went with Him* and the novel, *Mine Boy* by Peter Abrahams.

'Women in Africa, Social Transformation and Empowerment' is a 300 level seminar taught every two years. It investigates the conceptual and theoretical approaches to the study of women in Africa, through a comparative analysis of the social, economic, cultural and political roles of African women. It is conducted within the context of national and international development processes and the quest for social transformation and the empowerment of women. Most of the books, articles and material used in this course are written by African women scholars.

One of the objectives of the course is to increase our understanding and appreciation of African women's contributions to their societies. Another is to engage in a critique of Eurocentric studies and of the structure and development models that result in the marginalization of women. A third approach looks at women's associations and women's movements with a view to understanding women's collective action and the impact on gender relations. Among the books and articles used were Oyewumi's *The Invention of Women: Making an African Sense of Wester Gender Discourse;* Steady's *The Black Woman Cross-Culturally*; Steady's *Women and Leadership in West Africa;* Steady's *Women and Collective Action in Africa*; Tamale's *When Hens Begin the Crow*: *Gender and Parliamentary Politics in Contemporary Uganda* Maathai's *Unbowed: A Memoir* and Aidoo's *Changes: A Love Story.*

The seminar starts with a study of feminist theories, especially African feminism and other versions of African feminism such as negro feminism, aspects of womanism and emerging feminist theoretical insights from countries of the Global South. It also interrogates the term 'gender' both from the point of view of its epistemological genesis in the West, with its cultural specificities, and its imposition on countries in Africa. In the African context there is a tendency for African societies to adopt more flexible approaches to male/female designations, roles and expectations. These epistemological and theoretical discussions are exemplified in the work of scholars like Ifi Amadiume of the Igbo of Nigeria. The complexity of the concept of 'gender' when applied to Africa is examined against the dominant Western feminist discourses through various readings, notably *The Invention of Women* by Oyewumi and selected chapters in the anthology *The Black Woman Cross-Culturally*, edited by Steady. The course also explores the influence of matri-focal (mother-focussed) traditions of Africa and their overt and subtle persistence, even in patrilineal societies, in order to understand gender roles and gender relations over time.

Women's collective action is examined from various perspectives, focusing on theoretical explanations for female mobilization, the nature and function of women's associations and their impact on the international environment. One objective is to examine the constraints placed by the global economy on the economic and social development trends in Africa and on African women. Analyses are made of African women's resistance to these processes occurring within the unjust context of corporate globalization and the international division of labor.

Students are encouraged to work on research projects focusing on women's groups and associations; women's leadership and on their role in the development process and in the quest for full citizenship. Particular emphasis is placed on women's political roles and the impact of female agency on bringing about social transformation and their empowerment. Case studies are drawn from several countries representing the four sub-regions of Africa. These are Nigeria, Sierra Leone and Guinea for West Africa; Kenya and Uganda for East Africa; South Africa and Namibia for Southern Africa; and Mozambique, Angola and Guinea-Bissau for Lusophone Africa and Algeria, Morocco and Egypt for North Africa.

'The Black Woman Cross-Culturally: Gender Dynamics in The Africana World' is a 300 level seminar that uses a multidisciplinary approach to examine theories, methodological approaches and socio-cultural analyses of the lives, experiences and contributions of the Black women from a cross-cultural perspective. Case studies examine women's positions and gender dynamics in North and South America, the Caribbean, Europe, Asia and Africa. It also interrogates women's evolving positions in society; examines the dynamics of gender relations and analyzes the legacies of slavery, colonialism and liberation struggles within a post-colonial and post-modern context. The negative impact of corporate globalization, neo-liberalism and the challenges in the quest for democratization and human rights are central themes in the discussions. The take-off point of the course is the reading of *The Black Woman Cross-Culturally*, edited by Steady, now in its third edition.

The first part of the course is designed to cover major sections of feminist theory and methodologies, as they relate to women in Africa and the African Diaspora. This is particularly pertinent to the case studies in understanding common themes, evolving concepts of feminist modes of analysis related to the study of Black women in an international context. Theoretical insights include, inter alia, a study of Black feminism, African feminism, Nego feminism, womanism and Third World feminist discourses. The intersectionality of race, class, gender and sexuality is interrogated throughout the course.

The second part of the course examines two major themes, namely the idea of matriarchy and female-centered systems and studies of masculinity in the Africana world. The third part consists of case studies from Africa, the United States, Latin America and the Caribbean, reflecting theoretical and empirical studies along the lines of specific family and kinship structures; citizenship and participation in the public sphere; female leadership and authority. Also discussed is women's legal capacity in promoting the eliminating gender-based hierarchies and discrimination; women's movements and activism and the link between women's rights and human rights. Comparisons are drawn with women's movements that are not in the Africana world as well as the International Women's Movements.

The fourth part examines biographies and biographical novels to give a subjective and personal dimension to studies of women and to examine their testimonies, reflections, theories and views about their lives and their societies. In addition, films and other audio-visual aids are used to add texture to the readings and discussions. The final part of the course examines the Black women in international contexts and reviews international instruments, such as the United Nations Convention for the Elimination of All Forms of Discrimination Against Women; the Beijing Platform for Action; the Universal Declaration of Human Rights and the African Charter on Human and People's Rights.

The reading consists of classics as well as noteworthy books and articles on the subject. Emphasis is placed on using the works of scholars, especially female scholars from the Africana world. One resource that is under appreciated but used in this course is sometimes referred to as 'grey literature' produced by non-governmental organizations (NGOs.) This type of literature is essential to the growing body of feminist literature and sometime forms the core ideological and intellectual basis for the orientation, objectives and agenda of feminist activism. Exposing students to this literature in a critical and appreciable way enhances their knowledge. Among the regular texts used are the following: Collin's *Black Feminist Thought;* Angelou's *I know Why the Caged Bird Sings;* Hooks's *Ain't I a Woman;* Springfield's *Daughters of Caliban: Caribbean Women in the Twentieth Century;* Steady's edited *The Black Woman Cross-Culturally,* Third Edition and Harris' *The Sisters are Alright: Changing the Broken Narrative of Black Women in America.*

CHAPTER 27

Significant Events and Contributions
to Wellesley College

'This little light of mine, I'm going to let it shine' –
Matthew 5.14-16 and George G. Ivins

❖

There are five significant events and contributions which I am very proud to have made to Wellesley College and the department during my time there, in addition to teaching established and new courses, research and scholarly activities and administrative responsibilities as department chair. I also organized three international conferences on 'Gender, Technology and Science in Africa;' 'Black Women, Globalization and Economic Justice and 'Environmental Justice in the New Millennium: Race, Ethnicity and Human Rights.' With the exception of the first conference, the papers and presentations at two of these conferences were subsequently published in edited books of the same title. [18] The five other major contributions are as follows:

---

18 Steady, F., 2002, (ed.) **Black Women, Globalization and Economic Justice,** Rochester, VT: Schenkman Books

Steady, F., 2009, (ed.) **Environmental Justice in the New Millennium: Race, Ethnicity and Human Rights,** New York, Palgrave/Macmillan.

1. Establishing Environmental Studies as the first co-Chair of Environmental Studies

Environmental degradation and destruction are among the most serious challenges of the twenty-first century. The central role of the Academy in combatting these challenges has resulted in the field of Environmental Studies, one of the most important areas of study in the twenty first century. Professor of Biology Nick Rodenhouse and myself co-chaired the first inter-departmental major in Environmental Studies at Wellesley College in the late 1990s and also co-chaired a committee to establish Environmental Studies as a program of study at the college. Having worked as Special Advisor of the Earth Summit in Rio in 1992, I was able to bring some of my insights and experiences to the work of the committee. I was also the first professor at Wellesley to teach a popular social science course on the environment, titled 'Environmental Justice, "Race" and Sustainable Development' in the spring of 1998. The course has been described earlier in this book and needs no elaboration here. It is important to note that students were excited about the course and motivated to conduct research in the Boston community and also on the campus on environmental justice issues. The College itself had a history that is relevant to the study of environmental degradation. The town of Wellesley had to clean up contamination by the now defunct Henry Woods Sons Company Paint Factory, which was situated near the campus and its enclosures, including Lake Waban.

The Environmental Studies Committee worked very hard to develop a major that would have an introductory component, core requirements and an inter-disciplinary format. It faced an uphill battle in trying to get the proposal through Academic Council, due mainly to opposition from mainstream departments that were not always predisposed to programs of a multidisciplinary nature. The program was eventually approved, established and staffed. Unfortunately, none of the tenured or tenure-track faculty in Environmental Studies is a person of color. In addition, reports from students of color majoring or minoring in the program revealed a level of discomfort in the department and unresponsiveness to their educational needs and to issues of environmental racism. Students were disappointed at the lack of participation of the Environmental Studies faculty at the international conference on 'Environmental Justice in the New Millennium: Race, Ethnicity and Human Rights' that I organized at Wellesley in 2009. This was unfortunate since one of the people responsible for establishing the major at Wellesley is a woman of color. I hope that in the future there will be greater sensitivity to the teaching and research that will support of students of color in the department.

2. Strengthening Africana Studies Department

My contribution to Africana Studies spans my twenty-two years at Wellesley College as a professor and chair for most of this period. The field has enjoyed a period of growth and development of multi-disciplinary research, analyses and teaching from the late 1960s to the 1990s. Since then, the record has been uneven. Some of these programs and departments have flourished and a few of them, such as Harvard University, Columbia University and Ohio State University, offer doctorate degrees. Others have had a more difficult trajectory with diminishing support from their administration, or been marginalized and subsumed under larger units dealing with global education, international studies, area studies and the like. At Wellesley the department has faced many challenges, and despite constant requests and justifications for additional tenure-track positions, it has never been fully staffed to the level of five tenure-track faculty positions which it was promised in 1997 when I was first hired. By the time I was leaving, we were down to three tenure-track positions – Literature, history and political science.

The highest we have achieved was four tenure-track positions for history, literature, political science and social anthropology. In addition, we had two non-tenure-track positions for religion and Swahili, which are renewed on a short-term basis, and a professor and chair. The social sciences are essential to Africana Studies and the study of culture and religion are central to the study of people of Africa and the African Diaspora. It is also important to have an African language offered in the department as a core requirement for our majors and minors and as a valuable skill for students from other departments planning to study or work in a Swahili-speaking country in Africa. It is my hope that the current administration will keep their promise of strengthening Africana Studies as a vital and forward-looking part of the general college curriculum. The current faculty is outstanding with strong teaching and publication records. The department offers prizes at the end of the year that include the following: the Fannie Lou Hamer Prize; the Ella Smith Elbert Prize; the Zora Neale Hurston Prize and the Professor Filomina Steady Prize.

The department has strengthened the curriculum of the college in general and has offered many college and community-wide events in the form of conferences, symposia, lectures, cultural events. It also offers the Africana Studies Colloquium which is compulsory for majors and minors and features the research of faculty in the department and beyond. Students are central to the department which works closely with students organizations like Ethos, Caribbean Women and Development and Wellesley's African Students Association in co-sponsoring their cultural and other events on campus and beyond. Many professors take students on trips to New York to see Broadway shows and other events that are relevant to the study of Africa and The African Diaspora. In addition, the students publish a yearly newsletter, *The Griot.*

3. Establishing 'Wintersession in Jamaica' Course

Another important contribution to Wellesley College was establishing The Wintersession in Jamaica course. As part of the curriculum of Africana Studies, students are encouraged to participate in study -abroad programs, particularly in Africa and the African Diaspora. Three courses were developed by the department as Wintersession courses taught during the winter break in January each year for three weeks in Jamaica, Ghana and East Africa. I directed the Wintersession in Jamaica course titled: 'Culture and Heritage in Jamaica: A Wintersession Experience' over a six-year period with students from all disciplines and backgrounds.

Jamaica is a country that provides a unique opportunity for the study of multiculturalism *in action*. Its national motto is 'Out of many, one people'. The majority of its peoples are descendants of enslaved Africans until 1833, when slavery was abolished, and the tiny island served as the chief slave market of the Americas. From these tragic beginnings the country has achieved a remarkable transformation into a multi-racial democratic and open society.

Half of the population lives in urban areas and speaks English or the popular and expressive Creole lingua franca. The Christian religion and its many variations are the dominant religion, but African-centered and inspired religious traditions are still observed or combined with Christianity. Other religions, like Hinduism and Islam, are practiced by a minority.

The country has a vibrant cultural heritage, much of which has been exported to all parts of the world. Among the most famous are its reggae music, the carnival, its cuisine, fashion and the Rastafarian way of life. It has also produced internationally recognized heroes that include Marcus Garvey, Granny Nanny, Lucille Mair and Bob Marley. About one third of the people depend on agriculture, but Jamaica is best known for its tourism. Despite its legacy of slavery and colonialism, it is a democratic, modern and dynamic country endowed with natural and human resources and inhabited by a proud and spirited people. Many Jamaicans are proud of their country and heritage and emphasize education, economic and social development. The country continues to have close ties with Britain as a former British colony but has been increasing its ties with the United States due to its close geographical proximity and trade and other international relations.

Through this Wintersession course, Wellesley students benefitted from the rich historical and cultural traditions of this beautiful and remarkable country. Although I was the director of the course, most of the activities were decentralized, with Jamaicans playing a major role in the execution of the course. It was housed at the University of the West Indies, Mona campus, and involved several units of the campus including the Center for Gender and Development Studies and covered a period of three weeks. It was coordinated at the local level by Ms. Shirley Campbell, an expert and director of several study abroad programs. In addition, the general manager of the Social Investment Fund, Mrs. Scarlette Gillings, agreed to provide an opportunity for students to interact with experts in the field of development in the areas education, health and social services.

The program focused on the historical and cultural heritage of Jamaica as well as on current political and social-economic development trends. Students were asked to read a novel about Jamaica prior to their departure and *The Story of the Jamaican People* by Philip Sherlock and Hazel Bennett. These books were often used to initiate a thematic seminar which ran for a week and a half at the University of West Indies at The Social Welfare Training Center at U.W.I. Professors from the University of the West Indies gave lectures on the Caribbean including history, economics, religion, music, sociology, art, Women's Studies and the Jamaican language. Students were required to complete a paper based on prior and subsequent reading material, the seminar, workshops, field trips and study visits to rural areas. In addition, an analytical and reflective journal was assigned as well as a short quiz administered at the end of the lectures.

The main teachers from Jamaica included four University of West Indies professors, development practitioners, cultural heroes, artists, Maroon historians and rural community leaders. Students lived in Liguanea Gardens in the center of Kingston in town houses that can accommodate four to five students. Each building has at least three bedrooms and two bathrooms upstairs and a living room and kitchen downstairs. There is also a small porch in the back and a swimming pool in the beautiful landscape garden with lots of trees. Security is provided by electronic gates and nighttime security guards.

I lived about four blocks away at another hotel complex called Crystal Towers. In the beginning, I used to stay in the same complex as the students but found out after the first Wintersession that I needed a more quiet and tranquil environment. We would all travel by bus to and from our various activities. The students took turns in serving as monitors to ensure punctuality and the smooth running of the logistical and behavioral aspects of the program.

One weekend was devoted to homestays at a rural village in Woodside, St. Mary's Parish in the eastern section of the island. The population is about 1000. The students' stay is structured around the concept of 'educo-tourism'. This involves the process of exchanging knowledge with the local people. The villagers and students share aspects of their heritage and culture and make presentations individually or jointly. Students also participate in on-going projects in an old slave plantation. These activities include the mapping of caves, tracing kinship lines from slavery to the contemporary period. The objective of local development projects by the villagers is to get descendants of Woodside to contribute to the growth and development of the community and to document their cultural activities. Students also participated in the celebration of Woodside Day held on the first Thursday in January profiling the cultural and intellectual skills of the community.

The first year, 1996, was difficult because American students had to forego some of the luxuries and creature comforts to which they were accustomed. These included not having instant hot water for showers and dealing with mosquitoes and other pests and tiny lizards that sometimes live in people's houses. I had to quell their fears about the lizards by telling them that we had them in the houses in Sierra Leone also and that we referred to them as 'children of the house' since they were always around. Somehow this seemed to calm them down and they eventually accepted the lizards as harmless. Some also felt a lack of freedom during the first year and complained about the activities being too structured. After a few meetings with the students and the local coordinator, we decided to schedule more free time and supervised visits to social clubs in town.

Other activities during the rural home stays included history lecturers about the village before and during the time of slavery to the present. The students also were also led on hikes by a local hiker into the deep tropical forests, noting important landmarks such as monuments to 'Wan Bobi Susan' (Susan with one breast) and grave sites of ancestors of the current villagers. The local coordinator was Dr. Erna Brodber, a sociologist, noted novelist and lecturer in the Department of Sociology and Social Work at U.W.I. Other activities included lessons in arts and crafts from the villagers using local products like coconut shells, leaves, gourds and seeds. Students who were interested in going into the field of medicine spent time with traditional healers learning about the use of herbs in treating illnesses. We also learnt about Rastafarian culture, religion and way of life from the Rastafarian families in the village. These included their connection to Ethiopia and Haille Selassi, whom they believed to be a god and Africa as their homeland. Reggae music was also central to their lives as promoted by Bob Marley, a world-famous musician and Rastafarian. Also of significance to their religion and culture were their dreadlocks, the smoking of marijuana and the colors of red, green and gold with black added to signify the community. Most of the villagers had a vegetable garden and some took their surplus vegetables to the market about a mile away for sale.

Another home stay village was historic Accompong. This is a mountainous community of Maroons, African descendants of free and runaway slaves who set up an independent community in the hills of St. Elizabeth and neighboring Trelawny. In 1739, after years of guerrilla warfare, the British were forced to sign a peace treaty with the Maroons. Every year on January 6th, which is the birthday of Kudjo, the warrior leader of the Accompong Maroons, this community celebrates this event as an act of freedom and independence. This event is known as Maroon Peace Treaty Day. A gathering usually takes place under the kinder (family) tree where Kudjo and his soldiers had their meetings to plan their strategies on regaining their freedom from the British. A cultural ceremony involving the cooking and sharing of special ancestral meals is held, including ritual visits to the ancestral graves at midday.

Students would usually spend one night in Accompong and the next day hike to the peace cave. This is the cave in which the Maroons hid and ambushed the British soldiers, and also where the peace treaty was signed. The hike takes place along the route of the Kinder Tree and Old Town where the Maroons lived until they were forced to relocate to higher ground. The hike also includes a visit to Kudjoe's grave. In addition, oral presentations were made by elders and traditional dances were performed. This was usually a grand event, attracting dignitaries from the national government and numerous visitors who were happy to wind their way to one of the highest hilltops of the country, with spectacular views of the island nation along the way and at the top.

The first year in Accompong was full of tensions of all kinds. The ride to the top of the mountain was long and tiring and to make matters worse, the driver got lost on the way. By the time we arrived, the students were very tired and frustrated. They stayed with families, which worked for most of them, but for a few students the houses were small and they suddenly found out that they had to share the space with other guests from Kingston. We learned afterwards that the residents of Woodside rent rooms in their houses during this time to make extra money. Understandably, the students felt unsafe having strange house mates. To make matters worse, Accompong residents do not lock their doors as a rule because of the low crime rate, so the students were not provided with keys.

Some hardly slept and others ran away during the night to my place and slept on the porch. The next day many complained about their accommodation and about feeling unsafe. This was a reaction that was based on fears that would have been true in the United States but unfounded in Accompong. We found that Accompong is a very safe community and that there is hardly any crime. When a rare crime occurs, it is usually committed by people from outside.

After the first night and the hike the next day to the peace tent and Kudjoe's grave, I decided to take the group back to Kingston. I felt that this was a failure on the part of the students in terms of developing more tolerance and skills in international living and learning, but did not want to put them to the test any further. American students are generally spoiled and used to comforts that are not readily available in a Third World Country, especially in the rural areas. In addition, they have perceptions about crime derived from living in America that they project to another country, leading to unrealistic fears and anxieties. For these reasons, I thought it best to take them back to Kingston.

In Kingston, the program included opportunities to visit art galleries, the national heroes' park as well as to attend popular theater performances, including the famous Kingston pantomime and concerts. Students also enjoyed going to some of the night clubs and to ensure their safety, we hired a male administrative assistant to help with escorting them around town and to serve as a chaperon during visits to night clubs and other social events. They enjoyed shopping in the malls and the main shopping center in downtown Kingston as well as in the Craft Market. Other activities included hiking to the famous Blue Mountains, visits to tropical rain forests and sightseeing, all of which provided interesting and important opportunities for cross-cultural learning.

Opportunities and challenges for Study Abroad Programs

All of my Wintersession courses were important and successful learning experiences for students and myself. With the exception of a handful of students, most of them behaved well and were cooperative. Many developed excellent inter-cultural communication skills and were appreciative of the total immersion approach to international learning. Most of them made lasting friendships with students at the University of West Indies, their host families and people they met. Their courses were enlightening and presented from critical perspectives that may not be as readily available at Wellesley, a point made in many of our discussions. The students saw the history of slavery in a new light and appreciated the contribution of the Haitian Revolution to freedom of all of mankind because of its all- inclusive and extensive treatise on freedom.

There are several challenges in Study Abroad Programs which were evident in my four Wintersession in Jamaica courses. Before going to Jamaica, I tried to minimize the challenges by holding meetings with the selected students at Wellesley. One was a briefing on the course and expectations of the program, and the other was a security briefing involving a campus police officer and a nurse from the college's health department. I also ensured that each student signed the Jamaican 'Honor Code' which was inspired by the Wellesley Honor Code as a guide for behavior while overseas. One of my main concerns was that students would feel a sense of freedom and reckless abandon when they were overseas. They also needed to be protected from risky behavior and going to unsafe places on their own. The student in the classroom at Wellesley is usually well-behaved, but could change in a setting that is foreign and unfamiliar. On some Study Abroad Programs by other institutions unpleasant things have happened to students, including violent acts and risky behavior that could endanger their health.

One of the main challenges of being abroad for these courses is the rate at which a few students 'fall in love' with local men and want to spend more time with them, including overnight stays. One year when the students stayed in a convent, I found out afterwards that a few of them would climb over the wall at night to visit 'boyfriends' or visit shady night clubs and climb back in before daybreak. On one occasion, I had taken students out to a club on New Year's Eve and they were dancing with the local men, which was fine. After about an hour, I was shocked and could not believe my eyes when I noticed that a few of them were dancing very closely and intimately with men they had just met. In Jamaica, this is called 'rent a tile' where the couple are very close and hardly move during dancing.

The dancing by some students with strangers was so erotic that I decided to take them back as soon as the music stopped. Two of them refused to get on the bus, insisting that their parents did not impose curfews on them. I ordered them to get on the bus or be ready to fly back to Boston and Wellesley the next day. That did it and all of them got on the bus to go back to their hostel. I was disappointed at the behavior of some of these students because the coordinator had informed them during the orientation period of the dangers of mixing with strange men and engaging in any improper behaviour or other activity that would put them at risk. She had stressed the fact that a number of Jamaican men are womanizers and have the habit of chasing women, especially foreign women, with only one thing in mind.

Another challenge had to do with alcohol consumption and the smoking of marijuana. Wellesley had a policy of an age limit of eighteen for alcohol at the time and most establishments in the United States would ask for an ID from students to check their age. In Jamaica, there is no checking of IDs and students can obtain alcohol from any club, bar or supermarket, where they are widely available. On a trip to Ocho Rios to climb the famous waterfall, a student insisted on buying hard spirits from one of the local bars, which like all the bars in Jamaica, did not require proof of age. When I stopped her, she was indignant and told me that she was allowed to drink at home. I had to remind her that she was not at home and that I was the one in charge in Jamaica. She realized that there was no way she was going to drink hard liquor while I was around.

In addition to alcohol, marijuana is widely available and smoked in many public and private places. It is also a cultural requirement of the Rastafarians, whose religion is based on a belief in Haile Selassie of Ethiopia as a god. The religion is committed to Black emancipation and a return to Africa. On one of our rural homestays, we visited a Rastafarian family for the students to learn how to carve useful and decorative bowls from gourds from the father of the family. The mother sold vegetables in the market and the children went to school or stayed home with their father while their mother was away. Smoking marijuana seemed like a natural occurrence for the father, but we never saw the mother smoking it or the children.

Dealing with White privilege in young people was another challenge for which I was not prepared. On one of the Wintersession programs, I had a number of White students who felt that I owed them more attention and kept disrupting the plans in a number of ways. They tended to segregate themselves in terms of the selection of housemates and during meal times. No surprise there, since this was in keeping with the practice at Wellesley and many colleges and universities in the United States, where students tend to self- segregate on the basis of race. Tatum examines this phenomenon in a popular book titled: *Why Are All The Black Kids Sitting Together in the Cafeteria?: And Other Conversations.*[19] What was different in Jamaica was that the White students expected me to sit at their table and would actually call me on my way to another more diverse table and insist that I sit with them. When I refused and explained that I was already on my way to another table, they seemed offended.

On another occasion, I invited a diverse group of students to ride with me in the car to Moore Town on a trip to visit the Maroons. On the way back, three White students had quickly jumped into the back seat of the car to make sure that they rode with me instead on the return trip. I told them that I would like some diversity in the car and invited an Asian and Latin X student to ride with me on the way back. This feeling of White privilege in a predominantly Black country was something I had difficulty dealing with, especially coming from students who were so young. It was as if a few of them were having some kind of crisis by being surrounded by so many Black people. I am still trying to understand that type of behavior, since America is a multi-racial society and they should be used to diversity.

I also noticed that a couple of the White students liked to engage with me on conversations about race on a one-to-one basis to see what I thought. For example, out of the blue, one White student told me that she did not like the Reverend Al Shapton. I asked her why. She replied

19   Tatum, B., 1997, New York, Basic Books.

that her family thought he was a troublemaker. I asked her how else would one fight against racism without seeming to be a troublemaker and if she knew of another way to do it. In her reply, she indicated that racism was no longer a problem and could be overcome by just talking about it. I suggested that racism went deeper than talking and was embedded in institutions, and suggested that we bring it up to the main group for discussion, and she agreed.

A handful of White students found it difficult being a minority for the first time and were having problems with it. I used the opportunity to bring these subjects to our general discussions and to help them work out their guilt or sense of entitlement because of White privilege. For many of them, it was an eye opener and the students of color also benefited from these discussions by understanding some of the complexities of racial attitudes and the burden of White privilege, even at a young age.

Interestingly, when it came to adjusting to rural village life and the hardship of walking everywhere and taking cold showers and so forth, the White students adapted much better than the Black ones. Many of the Black students wanted to have the same comforts to which they were accustomed and did not make the necessary mental adjustment of being in a rural community in a Third World country. They saw Jamaica as a place of sunshine and beaches and luxury living as depicted on TV and could not withstand the hardship of rural life. Fortunately, these maladjusted students were among the minority and by the end of the rural homestays, many of them became accustomed to doing away with the comforts and even enjoyed taking cold showers and long walks through the village.

Excerpts from students' journals

In January 2007, the Africana Studies Department again offered students a Wintersession in Jamaica. The program included lectures, visits to museums and historical sites, and academic lectures. Below are excerpts from students' journals on various aspects of the Wintersession. They are from the Africana Studies website and copyrighted by the Trustees of Wellesley College.

'Heritage and Culture in Jamaica: A Wintersession Experience' – 2007[20]

Dunns' River Falls, Ocho Rios, Jamaica –
Wellesley Students climbing the Dunn's River waterfall

The following are excerpts from students' journals

On Arrival

■ I was amazed to see so many black people at the airport, and they were running the airport too. This was completely different from the airports that I am familiar with… where the majority of the staff behind the counters and all the official personnel are white. The sight of black Jamaican women checking our passports and making decisions of national importance about our admittance into their country made me feel so proud.

Lectures

---

20 Wintersession Journal Entry of Students - Copyright © Trustees of Wellesley College | Wellesley College 106 Central Street – Wellesley, MA 02481 (781) 283-1000. For further information: www.wellesley.edu/africana/Jamaica/index.html.

■ I was fascinated by the depth of knowledge and the passion that the professors had. I loved their approaches, quite refreshing and different from what I hear in the USA. I learned so much about Jamaica, but also about the world and about myself. I was inspired even more to go home and do something about making a better Africa… I remember Professor Hutton's words in particular, that most of what he teaches is his own research; that it is not enough to sit and listen but to explore, ask the 'whys' and 'hows', look beyond what is presented for a perspective that is missing in the academic world. Interacting with them brought a new sense of respect for teaching as a profession. Imparting knowledge to another generation is one of the most effective tools in facilitating change.

■ My favorite lecture was by Michael Witter. He made me re-evaluate the way I think and view things. Before this lecture I had not thought about the consequences of tourism. His energy and humor were great. I wish we had economics professors like him at Wellesley. I love my econ professors but very few of them make their students think the way he did. We all benefited from having been taught by him.

■ Professor Clinton Hutton lectured us about the Haitian revolution and both the popular and traditional music of Jamaica. On one point he was abundantly clear: the Haitian revolution gave to the world the idea that slavery was wrong and should not be inflicted on anyone. He unearthed the racism of the founding fathers of America and the revolutionaries of England and France. I was especially impressed by his charging each of us to become a "sovereign student' – that ninety percent of our knowledge should be what we acquire ourselves through our own research. I think this is so important, and sincerely hope that I can live my life this way.

■ I learned from Professor Hutton that Jamaica has promoted the idea of self-determination but at the same time this notion has been undermined. Jamaica will be fully emancipated when she can choose to follow her own destiny. Jamaica will reach its full emancipation when she is free from imposing demands and pressures to conform to the needs and wants of the international community. Jamaica will reach full independence when she can create economic developments that can serve to meet the needs and wants of her people.

■ I was really shocked when Dr. Hutton read Christopher Columbus' diary entries about the Native Americans in Jamaica when he first arrived there... As a child I grew up learning that Columbus was a significant man who "discovered" the Americas, when in actuality he was the person that started the slave trade. I find it extremely ironic that these facts were omitted from our American textbooks. Such facts make me wonder what were the reasons and logic for hiding such critical information from the American public.

■ Africa (and its descendants) has always been a source of art, creativity and intelligence. However, we learned from Professor Cecil Gutzmore today that world history denied the intellectual heritage of Africa because of the lack of a written history of its achievements. Nonetheless, Africa was the birthplace of human civilization and has several triumphs on which to pride itself.

■ Professor Gutzmore's account of Jamaican history was one I wish African Americans would develop for themselves. I felt that his approach in addressing history would have been considered radical, but I honestly envied what students at UWI are being taught in terms of their history because it seemed truthful and for once in the eyes of Black people instead of White. These types of courses, if made mandatory for students, could better them in terms of their success in life. It gives people in Jamaica a solid understanding of there they come from and... gives them some pride and sense of accomplishment.

■ Although psychologically women are socialized to be dependent on a man, they quickly learn to be independent. After listening to Dr. Leith Dunn's lectures I found it easy to make some similarities to the gender controversies in the United States... where the Blacks also experience the same type of matrifocal structure based on the same reasons – lack of the presence of fathers. Although there are some advantages to having a matrifocal family structure, it would be a lot more helpful if all of the responsibilities were shared with the father.

■ The most important thing that I learned on this trip was taught by Dr. Witter and Dr. Dunn on issues revolving around globalization. These professors together taught me that globalization in world history really began in Jamaica. If Christopher Columbus had not come to the Caribbean looking for the West Indies and discovered people that would be used as slaves, world trade and globalization would not have happened. World trade was based on the slave trade in which human beings and raw materials were traded between Africa and the Caribbean, the United States and Europe. Although Jamaica is a small island, its history is very significant to world history.

■ It was fascinating to learn about the Jamaican language, patois, from Joan Andrea Hutchinson. The language developed from Twi (an African language), English, and other African and European languages. Patois has all the features of an official language, but people tend not to accept it as such because it is the language of lower class people. In deep rural Jamaica 'she' and 'her' don't exist. When speaking about a woman they still use 'him', thus the language appears to be male dominated. Professor Hutchinson is involved in the protection and preservation of the language – which is as yet an unwritten language.

■ Dr. Imani Tafari-Ama during her lecture explained that lighter skin is associated with social mobility and dates back to slavery. As I observed the Jamaicans in Sovereign I noticed that the lighter skinned women in particular were often with middle class professionals. Also a lot of the wealthy looking people were of a lighter skin tone.

Museums, National Parks, Heroes Park

■ The Bob Marley Museum was a treat. I was walking through the halls of his home, seeing his bed, touching his awards. It was all too cool. I loved the colors that were vibrant throughout the museum. It was as if Bob Marley could have greeted us at the front steps and everything would fit into place. I looked at all the photos from then and now, and I saw no change. Everything was frozen in time perfectly, and I loved it.

■ Marcus Garvey Museum Tour and Liberty Hall. I was surprised to learn of the pivotal role Marcus Garvey had played in raising the morale of the African Diaspora, as well as his range of influence – he started the Universal Negro Improvement Association (UNIA), centers of which were set up all over the world. These centers were known as Liberty Halls, which are supported by the Friends of Liberty Hall. In the United States alone there are 837 Liberty Halls. He is a powerful and inspirational figure to African-Americans – an example of nobility and the greatest they are capable of.

■ About Jamaica I have noticed that although they may have been robbed of their history before slavery, they have made significant strides to preserve their history post-slavery. The museum was amazing and one lucky to have such an amazing man come out of their country. Marcus Garvey's idea, "Up you mighty race, you can accomplish what you will!" is something all Black people need to reconsider... Garvey planted the seeds of a revolution for Black people. It is now our responsibility to make sure those seeds grow into prosperity.

■ The pieces at the National Art Gallery really encompassed what it means to be Jamaican: images of a Coca-Cola bottle symbolizing Jamaica's participation in the global economy, pictures of Rastafarians smoking marijuana embracing the religion of more than one percent of the nation's population, portraits of women upon whom Jamaica's matrifocal society is hinged. One of my favorite pieces was one at the entrance showing a naked man and woman deep in conversation. It reminded me of Laura Facey's piece at Emancipation Park as well as some of the work by one of Zimbabwe's biggest sculptors. I felt as though the picture captured the essence of how both men and women had survived for centuries by operating as a unit, building and valuing their families and sharing domestic and administrative skills.

■ The Recognition of Heroes is seen throughout Jamaica and is something I will take away with me when I leave. The people's pride in their heroes is admirable. I can only hope that future generations can continue to learn the history of their country and understand the importance of these people.

Natural Beauty & Hikes

■ We drove for about two hours to Woodside. I don't think I've ever had such a breathtaking car ride. The view was amazing. Take a moment to imagine Paradise. Beautiful waterfalls, huge green mountains, a wide river cutting through the middle of a wonderfully lush valley, the sun shining though the clouds to cap the highest peaks of these mountains. It was perfect.

■ We were in Negril for only one night and a day... That was the Jamaica you see on postcards... The ocean was beautiful... I've never seen an ocean like that in the United States, with those deep blues and greens and aquamarines. The horizon never seemed so vast. Looking out on the ocean I thought I could see forever.

■ The hike to the waterfalls in Moore Town was probably one of the most spiritual experiences of this trip. There was such a sense of connectedness that I felt with the land, with the tour guides who worked hard to maintain and preserve their Maroon identity and community, as well as the fighting souls that once passed through the same paths centuries ago.... My lasting impression of the Maroons is one of complete awe. I admire their choice to live in the unknown rather than to be enslaved on plantations. They fought for what they believed in and did not compromise their values.

Interactions with Jamaicans: Rural Home Stay at Woodside, St. Mary's Parish

■ At Hellshire beach two young men approached [the two of us]. They introduced themselves and their friends who were off to the side. The first two boys told us that their two friends wanted us to go over and talk to them. I was offended, to say the least. The culture shock over the Caribbean machismo frustrated me. Why does the woman go to the man? Is it because he said so? I did not realize until that point, when I experienced it myself, that gender roles and identities in the United States are very different and, in may opinion, have been relatively progressive in terms of gender equality.

■ Sex Tourism. Negril may be nicknamed "the capital of casual" but I call it "a small place with big problems." Never in my life have I encountered a night such as Saturday January 13! After arriving at a hotel and five of us were waiting to get some food, a white couple constantly stared at us and appeared to be eavesdropping. That made me tense. But what made me most uncomfortable was the overt display of Sex Tourism. It was everywhere. I even got aggressively pursued. About six white men walked towards ____ and me, hollered at us like cattle, winked and exaggerated their eyes like we were animals wanting to have sex with them. I was completely offended and disgusted.

■ Talking to a herbalist was an amazing experience. He reminded me of my grandmother, whom I had never met but who herself was a herbalist. As he explained how each plant could be used for different illnesses, I could not help but notice the difference between this model and the western model. A few students kept asking questions like "How many times should you take this?", "How much of it?' – and I realized how most of us can hardly think beyond the 'three-times-a-day-for-a-week ' kind of medication. Here there was less emphasis on precision but on general well being. You stopped taking the medicine when your pain/rush (or whatever) was gone.

■ Saturday morning's visit to Dr. Erna Brodber was an experience of its own. I think the most inspiring thing I learnt from her is her willingness to come back and live in her community, and help build something for them. I do not know many people who would be willing to leave the city's comfort for a rural setting, and also be willing to do all that work without any payment. She is a very dedicated woman and an inspiration to us.

■ During a conversation with my host family we talked about why Jamaicans are so anxious to leave their country and go to America. They viewed America as a land of opportunity with endless amounts of jobs, a better way of living, and happiness. I was utterly confused, because to me Jamaica is a paradise. Right outside their window they have ample crops and food. They have beaches nearby and a community that cares about them… I tried to convince them that the US would not be much better.

■ One guy, a taxi driver at Woodside, would not let me pay for the taxi because he was so fascinated to have met an African. He was 'blessed' (in his words) to have an African ride in his taxi. I was flustered and again, I recognized that it is only fate that had led some of us here, and left others to be born in the motherland.

Woodside and Home Stays

■ We enjoyed the annual Woodside Day celebration, an invigorating and spiritual hike and herbal tutorial. I am also very appreciative of the family that graciously hosted me. I truly believe that my Woodside experience was the best of the entire trip so far, because it allowed me to be exposed to the African experience in the past and present. The Woodside community has a vibrant cultural heritage. My only regret is that I did not stay longer.

■ My host family at Woodside was very nice to me. Ms. Patricia and her daughter, Stacy, made sure I had a wonderful time. I must say I was shocked by the standard of living that I saw. Back in my rural home it is hard to imagine most people having TVs, DVD players, etc., but most people at Woodside had them, and a few more luxury items. In a way Woodside was not as rural as I thought it would be. I must admit that my language skills were tested… and I often emerged on the losing side. The accent was quite difficult for me, but it helped sharpen my hearing.

■ Being with my host family at Woodside showed me the meaning of true joy and happiness that does not depend on money or material possessions. Rather the meaning and purpose of life can be found in the love that a mother has for her family and the love a people have for their community – a community composed of people with different ideas and talents who are willing to listen to each other in hopes of attaining the same goal. I want to thank Woodside for making me a part of their community because I will never forget it.

Performance

■ Body poetry. Jamaicans have their own expression form called dub poetry – a fusion of dance, drumming and poetry. It seems that in the entertainment world, aside from musicians, dub poets definitely command a high level of respect in the public arena. A'dzioo Simba's performance was remarkable, and even more insightful were her carefully picked words. Her slim body gyrated at the sound of the drumbeat as she made profound though still elegant movements in unison with her verse – a breathtaking form of body-poetry. As she allowed us into her world for an hour it was clear that she represented the fusion of two central issues: the plight of women in Jamaica and the country's take on international politics. It seemed to me that a recurring motif was a strong anti-American sentiment, backed by widely exercised Afrocentrism.

■ The beat of the drums was so rhythmic, it was lively and I could feel the beat pulsating through my body. I really wanted to get up and dance too…The Manchioneal Cultural Group completed the show by performing another ceremony called Kumina that drove the spirits away. The ceremony could last as long as the spirits made it, but this time it lasted only five minutes. I had learned about revivalism and Kumina in class, but witnessing and experiencing the ceremonies allowed me to have greater understanding.

■ Another amazing opportunity was being able to attend a reading by Chinua Achebe at UWI. I took a look at the crowd and I was happy to see a wide range of people in attendance. There were blacks, whites,

Asians with dreads, Chinese Jamaicans, Indians, mulattoes and anything in between. It was so interesting and heartwarming. I even met a lady who had been a speaker at MIT's Caribbean conference.

Maroons

■ Visiting the Maroons was eventful. Climbing to Nanny Falls was a workout but really cool. We learned so much from Colonel Wallace Sterling. The community was humble. The Maroons showed us their lifestyle, taught us about their history and shared their culture with us. The amount of creativity and resourcefulness that the Maroons had was beyond comprehension. I felt completely at home!

■ We were able to hike through the mountains at Moore Town and experience the living of the Maroons who escaped slavery on the plantations, under the leadership of Ashanti warrior, Nanny. While moving though the thick forest trees, eating coconut and sugarcane straight from the trees and visiting the waterfalls, I felt a sense of freedom, a sense of peace, serenity and happiness. I can only imagine how the enslaved people felt when they escaped the plantations and developed communities among the greatness and fullness of the forests. What amazed me about the Maroons is that they were a resourceful, intelligent and willful people.

Identity, Nationalism, Class Issues

■ Cultural and national identity should be embraced, even if it is not perfect, because it was who you are. On the issue of the national anthem being sung in public venues (such as church or a movie theater) I think it is a good way to bring people together and instill a great sense of pride and love for Jamaica, so that the Jamaican people can have more of a reason to be proud of who they are, where they came from and, most importantly, where they are going in the future.

■ Apart from shaping the hinge of Jamaican society today in a global sense, the principles and teaching of Marcus Garvey are essentially the foundation upon which Rastafarianism is based. On Rastafarianism and Afrocentrism I have been astounded and somewhat impressed by the extent to which Jamaicans are in touch with their African roots, especially in the way that they identify themselves and the way they dress... The issue of identity is of key concern on a national level and is part of the public sentiment that Jamaican youth need to be educated on their culture and black identity. Perhaps my inability to see the real issue is rooted in the fact that I am a foreigner, and thus only have the opportunity to see things through a slightly biased lens.

■ Mark said that in Jamaica there is no true political leadership. The new Prime Minister is good, but enthusiasm and a charismatic personality alone cannot run a country. She needs to learn to make conscious policy decisions and needs more experience. Most Jamaicans are not anti-woman and are patient to see what she can do. It is a class problem that she is encountering, not an issue of ability.

■ One thing that surprised me about Jamaica is the overwhelming gap between the rich and the poor. In most other countries I have visited the rich and poor live in their own separate and distinct communities. In Jamaica I saw mansions and elaborate homes right next to and across from desperately poor communities.

Self -Transformation

■ I feel as though learning about the Maroons has brought us around full circle. We've been all over Jamaica, and we've seen everything a tourist needs to see as well as everything a 'sovereign learner' needs to see. I feel like an Honorary Jamaican.

■ I think that our psychological development is equally important as our social, political and economic development. I think we need to develop ourselves internally so that we can be comfortable with who we are as people. Marcus Garvey influential because he was able to encourage African Jamaicans to take pride in who they are. I think this is essential to our development.

■ Liguanea. I loved our house; it was so great. My roommates and I had a fabulous time. There was never any quarrel, we did almost everything together and enjoyed ourselves so much. The irony of it all is that we were the single group that wasn't really a group to begin with… I think the fact that we didn't know each other created an openness that enabled us to get to know each other even better and create a nice environment in the house.

■ It is easy for a white person in America to be unaware or to choose to ignore the division, but mostly, for me, I was raised completely color-blind. One thing my parents always made very clear to me, even when I was young, that at some points in history people have done horrible things to each other because of stupid, insignificant differences like race and color, but that people are all the same. I don't know how to think about the world in any other way.

■ During our orientation Ms. Campbell spoke about how stereotypes and biases affect our objective eye. I expect to engage my senses in my experience of Jamaican culture over the next couple of weeks. The most exciting thing about this journey is that I will probably walk away feeling a stronger sense of pride in who I am, as a Caribbean American and a person of African descent.

■ Even on a trip it's a good feeling to be at home in a place. The people here are warm and friendly, and so many of them want to open their hearts to us. I may be biased, but I don't see many Americans doing that. We could learn a thing or two from the people here. I'm making sure that I am always in sponge-mode while I'm here, ever absorbing.

4. Introducing Swahili to Wellesley College

Another important contribution to Wellesley College of which I am proud was the introduction of Swahili with the support of Provost Andrew Shennan. This was in response to years of lobbying by Black students and Black alumnae for an indigenous African course to be taught at Wellesley to support the major and minor in Africana Studies and other related programs of study. Swahili is one of the most popular and important languages in the world today and is spoken by a majority of people of African descent who represent one billion people worldwide. It carries the culture of many African peoples who are linked to ancestors that have existed since the dawn of humanity. It is also the most widely taught African language in the United States and the only indigenous African language taught at Wellesley College. Swahili holds a special place in the curriculum and its continuing existence is based on its intrinsic value that merits the commitment of a premier Liberal Arts College. To be competitive in global education and global career development, the college was urged to maximize the importance of its only indigenous African language by supporting its central place in the curriculum, with implications for the study of Africa and the African Diaspora in the Americas, the Caribbean, Europe and Asia.

Most students come to language programs because they have a dream of visiting, studying, or working in countries where the languages are spoken. The department felt that it was important to develop a supportive educational infrastructure that includes classroom Swahili as well as internships, study abroad opportunities and post-Wellesley language training like many of the other languages taught at Wellesley. The following was the first advertisement for the introduction of Swahili to Wellesley College:

Next year, 2009, Africana Studies will introduce Swahili, the most popular African language to Wellesley College for the first time. It will be taught in the fall and Spring semesters as Africana 101 and 102 – Elementary Swahili. This will enhance its curriculum and provide students with an opportunity to learn an African language. A number of our students study abroad in African countries where Swahili is spoken and this will be a valuable skill for them to have. Other students may be interested in learning an African language to expand their linguistic skills. The instructor will be Judith Mari from Tanzania, a native speaker, who has taught Swahili at several universities in the United States. Judith Mari has a B.Sc. in Public

Policy and Management and Geography and an M.A. in International Development. She also has several certificates in Teaching African Languages and has been a research fellow at the W.E.B. Dubois Institute at Harvard University.

5. Featured Speaker at 'African Women's Leadership Conference' 2018, Wellesley College

Wellesley College and the Mastercard Foundation organized a landmark and memorable conference on 'African Women's Leadership' from March 8th to 9th, 2018, in which I was a featured speaker. The conference brought a number of African women leaders, including former president of Liberia, President Ellen Johnson Sirleaf and Nobel Laureate to the campus as well as kansiime Ann, an African woman comedian of international repute. Other speakers included President Paula Johnson of Wellesley College; Dr. Agnes Binagwaho, Vice-Chancellor, University of Global Health Equity (UGHE) and former minister of health, Rwanda; Kakenya Ntaiya, a Kenyan educator and social activist; Farida Bedwei, Ghanaian software engineer and disability rights advocate; Hauwa Ibrahim, Nigerian international human rights activist and Sharia Law attorney and Mfoniso Udofia, first-generation Nigerian American story teller and educator. Several Mastercard scholars and officials also spoke on the panel titled 'Perspectives from young leaders.' Speakers included Tanyaradzwa Chinyukwi, Leah Nakaima, Ivy Mwai, Eunice Adjoa,Yeboah Adu and Jennifer Amuah.

This ground-breaking African Women's Leadership Conference brought together eminent African women leaders from Africa and around the world to discuss and reflect on the importance and contribution of women's leadership on the continent as well as the constraints to such leadership. Speakers and participants brought their experiences and knowledge in a pioneering expression and appreciation of the successes and challenges facing African women's influence and authority in providing leadership in the fields of health, education, politics, technology, law and the arts. Emphasis was placed on young African women leaders and the importance of mentoring the next generation of women who are going to help shape the future of the continent, promote gender equality and advance the empowerment of women.

This important conference was jointly organized by Wellesley College and the Mastercard Foundation to achieve the following: "expand our understanding of the many ways women leaders are transforming their communities and their nations; it promises to advance leadership and provide opportunities to learn from the women who are making a difference not only across Africa but around the world. In lectures, breakout sessions, and informal discussions, attendees explored what women's leadership looks like through the lens of four key leadership competencies – confidence, creativity, courage, and resilience – leading to a deeper appreciation of the challenges African women leaders face and offering productive strategies for addressing them."

Highlights from my speech: 'African Women's
Leadership Through the Ages'

As a resident professor at Wellesley College, I was asked to give the first lecture to set the stage for the conference. The title of my lecture was 'African Women's Leadership Through the Ages' moderated by Professor Lidwien Kapteijns, Professor of History. My presentation examined women and leadership in Africa through the ages through an exploration of various theoretical constructs used in the study of female leadership. It presented definitions of leadership and reviewed a history of leadership and the domination of men in leadership positions since classical times. Four types of leadership present in the literature were discussed, namely charismatic leadership, transactional leadership, transformational leadership, and servant leadership. I then gave examples of women leaders from Africa in each of the categories. Good examples of charismatic leadership are Winnie Mandikizela Mandela, popular anti-apartheid leader of South Africa and Alice Lenshina, renowned charismatic prophet of the Lumpa Church from Zambia.

The second type is transactional leadership, which was exemplified in a video of the South African parliament, presided over by a former female speaker, Baleka Mbete, and showing how she had to negotiate her position of authority against strong male resistance. The third was servant leadership, with an example of Canon Cassandra Garber JP from Sierra Leone who serves her nation and her ethnic group as an effective leader of the Krio Descendants Union and promotes minority rights and inclusive leadership. The fourth example was transformational leadership, depicting the former president of Liberia, Ellen Johnson Sirleaf, who skillfully shepherded her country from war to peace and to democratic governance. When she stepped down in 2018, she was rewarded by being awarded the Mo Ibrahim prize for leadership.

In my presentation, I pointed out three important contributions that African women's leadership has made to the world. The first is women's suffrage. In the 1792 elections in Sierra Leone, all heads of households, one third of whom were women, voted. According to Schama in his book *Rough Crossings: Britain, the Slaves and the American Revolution,* 'Female voting was something that even the French Revolution, in its most radical phase had not been able to contemplate. Indeed, the Jacobins were hostile to the idea. It was momentous then, that the first women to cast their vote for any kind of public office anywhere in the world were Black liberated slaves.'[21] This was 40 years before the suffragette movement gained the vote for women in Britain in 1832 and eighty- eight years for the United States where women got the vote in 1920.

The second is climate change. In 1977, the Greenbelt Movement of Kenya, led by Nobel Peace Laureate Dr. Wangari Maathai, a scientist, made the link between deforestation and climate change and noticed the impact of seasonal changes to the agricultural cycle. They

---

21 Schama, 2006, **Rough Crossings: The Slaves, the British and the American Revolution**, New York, Harper Collins Publishers, p. 374

started planting trees to combat this, long before the world held a UN conference and UN Earth Summit in 1992 to develop an International Convention on Climate Change.

The third highlights Africa's contribution to feminist epistemology. Africa was the laboratory for early anthropological studies of women and gender roles. In the pioneering book, *Women, Culture and Society* edited by Rosaldo and Lamphere in 1974, African-based studies helped prove that gender asymmetry was not a natural but socially constructed phenomenon.[22] Examples from egalitarian gender systems of hunter-gatherer societies, matrilineal societies and women in executive positions as rulers provided theoretical and methodological ammunition to scholars in deconstructing prevailing androcentric modes of analysis.

The lecture also commented on some of the indigenous mechanisms that provided opportunities for the development of female leadership and the role of colonialism in redefining structures of authority in ways that tended to favor men. Afro-centric perspectives on female leadership were contrasted with Euro-centric perspectives, including definitions of feminism. For Africa, female leadership revealed certain unique characteristics, namely: The legacy of female sanctioned executive authority; Motherhood and its matriarchal association with leadership; Parallel leadership: and the Queen Mother paradigm and armed conflict as a catalyst for the emergence of female leadership for peace. Emerging views both about leadership and followership were presented with a plea for an equal emphasis to be placed on the study of followership since this in an intrinsic aspect of leadership formation. Case studies were then presented from the findings of my research on 'Women and Leadership' in three of the Manor River Union countries of Liberia, Guinea and Sierra Leone which resulted in the publication of the book *Women and Leadership in West Africa:*

22 Rosaldo, M. and Lamphere, 1974, **Woman, Culture and Society**, Alto, Stanford University Press.

Mothering the Nation and Humanizing the State in 2012.[23]

Some of the findings of the research included the following characteristics of women leaders in the three of the four Mano River Union countries studied:

One, leadership qualities showed up at an early age through responsibilities in the home, birth order, namely the first child or the first girl, and having strong female role models in their primary group. Two, the role of fathers in encouraging and cultivating their leadership potential and providing educational and other opportunities was crucial. This was not so much a case of girls getting along better with their fathers, but a father's ability to navigate the largely male-dominated outside world and provide advice and guidance to their daughters.

Three, many of the leaders had good female mentors through their educational years and their careers, although some of their mentors were men. Four, most of the women had supportive husbands or partners. Five, traditional leaders, such as female chiefs, had the advantage of automatic loyalty and followership. They understood and internalized their constitutional power and unquestionable authority, which was not based on gender. One of them, Chief Melrose Forster Gbowee of Sierra Leone, explained how she settled a dispute among her male political officials: 'I had to stop power by using my own bigger power.' The constitution gave her that power and she knew how to use it. Gender was irrelevant.

Six, there is a moral and altruistic thrust to their concept and definition of leadership that is closely linked to concepts of motherhood and peace. Seven, although they all recognized problems of gender inequality and male domination in general, they universally identified one problem of female leadership that they blamed on women. That is the tendency for women to lack solidarity with other women and to bring each other down, especially women in leadership positions.

---

23   Steady, F. 2012, **Female Leadership in West Africa: Mothering the Nation and Humanizing the State,** New York, Palgrave/Macmillan.

Some described it as 'Crabitis', evoking the imagery of crabs trying to climb out of a bucket and in the process, bringing each other down. Eight, they did not believe that women in high political office necessarily promote gender equality because they could be mere tokens or become co-opted by the male-dominated political system and are also capable of abusing power.

In general, the following conclusions can be made: First, although women have made some progress in political leadership, we still have a long way to go. Second, although politics remains a male preserve and patrilineal and patriarchal ideologies still prevail, female leadership and the dynamics of power in Africa can be expressed in overt, covert and low-intensity ways in political and non-political spheres. Third, indigenous systems of female leadership, with executive power, continue to serve as models with built-in guarantees of constitutional authority and automatic followership. Fourth, motherhood and its derivative, 'matriarchy', continue to be relevant and to inspire, produce and sustain a type of female leadership with values that tend to be more egalitarian, compassionate and altruistic, with moral overtones.

Fifth, armed conflicts have had a catalytic effect in advancing female leadership, since the effects of wars on women can be devastating and continue long after the war ends. Sixth, my continuing research offers an alternative to the ways in which we view leadership. While recognizing that women can also abuse power, as in the case of Alice Lenshina of Zambia, it offers an alternative to the male-dominated, authoritarian and war-prone leadership that has affected the West African Mano River Union countries of Guinea, Liberia and Sierra Leone. It provides a powerful narrative for mothering the nation and humanizing the state.

In closing, I evoked an African saying which I mentioned earlier, credited to the Yoruba of Nigeria, that best expresses aspects of female leadership in Africa: 'Men may be the heads, but women are the necks that turn the heads.' In the African context, we may have to look in all the right places to fully appreciate the extent, complexity, richness and impact of African women's leadership through the ages.

The conference was organized around several major themes, including:

- Women's leadership through the ages.
- The challenge faced by African women leaders in the health sector.
- Creating movement: African women in the American theatre..
- Empowering girls, transforming communities: My journey to lead a bold vision for change.
- Young women leading the way: Transforming leadership in Africa....
- Coding my way to an empowered life.
- Mothers without borders: Steering youth away from violent extremism
- Conference insights and reflections
- The Kenner Lecture – 'If your dreams don't scare you:' A conversation on advancing African women's leadership by Ellen Johnson Sirleaf, President of Liberia -2006 -2018 and Nobel Laureate)-I am - - kansiime Ann: a performance by world-renowned Ugandan Comedian Anne Kansiime

CHAPTER 28

Retirement and Beyond

'A feminist's work is never ever done' – Filomina Steady

⬥

I have always been a woman in action, both in my personal and professional life. After serving twenty-two years at Wellesley College, mostly as professor and often as chair of the Africana Studies Department, I felt it was time to retire. Retirement is a life cycle event that marks the end of a professional career in a formal sense but also signals the beginning of a new life and the next chapter in one's life. It can therefore be a life-changing event that helps you reflect on the past and prepare for the future. I feel blessed and lucky to have had the opportunities that I had, starting from being born into a family that valued baby girls and daughters and gave equal educational opportunities to all children, regardless of gender. Being a woman in action and a feminist came naturally to me.

The predominantly all-female educational institutions that I attended and spent my professional life in also helped me to develop an understanding of the life cycle and position of women in society and a motivation to work for gender equality and the advancement of women. I had many good female role models as family members, teachers, professors, Girl Guide leaders and eminent women holding high positions in Freetown society. I was fortunate to have very good and productive positions in academia, where my teaching and research helped to develop the minds of young students, many of whom went on to make significant contributions in the professions as well as in politics and community service. I was equally fortunate to hold executive positions as Deputy Director and Special Advisor at the United Nations, which promoted gender equality and the advancement of women at a critical time of international policy development in these important areas.

As a professor and an academic, it was a distinct honor to have a symposium dedicated to my work as a tribute to me during my retirement. The events surrounding the Filomina Steady Symposium are recounted below:

The Filomina Steady Symposium: Honoring the Work of Professor Filomina Steady on the occasion of her retirement – April 26, 2019. (Center)

An international symposium was held in honor of my work during my retirement from Wellesley in spring 2019. It was sponsored by the Africana Studies Department, Wellesley Center for Women, the Provost's Office, the Departments of Anthropology, Art, East Asian Languages and Cultures, Education, English, French, History, Music, Philosophy, Psychology, Religion, Sociology, Spanish, Women and Gender Studies, Dean of Students, Harambee House, Slater International Center, the Black Task Force, the Freedom Project, Committee on Lectures and Cultural Events and some student organizations.

The program was rich and extensive and included a welcome address from President Paula Johnson and an introduction by Professor Layli Maparyan, Executive Director of The Wellesley Centers for Women and Professor of Africana Studies. Some of my faculty colleagues in Africana Studies, namely Kellie Carter Jackson, Lizeli Fitzpatrick and Geofred Osoro, participated in the introductory panel. Other panels included a faculty panel, an alumnae panel, a student panel and special tributes from Wellesley African Students' Association. Impromptu remarks were also made by others present at the symposium, which included Professor Johnetta Richards and representatives of the Krio Descendants Union of Sierra Leone.

Specifically, my scholarly contributions to African feminism and women's leadership were being highlighted at the symposium. My books were also on display and numerous references were made to the award-winning book *The Black Woman Cross-Culturally*, which I edited and which is now in its third edition. It was an award-winning book viewed by some as a classic and has been referenced hundreds of times. The keynote speaker, Chancellor's Professor Obioma Nnaemeka of the University of Indiana and of international repute, gave an outstanding lecture on 'Expanding Feminist Visions' and emphasized my pioneering efforts at bringing and centralizing African women in the discourse on feminism and women's and gender studies.

A noted theoretician, Professor Asoka Bandarage, on the faculty panel stressed the relevance of my work for early studies of women of the Global South and women of color in general. My contributions to the definition of African feminism as humanistic feminism was also commended, as was my contribution to environmental studies by Professor Lidwien Kapteijns, a distinguished faculty colleague at Wellesley College who also emphasized the breath of my teaching fields in keeping with my global, cross-cultural and wholistic approaches. Other speakers included Professor Stanlie James, one of the leading experts on Black feminism, who gave an update on her book on the contribution of Black women to international human rights and my important role as an academic activist in pushing the agenda of human rights and women's rights at the United Nations.

Professor Oyewumi Oyeronke, the award-winning author of *The Invention of Women: Making an African Sense of Western Gender Discourses* appreciated my pioneering role, especially in presenting a road map for junior women faculty working in the area of feminist theory and methodology, and stressed the importance of the 'sense of history' which undergirded my work. My compatriot, distinguished professor and expert on adult literacy Daphne Ntiri, spoke passionately of the importance of women studies and feminist and womanist theories and my contribution to these lines of enquiry. She also credited my background for some of my success and spoke of the grounding that I had received as a Krio woman in Sierra Leone and the foundational role of my secondary school, the Annie Walsh Memorial School, founded in 1849, in shaping the course of my career and my contributions.

The speakers on the alumnae panel, Charlotte Ashamu, Katherine Jenkins, Lilly Marcelin and Fiona Almeida, were all hard-working and successful professionals in various fields at national and international levels. They expressed their appreciation of my work as a professor when they were students at Wellesley College and my serving as a mentor and role model to them. Halimatou Hima Moussa Dioula from Niger sent a moving tribute of how I had helped steer her journey into being a PhD student at Cambridge University. I was particularly touched by the warm tributes read by Nigerian student Chika Egbuzie, class of 2019 of alumnae from the Wellesley African Students Association (WASA) from all over the world, some of whom were pursuing important careers that would make a difference in the world, especially in Africa.

A students' panel was chaired by Professor Craig Murphy, one of the best professors and authors of political science, African Studies and International Relations at Wellesley College. These included outstanding Wellesley students like Dominique Copeland, Sandra Ohemeng, Kennedy Austin, Hawah Kallon and Penny Hawthorne. They spoke of their experiences at Wellesley College and their work with me in their various classes. They noted how my classes provided fresh insights and analyses and helped fill in the gap in terms of diversity of the curriculum and critical insights on gender, race and environmental justice. They were particularly appreciative of the importance of having representation in the form of Black female professors as role models in the classroom at Wellesley.

Throughout the event, I felt both proud and humble, and had no idea that my contributions to academia had had such a lasting impact. I was reminded of the time I spent with my father, who was an architect and a builder. I used to marvel at the way in which each building block was carefully installed, reinforcing the others. This symposium made me realize that what I had been doing all these years was also putting down building blocks in the academic environment. I was filled with gratitude that so many of my colleagues and students were adding bigger and better blocks to mine and making the academy stronger for it. One cannot ask for anything more! Listening to the various speakers on the panels, I was reassured that the important work of research, teaching and encouraging critical analyses will continue and flourish at Wellesley College.

The following tributes from faculty colleagues at Wellesley and beyond and Wellesley college alumnae were read at the symposium. The full program of the Filomina Steady Symposium is presented in Appendix 1.

Tributes from faculty and alumnae at Wellesley and beyond

Dear Filomina,

"I write to express my regrets for not being able to attend the symposium celebrating your retirement on Friday. I will be out of town. I have many fond memories of collaborating with you at Wellesley: as dean, as your faculty colleague, and as your peer on R&P committees for the anthropology department. You were always wise, generous and gracious in your dealings with others, and I learned a great deal from you. I know from many one-on-one encounters with your students that they would say much the same. I will miss you. Thank you for all that you've given me. And I wish you all good things in the years to come."

Warm regards,

Lee

Professor Lee Cuba, Department of Sociology, Wellesley College

"Thank you for sending this announcement of Professor Steady's retirement. She was Director of Women's Studies at Sacramento State University for two years. Though she was with us for a short period of time, she had a lasting impact on this campus. Hers has been an exceptional life of scholarship, womanism, and contribution to the well-being of humanity. We are proud and grateful for having had the privilege of knowing her. We hope her retirement proves as fulfilling as her life has been to this point, and we're sure it will be."

David Covin, Emeritus Professor of Pan African Studies and
Political Science, Sacramento State University, California

"Dear Illustrious Sister Filomina,

I received the first email/flyer about this major event on April 10, 2019, when I had just returned from a trip to Kenya and preparing to go to San Francisco for another conference. If I had known I would have joined to celebrate you and your remarkable and inspiring career. I had already finalized my annual trip to the UN in New York City with Cornell students. Since it is the end of the academic year, we do not have the possibility of postponing it. Otherwise I would so that I can join you. I am sure it will be quite a memorable day of reflection and debate. Congratulations!"

N'Dri Thérèse ASSIÉ-LUMUMBA, Ph D
Professor, Africana Studies and Research Center, Cornell University.

From alumnae

"Dr. Steady,

It is so wonderful to hear from you! Congratulations on your upcoming retirement! I am so humbled and honored to be invited to participate in the symposium, but I will unfortunately be traveling for a family obligation that day. I am so sorry to miss this event. I remember your Environmental Justice class so fondly and think of the material and concepts it covered regularly. After Wellesley, I went back to school to earn a Bachelor of Science in Nursing and began working as a nurse in a neonatal intensive care unit. This past year, I earned my Masters of Science in Nursing and am now practicing as a Neonatal Nurse Practitioner at the Women's and Children's hospitals in Pittsburgh, Pennsylvania. I think often of the systematic and personal social and environmental injustices that play a role in many of the health sequelae that lead to the preterm births and congenital anomalies that I see on a daily basis in my clinical practice. I often consider how I can go on to start to address some of these issues in the perinatal area, and know so much of my interest in this topic was stoked by your guidance in the Environmental Justice course.

I wish you a happy and full retirement. You will be greatly missed in the Wellesley academic community. You have touched so many with your thoughts, teachings, and kindness."

All the best,
Phoebe Handler - Alumna

"Dear Professor Steady,

I can hardly imagine Wellesley College without you, as you were a key figure during my years there. Your classes have made a tremendous impact in my undergraduate experience, and I am grateful to have had you as my major and thesis adviser. I wish I could attend the symposium, to be once more in an academic environment! I've always looked up to you, and still today I do. As much as I have learnt to be opened to the opportunities life has opened along my path, I hope that in some years from now, I will return to school and pursue higher education teaching and research. In my current work, I find myself showing partiality towards young females, teaching them skills that take them beyond cleaning positions, and reminding them that they can do anything a man does. This is important in a culture where women are regarded as minors, and men as leaders in society. And so I find fulfillment in my current work, even though it is not the academic environment that I aspire to be in. I imagine you are looking forward to retirement. Wellesley will miss you I am sure. Please send me your personal email so we continue to keep in touch.

Lastly, thank you so much for your donation. Relatives are starting to rebuild homes, and they couldn't have done much without the help being offered. You are part of making that possible. It will take time for the inhabitants of Beira to fully recover from the devastation,and any amount of help goes a long way. Thank you.

Wishing you a successful symposium. I hope it will be filmed and posted on Youtube so I watch the presentations and lectures online."

Warm regards, Andrea Kine - Alumna

"Wow! Professor Steady!

It is amazing that it is time for you to retire. I hope you look back on your life and legacy with great pride in remembering the large scope of your work and remembering each of us grateful alumnae/i who have benefitted from your incredible research, teaching prowess, and care nurturing us to do the work and staying motivated in the movement. I'm so glad to see two former students who I consider personal friends, Charlotte and Katherine, on the program to honor you with their words at the symposium. Though I cannot attend, I am no less enthusiastic about sending you a fond farewell and many thanks. You have done a great service at Wellesley College and I wish that you continue your impact in whatever way fills your spirit in the days, weeks, months and years to come!"

Fondly,
Rabbi Heather Miller - Alumna

"My well wishes from East Africa for Professor Steady upon her retirement from Wellesley College. Professor Steady's contributions to African Studies and Women's Studies are widely celebrated. I would like to add mention of her contribution to Environmental Studies as well. At Wellesley she taught the only course (available while I was there) that focused on minoritized populations' interactions with the environment and environmental justice. This work may be less well known but it has had an impact at Wellesley amongst many students, and beyond the academic world such as when we discussed Prof Steady's book "Environmental Justice in the New Millennium" with my activist collective 'Decolonizing Environmentalism'. For me, it is incredibly important to remember that the environment is core to the lives of African(a) peoples and African(a) women, contrary to popular stereotypes of our apathy towards environmental issues.

Professor Steady served as one of my advisors for my individual major but my own personal relationship with Professor Steady has grown after Wellesley, testament to her continued care for her students even after they leave the institution. Thanks to Professor Steady I have grown into my advocacy and activism self for example through advocating for the Africana Studies department to retain a hiring position. I am delighted to wish Professor Steady all the very best in the new paths she is moving onto after her retirement. May the ancestors continue to hear you and see you as they have done throughout these years in academic life. Àṣẹ, àṣẹ, ashe oleng."

Wangũi wa Kamonji, '13
Environmental Studies and (Individual major) Urban Studies

"It would be great to see if there's a way that those of us who are away from the US can attend parts of the symposium via Skype or video. Can't imagine Africana Studies without Professor Steady. She was a great inspiration."

Elishibah Mesengheti - Alumna

"When I reflect on my time at Wellesley, my experiences with Professor Steady shine bright. Professor Steady's classes were not only informative but they were inspirational as they helped me to deepen and cement my journey into being a learner and advocate for the African Diaspora. Professor Steady taught her classes with passion and brought a unique perspective. She had an intersectional approach to the coursework she taught, and students from a variety of disciplines could find something to take away from the subject material. In fact, some of the books and articles that were discussed in those classes can be found on bookshelves in my home. In addition to being one of my professors, Professor Steady was an advisor and mentor. She was very understanding about the difficulties that can arise for some students as they navigate tough academic schedules with the rest of their lives. She gave wonderful advice for my work and supported me as a student. One of the most memorable moments with Professor Steady is her taking me among other students to a Wintersession in Jamaica. The Jamaican trip had a profound impact on me. I hold on to the memories because I learned so much, got to deepen some friendships (that I hold near and dear today), and got to travel throughout the country. I am so thankful for my time with Professor Steady. I wish her well in her next steps as she embarks on retirement.' With love, Akua – Alumna.

Symposium remarks by Filomina Steady

"It is indeed a supreme honor to be standing before you today in celebration of my retirement. I would also like to congratulate the highly accomplished faculty members that are also retiring this year and wish them the best for this important life cycle transition. I cannot say enough kind words of appreciation to my faculty colleagues who have supported me and my department and who continue to excel in all areas, and to provide an atmosphere of friendly academic debate and discussion at Wellesley and beyond. I also want to thank my wonderful family, my devoted husband, Dr. Henry Maduka Steady, and my sons Filo Chinaka Steady, Henry Maduka Steady, Junior and daughter, Azania Kezia Agnes Steady, for their love and support over the years.

When I came to Wellesley in 1997, I brought with me experiences as a professor in other institutions and at the international level as a director in the United Nations' Division for the Advancement of

Women. I helped prepare a number of plans of action for gender equality and the advancement of women as an executive member of the UN secretariat and as one of the leaders of the research and policy analysis team. In many ways the work was similar to academia in terms of the research but the political climate, power dynamics and the high stakes involved at the UN make academic politics seem like child's play. I remember the pride I felt in contributing to the drafting of the recommendation that all institutions of higher learning establish Women's Studies Programs. Today, these programs and departments are flourishing all over the world.

In my 22 years at Wellesley, a large number of which were spent chairing the Africana Studies Department, I can say that the future of the department looks bright and exciting with a highly accomplished and established faculty of international repute and newly recruited faculty who are not only rising stars in their fields but also first-rate human beings. We are also proud of our multidisciplinary focus, which is being increasingly appreciated, and we have seen a significant expansion in the number of our majors and minors. We hope to continue to have the support of the president and the administration and to strengthen our collaborative efforts with colleagues in other departments.

During my tenure at Wellesley, much has changed, but so much remains the same. I have been through the administration of three presidents, Walsh, Bottomly and Johnson; all of whom had different leadership styles but were committed to excellence in scholarship, teaching, service and in building an inclusive and diverse community within and beyond Wellesley. When I came to Wellesley, there were slightly more male faculty in 1997 than female faculty, but the data for 2018 show that the gap is closing and women have surpassed men in terms of full-time faculty in all ranks, with male faculty at 28% and female faculty at 44%. However, if one examines the data closely, it becomes clear that there is gender disparity in terms of the nature of their contracts. Female faculty outnumber male faculty in the non-tenure-track positions of lecturer and visiting lecturer and so forth. With regard to Black faculty, the numbers of tenure track faculty have actually declined from 15 in 1997 to 11 in 2018. For students of African descent there was a slight increase of 86 students between 1997 to 2018 but it took 21 years to achieve that. I hope that going forward, these numbers will increase to truly reflect Wellesley's commitment to diversity and inclusive excellence.

On the level of the administration there have been some notable improvements. We now have five African-American women in high leadership positions, something I never thought I would see happen at Wellesley. It is to the credit of the college that we have African-American women in the positions of President, Dean of Students, Dean of Admissions, Director of Institutional Research and Executive Director of Wellesley's Centers for Women. All of these women are outstanding examples of role models for *every* woman in terms of their qualifications, personalities and ability to motivate others and provide enlightened leadership.

Wellesley has had many challenges over the years, including challenges of difference, racial incidents and political protests. As a community of scholars, teachers, staff and students, we still have a long way to go to unlearn some of our old prejudices and conscious as well as unconscious biases. We have had to face the constant challenges of budget cuts that affect faculty and staff positions and the curriculum. That's why it is so difficult to understand how Wellesley can have so many challenges in rationalizing its budget, with repeated complains of financial crises, despite its large endowment of about 1.8 billion dollars and record-breaking capital mobilization campaigns as recently as last year.

To my students, what can I say? I will miss you the most, but you will always have a place in my heart and mind. You are so special, so bright, so ambitious and so empathetic. You are so well behaved as well – now I sound like grandma, right? I hope you will break all kinds of ceilings, not only the gender-biased glass ceiling but ceilings of ignorance, bigotry, intolerance, discrimination and exclusion. You have inspired me so much and I have learnt how to think like a member of your generation and that has brought new meaning to my life. By being around you, I have remained young at heart because of you. That's how much you have influenced me and I thank you for that.

My future plans are simple. I will continue to be driven by my insatiable curiosity. My research interests in female leadership will expand to include more focus on the followers of leaders as much as the leaders themselves and the connection between the two. I will also be driven by my outrage over the alarming rate of maternal mortality, especially in Black women in Africa and the African Diaspora, where numbers can be as high as 800 maternal deaths per 100,000 live births in some African countries. I plan to work with a team and examine some of the ways in which the political economy and cultural determinants can contribute to both creating and alleviating the problem. In bringing forth new life, these mothers are dying needlessly from preventable causes. We have to look for solutions outside of the medical system, which is failing these women. The team plans to examine the problem in the US, Haiti and Sierra Leone and see how cultural systems can be harnessed to arrest this alarming problem.

I am honored by this tribute and wish to thank the organizers of this symposium, especially Professors Layli Marpayan who initiated it and Liseli Fitzpatrick, who gave me such a splendid introduction and the many sponsors for their generous contributions. I would also like to thank the other amazing members of my department, namely, Professors Selwyn Cudjoe, Kellie Carter Jackson and Geofred Osoro. I am sure we are going to have a productive and successful exchange of ideas; a celebration, and a warm appreciation of each other and of our collective contributions to the Academy, to our students and to humanity. I will miss Wellesley but I will be taking many fond memories of Wellesley with me. Wellesley is a part of me and I like to think that I will always be a part of Wellesley. Thank You very much!"

Filomina Steady Symposium on Youtube

https://www.youtube.com/results?search_
query=filomina+steady+symposium+2019

Postscript

The Africana Studies Department established a prize in my honor titled: 'Professor Filomina Steady Prize' given for research on Women of African Descent.

CHAPTER 29

Reflections on Some of Life's Lessons

" Life is the sum total of successfully overcoming challenges and seizing opportunities " – Filomina Steady

───❖───

In this final chapter, I discuss and reflect on some of the lessons I have learnt from life, including the following: Retirement as an elevation of one's status; upbringing and preparation for life; racism in the United States and Europe; Blacks in White academic institutions; the challenge of raising African children in the United States; Living through and learning from loss and grief; Feminism takes many forms; African Feminism as Humanistic Feminism; Being average is alright and 'The family is everything.'

Retirement as an elevation of one's status

Retirement could be a cause for celebration or a lament, depending on the cultural meanings attached to it in different societies. As an African, I value retirement and old age as important transitions to be celebrated, since they elevate one's status to that of an elder which comes with special respect and expectations to serve as counselor and adviser to the young. Women in particular play a more active role in public affairs, including, in some African societies, taking up political positions. So the idea of getting old for an Africa is different from that of an American, where youth is worshiped and old age is generally devalued.

Retirement also brings into focus the inevitable physical changes that come with aging and eldercare becomes central and requires special attention, as analyzed in the book *Eldercare as Art and Ministry* by my friend Dr. Irene Jackson Brown.[24] Although I have been very lucky to have enjoyed good health most of my life, health challenges come with my advancing years, such as arthritis, glaucoma, cataracts and hypertension. All of these conditions are well controlled with medication, exercise, diet and surgical interventions. If you are ageing in the United States, you will likely be on several medications and have frequent visits to the doctor for all kinds of tests, exams and consultations, as part of a profit-oriented medical system. Despite my critical evaluation of these excessive interventions, I found myself succumbing to the pill-popping habit of most senior citizens living in the United States.

My husband Henry, on the other hand, has not been so lucky health-wise and has had health challenges since 2014. He has problems with his legs and his stomach and has had two surgeries. Interestingly, he escaped many of the serious health challenges that come with aging and his vital signs remain good. He retired about ten years earlier than I did and spent most of his time in Brookline, Massachusetts, our family home, while I continued to teach at Wellesley College in Massachusetts until my retirement in 2019. As part of our family tradition, we have been spending Christmas in Freetown, Sierra Leone, joined by our children, Duka and Azania, on several occasions. Our regular visit to Freetown for 2019 was different. Henry and I were to return to the States in March 2020 but the Covid-19 pandemic stopped

---

24 Jackson Brown, I., 2020, **Eldercare as Art and Ministry,** New York, Church Publishing.

us in our tracks because of the closure of the airport and we were stuck in Freetown for several months. Now that the airport has reopened, we plan to continue spending six months in the USA and six months in Sierra Leone as cosmopolitan and happy senior citizens of the world.

Upbringing in preparation for life

My upbringing contributed a lot to the path that I charted in life and helped to steer me into a field concerned with gender equality and social justice. It helped to shape me into a woman of action. It provided me with a level of self-confidence that was necessary to navigate a world in which racial, gender and other demographic differences, as well as class, were the dominant organizing principles of society. Good behavior, strict discipline and decorum were stressed in my upbringing, which prepared me for life but can become a disadvantage in societies where assertiveness and aggression are sometimes required. The guide to behavior is rooted in a history of religious devotion and respect for the elders. Other values included 'ajo', which means having a generous spirit, helping others, being supportive and showing compassion. As can be expected, these are lofty goals and a lot to ask of someone growing up in this society, so not everyone adheres strictly to them. They can also be a disadvantage in a highly cut-throat and competitive environment which was more prevalent in the United States and at the United Nations where I studied, lived and worked. I had to develop a more assertive character in these situations to survive and thrive.

Racism in the United States and Europe

I did not experience racism or think about color until I went to England and the United States. Racism is embedded in the history and institutional structures of both countries but is more systemic and persistent as an organizing principle of society in the United States. Every Black person, regardless of national origin or social class experiences racism, overtly or covertly in a predominantly White country. It is now fashionable to talk of 'unconscious bias' in the United States, but this is misleading; all bias is conscious, whether expressed or not. It is apparent in the institutions as well as in the attitudes and behavior that continue to support notions of White supremacy, White privilege and White power.

Although many Whites are openly against racism, some cover up their own racism by making contributions to Black causes, tutoring Black youth or adopting the posture of being a good Christian missionary. Racism can also take the form of blaming the victim or ascribing some pathological problem by recommending counselling or medical attention just before a Black person is fired or demoted. This is what Robin DiAngelo referred to as 'nice racism' in her book of the same name.[25] It takes a strong, politically conscious and savvy individual to confront, navigate and challenge insidious and destructive racism in the United States. Racism is an ideology and is part of a reward system which benefits Whites. The worst form is organized, vicious, anti-democratic, fascistic and sexist. Although racism also exists in European countries, in my observation, having lived in both the United Kingdom and the United States, in Europe it is modified to some extent by class. Its manifestation in America is the most destructive although it has been mediated to some extent by the Civil Rights Movement of the 1960s, which does not have an exact equivalen in Europe. For all its achievements and position of leadership in the world, racism is a stain on American conscience and democracy and continues to expose the ugly side of its history of slavery, Jim Crowism, segregation, discrimination and racial terror.

Blacks in White academic Institutions

Working in predominantly White academic institutions is a challenge for many Black professionals, although there are many success

---

25   DiAngelo, R. 2021, **Nice Racism: How Progressive White People Perpetuate Racial Harm**, Boston, Beacon Press.

stories and supportive White colleagues. One is constantly being tested and challenged in a way a White colleague is not, and most Blacks carry the burden of representing their group at all times. It can also be lonely and requires good social skills to navigate the many invisible barriers inhibiting one's ability to succeed. Black professors are often not mentored adequately and take on extra work of service to the institution. They are also not in the networks that facilitate publications in peer review journals and presses, which can negatively affect their chances of promotion. Black professionals are sometimes regarded as 'affirmative action' hires and therefore less qualified even when they are not, ignoring the fact that Blacks often have to be twice as qualified with higher expectations of performance than Whites. A few Black professionals in academia run the risk of forging alliances solely with White colleagues to the detriment of building alliances with Blacks, to whom they often have to turn when they are in trouble or at the risk of being denied tenure or promotion.

One gets the impression that the perception of Blacks in White academic institutions is that they should be grateful for having been given a job at all and are not deserving of any further accolades. Special recognitions like endowed chairs and prizes are often more difficult for Black professors to obtain unless there is a pro-active, fair and just administration or protests by students and faculty.

Discrediting Black leaders to their supervisors is another way of weakening their influence in White institutions. Equally significant is discrediting Black intellectual thought, the most recent being the irrational attack on Critical Race Theory.[26] In brief, Critical Race Theory supports the idea of systemic racism by arguing that social institutions, especially the legal system, are set up to benefit the powerful and uphold White supremacy and White privilege. It is an intellectual Civil Rights Movement of a sort, fighting against structural racism and racial ideologies. It is therefore under attack by political operatives with hegemonic proclivities that are determined

---

26 See Delgado, R, Stenphancic, J., 1917, **Critifcal Race Theory: An Introduction, Third Edition,** New York, New York Press.

to constrain and undermine democracy and democratic institutions through aggressive nationalism and racist ideologies.

One of my observations in academia and the United Nations was the tendency for supervisors to automatically believe negative rumors about Blacks in position of leadership from Whites without first checking their veracity. This undermines Black leadership as well as Black integrity and influence in advancing Black causes and challenging racism in predominantly White institutions. The difference between the United Nations and academia is that the United Nations has a rigid hierarchical structure which protects Black professionals at a high level, since insubordination carries a heavier penalty than in Academia. Although all Blacks at international institutions are likely to face some form of racism in their careers, those at a lower level at the United Nations, for an example, can experience fairly regular discrimination and harassment similar to those experienced in Academia.

The challenge of raising African children in the United States.

The clash of cultures is the main challenge in raising African children in the United States. American society celebrates youthfulness and devalues the elderly, which can lead to the excessive empowerment and entitlement of children and youngsters. Most African cultures, on the other hand, emphasize modesty and obedience in children and youth and require respect for age and elders. Another difference is the tendency in the US to have the state involved in the upbringing of children, whereas in Africa it is the family and the extended family that generally assume this responsibility. The African approach to discipline tends to be strict and in some instances could involve corporal punishment at home and in the schools. This is generally unacceptable in the United States and can lead to the intervention of state authorities in the affairs of the home and in the discipline of children.

There is therefore a fine line that African parents have to walk to preserve and transmit the best elements of African culture, while adopting the desirable elements of American culture and cleverly editing and eliminating the negative aspects of both. African children growing up in the United States have to learn to navigate between the two cultures and apply the practical politics of survival and prosperity in the US. Growing up in White suburbs poses a special challenge for Black children in being the rare minority student in their classes from an early age on for many years. This puts them under the 'social microscope' and subjects them to indirect and direct acts of racism which they have to challenge, resist and ignore. For an example, if they speak good English they may be taunted as 'acting White' or called 'Oreo cookies' which means Black outside and White inside.

Living through and learning from loss and grief

The 1980s were described as 'the lost decade for African development.' For me, the 1980s were the decade of loss of family members. First my mother, Keziah Letitia Lolloh Forster-Jones, who died in 1982 at the age of seventy. The loss of a mother is probably the most difficult since a major physical bond is separated forever. Second, my father, Filomeno Whitfield Forster-Jones, who died in 1987 at the age of eighty-three. I was very close to my father, so his loss was deeply felt and seemed as much of the loss of a friend and confidant as a father. The most painful loss of all was that of my son, Filo Chinaka Steady, in 1989 at the age of twenty-one while he was a graduate student at Yale University. His loss led me to understand motherhood in a profound way and to give it a new definition. I had to come to terms with the intensity of being a mother and accept the fact that it can bring both joys and sorrows. I had to face the emptiness and reality of the physical absence of a child and the fact that one is more intensely a mother at the death rather than at the birth of a child.

Feminism takes many forms

Universal feminism is necessary but impossible. Historical factors have constructed various categories for women, based on their relationship to Eurocentric patriarchy, the dominant ideology and institutional manifestation of absolute power. Women closest to Eurocentric patriarchy enjoy the benefits of that position, even if they are subordinate to men. Together, they and their families are privileged by it and benefit from this hegemonic reality. As a result, they are directly or indirectly responsible for the domination of women and men from countries of the Global South and minority groups of color within the Global North through slavery, colonialism, neo-colonialism, internal colonialism, racism and corporate globalization. It is therefore not possible to use Western-derived feminisms, be they bourgeois feminism, cultural feminism, radical feminism and so forth to liberate women of the Global South or women minorities of color of the Global North from absolute patriarchy. In absolute patriarchy, all men are also victims of ideologies of domination.

African feminism as humanistic feminism

African feminism, first defined and explored by me in the book *The Black Woman Cross-Culturally,* concluded that the African woman was the original feminist and continues to be central to studies of feminism. African Feminism is a feminism that operates within a global political economy in which sexism cannot be isolated from the larger political and economic forces responsible for the exploitation and oppression of both women and men, especially in Africa and the African Diaspora. African Feminism is rooted in the history of Africa as the birthplace of *Homo sapiens;* the transatlantic slave trade; colonialism, nationalism, post-colonial experiences, patriarchal ideologies and structural racism, manifested today as systemic and institutionalized racism. It continues to challenge the racial and gendered nature of corporate globalization. This results in a kind of feminism that promotes a vision and a pragmatism in human and social terms, rather than in personal, individualistic and sexist terms. African feminism moves us towards a more inclusive, humanistic feminism that links theory and praxis as it seeks to resist multiple and compounded forms of discrimination and provide sustainable and human-centered alternatives.[27] African feminism can be viewed as having the power of total liberation and is a feminism that takes into account the history of domination of both women and men by the exigences of Eurocentric patriarchy. African feminism is inclusive of all *Homo sapiens* in its diversity and richness and seeks to liberate humans from all kinds of domination.

Being 'average' is all right

One of the most important lessons that I learnt in life is that it is all right to be average. Some of the happiest people I know can be described as 'average' with no pretentions and are at peace with themselves. I am thankful for being highly motivated and for having a mission and a vision in life directed towards the promotion of women's rights and social justice. I am also thankful for the opportunities and experiences I have had and to have attended some of the best and most prestigious schools and universities in the world. I am grateful for the professional successes I achieved both in academia and in the United Nations. Nonetheless, I have come across many people who can be described as 'average' who also live fulfilled and happy lives and do not have to succumb to the pressure of overachievement. The drive to achieve is good in a competitive world, but it can be overwhelming.

Being average is all right and significant. One of the most impactful books that is used in my class on 'Environmental Justice' is titled: *American Mania: When More is Not Enough* by Peter Whybrow. It examines the danger of excesses in American culture and the risk to one's health and happiness in what he describes as 'the fast new world.'[28] Choosing a more low key and average lifestyle enhances

27 Steady, F. 2005. 'African Feminism: Theory and Agenda' in B. Graig and A. Appiah, eds. **Routledge Encyclopedia of Philosophy,** New York. Routledge.

28 Whybrow, P., M.D., 2006, **American Mania: When More is Not Enough,** New York, W.W. Norton

social relationships and well- being. I have come to appreciate the more aesthetic aspects of life and the value of social relationships. These are important in helping to avoid the trappings of a stressful life dominated and propelled by social media and the need to be successful, perfect and popular.

'The family is everything'

Although Friedrich Engels, writing in the nineteenth century, blamed the origin of the family as the root of the subordination of women, in today's world the matter is more complicated. As a feminist, I agree with Engels to some extent and recognize that much remains to be done to achieve equal rights for women, especially in the care economy that is responsible for the reproduction, nurturing and care-giving activities of the present and future generations. Nonetheless, the family has been evolving and women have been gaining greater equality both inside and outside of the family. As a social anthropologist, I also recognize that there are many types of families, ranging from the nuclear family to extended, polygynous, single-parent, blended, same-sex and gender-neutral families. However, regardless of the type of family, a good, loving and functioning family is the greatest of life's experiences. In my view, no matter what else one achieves, the family comes first, and successful families are the most valuable of human institutions.

I have been blessed with both a strong and loving 'family of orientation', to use sociological terms, in which I was raised and an equally strong and loving 'family of procreation', which my husband, children and I created and maintain till this day. The first lesson is the obvious one, namely that unconditional love, reinforced from time to time with tough love for children, should always be at the center of family life. The second is the necessity for each individual in the family to be given space to grow and thrive. The third is that the home should always be a refuge and a place of peace. I used to tell my children to leave all their troubles behind the moment they open the front door to the house and view it as a welcoming haven of safety, tranquility, harmony and love. This is not to ignore the fact that conflicts are a part of life and families have their share of them. Nonetheless, peace, love and harmony in the home have to be valued and well entrenched to withstand both internal and external conflicts.

Finally, I am grateful to have had a family of talented achievers. My husband, Henry Maduka, a physician who received his medical degree from Oxford University, was the head of the blood bank at the Meriter Hospital in Madison, Wisconsin, USA, until his retirement. Our son Chinaka graduated with honors in biological sciences from the University of Wisconsin, Madison, and was a graduate student at Yale University when he passed away in 1989. Our second son, Henry Maduka Steady, earned a bachelor's degree with honors in Theatre from Carnegie Mellon University and a Master's Degree in Computer Imaging and Design at New York University. He has a successful career in the performing arts as an actor and in film production and post-production as an award-winning film editor.

Our daughter Azania received an international baccalaureate from Collège du Léman in Switzerland and a Bachelor's and Master's Degree in International Business at Webster University also in Geneva, Switzerland. She is the president and CEO of Singer Elite Academy and a successful vocalist and songwriter performing concerts in Geneva, Switzerland and other parts of Europe and the United States. She is an award-winning international singer, who won the 'Graines des Stars' award, equivalent to 'American Idol' on French TV6.

My name 'Filomina', as told to me by a group of Catholic nuns and monks from Italy at the 1992 Earth Summit means 'One who must be loved'. They were right. This has been borne out in both my 'family of orientation' and my 'family of procreation' and I will forever be grateful for that love. I therefore end this memoir by paying tribute to the family and reiterating that the family is indeed everything.

References

Blyden, 2000, *West Indians in West Africa, 1808-1880: The African Diaspora in Reverse,* New York, University of Rochester Press.

Brown-Davies, N, 2019 'The Emergence of Creoledom and the Future: 1792 to the Present,' Keynote Speaker, Boston, Krio Descendants Union Global, Family Reunion.

Campbell, 1993, M. *Back to Africa: George Ross and the Maroons: From Nova Scotia to Sierra Leone,* Trenton, N.J. Africa World Press.

Cole, G., 2013, *The Krio of West Africa: Islam, Culture, Creolization and Colonialism in the 19th Century,* Athens, Ohio University Press.

Cummings John C., 1995, *Constance Agatha Cummings-John: Memoires of a Krio Leader,* Ibadan, Sam Bookman.

Denzer L., 1981, 'Constance Cummings-John: Her Early Political Career in Sierra Leone' *Tarikh,* vol. 7 no. 1

DiAngelo R. 2021, *Nice Racism: How Progressive White People Perpetuate Racial Harm*, Boston, Beacon Press.

Dixon-Fyle, M., 1999, l, Rochester, University of Rochester Press.

Foray, C., 1977, *Historical Dictionary of Sierra Leone,* London.

Fyfe, 1962, *A History of Sierra Leone,* New York, Oxford University Press.

Jackson -Brown, I., 2020, *Eldercare as Art and Ministry,* New York, Church Publishing.

James, E. et. als., 2006, *Den Ol Bod Os: Creole Architecture in Sierra Leone,* Freetown, The British Council

Rosaldo, M. and Lamphere, 1974, *Woman, Culture and Society,* Alto, Stanford University Press.

Schama, S., 2006, *Rough Crossings: The Slaves, the British and the American Revolution,* New York, Harper Collins Publishers.

Spitzer, 1974, *The Creoles of Sierra Leone: Responses to Colonialism, 1870-1945,* Madison, University of Wisconsin Press.

Steady, F. 1981, *The Black Woman Cross-Culturally,* Cambridge, Schenkman Books, Now in its Third Edition.

Steady, F., 1993 *Women and Children First: Poverty, Environment and Development,* Rochester, Schenkman Books

Steady, F. 2001, *Women and the Amistad Connection: Sierra Leone Krio Society,* Rochester, Schenkam Books.

Steady, F. 2005. 'African Feminism: Theory and Agenda' in B. Graig and A. Appiah, eds. *Routledge Encyclopedia of Philosophy,* New York. Routledge.

Steady, F. 2006, *Women and Collective Action: Development, Democratization and Empowerment,* New York, Palgrave/Macmillan.

Steady, F. 2007. *Women, Globalization and Economic Justice,* Rochester, VT: Schenkman Books.

Steady, F., 2009, (ed.) *Environmental Justice in the New Millennium: Race, Ethnicity and Human Rights,* New York, Palgrave/Macmillan.

Steady, F. 2012, *Female Leadership in West Africa: Mothering the Nation and Humanizing the State,* New York, Palgrave/Macmillan.

Steady, F. 2018, *Krio Women of Sierra Leone: Embracing a Culture of Many Parts,* Linus Learning, Ronkonkoma, New Jersey.

Tatum. B., 1997, *Why Are All The Black Kids Sitting Together in the Cafeteria?: Another Conversations About Race,* New York, Basic Books.

Toure, R., and Steady, F., 1995, *Women and the United Nations: Reflections and New Horizons*, Rochester, Schenkman Books.

United Nations, 1980, *The Copenhagen Program for Action,* United Nations, New York.

United Nations, 1986, *The Nairobi Forward-Looking Strategies for the Advancement of Women,* United Nations, New York.

United Nations, 1992, *Agenda 21: The Program of Action from Rio,* New York, United Nations.

United Nations, 1995, *The Beijing Platform for Action,* United Nations, New York.

Whybrow, P., M.D., 2006, *American Mania: When More is Not Enough,* New York, W.W. Norton

Wyse, A. 1991, *The Krios of Sierra Leone: An Interpretive History,* Washington, D.C. Howard University Press.

Videos of Filomina Steady on Youtube

❧

1.Filomina Steady's Lecture on Women and Leadership in Africa Through the Ages

https://www.youtube.com/
watch?v=vt7EkRgHLcw&list=PLFWQ1g8jNXn9SJ3G4bzK6vK25_
x3wkQ8j&index=5

or search Youtube: 'Filomina Steady Women and Leadership Through the Ages'

2. The Youtube videos of the Conference on 'Women and Leadership in Africa' Wellesley College, 2018 is presented below

https://www.wellesley.edu/AWLC#live

3. The Filomina Steady Symposium: Honoring the Work of Professor Filomina Steady on the occasion of her retirement – April 26, 2019. Youtube link below

https://www.youtube.com/results?search_query=filomina+steady+symposium+2019

Appendix

Filomina Steady Symposium Program

❖

Symposium in Honor of the Retirement of Professor Filomina C. Steady
Chair of Africana Studies, Wellesley College
Friday, April 26ᵗʰ, 9.30am to 5.00pm

Collins Cinema
'African(a) Feminism and Women's Leadership in Global Context: Honoring the
Work of Professor Filomina Steady.'
Livestreaming

9.30am

Welcome and Introduction

Welcome – Professor Layli Maparyan, Executive Director, Wellesley Centers for
Women and Professor of Africana Studies

Greetings – President Paula Johnson, M.D., Wellesley College

Thanks to Sponsors – Geofred Osoro, Lecturer, Africana Studies

Introduction of Professor Filomina Steady – Dr. Liseli Fitzpatrick, Visiting Lecturer,
Africana Studies

Remarks by Professor Filomina Steady, Africana Studies.

10.00am - 11.00am

Keynote Address

Introduction of the keynote speaker – Prof. Kellie Carter-Jackson, Africana Studies,
Wellesley College

Keynote Address: 'Expanding Feminist Visions' Chancellor's Professor Obioma
Nnaemeka, University of Indiana – Indianapolis

11.00am - 12.30pm

Faculty Panel

Professor Stanlie James, Vice Provost and Professor, Arizona State University.

'The Impact of Filomina Steady and her work on international human rights.'

Professor Oyeronke Oyewumi, Professor of Sociology, Stony Brook University, New York

'Motherhood as the Practice of Leadership: Appreciating Filomina Steady's Research Insights on the Pioneers called African Women'

Professor Asoka Bandarage, Visiting Professor, Colorado College and Georgetown University, Washington, DC.

"Women's Leadership in a Changing World.'

Professor Lidwien Kapteijns, Professor of History, Wellesley College

"Filomina Steady – The Contribution of a Leading Scholar, Teacher, Theorist and Practitioner to African(a) Women's Lives, Collective Action and Humanistic Feminism."

Professor Daphne Ntiri, African-American Studies, Wayne State University, Discussant

Chair: Professor Layli Maparyan, Executive Director, Wellesley Centers for Women, Wellesley College and Professor of Africana Studies.
Leading Scholar and Author on 'Womanism'

12.30pm - 1.30pm

Lunch - Jewett Sculpture Court

MC for lunch – Sarah Abramson, class of 2021. Africana Studies Major

1.30pm - 2.50pm

Alumnae Panel

MC for Alumnae Panel – Sarah Abramson, class of 2021. Africana Studies Major.

Video messages and accolades from Wellesley Alumna

Charlotte Ashumu, class of 2001. Associate Director at the Smithsonian's National Museum of African Art.

"Feminism and Women's Leadership: Reflections of my work in five African Countries"

Katherine Jenkins, class of 2003, Educator, Mather Elementary School, Boston Public Schools, Massachusetts

"Reflections on the personal & professional impact of Afrocentric feminism from a 'White' Alumna."

Rhobi Matinyi, class of 2007. Associate Partner at Dalberg Advisors, a South African-based strategy consulting firm that focuses on emerging and developing markets.

"Can Women's Participation in Leadership Change the Trajectory of the Continent of Africa?"

Lilly Marcelin, class of 2012. Community activist, organizer and founder of Resilient Sisterhood, an NGO focusing on underserved women and reproductive health.

"'A Racial Prism and Analysis on the Impacts of Infertility in Black Women"

Fiona Almeda, Class of 2015. Chair. Teacher, researcher and project designer, working both in the US and internationally, especially in India and South Africa, her home country.

Tributes from Alumnae of the Wellesley African Students Association – Read by Chika Egbuzie, class of 2019

2.50 to 3.00p.m

BREAK

3.00pm – 4.10pm

Students Roundtable

Topics on 'Reimagining Feminism; African(a) Feminism and Women's Leadership in honor of Professor Filomina Steady by Wellesley's students.

Chair: Professor Craig Murphy, Political Science.

Dominique Copeland – Major -Economics - 2019

Sandra Amponsah Ohemeng – Major- Economics - 2020

Kennedy Austin – Major- Africana Studies & Sociology - 2019

Hawah Kallon – Major -Africana Studies & Psychology - 2019

Penny Hawthorne - Undeclared major- 2021

4.10pm

Closing Remarks
Professor Steady and Professor Maparyan.

4.20pm – 5.00pm

Reception - Collins Café

Filomina Steady Symposium Videos on Youtube
https://www.youtube.com/results?search_query=filomina+steady+symposium+2019

Postscript

※

For Professor Steady's Youtube talk on 'African Women's Leadership Through the Ages' at Wellesley College, March 8th 2018, go to the link below:

https://www.youtube.com/watch?v=vt7EkRgHLcw&t=16s

Books by Professor Steady will be available at the bookstore (Wang Campus Center, 4th. floor) and at Collins Cafe.

Index

Aboderin, Akin, 176

Abortion, 285, 288, 293, 323-4, 330,

Accompong, village, 373-4

Achola Pala Okeyo, Dr., xii, 224,

African Scholarship Program of American Universities (ASPAU), 99-103, 110, 121, 126, 130, 150, 154, 162, 248,

African Studies Center, Boston University, 167, 169, 213, 217-219

African Women's Leadership Conference, 393

Africana Studies, ix, 334, 336, 339, 341, 342, 368, 369, 379, 400, 401, 408, 410, 414

African-American Institute, 100, 102, 107, 162

Agenda 21, Proghram of Action from Rio 1992, xi, 311, 314, 315, 316, 319, 320, 321, 322

Ahmed, Sjamsiah, xi

Akerle, Olubanke King, xi,

Aki Sawyer, Mrs. Yvonne, 15, 20

Akus, of the Gambia, 1

Alakija, Sharon Caperling, xi, 308

Almeida, Fiona, 403

Amherst College, 133

Anglican Church Missionary Society (CMS), UK, 3, 16, 56, 71

Annie Walsh Memorial School, xii, 403, 4, 6, 55-56, 71, 86, 123,

Anti-Apartheid Movement, 139, 170, 342

Apapa, ship, 73, 81

Apartheid, 94, 141, 142, 167, 224, 232, 288, 289, 294, 347, 361-2

Ardener, Edwin, 192, 212

Ashamu, Charlotte, 403

Ashwood, Mrs. Ethel, 15

Association of African Women for Research and Development (AAWORD), xii, 222, 323

Astolfi, Betty, xi, 309

Atchouk Tcheknavorian Asenbauer, xi

Awori, Thelma, ix

Baden-Powell, Lady, 77, 78

Bandarage, Professor Asoka, 402

Bedwei, Farida, 393

Belmont Williams, Dr, 239

Benjamin Family, 6

Benka Coker, Mrs. Hannah, 15, 54

Bennett College, North Carolina, 100, 110, 114-129, 137, 145

Beoku-Betts, Josephine, xii

Binagwaho, Dr. Agnes, 393

Bishop Crowther Memorial Church, 9, 28, 29

Bishop Crowther Memorial School, 50-51

Boston University, xii, 162, 164, 167, 168, 172, 173, 214, 217-219, 248

Cline Town (Kanike), 9, 11, 29, 30, 50, 203, 209

Collège du Léman, 317, 318, 425

Collor De Mello, President Fernando, 320

Columbia University, 154, 230, 368

Comparative Religion, 138

Connaught Hospital, Freetown, 88

Convention on the Elimination of All Forms of Discrimination Against Women, xi, 252

Copenhagen Programme of Action, 1980, xi

Covin, Professor David, 405

Cox George, Professor William, 206

Cromwell, Otelia, 133, 247

Cuba, Professor Lee, 404

Cummings-John, Mrs Constance, 15, 46, 54

Davies, Juliet, xii, 56

Davies, Mrs. Muriel, 70

Diaspora, African, 158, 226, 232, 247, 336, 337, 350, 356, 364, 369, 384, 392, 409, 412, 422

Dillsworth, Miss Florence, 15

Division for the Advancement of Women, x, xi, 410

Dorcas Association, 46

Dove Danquah, Mrs. Mabel, 54

Downs-Thomas, Felix, 176

Dumbuya, Dr. Moses, 206, 207

Freemasons, 46, 298, 299, 300

Freetown, Sierra Leone, 1, 2, 13, 14, 16-20, 25, 28-31, 32, 38, 45, 48, 53-55, 61, 65-69, 168, 185-187

Freire, Paolo, 211

Friedan, Betty, 133, 145

Fynch, Clarice, 2, 6, 37

Gandhi, Indira, 313

Garber, Mrs. Eudora, 70

Garber, Canon Cassandra JP, 18, 395

Garvey, Marcus, 337, 340, 370, 384, 389, 390

Gbowee, Chief Melrose Forster, 397

Gierycz Dorota, xi

Gilpin, Josephine, 63

Girl Guide movement, 72, 73, 77, 81

Gorbachev, President Mikhail, 218, 312

Government Model School, 52

Government Municipal School, 87

Greensboro, North Carolina, 100, 110, 114, 115, 119-121, 126

Group of 77 (Third World Countries), 218

Gulliver, Professor Adelaide, 219

Hampshire College, Massachusetts, 133

Holst Roness, Dr. June, 15

Horton, Dr. Africanus, 15, 17

Ogundipe-Leslie, Omolara, xii, 224

Oku group (Muslim Krios), 30-31

Omolara Ogundipe-Leslie, Professor, xii, 224

Osoro, Geofred, 401, 412

Otelia Cromwell Distinguished Alumna Award, 247

Outdooring ceremony, 8

Oxford University, xii, 173, 188-190, 195, 197, 199, 202, 211, 212, 213, 263, 425

Oyeronke, Professor Oyewumi, 402

Pala, Achola (Achola Pala Okeyo), xii, 224

Pan-African Congress (PAC), 141

Peters, Mr. Ishmael, 70

Princess Margaret, HRH, 77

Queen Elizabeth II, HM, 77

Queen Elizabeth the Queen Mother, HRH, 77, 396

Race relations in England, 92

Radcliffe Infirmary, Oxford, 195, 200, 212, 303

Remi Toure, ix

'Rio Declaration', The, 321

Riots in Freetown, 1955, 66-69

Rodenhouse, Professor Nick, 367

Ronsho devil (myth), 27

www.ingramcontent.com/pod-product-compliance
Lightning Source LLC
Chambersburg PA
CBHW062045270326

41930CB00031B/1491